Exam Ref MD-100
Windows 10

Andrew Bettany
Andrew Warren

Exam Ref MD-100 Windows 10

Published with the authorization of Microsoft Corporation by:
Pearson Education, Inc.

Copyright © 2019 by Pearson Education, Inc.

ISBN-13: 978-013-556059-4
ISBN-10: 0-135-56059-4

Library of Congress Control Number: On file

3 2019

Trademarks

Microsoft and the trademarks listed at http://www.microsoft.com on the "Trademarks" webpage are trademarks of the Microsoft group of companies. All other marks are property of their respective owners.

Warning and Disclaimer

Special Sales

For information about buying this title in bulk quantities, or for special sales opportunities (which may include electronic versions; custom cover designs; and content particular to your business, training goals, marketing focus, or branding interests), please contact our corporate sales department at corpsales@pearsoned.com or (800) 382-3419.

For government sales inquiries, please contact governmentsales@pearsoned.com.

For questions about sales outside the U.S., please contact intlcs@pearson.com.

Editor-in-Chief	Brett Bartow
Executive Editor	Loretta Yates
Assistant Sponsoring Editor	Charvi Arora
Development Editor	Rick Kughen
Managing Editor	Sandra Schroeder
Senior Project Editor	Tracey Croom
Copy Editor	Rick Kughen
Indexer	Cheryl Lenser
Proofreader	Abigail Manheim
Technical Editor	Boyd Nolan
Editorial Assistant	Cindy Teeters
Cover Designer	Twist Creative, Seattle

Contents at a glance

Contents

Chapter 4   Maintain Windows   263

Acknowledgments

I would like to dedicate this book to Annette and Tommy for being so supportive and encouraging whenever I work on projects that sometimes eat into our quality time together. This book is also for the reader. Having taught thousands of IT Professionals over my career, I hope this book helps you to become proficient with Windows 10. Work hard and aim for the stars!

—Andrew Bettany

I took my first Microsoft exam in 1996, and it was a daunting prospect going into that room armed only with what I could remember. It turned out alright, though, and I've taken a fair number since. My aim with this book is to arm you with what you need to know to take and pass the MD-100 Windows 10 exam and work towards your Microsoft 365 Certified: Modern Desktop Administrator Associate qualification. As always, this book is a collaborative effort, and I'd like to thank my co-author, Andrew, and the team at Microsoft Press for helping get this book out there.

—Andrew Warren

About the authors

ANDREW BETTANY is a Microsoft Most Valuable Professional (Windows and Devices for IT), dad, IT Geek, training mentor and consultant, entrepreneur, and author.

As a Microsoft MVP, Andrew is recognized for his Windows expertise, and he is the author of many publications, including several Windows exam certification prep guides and Microsoft official training materials. He is the author of video training materials for LinkedIn Learning and Pluralsight. As a Microsoft Certified Trainer, Andrew delivers learning and consultancy to businesses on many technical areas, including Microsoft 365, Azure, and Windows.

He has co-founded the "IT Masterclasses" series of short intensive technical courses (see www.itmasterclasses.com), and he is passionate about helping others learn technology. He is a frequent speaker at Microsoft Ignite and other technical conferences worldwide.

Andrew is active on social media and can be found on LinkedIn, Facebook, and Twitter. He lives in a village just outside the beautiful city of York in Yorkshire, England.

ANDREW WARREN, MCT, has been writing for Microsoft for many years, helping to develop their official curriculum of instructor-led training material. He has served as a subject matter expert on many of the current Windows Server 2016 courses, was technical lead on several of the Windows 10 titles, and was involved in Microsoft 365, Azure and Intune course development. When not writing about Microsoft technologies, he can be found in the classroom, teaching other IT professionals what they need to know to manage their organization's IT infrastructure.

Introduction

With the new Microsoft 365 Certified: Modern Desktop Administrator Associate certification, Microsoft have changed the way that IT Pro certifications work. Rather than being based on a technology area, they are focused on a specific job role. The Microsoft MD-100: Windows 10 exam provides the foundation of this new Modern Desktop Administrator Associate certification.

This book covers every major topic area found on the exam, but it does not cover every exam question. Only the Microsoft exam team has access to the exam questions, and Microsoft regularly adds new questions to the exam, making it impossible to cover specific questions. You should consider this book a supplement to your relevant real-world experience and other study materials. If you encounter a topic in this book that you do not feel completely comfortable with, use the "Need more review?" links you'll find in the text to find more information and take the time to research and study the topic. Great information is available on the Microsoft website at docs.microsoft.com.

Organization of this book

This book is organized by the "Skills measured" list published for the exam. The "Skills measured" list is available for each exam on the Microsoft Learn website: http://microsoft.com/learn . Each chapter in this book corresponds to a major topic area in the list, and the technical tasks in each topic area determine a chapter's organization. If an exam covers six major topic areas, for example, the book will contain six chapters.

Microsoft certifications

Microsoft certifications distinguish you by proving your command of a broad set of skills and experience with current Microsoft products and technologies. The exams and corresponding certifications are developed to validate your mastery of critical competencies as you design and develop, or implement and support, solutions with Microsoft products and technologies both on-premises and in the cloud. Certification brings a variety of benefits to the individual and to employers and organizations.

> **MORE INFO   ALL MICROSOFT CERTIFICATIONS**
>
> For information about Microsoft certifications, including a full list of available certifications, go to *http://www.microsoft.com/learn.*

Check back often to see what is new!

Errata, updates, & book support

We've made every effort to ensure the accuracy of this book and its companion content. You can access updates to this book—in the form of a list of submitted errata and their related corrections—at:

MicrosoftPressStore.com/ExamRefMD100/errata

If you discover an error that is not already listed, please submit it to us at the same page.

For additional book support and information, please visit

https://MicrosoftPressStore.com/Support.

Please note that product support for Microsoft software and hardware is not offered through the previous addresses. For help with Microsoft software or hardware, go to *http://support.microsoft.com.*

Stay in touch

Let's keep the conversation going! We're on Twitter: *http://twitter.com/MicrosoftPress.*

Important: How to use this book to study for the exam

Certification exams validate your on-the-job experience and product knowledge. To gauge your readiness to take an exam, use this Exam Ref to help you check your understanding of the skills tested by the exam. Determine the topics you know well and the areas in which you need more experience. To help you refresh your skills in specific areas, we have also provided "Need more review?" pointers, which direct you to more in-depth information outside the book.

The Exam Ref is not a substitute for hands-on experience. This book is *not* designed to teach you new skills.

We recommend that you round out your exam preparation by using a combination of available study materials and courses. Learn more about available classroom training and find free online courses and live events at *http://microsoft.com/learn*. Microsoft Official Practice Tests are available for many exams at *http://aka.ms/practicetests*.

This book is organized by the "Skills measured" list published for the exam. The "Skills measured" list for each exam is available on the Microsoft Learn website: *http://aka.ms/examlist*.

Note that this Exam Ref is based on this publicly available information and the author's experience. To safeguard the integrity of the exam, authors do not have access to the exam questions.

CHAPTER 1

Deploy Windows

The MD-100 Windows 10 exam focuses on how to install Windows 10 efficiently and with the least amount of administrative effort. You need to understand how to plan and prepare the Windows 10 installation, along with the installation process itself, activation, and any blockers along the way. You'll be expected to know how to perform an in-place upgrade from another version of Windows and how to migrate user data, configure hardware devices, how to manage device drivers, and how to perform post-installation configuration. For users who operate Windows 10 using a different language, you also will be expected to know how to configure additional languages and regional settings.

Skills covered in this chapter:

- Skill 1.1: Deploy Windows 10
- Skill 1.2: Perform post-installation configuration

Skill 1.1: Deploy Windows 10

Devices will be shipped with a ready-to-use version of Windows. For a number of reasons, you may want to replace it with a newer version of Windows. In a corporate environment, you may need to install Windows 10 on many devices, which requires careful consideration, planning and preparation. This skill explores the requirements and preparations necessary for the deployment of Windows 10.

It is important to select the appropriate edition of Windows 10 for your users. Windows 10 is available across many device types, including tablets, laptops, and desktop computers. Also, also it is available in multiple editions and in both 32-bit and 64-bit architecture versions. You need to choose the appropriate edition and version to provide the necessary capabilities that your users require.

After determining which edition you want to install, consider how best to deploy Windows 10. You can choose between simple interactive installations using local Windows 10 media, or you can deploy Windows 10 to your organization's devices by using one of several deployment technologies.

This skill covers how to:

- Select the appropriate Windows edition
- Perform a clean installation
- Perform an in-place upgrade
- Migrate user data
- Configure Windows for additional regional and language support
- Implement activation

Select the appropriate Windows edition

Windows 10 is available in several different editions and you should choose the most appropriate version for your personal or business needs. The specific editions of Windows 10, listed in Table 1-1, are designed to address the varying needs of this diverse user base.

TABLE 1-1 Windows 10 editions

EDITION	FEATURES
Windows 10 Home	Designed primarily for home users and includes similar features to those found in Windows 8.1 Home, plus: ■ Microsoft Edge ■ Continuum Tablet Mode for touch-capable devices ■ Cortana ■ Windows Hello ■ Virtual Desktops ■ Projecting To his PC ■ Activity History ■ Windows Ink ■ A number of built-in universal Windows apps, such as Photos, Maps, Mail, Calendar, Music, and Video ■ Supports maximum 128 GB of RAM Note that in Windows 10 Home, you cannot control Windows feature and quality updates as was possible on earlier Windows versions; these are received and installed automatically.
Windows 10 Pro	Includes the same features as in Windows 10 Home but additionally provides: ■ Domain Join And Group Policy Management ■ Microsoft Azure Active Directory Join ■ BitLocker Drive Encryption ■ Enterprise Mode For Internet Explorer 11 ■ Client Hyper-V ■ Storage Spaces ■ Remote Server Administration Tools For Windows 10

EDITION	FEATURES
	■ Microsoft Store For Organizations ■ Windows Information Protection (WIP) ■ Support for 2 CPUs and maximum 2 TB of RAM In Windows 10 Pro, updates are provided by Windows Update for Business. This provides control over when and how devices can receive Windows feature and quality updates.
Windows 10 Pro for Workstations	Includes the same features as in Windows 10 Pro but additionally provides: ■ SMB Direct using RDMA (Remote Direct Memory Access) ■ Resilient File System (ReFS) ■ Licensed for installation on PCs using server-grade Intel Xeon and AMD Opteron processors ■ Persistent Memory using NVDIMM-N hardware ■ Support for 4 CPUs and 6 TB of RAM ■ Ultimate Performance power plan for desktop devices In Windows 10 Pro for Workstations, you can utilize powerful PC hardware with up to 4 CPUs and 6 TB of memory.
Windows 10 Enterprise	Windows 10 Enterprise builds on the features of Windows 10 Pro, providing additional features of relevance to larger organizations, including: ■ Always On VPN ■ DirectAccess ■ Windows To Go Creator ■ AppLocker ■ BranchCache ■ Start Screen Control with Group Policy ■ Managed User Experience ■ Windows Defender Credential Guard ■ Windows Defender Device Guard ■ Windows Defender Advanced Threat Protection ■ Virtual Desktop Infrastructure enhancements ■ Application Virtualization In addition to the ability to manage updates to Windows with Windows Update for Business, Enterprise customers can also access the Long-Term Servicing Channel (LTSC) deployment version of Windows 10 Enterprise.
Windows 10 Enterprise LTSC	This specialized edition of Windows 10 Enterprise receives security and other important updates in the normal way but does not receive feature updates. This enables organizations to know that their environment does not change over time. Windows 10 Enterprise LTSC does not include built-in apps that are subject to change including: ■ Microsoft Edge ■ Microsoft Store client ■ Cortana ■ Many built-in universal Windows apps
Windows 10 Education	Provides the same features as Windows 10 Enterprise but does not offer support for LTSC. Windows 10 Education is only available through Academic Volume Licensing.
Windows 10 Mobile & Windows 10 Mobile Enterprise	Designed for phones and smaller tablets, with broadly the same feature set as the Windows 10 desktop edition. It includes many of the same universal Windows apps as well as a touch-optimized version of Microsoft Office. Microsoft has ended development of the Windows 10 Mobile platform, and the most recent version released in October of 2017, is scheduled to have support end on December 10, 2019.

Following the Windows 10 April 2018 Update, the Windows 10 S edition was replaced with Windows 10 in S mode. This is a mode of Windows 10 and not an edition. It is designed to be the safest and most stable version of Windows ever. Windows 10 in S mode is a limited, locked-down version of Windows 10. To reduce the total cost of ownership (TCO) you can only install applications from the Microsoft Store and browse the Internet using the Microsoft Edge browser.

- Microsoft Edge only.
- Bing search engine.
- Microsoft Store apps only.
- Not able join Active Directory Domain Services (AD DS) domain.
- Azure AD Domain Join is available in Windows 10 Pro in S mode and Windows 10 Enterprise in S mode.

PCs ship with one of three versions of Windows 10 in S mode:

- Windows 10 Home in S mode
- Windows 10 Professional in S mode
- Windows 10 Enterprise in S mode

Users can freely opt to leave S mode—for example, to switch to Windows 10 Pro—by installing the Switch out of S mode app from the Microsoft Store. This action is a one-time decision—once you've taken the PC out of S mode, it cannot be put it back into S mode.

> **NOTE WINDOWS 10 BUSINESS**
>
> Microsoft also provides a special business-focused license that can be applied to the Windows 10 Pro edition. This is called Windows 10 Business, and the upgrade license is included as part of Microsoft 365 Business. You can upgrade Windows 7, 8, and 8.1 Professional to Windows 10 Pro and then apply the Windows 10 Business license. You cannot purchase the standalone version of Windows 10 Business edition; therefore, it is not listed in Table 1-1. To review further details about Microsoft 365 Business, visit the Microsoft website at *https://docs.microsoft.com/microsoft-365/business/support/microsoft-365-business-faqs*.

Also, Microsoft has released Windows 10 Internet of Things (IoT) editions—Windows IoT Core and Windows IoT Enterprise. These can be used to operate small industrial devices, such as control devices and specialist industrial computing systems.

For businesses that require a long period of support for their IoT installations, Microsoft has released Windows 10 IoT Core Long Term Servicing Channel (LTSC) together with Windows 10 IoT Core Services, which provides a subscription with access to 10 years of support for the IoT releases.

CHOOSE 32-BIT OR 64-BIT VERSIONS

You can choose between 32-bit and 64-bit versions of all desktop editions of Windows 10.
Nowadays, you should choose 64-bit versions unless there is a compelling reason to use 32-bit
versions, such as your hardware does not support the 64-bit architecture.

The various edition features described in Table 1-1 are applicable for both 32-bit and
64-bit versions. However, 64-bit versions of Windows 10 do provide a number of advantages,
including:

- **Memory**   The 64-bit versions of Windows 10 can address more physical memory than
  32-bit versions. Specifically, 32-bit versions are physically limited to just under 4 GB of
  RAM, whereas 64-bit versions of Windows are limited by the edition of Windows 10
  installed.

- **Security**   Features such as Kernel Patch Protection, mandatory kernel-mode driver
  signing, and Data Execution Prevention (DEP) are available only in 64-bit versions of
  Windows 10.

- **Client Hyper-V**   This feature is only available on 64-bit versions of Windows 10. Your
  hardware must also support second-level address translation (SLAT).

- **Performance**   The 64-bit processors can handle more data during each CPU clock
  cycle. This benefit is only realized when running a 64-bit operating system.

EXAM TIP

You cannot perform a direct upgrade from a 32-bit version of Windows 10 directly to the
64-bit version. Therefore, ensure that you know that in this scenario, you must perform a
wipe-and-load installation.

Determine Windows 10 Edition requirements for particular features

A number of general and security features available in some editions of Windows 10
require specialist hardware or software configuration that you should know. This section
covers how to

- Identify hardware and configuration requirements for general Windows 10 features
- Identify hardware and configuration requirements for Windows 10 security features

GENERAL FEATURES

These features provide for general usability and functional improvements and include:

- **Client Hyper-V** Enables you to create, manage, and run virtual machines that you can install with different guest operating systems to support, perhaps, earlier line-of-business (LOB) apps that will not run natively on Windows 10. Requirements of the Client Hyper-V feature are:

  - A 64-bit version of either the Windows 10 Pro or Windows 10 Enterprise edition.

  - A computer that supports SLAT.

  - Additional physical memory to support running the virtual machines. A minimum of 2 GBs of additional memory is recommended.

- **Cortana** You can use Cortana as a digital assistant to control Windows 10 and perform tasks such as writing email, setting reminders, and performing web searches. Because Cortana is voice-activated and controlled, your Windows 10 device requires a microphone.

- **Continuum** Windows 10 is available on a variety of devices types and form factors. With Continuum, Microsoft endeavors to optimize the user experience across device types by detecting the hardware on your device and changing to that hardware. For example, Windows 10 determines when you are using a non-touch desktop computer and enables traditional interaction with the operating system by use of a mouse. For users of hybrid devices, such as the Microsoft Surface Pro, when you disconnect a keyboard cover, Windows 10 switches to Tablet Mode.

- **Miracast** Windows 10 uses Miracast to connect your Windows device wirelessly to an external monitor or projector. You will need a Miracast-compatible external monitor or projector to use this functionality. If your display device doesn't support Miracast, you use a Miracast adapter, such as a Microsoft Wireless Display adapter.

- **Touch** Windows 10 is a touch-centric operating system. Although you do not need touch to use Windows 10, some features are made more usable through the use of touch. To use touch, your tablet or display monitor must support touch.

- **OneDrive** Users of OneDrive are entitled to 5 GB free online storage. OneDrive provides this storage. OneDrive functionality is built into the Windows 10 operating system and it is easy to use. You must have a Microsoft account to use OneDrive.
- **Sync your settings** When you use more than one Windows 10 device, it is convenient for your user settings to move with you to the new device. You can use the Sync Your Settings feature of Windows 10 to ensure that settings such as theme, Internet Explorer and Edge settings (including favorites), passwords, language, and ease of access are synchronized between your devices. You must have a Microsoft account to use this feature.

> **NOTE   ACTIVE STYLUS SUPPORT**
>
> Some touch devices have screens that support active stylus input. Active styluses provide for pressure-sensitive input and enable you to use your device for accurate note taking and drawing. Passive styluses are supported on all touch devices but do not support these more advanced features.

SECURITY FEATURES

Windows 10 also includes a number of features that can help make your device more secure, including:

- **BitLocker Drive Encryption** A Trusted Platform Module (TPM) version 1.2 or higher works with BitLocker to store encryption keys. This helps protect against data theft and offline tampering by providing for whole-drive encryption. Requirements for BitLocker include:
  - A device installed with either Windows 10 Pro or Windows 10 Enterprise.
  - Optionally, you should use a TPM. Using a TPM with BitLocker enables Windows to verify startup component integrity. You do not require a TPM in your computer to use BitLocker, but using a TPM does increase the security of the encryption keys.
- **Device health attestation** With the increase in use of users' own devices, it is important to ensure that Windows 10 devices connecting to your organization meet the security and compliance requirements of your organization. Device health attestation uses measured boot data to help perform this verification. To implement device health attestation, your Windows 10 devices must have TPM version 2.0 or higher.
- **Secure Boot** When Secure Boot is enabled, you can only start the operating system by using an operating system loader that is signed using a digital certificate stored in the UEFI Secure Boot signature database. This helps prevent malicious code from loading during the Windows 10 start process. Requirements for Secure Boot include
  - Computer firmware that supports Unified Extensible Firmware Interface (UEFI) v2.3.1 Errata B, and for which the Microsoft Windows Certification Authority is in the UEFI signature database.

- **Multifactor authentication (MFA)**   This is a process that provides for user authentication based on at least two factors: something the user knows, such as a password; and something the user has, such as a biometric feature (fingerprint or facial features), or a device, such as a cell phone. Requirements for two-factor authentication include:
  - Biometric devices that support the Windows Biometric Framework, such as a fingerprint reader, a smartphone, or an illuminated infrared camera using Windows Hello.
  - A biometric attribute, such as facial recognition, iris detection, or a fingerprint.

> *NOTE* **WINDOWS HELLO**
>
> When Windows 10 first shipped, it included Microsoft Passport and Windows Hello. These components worked together to provide multifactor authentication. With Windows 10, version 1703, to help to simplify deployment and improve supportability, these technologies are combined into a single solution called Windows Hello. Windows Hello for Business provides enterprises with the tools and policies to implement and manage multifactor authentication within their organization's infrastructure.

- **Virtual Secure Mode**   This feature moves some sensitive elements of the operating system to *trustlets* that run in a Hyper-V container that the Windows 10 operating system cannot access. This helps make the operating system more secure. Currently, this is only available in the Windows 10 Enterprise edition.
- **Virtual Smart Card**   This feature offers comparable security benefits in two-factor authentication to that provided by physical smart cards. Virtual smart cards require a compatible TPM (version 1.2 or later).

EXAM TIP

If your organization requires the use of Windows Hello and your existing devices do not have the necessary hardware, then you can use an aftermarket add-on. You can purchase USB-connected infrared cameras, which provide secure facial recognition and USB-connected external fingerprint readers to the specifications required to support Windows Hello.

Perform a clean installation

Although most computers are purchased preinstalled with Windows 10, many organizations prefer to reinstall the operating system to avoid the additional software that original equipment manufacturers (OEMs) often include with their computers. This software is often referred to as *bloatware* and can include utilities and tools or trial versions of software such as Microsoft Office or anti-spyware software that are unwanted.

As shown in Table 1-2, there are several methods of installing Windows 10 on a device, and you should familiarize yourself with each prior to taking the exam.

TABLE 1-2 Windows installation methods

INSTALLATION METHOD	DESCRIPTION
Install from DVD	Windows 10 is no longer shipped on DVDs. You can use the downloadable media obtained from the Microsoft Windows 10 website, Microsoft Volume Licensing Service (MVLS), or Visual Studio Subscriptions and burn it to DVD media.
Install from USB	Use this method to install the operating system on one computer at a time. Installation from a USB device is quicker than using a DVD. You must modify BIOS or UEFI settings to enable booting from USB.
Install from Windows Deployment Services	Requires Windows Deployment Services (WDS), which is a role installed on Windows Server 2019. WDS also requires Dynamic Host Configuration Protocol (DHCP) on the network. The target computer network card must support Pre-Boot Execution Environment (PXE). Using WDS allows automated installation of system images and deployment of Windows to multiple computers simultaneously by using multicast.
Install an image from Windows Preinstallation Environment (Windows PE)	Boot the device by using Windows PE, and then use one of the following deployment options. <ul><li>Use Deployment Image Servicing and Management (DISM) to apply the Windows image.</li><li>Use the Microsoft Deployment Toolkit (MDT) deployment solution.</li><li>Use the System Center Configuration Manager (Current Branch) deployment solution (Configuration Manager).</li></ul> Both MDT and Configuration Manager are enterprise-level solutions that enable you to deploy Windows to hundreds or thousands of devices at once and configure lite-touch installation (LTI) or zero-touch installation (ZTI) for either minimal user interaction or no user interaction, respectively, during the deployment.
Install over the network	Start the computer by using Windows PE and connect to a copy of the installation files stored on a shared network folder. You would use this method when you are unable to use a USB device, WDS, MDT, or Configuration Manager.

> **NOTE CREATE WINDOWS 10 INSTALLATION MEDIA**
>
> To obtain the latest version of Windows 10 that you can use to upgrade a device or download to create installation media on a DVD or USB, you should visit *https://www.microsoft.com/software-download/windows10*.

If you intend to start your PC from your installation media, such as a USB drive, you may need to configure your BIOS or UEFI to allow this. This can be achieved by modifying the BIOS or UEFI setting or choosing a custom boot order during the startup process.

During a clean installation on a new hard drive, perform the following steps to install Windows 10.

1. Insert your installation media and start your computer.

2. At the Windows Setup screen, choose the appropriate language and regional settings and then click Next.

3. In the Windows Setup window, click Install Now.

4. On the Applicable Notices And License Terms page, accept the License Terms and click Next.

5. On the Which Type Of Installation Do You Want? page, choose Custom: Install Windows Only (Advanced).

6. On the Where Do You Want To Install Windows? page, select Drive 0 Unallocated Space and click Next.

> **NOTE   EXISTING OPERATING SYSTEM DRIVE**
>
> For a clean installation of Windows 10 on a device on which an operating system is already installed, erase this partition either by formatting or deleting any partitions present during the setup process.

The installation begins. To install Windows 10 for personal use, perform the following steps:

1. On the Let's Start With Region. Is This Right? page, select the regional settings.

2. On the Is This The Right Keyboard Layout? page, select the keyboard layout settings.

3. On the Want To Add A Second Keyboard Layout? page, add a layout, or select Skip.

4. On the Let's Connect You To A Network page, select a network connection.

5. On the How Would You Like To Set Up? Page, choose Set Up For Personal Use and click Next.

6. On the Sign In With Microsoft page, create a local offline account by selecting Offline Account. Or enter your Microsoft account and password or select Create Account.

7. On the Create A PIN page, click Create PIN and enter a PIN.

8. On the Link Your Android Or iPhone To This PC page, enter your phone number and click Send and then click Next. Or click Do It Later to skip this step.

9. On the Protect Your Files With OneDrive page, click Next. Or click Only Save Files To This PC to skip this step.

10. On the Make Cortana Your Personal Assistant? page, choose whether to enable Cortana.

11. On the Do More Across Devices With Activity History page, choose whether to enable the timeline feature.

12. On the Choose Privacy Settings For Your Device page, choose the privacy settings that you require.

13. The remainder of the setup process will continue.

14. You are now signed in.

Depending on your hardware performance, Windows should complete the clean install process within 10–15 minutes, and the machine will restart several times. A device with a solid-state drive (SSD) will outperform slower traditional hard drives with spinning platters. During the final stages of installation, the Getting Ready notification appears while Windows installs device drivers specific to the hardware.

Identify an installation strategy

You can choose from among a number of methods when considering how best to install Windows 10. Generally, the size of your organization and the number of devices that you must install will determine the strategy that you select. The available strategies have different prerequisites, and some might require additional software components and configuration before you can begin installing Windows 10. Table 1-3 describes the strategies available.

TABLE 1-3 Windows 10 installation strategies

DEPLOYMENT OPTION	DESCRIPTION
High-touch retail media deployment	Suitable for small organizations with few devices to install with Windows 10. Requires no specialist IT skills or additional services or components. All that is required is one or more copies of the Windows 10 installation media, which can be provided on a DVD, or on a USB storage device, or even from a shared folder on a network file server.
Low-touch deployment	Suitable for larger organizations that intend to install a few hundred devices, using limited installer intervention. Because the strategy relies on the use of image deployment and additional services, such as Windows Deployment Services (WDS) and, optionally, Microsoft Deployment Toolkit (MDT), some specialist IT skills are also required.
Zero-touch deployment	For very large organizations with thousands of devices. Requires a considerable investment in IT skills to facilitate this strategy. Also requires the use of MDT and System Center Configuration Manager (Current Branch) to deploy Windows 10, using no installer intervention.

Determine the appropriate installation media

Windows 10 uses an image-based installation and deployment model with the Windows operating system installation files packaged inside an image file that is used as an installation source during the installation process.

A default installation image, Install.wim, is provided on the installation media in the \Sources folder. Although you can choose to use this default image, you can also configure it to create custom installation images that better suit the needs of your organization. Customizations might include:

- Selecting a particular edition of Windows 10.
- Choosing which Windows features are enabled.
- Including Wi-Fi profiles and virtual private network (VPN) profiles.
- Adding universal apps or desktop applications.

The Windows Assessment and Deployment Kit (Windows ADK) contains a number of tools that you can use to create and manage Windows 10 images to support your installation needs. These are:

- **DISM**   The Deployment Image Servicing and Management (DISM) command-line tool enables you to capture, deploy, and manage Windows images. You can use the tool to install, uninstall, configure, and update Windows features, packages, drivers, and international settings in a .wim file or VHD, which can be either online or offline.

- **Windows Configuration Designer**   This tool, as shown in Figure 1-1, enables you to provision Windows 10 features and runtime settings by using provisioning packages (.ppkg) to quickly configure a Windows 10 device without having to install a new image.

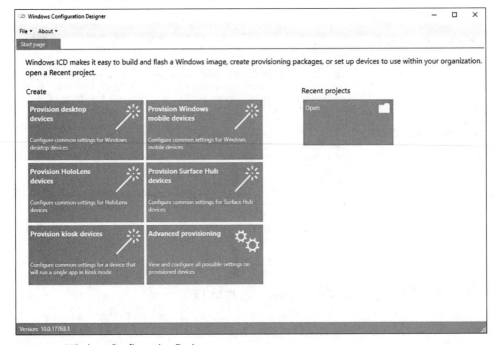

FIGURE 1-1 Windows Configuration Designer

You can then deploy these custom images and packages to target computers within your organization that require Windows 10. You can perform this deployment in a number of ways and by using a variety of deployment technologies and tools, depending on the installation strategy you previously selected. Options include:

- **DVD installation**   You can create installation DVD media, or you can use a customized image that you created. The device you are installing to requires an optical drive.

- **USB installation**   You can use the default or custom Windows images. This method is quicker than DVD, and although it does not require an optical drive, you might need to reconfigure your computer's BIOS or UEFI firmware settings to support startup from USB.

EXAM TIP

You can perform an unattended installation using these methods, provided an unattended answer file is present on the media. Answer files are discussed in the following section.

- **WDS deployment**   To use this method, Dynamic Host Configuration Protocol (DHCP) must be available to network clients on your network, and your target computers running Windows 10 must support Pre-Boot Execution Environment (PXE). Combined with unattended answer files and custom images, you can use this method to deploy multiple images to multiple computers at the same time by using multicast.

- **Image-based installation**   By starting your computer into Windows Preinstallation Environment (Windows PE), you can use DISM to apply an image locally to the target computer. Alternatively, you can use MDT and System Center Configuration Manager (Current Branch) to deploy the image and desktop apps to the target devices.

- **Shared network folder installation**   You can use Windows PE to start your computer and map a network drive to installation files and images on a network file shared folder. This is a comparatively inefficient method and has been replaced by the other methods previously described.

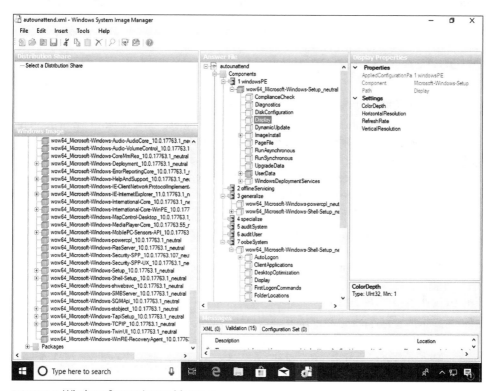

FIGURE 1-2 Windows System Image Manager

- **Windows SIM** The Windows System Image Manager (Windows SIM) shown in Figure 1-2 enables you to create installation answer files for use in automated deployments. These answer files contain the configuration options used to install Windows 10. You can then associate these answer files with a local copy of the installation media, perhaps on a USB memory stick to provision Windows 10 using a semi-automated interactive installation.

> *NOTE* **NAMING THE ANSWER FILE**
>
> If you copy the answer file you create by using Windows SIM to the location of the installation media, name the file **autounattend.xml.** Windows setup knows to search for this named file in the root of the installation media.

- **Windows PE** Windows PE (WinPE) is used to start a computer that is being deployed with Windows 10. It enables access to Windows file systems and is, in essence, a small Windows operating system. You can use the generic Windows PE provided on the product DVD, or you can create your own using tools found in the Windows ADK to address your specific deployment needs. You can then launch Windows PE from a DVD or a USB memory stick or across the network using PXE.

Perform an in-place upgrade

The most efficient method of installing Windows 10 on existing computers is to perform an in-place upgrade. This method is fully supported and recommended by Microsoft.

It is important to understand the terminology used when describing the process of upgrading to Windows 10. *Upgrade* is often used generically to explain the licensing process of upgrading from an earlier version of Windows to a later version. You can also upgrade the edition of Windows which replaces an existing operating system, such as Windows 7 Home edition to Windows 10. On a semi-annual basis, Windows 10 will automatically perform an in-place upgrade of Windows 10 to the latest version of Windows 10.

When manually upgrading to Windows 10, you update the existing operating system and perform what is called an *in-place upgrade* on existing hardware. All user data and settings are retained. For most users, this is now the recommended procedure.

Supported upgrade paths

Performing an *in-place upgrade* can be the simplest option, especially when you have only a few computers to upgrade. However, you cannot perform an in-place upgrade on computers running a Windows version that does not share the same feature set as the edition of Windows 10 that you want to install.

Table 1-4 lists the supported upgrade paths based on the Windows edition.

TABLE 1-4 Supported upgrade paths to Windows 10

EARLIER WINDOWS EDITION	WINDOWS 10 HOME	WINDOWS 10 PRO	WINDOWS 10 ENTERPRISE
Windows 8/8.1	X		
Windows 8/8.1 Pro		X	
Windows 8/8.1 Enterprise			X
Windows 7 Starter	X		
Windows 7 Home Basic	X		
Windows 7 Home Premium	X		
Windows 7 Professional		X	
Windows 7 Ultimate		X	
Windows 7 Enterprise			X

You will notice from Table 1-4 that direct upgrades between different editions are not supported. That is, you cannot upgrade directly from Windows 7 Home to Windows 10 Enterprise.

> *NOTE* **UPGRADING FROM WINDOWS 7 HOME**
>
> If you want to upgrade from Windows 7 Home to Windows 10 Enterprise, you can achieve that in a two-stage process. First, upgrade to Windows 10 Home and then upgrade to Windows 10 Enterprise.

After you have determined whether your upgrade path is supported, choose how to perform the process of upgrading to Windows 10.

CONSIDERATIONS FOR PERFORMING AN IN-PLACE UPGRADE

When determining whether to use the in-place upgrade method to upgrade to Windows 10, consider the following factors.

- It is a simple process and is ideal for small groups of computers.
- It provides for rollback to the earlier version of Windows.
- User and application settings and user data files are retained automatically.
- Installed applications are retained; however, retained applications might not work correctly after upgrading from an earlier Windows version.

- You do not need to provide for external storage space for data and settings migration.
- It does not allow for edition changes and is available only on supported operating systems (see Table 1-4).
- It does not provide the opportunity to start with a clean, standardized configuration.

Perform an in-place upgrade to Windows 10

As you have seen, there are three ways to upgrade to Windows 10. The recommended method by Microsoft is to use an in-place upgrade. This is the method that will be utilized for all future upgrades of Windows 10 using Windows Update. Using an in-place upgrade enables you to retain all the users' applications, data files, and user and application settings. During the in-place upgrade, the Windows 10 setup program automatically retains these settings.

> **IMPORTANT**   **BACK UP DATA FILES**
>
> It is important to perform a backup of user data files that may be stored locally prior to launching an in-place upgrade to guard against possible data loss.

You perform an in-place upgrade to Windows 10 when your users will continue to use their existing computers. To perform an in-place upgrade, complete the following procedure.

1. Evaluate the user's computer to determine that it meets minimum hardware requirements for Windows 10 and that Windows 10 supports all hardware.
2. Verify that all applications work on Windows 10.
3. Optionally, back up the user's data files.
4. Run the **Setup.exe** program from the root of the Windows 10 installation media.
5. Choose Upgrade when prompted and complete the setup wizard.

> **NOTE**   **UPGRADING DEVICES WITHIN A CORPORATE ENVIRONMENT**
>
> If your existing operating system is unstable or runs slowly, you may not want to perform an in-place upgrade to Windows 10. If the device is in a corporate environment and you previously deployed the earlier version of Windows using an automated deployment method, you can re-deploy the operating system again. Once complete, allow the corporate apps and settings to be applied and then perform an in-place upgrade to Windows 10. This two-stage process will take longer to perform, but it can provide an alternative method of deploying Windows 10 until you evaluate your deployment strategy.

The in-place upgrade process works well and is now the recommended deployment method Microsoft suggests for upgrading devices that run Windows 7 or Windows 8.1 to Windows 10.

Upgrade using installation media

An enterprise will normally obtain Windows 10 media through the volume licensing channel and can download it from the Volume Licensing Service Center (VLSC) at *https://www.micro-soft.com/licensing/servicecenter/default.aspx*. VLSC media use either a Multiple Activation Key (MAK) or Key Management Service (KMS) which is used during the installation process and is tied to the enterprise license agreement with Microsoft.

Alternatively, purchased retail media can be used, which is supplied on a USB thumb drive or by a direct download from the online Microsoft Store.

Another option is to use the Media Creation Tool (MCT), which generates a ready-to-use, bootable USB flash drive. You can also download an ISO file that can be used for the installation, which would need to be burned to a writeable DVD. Media created with the MCT cannot be used for upgrading a Windows Enterprise edition client. When you run the MCT, when prompted, on the What Do You Want To Do? page, click Create Installation Media and then click Next.

> **NOTE MEDIA CREATION TOOL (MCT)**
>
> You can download the MCT at: *https://www.microsoft.com/software-download/windows10.*

If you encounter issues while upgrading to Window 10, you should inspect the installation log file found at C:\Windows\Panther\UnattendGC\SetupAct.log. If you are trying to use the wrong media or if you are trying to upgrade from an unsupported operating system, there should be an entry such as the following:

```
Info [windeploy.exe] OEM license detected, will not run SetupComplete.cmd
```

With all upgrades, you must ensure that you understand the requirements for a successful upgrade, such as having at least 2 GB RAM and enough disk space. In the exam, you might face scenarios in which you are asked to upgrade from one architecture to another architecture which is not supported. You may be presented with the current system drive having insufficient disk space. To resolve disk space issues, you could attempt one of the following resolutions to complete the upgrade:

- Run Disk CleanUp Wizard, remove any unwanted files, and empty the Recycle Bin.
- Uninstall apps, files, and language packs that you do not need.
- If possible, expand the volume by using the Disk Management tool.
- Move personal files off the system drive and onto another drive or external drive.

If the system fails during the upgrade due to a compatibility issue, you can troubleshoot the cause by reviewing the setupact.log found at: C:\$Windows.~BT\Sources\panther\setupact.log. Some of the most common codes are shown in Table 1-5.

TABLE 1-5 Setuperr.log errors relating to upgrading

ERROR CODE	DESCRIPTION
CsetupHost::Execute result = 0xC1900200	PC not meeting the system requirements for Windows 10.
CsetupHost::Execute result = 0xC190020E	Insufficient free hard drive space.
CsetupHost::Execute result = 0xC1900204	Migration choice (auto upgrade) not available—wrong Windows 10 SKU or architecture.
CsetupHost::Execute result = 0xC1900208	Compatibility issues found (hard block).
CsetupHost::Execute result = 0xC1900210	No issues found.

If you want to check the system for compatibility only, you can run Setup.exe with a command-line switch, which will check for compatibility but not perform the actual upgrade.

An example command is:

```
Setup.exe /Auto Upgrade /Quiet /NoReboot /DynamicUpdate Disable /Compat ScanOnly
```

Windows 8.1 supports mounting an ISO disk image directly in File Explorer. You can download the Windows 10 ISO and upgrade Windows 8.1 without first having to create installation media such as a DVD or bootable USB. For Windows 7, you must use bootable media, extract the files contained in the ISO, or use a third-party tool to mount the ISO.

A major advantage of upgrading rather than performing a clean installation (sometimes referred to as a *wipe-and-load* scenario) is that all the applications, settings, and data on the PC are retained during an upgrade. This often results in a much quicker process, and the device can be returned to the user in the shortest possible time.

> ***NEED MORE REVIEW?*** **WINDOWS 10 ENTERPRISE: FAQ FOR IT PROFESSIONALS**
>
> This Microsoft resource is useful to obtain answers to common questions about installation for Windows 10 Enterprise. Visit *https://docs.microsoft.com/windows/deployment/planning/windows-10-enterprise-faq-itpro#administration*.

As part of the pre-upgrade checks, Windows 10 will validate the following.

- Whether UEFI is used (UEFI v2.3.1 or later is required for Secure Boot).
- System Host is not configured to boot from VHD.
- The system is not installed as a Portable Workspace (for example, using Windows To Go).

Details of the setup compatibility checks can be reviewed in the log file found at C:\$WINDOWS.~BT\Sources\Panther\setupact.log. The installation process proceeds in the same way as the in-place upgrade using Windows Update.

Migrate user data

With the rapid adoption of Office 365, more data than ever before is now stored in cloud-based storage such as OneDrive for Business and SharePoint Online. Despite this trend, file server-based shared storage and local storage is still the most common data storage location for businesses.

Both cloud-based and server-based storage data storage backup and migration are outside of the scope of this exam, but you need to know how enterprises can migrate both user data and Windows settings from an earlier version of Windows to Windows 10. The procedure for migrating user data has not changed over the years, but you will be expected to understand the process.

> **This section covers how to:**
> - Migrate from previous versions of Windows
> - Migration strategies
> - Perform a user state migration

Migrate from previous versions of Windows

The amount of user affinity with their devices is often overlooked by support professionals. If allowed, users can invest significant time and effort to customize and personalize their working environment, and this can include the Windows operating system and applications. When upgrading from an older operating system, it is very common for the user to be presented with a new device running the new version of Windows after the old device is removed. This can sometimes cause significant loss of productivity while the user becomes familiar with the updated operating system and reconfigures settings to their preferences.

The level of user personalization of the device can include the following.

- Desktop appearance, sounds, themes, and backgrounds
- Start-menu customization
- Icons and file associations
- Files and folders stored locally
- Device and power settings
- Application settings, such as autotype and template locations

Migration strategies

You perform a migration to Windows 10 when your users have new computers on which to install Windows 10 and you want to preserve settings and data from their old computers. During the process, you perform the following high-level procedures.

1. Verify that all existing required applications work on Windows 10.
2. Ensure that the appropriate edition of Windows 10 is installed on the user's new computer.
3. On the new computer, install the required applications.
4. Back up the user's data files and settings from the old computer using USMT (User State Migration Tool).
5. Restore the user's data files and settings on the new computer using USMT.

You can use either a side-by-side migration or wipe-and-load migration strategy to perform a migration. These migration scenarios are summarized as follows.

- **A side-by-side migration**   In this scenario, the source and destination computers for the upgrade are different machines. You install a new computer with Windows 10 and then migrate the data and most user settings from the earlier operating system to the new computer.

- **A wipe-and-load migration**   In this scenario, the source and destination computer are the same. You back up the user data and settings to an external location and then install Windows 10 on the user's existing computer. Afterward, you restore user data and settings.

PERFORM A SIDE-BY-SIDE MIGRATION

When you opt to use the *side-by-side* migration strategy, illustrated in Figure 1-3, use the following procedure to complete the task.

1. Either obtain a computer with Windows 10 preinstalled or install Windows 10 on a new computer. When Setup.exe prompts you, choose Custom (Advanced). This is the destination computer.
2. Install the same applications on the destination computer as are presently on the source computer.
3. Create an external intermediate storage location, such as a file server–shared folder or an external hard drive, for the storage of user data and settings. This storage must be accessible from both the source and destination computers.
4. Use the USMT to collect the user's data and settings from the source computer and store them to the external intermediate store.
5. Use the USMT to collect the user's data and settings from the external intermediate store and install them in the destination computer.

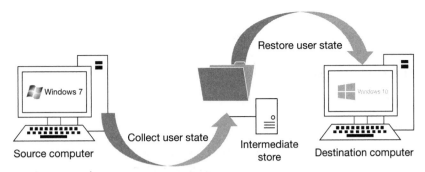

FIGURE 1-3 Side-by-side migration to Windows 10

PERFORM A WIPE-AND-LOAD MIGRATION

When you opt to use the *wipe-and-load* migration strategy, illustrated in Figure 1-4, use the following procedure to complete the task.

1. Create an external storage location, such as a file server-shared folder or an external hard drive, for the storage of user data and settings.

2. Use the USMT to collect the user's data and settings and store them in the external location.

3. Install Windows 10 on the existing computer. When Setup.exe prompts you, choose Custom (Advanced).

4. Reinstall the applications on the computer.

5. Use the USMT to restore the user's data and settings from the external location.

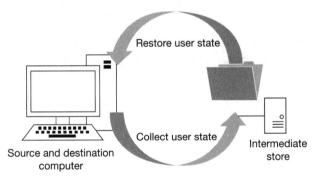

FIGURE 1-4 Wipe-and-load migration to Windows 10

CONSIDERATIONS FOR PERFORMING A MIGRATION

When determining whether to use one of the two migration methods outlined to upgrade to Windows 10, consider the following factors.

- You have an opportunity to create a clean installation, free from remnant files and settings.
- You can reconfigure the existing disk partitions.

- You can upgrade to any Windows 10 edition, irrespective of the earlier Windows edition.

- Migration is a more complex process, and you must use migration tools such as User State Migration Tool (USMT) to migrate user data and settings.

- You need to provide storage space for user settings and files to be migrated.

- Applications are not retained, and you must manually reinstall these.

Perform a user state migration

When computers are being replaced or refreshed on a large scale, the loss of user productivity can be significant. In this scenario, you can use the User State Migration Tool version 10 which is available as part of the Windows ADK.

EXAM TIP

You should always use the version of the Windows ADK for your version of Windows 10. For example, ensure you download Windows ADK, version 1809, if that's the version of Windows 10 you are deploying. At the time of writing this book, Windows 10 1809 is the current feature release.

The Windows ADK is available from the following Microsoft website at: *https://developer.microsoft.com/windows/hardware/windows-assessment-deployment-kit.*

User state migration is performed in two phases as follows.

1. Settings and data are captured (collected) from the source computer and stored in a secure migration store using the ScanState tool.

2. Captured settings and data are restored on the destination computer, using the LoadState tool.

USMT is a collection of three command-line tools that can be scripted to capture and migrate data efficiently and securely and is intended for performing large-scale automated deployments.

- ScanState.exe
- LoadState.exe
- UsmtUtils.exe

You choose which data is captured, and these settings are stored in migration XML files as follows.

- MigApp.xml
- MigDocs.xml
- MigUser.xml
- Custom XML files that you can create

The XML files provide the migration rules that USMT needs to process.

You can also create a Config.xml file that is used to specify files or settings, which will be excluded from the migration.

IMPORTANT **INSTALL APPLICATIONS**

The USMT does not migrate applications; only the supported applications' settings are migrated. Therefore, any required applications must be already installed on the destination computer so that the captured app settings can be reinstated.

As part of both migration strategies, you must migrate user data and settings to the destination computer. Consequently, it is important to determine where these data and settings reside. The types of data that USMT can capture and migrate are shown in Table 1-6.

TABLE 1-6 Data types accessible by USMT

DATA TYPE	EXAMPLE	DESCRIPTION
User data	Documents, Video, Music, Pictures, Desktop files, Start menu, Quick Launch settings, and Favorites	Folders from each user profile.
	Shared Documents, Shared Video, Shared Music, Shared Desktop files, Shared Pictures, Shared Start menu, and Shared Favorites	Folders from the Public profiles.
	File	USMT searches fixed drives, collecting files that have any of the file name extensions that are defined in the configuration XML file.
	Access control lists (ACLs)	USMT can migrate the ACL for specified files and folders.
Operating system components	Mapped network drives, network printers, folder options, users' personal certificates, and Internet Explorer settings.	USMT migrates most standard operating system settings.
Supported applications settings	Microsoft Office, Skype, Google Chrome, Adobe Acrobat Reader, Apple iTunes, and more	USMT will migrate settings for many applications, which can be specified in the MigApp.xml file. Version of each application must match on the source and destination computers. With Microsoft Office, USMT allows migration of the settings from an earlier version of an Office application.

The following settings are not migrated when you use USMT.

- Local printers, hardware-related settings
- Device drivers
- Passwords
- Customized icons for shortcuts
- Shared folder permissions
- Files and settings, if the operating systems have different languages installed

After you have installed the USMT included in the Windows ADK, you have the following components as described in Table 1-7.

TABLE 1-7 USMT components

COMPONENT	DESCRIPTION
ScanState	Scans a source computer and collects files and settings, writing them to a migration store. (The store file can be password protected and can be compressed and encrypted if required, although you cannot use the /nocompress option with the /encrypt option.) You can turn off the default compression with the /nocompress option.
LoadState	Migrates the files and settings from the migration store to the destination computer.
USMTUtils	Compresses, encrypts, and validates the migration store files.
Migration XML files	MigApp.xml, MigUser.xml, or MigDocs.xml files, and custom XML files USMT uses to configure the process.
Config.xml	Used with /genconfig to exclude data from a migration.
Component manifests	Controls which operating system settings are to be migrated. These manifests are specific to the operating system and are not modifiable.

To initiate the collection of the files and settings from the source computer, use the following steps.

1. Ensure that you have a backup of the source computer.

2. Close all applications.

3. Open an elevated command prompt, and run ScanState, using this command:

   ```
   ScanState \\remotelocation\migration\mystore /config:config.xml / i:migdocs.xml
   /i:migapp.xml /v:13 /l:scan.log
   ```

4. Run UsmtUtils with the /verify switch to ensure that the migration store is not corrupted, using UsmtUtils /verify C:\mystore\storename.img.

5. On the destination computer, install the operating system, install any applications that were on the source computer, and then close any open applications.

6. Run the LoadState command, specifying the same .xml files that you used when you ran ScanState using the command

   ```
   LoadState \\remotelocation\migration\mystore /config:config.xml / i:migdocs.xml
   /i:migapp.xml /v:13 /l:load.log
   ```

7. Restart the device and verify whether some of the settings have changed.

> **NOTE USMT TOOLS**
>
> You can find the USMT tools within the C:\Program Files (x86)\Windows Kits\10\Assessment and Deployment Kit\User State Migration Tool folder on your computer. You need to use the tools that match your architecture (amd64, arm64, and x86).

The ScanState tool can also migrate user settings from an offline Windows system including the Windows.old folder. A Windows.old folder is created when you perform an in-place upgrade of a modern version of Windows to Windows 10. The ability to access user settings contained within the offline Windows.old folder can be advantageous in the following scenarios.

- Improved performance if the Windows.old folder is local
- Simplified end-to-end deployment process by migrating data from Windows.old by enabling the migration process to occur after the new operating system is installed
- Improved success of migration because files will not be locked for editing while offline
- Ability to recover and migrate data from an unbootable computer
- The migration can be performed at any time

> **NEED MORE REVIEW? USMT TECHNICAL REFERENCE**
>
> Microsoft has updated the technical reference relating to USMT 10, including support for Microsoft Office 2016; You can find it at *https://docs.microsoft.com/windows/deployment/usmt/usmt-technical-reference*.

Configure Windows for additional regional and language support

When Windows 10 was released, it offered support for 111 languages spanning 190 countries and regions. You can download any of the additional languages for Windows 10, which allows users to view menus, dialog boxes, and other user interface items in their preferred languages.

To add an additional input language to your device, perform the following steps.

1. Open Settings > Time & Language > Language.
2. Under Language, click Add A Language.
3. Select the language you want to use from the list or enter the language name in the search bar.
4. Click Next.
5. Choose to install the optional language features available for the selected language as shown in Figure 1-5.
6. The language pack is downloaded and installed.
7. Log out of the device and then sign in to display the new default display language.

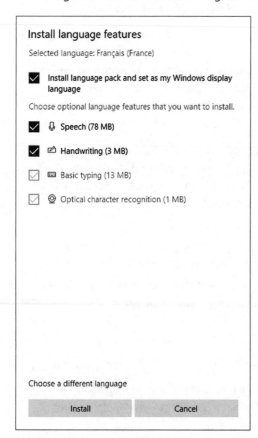

FIGURE 1-5 Choose a language to install

When adding an additional language to Windows 10, you can see which language features are available. These include.

- Display language
- Text-to-speech
- Speech recognition
- Handwriting support

You also have the option to set the language as your primary Windows display language after the language pack has been installed. There are additional language options available for common languages. Select the installed language and then click the Options button to configure features such as region-specific fonts (such as accents), regional formats, handwriting, pen settings, keyboards, and spell-checking options.

INSTALLING LOCAL EXPERIENCE PACKS

You can also modify the default language used by Windows 10 by adding a Local Experience Pack from the Microsoft Store. These packs perform the same configuration changes as the Language options within the Settings app, allowing you to enhance Windows with your chosen language, including navigation, menus, settings, and help topics.

To add a local language using the Microsoft Store, search for the required language and download it or use the link to add a Local Experience Pack on the Language page within the Settings app. If you need to add a Local Experience Pack to an offline image, you can add the Language Interface Packs (LIPs) .appx files and their associated license files, which can be found in the LocalExperiencePack folder on the Language Pack ISO. OEMs and System Builders with Microsoft Software License Terms can download the Language Pack ISO and Feature on Demand ISO from the Microsoft OEM site or the Device Partner Center. IT Professionals can find ISOs containing all available Language resources on the Microsoft Next Generation Volume Licensing Site at *https://licensing.microsoft.com*.

EXAM TIP

In previous versions of Windows 10, LIPs are delivered as .cab files, for example, C:\Languages\es-ES\lp.cab. Ensure that you know that since Windows 10, version 1809, LIPs are delivered as Local Experience Packs (LXPs) .appx files, for example, LanguageExperiencePack.am-et.neutral.appx.

After the language is installed, you can set it to be the default language for your device or remove the language. Within the Language page in the Settings app, you can also configure the Administrative Language Settings to copy your international settings to the Windows welcome screen, system accounts, and new user accounts as shown in Figure 1-6. System-wide changes require administrative privileges.

FIGURE 1-6 Modify administrative language settings

To save space, you can remove language components; for example, you could remove English when deploying devices to non-English regions.

USING THE DISM COMMAND LINE TOOL

You can also use the DISM command prompt to perform deployment of language components. As an example, if you want to modify an offline Windows image to add a language pack, first mount the Windows image, mount the Language Pack ISO and the Features on Demand ISO with File Explorer, and then use the following command.

```
Dism /Image:"C:\mount\windows" /Add-Package /PackagePath="D:\x64\langpacks\Microsoft-
Windows-Client-Language-Pack_x64_fr-fr.cab"
```

To add the Luxembourgish language, which requires the fr-FR base language and is delivered as an LXP, use the following command.

```
DISM /Image:"C:\mount\windows" /Add-ProvisionedAppxPackage /PackagePath=
"D:\LocalExperiencePack\lb-lu\LanguageExperiencePack.lb-LU.Neutral.appx" /LicensePath:
"D:\LocalExperiencePack\lb-lu\License.xml"
```

To remove the same LIP, which was added through LXP, you would use the following command.

```
Dism /remove-provisionedappxpackage /packagename:Microsoft.LanguageExperiencePack.
lb-LU._neutral__8wekyb3d8bbwe
```

Once you have completed the configuration, you need to capture the changes by committing the changes to the Windows image using the following command.

```
Dism /Commit-Image /MountDir:"C:\mount\windows"
```

USING THE LPKSETUP COMMAND LINE TOOL

You can also use the Lpksetup tool to perform language pack operations on language pack CAB files.

To launch the Lpksetup wizard, use the following steps:

1. Download and then mount the Language Pack ISO.

2. Press the Windows logo key+R to open the Run dialog box.

3. Type **lpksetup.exe**, and then select OK.

4. Step through the wizard and browse to the Language Pack location on the mounted ISO.

5. Locate the language pack as shown in Figure 1-7 and click Next.

6. On the Review And Accept The Microsoft Software License Terms dialog box, click I Accept The License Terms and click Next.

7. The language pack installation completes.

8. Click Close.

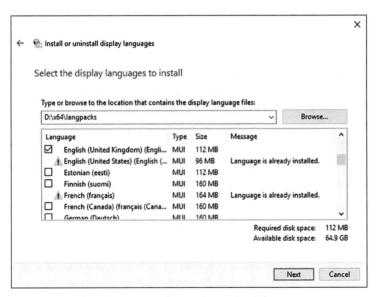

FIGURE 1-7 Perform language pack operations using Lpksetup

If you want to automate the process or bypass the user interface (UI) and perform unattended or silent-mode language pack installations, you can also use the Lpksetup command-line tool. You need to run Lpksetup using an elevated command prompt. The syntax is:

```
lpksetup.exe /i * /p <path>
```

This example installs all language packs that are located on installation media specified in the *<path>* location. The command-line options available for Lpksetup.exe are shown in Table 1-8.

TABLE 1-8 Lpksetup.exe command-line options

OPTION	DESCRIPTION
/i	Installs the specified language packs. If you do not include * or language after **/i**, you are asked to continue the installation through the UI.
*	Wildcard character that represents all language packs found in the language_pack_path or the directory where lpksetup.exe is located.
Language-region	Specifies the language pack or packs to be installed or uninstalled.
/u	Uninstalls the specified language packs. If you do not include * or a language after **/u**, you are asked to continue the uninstall through the UI.
/r	Suppresses the need to restart after an operation is complete.
/p language_pack_path	Indicates the path of the language packs to install.
/s	Performs a silent and unattended operation that requires no user input.
/f	If the computer is required to restart, forces a restart even if other users are logged on to the computer.

> **NOTE** **FULL LANGUAGE PACKS ARE NOT INTERCHANGEABLE**
>
> Language components are not interchangeable between Windows 10 and Windows Server, but some LIPs are. You must also match the version of Windows to the language pack. For example, Windows 10, version 1809 must use the Windows 10, version 1809 language pack.

Implement activation

Activation is a very important part of configuring and managing Microsoft products and remaining within the Microsoft Software License Terms.

In some environments, the activation process will be fully automated, or silent, and it is easy to overlook it. This section explores Windows 10 activation options and procedures that you need to understand.

Like most Microsoft products, Windows 10 requires activation. Activation verifies that your copy of Windows 10 is genuine and that it hasn't been used on more devices than the license terms allow. Only a valid product key can be used to activate Windows 10. Figure 1-8 shows the current activation status of a computer running Windows 10 Professional.

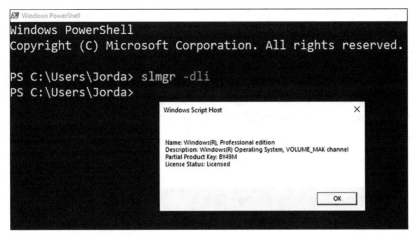

FIGURE 1-8 Viewing the activation status of Windows 10

You can activate Windows 10 in several ways—by using an Internet-accessible service at Microsoft, by telephone, and by using bulk activation methods such as Key Management Service (KMS) and Active Directory–based activation. This section explores activation and the methods you can use to manage your organization's Windows 10 activation.

> **This section covers how to:**
> - Select an activation method
> - Volume activation services
> - Activate Windows 10
> - Activate Windows 10 Virtual Machines
> - Troubleshoot Activation Issues

Select an activation method

To activate Windows 10, you might need a *product key*, a 25-character code which looks like this:

PRODUCT KEY: XXXXX-XXXXX-XXXXX-XXXXX-XXXXX

Not all Windows 10 installations require the use of a product key to activate, relying instead on a *digital license* (called a digital entitlement in Windows 10, Version 1511). A digital license is a method of activation in Windows 10 that doesn't require you to enter a product key; instead, digital licenses are connected to your Microsoft account. Once your PC is connected to the Internet and you log in to your Microsoft account, the activation takes place.

You must use a product key for activation when:

- You purchase Windows 10 from a retail store or authorized reseller, either as a physical product or as a digital download.
- You do not have a digital license.
- Your organization has a Microsoft volume licensing agreement for Windows 10.
- You purchased a new device on which Windows 10 is preinstalled.

You do not need a product key for activation and can rely on a digital license when:

- You upgrade to Windows 10 from an eligible device running a genuine copy of Windows 7 or Windows 8.1.
- You purchase Windows 10 from the Microsoft Store.
- You purchase Windows 10 Pro upgrade from the Microsoft Store.
- You use Windows 10, version 1803 or later on a device with a firmware-embedded activation key.
- You are a Windows Insider and upgrade to the newest Windows 10 Insider Preview build on an eligible device that was running an activated earlier version of Windows and Windows 10 Preview.

The method you use to activate Windows 10 is determined by a number of factors, including how you obtained Windows 10 and whether your organization has a volume license agreement in place with Microsoft. The following scenarios determine how you activate Windows 10.

- **Retail**   If you purchase Windows 10 from a retail store or from an authorized retailer, it should come with a unique product key, which can be found on a label inside the Windows 10 box. For a digital copy of Windows 10, you should have access to the product key, which may be stored in a digital locker accessible through the retailer's website. You can enter the key during or after installation to activate your copy of Windows 10.
- **OEM**   If you purchase a new computer on which Windows 10 is preinstalled, it comes with a product key, which is included with the device packaging or included as a card or on the Certificate of Authenticity (COA) attached to the device. You can activate Windows by using this product key.
- **Microsoft volume licensing**   Microsoft offers several volume licensing programs to suit different organizational sizes and needs. These programs support both Active Directory–based activation and KMS.

EXAM TIP

Retail versions of Windows 10 cannot be activated using volume licensing methods.

Volume Activation Services

For large organizations with many hundreds or even thousands of devices, using manual product key entry and activation is impractical; it is both error prone and time-consuming. For these reasons, Microsoft provides three methods for volume activation. These are:

- **Key Management Service (KMS)**   You can use this Windows Server role service to activate Windows 10 in your organization's network. Client computers connect to the KMS server to activate, thereby negating the need to connect to Microsoft for activation. It is not necessary to dedicate a server computer to perform activation with the KMS role.

EXAM TIP

KMS is designed for organizations with either 25 (physical or virtual) client devices persistently connected to a network or organizations with five or more (physical or virtual) servers. KMS requires a minimum threshold of 25 computers before activation requests will be processed.

- **Active Directory–based activation**   Any device running any Windows 10 that is connected to your organization's domain network and is using a generic volume license key (VLK) can use Active Directory–based activation. Periodically, the client must renew the license from the licensing service. Therefore, for the activation to remain valid, the client device must remain part of your organization's domain. As with KMS, you do not need to dedicate a server to the Active Directory–based activation role.

EXAM TIP

You cannot use Active Directory–based activation to activate devices running Windows 10 that are not members of your domain.

- **Multiple Activation Key**   Multiple Activation Key (MAK) uses special VLKs that can activate a specific number of devices running Windows 10. You can distribute MAKs as part of your organization's Windows 10 operating system image. This method is ideal for isolated client computers, which will benefit from a one-time activation using the hosted activation services provided by Microsoft.

To use either KMS or Active Directory–based activation to manage your volume activations, the Volume Activation Services server role must be running on a Windows Server 2016 or Windows Server 2019 computer and be configured to use either KMS or Active Directory–based activation. You need to activate the role with Microsoft so that the service can activate devices. This involves entering and validating a KMS host key with Microsoft, either online or by telephone.

An administrator can manage the organization's volume activations centrally using the Volume Activation Management Tool (VAMT) from a Windows 10 or Windows Server 2016 R2 computer. You can download the VAMT as part of the Windows Assessment and Deployment Kit (Windows ADK).

Activate Windows 10

If you are using one of the volume activation methods, you do not need to perform any task on your Windows 10–based devices because Windows 10 will automatically remain in an activated state whilst the volume license agreement is in place. However, if you are manually managing activation on Windows 10–based devices following installation, you must complete the following procedure.

1. Click Start > Settings.
2. Click Update & Security > Activation > Change Product Key.
3. In the Enter A Product Key dialog box, type your 25-character product key.
4. On the Activate Windows page, click Next.
5. When prompted, click Close.

After you have activated Windows 10, you can view the activation status on the Activation tab of the Update & Security section of the Settings app. Also, you can view and manage the activation status of your Windows 10–based product by using the Slmgr.vbs command. For example, Figure 1-8 showed the result of typing the **Slmgr.vbs -dli** command. You can see that Windows 10 Pro is licensed properly.

Activate Windows 10 Virtual Machines

For Windows 10 virtual machines running on Windows 10, version 1803, a new feature called Inherited Activation allows Windows 10 virtual machines to inherit an activation state from their Windows 10 hosts.

When a user creates a new Windows 10 virtual machine (VM) using a Windows 10 local host, the VM will automatically inherit the activation state from a host machine. Inherited Activation requires that both the host computer and the VM are running Windows 10, version 1803 or later and that the host computer has been activated using a Windows 10 E3 or E5 license.

Troubleshoot activation issues

When a device running Windows 10 is not activated, the user is presented with a watermark on the lower-right corner of the screen requesting that you activate Windows. Additionally, you cannot personalize the device, such as changing wallpaper, accent colors, lock screen, themes, or sync settings between devices.

Unlike earlier versions of Windows, there is no grace period for how long you can use Windows 10 without activation. In the Windows 10 license agreement, users are authorized to use Windows 10 only if they are properly licensed and the software has been properly activated with a genuine product key or by another authorized method.

If you are having trouble activating Windows 10, you could try these actions to resolve common activation issues.

VOLUME LICENSE ACTIVATION RENEWAL

If you are using one of the volume activation methods, and your device falls out of activation, you should ensure that the device has network connectivity and that the user has signed onto the device successfully using their corporate credentials. If the activation process does not trigger automatically within two hours there may be an issue with KMS.

Client computers that use KMS must have their activation status renewed at least once every 180 days. Clients achieve renewal by connecting to the network-located KMS host. By default, devices will attempt to renew their activation every seven days following a reboot, or restart of the KMS client service. If KMS activation fails, then the client will retry every two hours, and after 180 days have elapsed following activation, the device will fall out of activation.

If client devices are within the renewal window but fail to automatically activate (perhaps they are present on the network for only a short time), you can force a manual activation while the device is on the network by running or scripting the command **slmgr /ato** using administrative privileges.

CHECKING ACTIVATION STATUS

To check activation status in Windows 10, follow these steps:

1. Open the Settings App.
2. Select Update & Security and then click Activation.
3. View the activation status.
4. If Windows 10 isn't activated, click the Troubleshoot link, as shown in Figure 1-9.

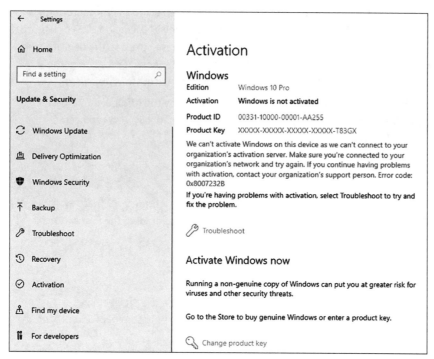

FIGURE 1-9 Troubleshoot activation

ACTIVATING WINDOWS 10 FOR THE FIRST TIME

Most new devices purchased are pre-installed with Windows 10. These devices will automatically activate once the device is connected to the Internet.

If you manually install Windows 10 on a device that has not previously had an activated copy of Windows 10 on it, you'll need to use a valid product key to activate the device. This scenario also covers if you install a different edition of Windows 10 that wasn't previously activated on the device. For example, if you install Windows 10 Pro on a device that had Windows 10 Home installed on it, then you will need to provide a valid Windows 10 Pro product key to activate the device.

ACTIVATING AFTER REINSTALLING WINDOWS 10

If you need to reinstall Windows 10, this could cause issues with your activation status depending on how Windows 10 was originally installed on your device.

If you bought Windows 10 from the Microsoft Store, or if you activated a free upgrade to Windows 10, then you have a digital license for the device.

So long as you reinstall the same edition of Windows 10 onto your device, you won't need a product key. If you're asked to enter a product key during reinstallation, you should skip this step. Windows 10 will automatically activate online after the installation is complete.

ACTIVATION ISSUES AFTER A HARDWARE CONFIGURATION CHANGE

If significant hardware changes are made to a device (such as replacing the motherboard), Windows 10 might fall out of activation. Devices running Windows 10, version 1607 or later that have been used with a Microsoft account will have a digital license linked to the device. If the activation error codes 0x803f7001 or 0xC004C008 appear on the Activation page of the Settings app, you should use the Activation troubleshooter to reactivate Windows.

If the motherboard was replaced under warranty—such as by the original equipment manufacturer (OEM)—then the device should reactivate automatically, or a replacement product key should have been provided.

> **NOTE FIRMWARE UPGRADE**
>
> Consider checking whether the motherboard manufacturer has a firmware update available. This should be applied prior to installing Windows; otherwise, upgrading the firmware after activation might require the system to fall out of activation.

ACTIVATING REFURBISHED DEVICES RUNNING WINDOWS 10

A refurbished device running Windows 10 can be activated using the product key on the Certificate of Authenticity label that will be attached to the device using the following procedure.

1. Open the Settings App.
2. Select Update & Security and then click Activation.

3. Select Change product key.

4. Enter the 25-character product key found on the Certificate of Authenticity and follow the instructions.

USE THE ACTIVATION TROUBLESHOOTER

The Activation troubleshooter is available for all users on the Activation tab within the Settings app. If the device has not been activated, running the troubleshooter can locate a digital license linked to the Microsoft account used on the computer and then prompt you to try activation again.

Sometimes when you run the Activation troubleshooter or attempt to activate a device the activation will fail, and an error code and message will be presented to the user.

COMMON ACTIVATION ERRORS

If you see an error code relating to Windows 10 activation, you can check the list of error codes in Table 1-9 and follow the suggested steps to resolve it. It is not necessary to remember the error codes for the exam, though it is useful to understand the various issues that can arise when activating Windows.

TABLE 1-9 Windows 10 activation errors

ERROR	DESCRIPTION
0xC004F211	Windows reported that the hardware of your device has changed. Use the Activation troubleshooter to reactivate Windows 10 after a hardware change or purchase a new Windows license.
0xC004F212, 0xC004F034, 0xC004F210, 0xC004E016	The product key does not match the installed edition of Windows 10. Re-install the correct edition of Windows 10 or enter a different product key. You might also see this error if the current edition of Windows installed on the device doesn't match the edition of the digital license.
0xC004F213	Windows reported that no product key was found on your device. A digital license is associated with the device hardware, but this is no longer available if the hardware of the device has changed. Use the Activation troubleshooter to reactivate Windows 10 after a hardware change or purchase a new Windows license.
0x803f7001 or 0x800704cF	A valid Windows 10 license couldn't be found to activate Windows 10. If you have a valid product key, select Change product key, and then enter the 25-character product key. If you don't have a valid product key, you will need to purchase a new Windows license.
0xC004C060, 0xC004C4A2, 0xC004C4A2, 0x803FA067L, 0xC004C001, 0xC004C004, 0xC004F004, 0xC004C007, 0xC004F005, 0xC004C00F, 0xC004C010, 0xC004C00E, 0xC004C4A4, 0xC004C4A5, 0xC004B001, 0xC004F010, 0xC004F050	The product key entered can't be used to activate Windows. Enter a different product key or buy a new product key. The activation servers were busy, wait a while and then select Activate. If you upgraded to Windows 10 using the free upgrade offer, Windows 10 should automatically be activated if you didn't make any significant hardware changes to your device (such as replacing the motherboard). If you continue to have problems with activation, contact customer support.

(Continued)

ERROR	DESCRIPTION
0xC004C003	The Windows 10 product key entered isn't valid. Product keys are unique; if a key has already been used, it's marked as not valid.
0xC004FC03	If you're not connected to the Internet or your firewall settings are preventing Windows from completing the activation process online, Windows will not be able to activate. You could try to activate Windows by phone.
0xC004E028	This error is shown if a device is already in the process of activation. Wait for the first request to complete.
0x8007267C	This error appears if the device is not connected to the Internet or the activation server is temporarily unavailable.
0xD0000272, 0xC0000272, 0xc004C012, 0xC004C013, 0xC004C014	If the activation server is temporarily unavailable, Windows will automatically be activated when the service comes back online.
0xC004C008, 0xC004C770, 0x803FA071	The product key has already been used on another PC, or it's being used on more PCs than the Microsoft Software License Terms allow.
0xC004F00F	You might see this error if a product key for the Enterprise edition of Windows is used to activate Windows 10 Home or Windows 10 Pro.
0xC004C020	A Volume License has been used on more PCs than the Microsoft Software License Terms allow.
0x8007232B, 0xC004F074, 0xC004F038, 0x8007007B	A product key for the Enterprise edition of Windows has been used to activate Windows 10 Home or Windows 10 Pro, or a work device is trying to activate, but the device is not connected to the workplace's network.
0x80072F8F	The date and time for the PC is incorrect, or Windows has trouble connecting to the online activation service and can't verify your product key. Use the network troubleshooter to identify and repair any network problems.
0xC004E003	If third-party software has changed system files, then Windows activation may fail. Restore the system files back to an earlier point in time and try to activate again.
0x80004005	Windows activation has failed. Use the Activation troubleshooter, and if this doesn't work, you might need to reset your PC.
0x87e10bc6	An error occurred with the activation server or licensing service. Wait a few minutes, try again, and then use the Activation troubleshooter. Alternatively, launch the Microsoft Store app and if the Microsoft Store app shows there was a problem, select Try Again, which should resolve the issue.

NOTE **ACTIVATE WINDOWS BY PHONE**

Sometimes, you will not be able to connect to the Internet to complete the activation process. You can activate Windows 10 by phone. To find your local freephone telephone number, type **SLUI 04** in the search box on the taskbar and select the SLUI 04 command. Select your country and then use the telephone number and installation ID provided to access the automated phone system to activate Windows. Phone activation cannot be used for Windows 10 Pro, Edu or Windows 10 Pro for Workstations editions.

Skill 1.2: Perform post-installation configuration

After you have provisioned Windows 10, you must ensure that the user is productive as soon as possible. Enabling a consistent Windows environment that looks and behaves the same regardless of the device used can be helpful. Users should be able to browse the Internet safely and in accordance with corporate policies. Devices that are used by mobile users can be configured dynamically to provide them with optimal power settings, and pre-configured connectivity to resources such as secure VPNs and Wi-Fi networks.

This skill covers how to:

- Configure sign-in options
- Customize the Windows desktop
- Configure Microsoft Edge
- Configure Internet Explorer
- Configure mobility settings

Configure sign-in options

After you have activated Windows 10, you can customize the user interface. In some respects, the Windows 10 user interface is familiar to users of Windows 7. It has a Start menu, a desktop, and a taskbar. These things all appear in Windows 7. However, because Windows 10 is designed to work across a variety of device types, including phones, tablets, and traditional desktop computers, it provides additional ways for users to interact.

As an IT pro, it is important for you to understand how to customize the Windows 10 user interface, including Start, taskbar, desktop, and notification settings. This enables you to ensure that the operating system interface meets the needs of the users in your organization.

This section covers how to:

- Configure Microsoft accounts
- Understand multifactor authentication
- Configure Windows Hello and Windows Hello for Business
- Configuring PIN
- Configuring Picture Password
- Configure Dynamic Lock

Configure Microsoft accounts

A Microsoft account (previously called Windows Live ID) provides you with an identity that you can use to securely sign in on multiple devices and access cloud services. You can also use the account to synchronize your personal settings between your Windows-based devices.

If Windows 10 detects an Internet connection during setup, you are prompted to specify your Microsoft account details, though you can skip this step and create a local account instead. You can link your Microsoft account to a local or AD DS domain account after setup is complete.

Microsoft accounts are primarily for consumer use. Domain users can benefit by using their personal Microsoft accounts in your enterprise, though there are no methods provided by Microsoft to provision Microsoft accounts within an enterprise. After you connect your Microsoft account to Windows 10, you can:

- Access and share photos, documents, and other files from sites, such as OneDrive, Outlook.com, Facebook, and Flickr.

- Integrated social media services providing contact information and status for your users' friends and associates are automatically maintained from sites such as Hotmail, Outlook, Facebook, Twitter, and LinkedIn.

- Download and install Microsoft Store apps.

- App synchronization with Microsoft Store apps. After user sign-in, when an app is installed, any user-specific settings are automatically downloaded and applied.

- Sync your app settings between devices that are linked to your Microsoft account.

- Use single sign-on with credentials roaming across any devices running Windows 10, Windows 8.1, Windows 8, or Windows RT.

EXAM TIP

You can browse the Windows Store even if you do not sign in using a Microsoft account. However, you cannot install Store apps without using a Microsoft account.

If Microsoft accounts are allowed in an enterprise environment, you should note that only the owner of the Microsoft account is able to change the password. A user can perform a password reset in the Microsoft account sign-in portal at *https://account.microsoft.com*.

SIGNING UP FOR A MICROSOFT ACCOUNT

To sign up for a Microsoft account, use the following procedure.

1. Open a web browser and navigate to *https://signup.live.com*.

2. To use your own email address for your Microsoft account, type it into the web form; otherwise, provide a telephone number to verify that you are not a robot.

3. To create a new Hotmail or Outlook.com account, click Get A New Email Address and then complete the email address line, specifying whether you want a Hotmail or Outlook suffix.

4. Press Tab to verify that the name you entered is available.

5. Complete the rest of the form and then agree to the privacy statement by clicking I Accept.

After you have created your Microsoft account, you can connect it to your local or domain account and access cloud services.

CONNECTING YOUR MICROSOFT ACCOUNT TO YOUR DEVICE

To connect your Microsoft account to your local or domain user account, use the following procedure.

1. Sign in with your local account.

2. Open the Settings app and click Accounts.

3. On the Your Info page, click Sign In With A Microsoft Account Instead.

4. On the Make It Yours page, enter the email address and then click Sign In.

5. On the Enter Password page, enter the password associated with your Microsoft account and click Sign In.

6. If prompted, enter your local account password to verify your local identity and click Next.

7. The device will now use your Microsoft account to log on.

8. If you want to add additional Microsoft accounts to Windows 10, you can use the Add A Microsoft Account option found on the Email & Accounts tab of the Accounts page in the Settings app.

NEED MORE REVIEW? **SETTING UP MICROSOFT ACCOUNTS ON DEVICES**

For more information about setting up Microsoft accounts on devices, refer to the Microsoft website at *https://account.microsoft.com/account/connect-devices*.

LIMITING THE USE OF MICROSOFT ACCOUNTS

Within an enterprise, you may want to prevent users from associating their Microsoft accounts with a device and block users from accessing cloud resources using their Microsoft accounts.

You can configure Microsoft account restrictions using two GPOs:

- **Block All Consumer Microsoft Account User Authentication**   This setting can prevent users from using Microsoft accounts for authentication for applications or services. Any application or service that has already been authenticated will not be affected by this setting until the authentication cache expires. It is recommended that you enable this setting before any user signs in to a device to prevent cached tokens from being present. This GPO is located at Computer Configuration\Administrative Templates\ Windows Components\Microsoft account.

- **Accounts: Block Microsoft Accounts**   This setting prevents users from adding a Microsoft account within the Settings app. There are two options: Users Can't Add Microsoft Accounts and Users Can't Add Or Log On With Microsoft accounts. This GPO is located at Computer Configuration\Windows Settings\Security Settings\Local Policies\Security Options.

Understand Multifactor Authentication

Traditional computer authentication is based on users providing a name and password. This allows an authentication authority to validate the exchange and grant access. Although password-based authentication is acceptable in many circumstances, Windows 10 provides for a number of additional, more secure methods for users to authenticate with their devices, including multifactor authentication (also referred to as two-factor authentication).

Multifactor authentication is based on the principle that users who wish to authenticate must have two (or more) things with which to identify themselves. Specifically, they must have knowledge of something, they must be in possession of something, and they must be some-thing. For example, a user might know a password, possess a security token (in the form of a digital certificate), and be able to prove who they are with biometrics, such as fingerprints.

EXPLORE BIOMETRICS

Biometrics, like a fingerprint, provides more secure and often, more convenient methods for both user and administrator to be identified and verified. Windows 10 includes native support for biometrics through the Windows Biometric Framework (WBF), and when used as part of a multifactor authentication plan, biometrics is increasingly replacing passwords in modern workplaces.

Biometric information is obtained from the individual and stored as a biometric sample which is then securely saved in a template and mapped to a specific user. To capture a person's fingerprint, you can use a fingerprint reader (you "enroll" the user when configuring this). Also, you can use a person's face, her retina, or even her voice. The Windows Biometric service can be extended to also include behavioral traits such as body gait and typing rhythm.

Windows includes several Group Policy settings related to biometrics, as shown in Figure 1-10, that you can use to allow or block the use of biometrics from your devices. You can find Group Policy Objects here: Computer Configuration\Administrative Templates\ Windows Components\Biometrics.

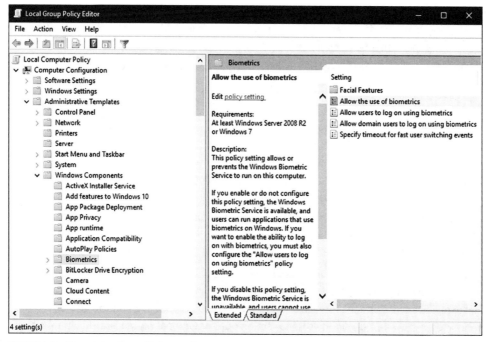

FIGURE 1-10 Biometrics Group Policy settings

Configure Windows Hello and Windows Hello for Business

Windows Hello is a two-factor biometric authentication mechanism built into Windows 10, and it is unique to the device on which it is set up. Windows Hello allows users to unlock their devices by using facial recognition, fingerprint scanning, or a PIN.

Windows Hello for Business is the enterprise implementation of Windows Hello and allows users to authenticate to an Active Directory or Azure Active Directory account, and it enables them to access network resources. Administrators can configure Windows Hello for Business using Group Policy or mobile device management (MDM) policy and uses asymmetric (public/private key) or certificate-based authentication.

Windows Hello provides the following benefits.

- Strong passwords can be difficult to remember, and users often reuse passwords on multiple sites which reduces security. Windows Hello allows them to authenticate using their biometric data.

- Passwords are vulnerable to replay attacks, and server breaches can expose password-based credentials.

- Passwords offer less security because users can inadvertently expose their passwords because of phishing attacks.

- Windows Hello helps protect against credential theft. Because a malicious person must have both the device and the biometric information or PIN, it becomes more difficult to hack the authentication process.

- Windows Hello can be used both in cloud-only and hybrid deployment scenarios.

- Windows Hello logs you into your devices three times faster than a password.

To implement Windows Hello, your devices must be equipped with the appropriate hardware. For example, facial recognition requires that you use special cameras that see in infrared (IR) light. These can be external cameras or cameras incorporated into the device. The cameras can reliably tell the difference between a photograph or scan and a living person. For fingerprint recognition, your devices must be equipped with fingerprint readers, which can be external or integrated into laptops or USB keyboards.

If you have previously experienced poor reliability from legacy fingerprint readers, you should review the current generation of sensors, which offer significantly better reliability and are less error-prone.

After you have installed the necessary hardware devices, you can set up Windows Hello by openings Settings, clicking Accounts, and then, on the Sign-In Options page, under Windows Hello, reviewing the options for face or fingerprint. If you do not have Windows Hello-supported hardware, the Windows Hello section does not appear on the Sign-In Options page.

To configure Windows Hello, follow these steps:

1. Open the Settings App and select Accounts.

2. On the Accounts page, click Sign-in options.

3. Under the Windows Hello section, click Set Up under Face Recognition.

4. Click Get Started on the Windows Hello setup dialog page.

5. Enter your PIN or password to verify your identity.

6. Allow Windows Hello to capture your facial features, as shown in Figure 1-11.

7. Once complete, you are presented with an All Set! message that you can close.

Users can use Windows Hello for a convenient and secure sign-in method that is tied to the device on which it is set up.

For Enterprises that want to enable Windows Hello, they can configure and manage Windows Hello for Business. Windows Hello for Business uses key-based or certificate-based authentication for users by using Group Policy or mobile device management (MDM) policy or a mixture of both methods.

NEED MORE REVIEW? **WINDOWS HELLO BIOMETRICS IN THE ENTERPRISE**

To review further details about using Windows Hello in the enterprise, refer to the Microsoft website at *https://docs.microsoft.com/windows/access-protection/hello-for-business/hello-biometrics-in-enterprise.*

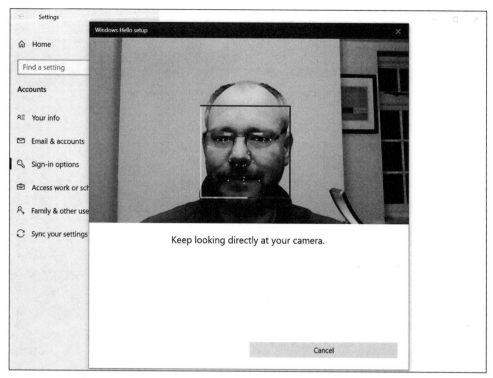

FIGURE 1-11 Configuring Windows Hello

Configure PIN

To avoid authentication with passwords, Microsoft provided an authentication method that uses a PIN. When you set up Windows Hello, you're asked to create a PIN first. This PIN enables you to sign in using the PIN as an alternative to when you can't use your preferred biometric because of an injury or because the sensor is unavailable or not working properly. The PIN provides the same level of protection as Windows Hello.

Windows Hello PIN provides secure authentication without sending a password to an authenticating authority, such as Azure AD or an AD DS domain controller. Windows Hello for Business provides enterprises compliance with the new FIDO 2.0 (Fast IDentity Online) framework for end-to-end multifactor authentication.

Within a domain environment, a user cannot use a PIN on its own (known as a Convenience PIN). You will see from the user interface shown in Figure 1-12, that the PIN settings are within the Windows Hello section of the Sign-In Options. A user must first configure Windows Hello and be already be signed in using a local account, a domain account, a Microsoft account, or an Azure AD account. The user is then able to set up PIN authentication that is associated with the credential for the account.

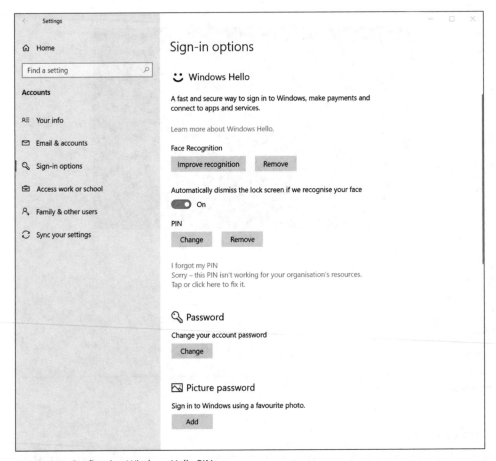

FIGURE 1-12 Configuring Windows Hello PIN

After a user has completed the registration process, Windows Hello for Business generates a new public-private key pair on the device known as a *protector key*. If installed in the device, the Trusted Platform Module (TPM) generates and stores this protector key; if the device does not have a TPM, Windows encrypts the protector key and stores it on the file system. Windows Hello for Business also generates an administrative key that is used to reset credentials if necessary.

> **NOTE** **PAIRING OF CREDENTIALS AND DEVICES**
>
> Windows Hello for Business pairs a specific device and a user credential. Consequently, the PIN the user chooses is associated only with the signed-in account and that specific device.

The user now has a PIN *gesture* defined on the device and an associated protector key for that PIN gesture. The user can now securely sign in to his device using the PIN and then add support for a biometric gesture as an alternative for the PIN. The *gesture* can be facial recognition, iris scanning, or fingerprint recognition, depending on available hardware in the device. When a user adds a biometric gesture, it follows the same basic sequence as mentioned in the previous section. The user authenticates to the system by using the PIN and then registers the new biometric. Windows generates a unique key pair and stores it securely. The user can then sign in using the PIN or a biometric gesture.

NEED MORE REVIEW?   **WINDOWS HELLO FOR BUSINESS**

To review further details about Windows Hello for Business, refer to the Microsoft website at *https://docs.microsoft.com/windows/security/identity-protection/hello-for-business/hello-identity-verification*.

You can use MDM policies or GPOs to configure settings for Windows Hello for Business in your organization. For example, you can configure a policy that enables or disables the use of biometrics on devices affected by the policy.

NOTE   **ENHANCING THE SECURITY OF A PIN**

When we think of a PIN, we generally think of ATM cash machines and 4-digit PINs. For securing Windows 10 with Windows Hello for Business, you can significantly increase the level of security by imposing rules on PINs so that, for example, a PIN can require or block special characters, uppercase characters, lowercase characters, and digits. Something like t496A? could be a complex Windows Hello PIN. The maximum length that can be set is 127.

To configure Windows Hello for Business in your organization, you use the appropriate GPOs within the following location:

Computer Configuration\Policies\Administrative Templates\Windows Components\Windows Hello for Business

To configure PIN complexity with Windows 10 (with and without Windows Hello for Business), you can use the eight PIN Complexity Group Policy settings, which allow you to control PIN creation and management.

These policy settings can be deployed to computers or users. If you deploy settings to both, then the user policy settings have precedence over computer policy settings and GPO conflict resolution is based on the last applied policy. The policy settings included are:

- Require digits
- Require lowercase letters

- Maximum PIN length
- Minimum PIN length
- Expiration
- History
- Require special characters
- Require uppercase letters

In Windows 10, version 1703 and later, the PIN complexity Group Policy settings are located at: Administrative Templates\System\PIN Complexity under both the Computer and User Configuration nodes.

NEED MORE REVIEW? **WINDOWS HELLO FOR BUSINESS GROUP POLICY SETTINGS**

To review more detailed configuration steps for Windows Hello for Business, refer to the Microsoft website at *https://docs.microsoft.com/windows/security/identity-protection/ hello-for-business/hello-cert-trust-policy-settings*.

If an organization is not using Windows Hello for Business, they can still use the option to set a Convenience PIN. A Convenience PIN is very different to a Windows Hello for Business PIN because it is merely a wrapper for the user's domain password. This means that the user's password is cached and substituted by Windows when signing in with a Convenience PIN.

Since the Anniversary release (Windows 10, version 1607), the option to allow a Convenience PIN is disabled by default for domain-joined clients. To modify the option to sign in with the Convenience PIN you can use the Turn On Convenience PIN Sign-In GPO at Group Policy\ Computer Configuration\Administrative Templates\System\Logon.

Configure Picture Password

A picture password is another way to sign in to a computer. This feature does not use Windows Hello or Windows Hello for Business and therefore, it is not available to be used within a domain-based environment.

You sign in to a touch-enabled device by using a series of three movements consisting of lines, circles, and/or taps. You can pick any picture you want and provide a convenient method of signing in to touch-enabled, stand-alone devices. Picture password combinations are limitless because the pictures that can be used are limitless. Although picture passwords are considered more secure for stand-alone computers than typing a 4-digit PIN, a hacker may be able guess his way into a device by holding the screen up to a light to see where most of the gestures are (by following the smudges on the screen). This is especially true if the user touches the screen only to input the password and rarely uses touch for anything else.

To create a picture password follow these steps:

1. Open the Settings App and click Accounts.
2. Click Sign-in options.
3. Under Picture Password, click Add.
4. Input your current account password and click Choose Picture to browse to and select the picture to use.
5. Adjust the position of the picture and click Use This Picture.
6. Draw three gestures directly on your screen.

Remember that the size, position, and direction of the gestures are stored as part of the picture password.

7. You are prompted to repeat your gestures. If your repeated gestures match, click Finish.

There is only one GPO relating to this feature. To disable Picture Password using Local Group Policy, you can use the Turn Off Picture Password Sign-In GPO in the following location:

Computer Configuration\Administrative Templates\System\Logon.

Configure Dynamic Lock

Users with smartphones can take advantage of Dynamic Lock, which was introduced with the Creators Update for Windows 10. Dynamic Lock allows users to automatically lock their devices whenever they are not using them. (At the time of writing, the iPhone does not support this feature.)

The Dynamic Lock feature relies on a Bluetooth link between your PC and paired smartphone.

To configure Windows 10 Dynamic Lock, use the following steps:

1. Open the Settings App and click Accounts.
2. Click Sign-in options and scroll to Dynamic Lock.
3. Check the Allow Windows To Detect When You're Away And Automatically Lock The Device option.
4. Click the Bluetooth & Other Devices link.
5. Add your smartphone using Bluetooth and pair it.
6. Return to the Dynamic Lock page and you should see your connected phone, as shown in Figure 1-13.
7. Your device will be automatically locked whenever Windows detects that your connected smartphone has moved away from your desk for 30 seconds.

You can configure dynamic lock functionality for your devices using the Configure Dynamic Lock Factors GPO. You can locate the policy setting at Computer Configuration\Administrative Templates\Windows Components\Windows Hello for Business.

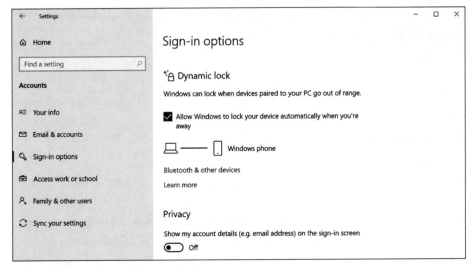

FIGURE 1-13 Configuring Dynamic Lock

Customize the Windows desktop

After Windows 10 has been activated, you can customize the user interface and personalize Windows. Devices enrolled in Microsoft Intune or joined to Azure Active Directory will be activated automatically if a digital license has been assigned. The Windows 10 user interface may be familiar to users of Windows 7 because it has a Start menu, a desktop, and a taskbar.

It is important for you to understand how to customize the Windows 10 user interface, including Start and taskbar layout, desktop, and notification settings. This allows you to ensure that the operating system interface meets the needs of the users in your organization.

> **This section covers how to:**
> - Customize Windows 10 Start
> - Configure the Action Center and taskbar

Customize Windows 10 Start

For users of earlier versions of Windows, the appearance of Start may be significantly different to what they have been used to. Start is dynamic, and its appearance depends on your device type. For example, a device with a small screen such as a tablet, Start appears full-screen, by default, which is easier to navigate when using a touch device.

If you are using a non-touch device, then, by default, Windows 10 displays Start as a menu that combines aspects that may be similar to the Start menu found in Windows 7 and Windows 8.1 (see Figure 1-14). This is more easily navigable by using a mouse than by using touch.

FIGURE 1-14 Start displayed as a partial screen

You can configure the Start menu behavior from the Settings app. Open the Settings App, click Personalization, and then click the Start tab. You can then select the option to Use Start full screen, as shown in Figure 1-15.

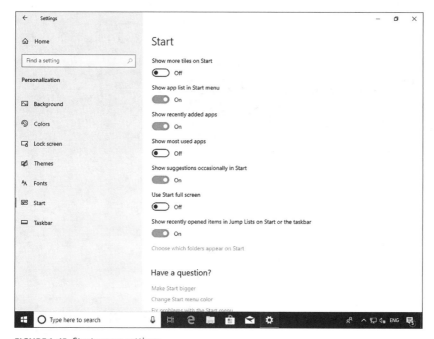

FIGURE 1-15 Start menu settings

The Start customizations shown in Figure 1-15 are:

- **Show More Tiles On Start** This setting enables you to display more tiles when Start is configured for partial-screen mode.
- **Show App List In Start Menu** Enables an alphabetical list of all apps on the left side of the Start screen.
- **Show Recently Added Apps** Any recently installed apps are marked as new in Start.
- **Show Most Used Apps** Windows 10 tracks your app usage and lists your most frequently used apps in a Most Used Apps list in Start.
- **Show Suggestions Occasionally In Start** This setting enables or disables app suggestions in Start.
- **Use Start Full Screen** Enables Start to display full screen. This is more useful on a tablet device than on a device with a mouse.
- **Show Recently Opened Items In Jump Lists On Start Or The Taskbar** This setting enables Windows 10 to remember recently opened files and list those in the context menu of apps appearing in Start or on the taskbar.
- **Choose Which Folders Appear On Start** This setting enables you to set shortcuts for the following folders on Start: File Explorer, Settings, Documents, Downloads, Music, Pictures, Videos, Network, and Personal Folders.

CONVERTIBLE DEVICES

Convertible devices, including the Microsoft Surface Pro, can switch in and out of Tablet Mode with the removal and reattachment of the keyboard, or by reorienting the device. When a device switches like this, you can choose whether Windows should switch to full-screen Start (Tablet Mode) automatically, as shown in Figure 1-16.

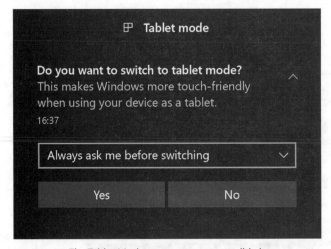

FIGURE 1-16 The Tablet Mode prompt on a convertible laptop

You can configure the default behavior through the Settings app. Click System and then open the Tablet Mode tab. As shown in Figure 1-17, you can then configure the following options.

- When I Sign In:
  - Use Tablet Mode
  - Use Desktop Mode
  - Use The Appropriate Mode For My Hardware
- When This Device Automatically Switches Tablet Mode On Or Off:
  - Don't Ask Me And Don't Switch
  - Always Ask Me Before Switching
  - Don't Ask Me And Always Switch
- Hide App Icons On The Taskbar In Tablet Mode
- Automatically Hide The Taskbar In Tablet Mode

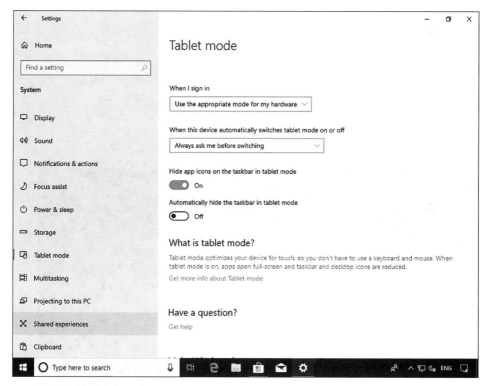

FIGURE 1-17 Tablet Mode options

NOTE **TABLET MODE**

Tablet Mode also changes applications so that they run full screen.

CONFIGURING START TILES

In addition to enabling or disabling Start Full-Screen behavior, you can also customize the application tiles that appear on Start and how those tiles look and behave. From Start, right-click the appropriate app, as shown in Figure 1-18. Click Pin To Start.

When a tile is pinned to Start, you can configure it. Right-click the tile and, from the context menu, you can choose:

- Unpin From Start
- Resize
    - Choose from Small, Medium, Large, and Wide, depending on the app.
- More
    - If the app is a Microsoft Store app, choose from Turn Live Tile Off, Pin To Taskbar, App Settings, Rate And Review, and Share.
    - If the app is a desktop app, choose from Pin To Taskbar, Run As Administrator, and Open File Location.
- Uninstall

> *NOTE* **UNINSTALLING DESKTOP APPS FROM START**
> If the app you select to uninstall is a desktop app, Programs And Features opens in Control Panel allowing you to manually remove the desktop app.

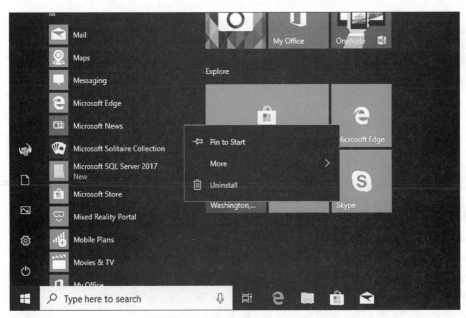

FIGURE 1-18 Customizing Start screen with a mouse

If your device is touch-enabled, the procedure is slightly different from using a mouse to configure tiles. Rather than right-clicking a tile from Start, you must touch and hold a tile. Then you can unpin the tile by using the Unpin icon. Use the ellipse button (three dots) to access the context menu, as shown in Figure 1-19.

FIGURE 1-19 Customizing Start screen with touch

GROUPING START TILES

After you have added the required tiles to Start, you might want to group the tiles. You can perform the following actions on groups.

- To create a new group of tiles, simply drag a tile to an area of unused space on Start.
- To name a group, hover your mouse or tap the screen immediately above the group of tiles and then type the name for your group in the text box that appears.
- To move tiles between groups, drag the required tile to the new group.

EXPORT START LAYOUT

Although you can manually drag and resize tiles on Start for each computer in your organization, this is not practical at scale. Within a corporate environment, you can control the Start layout by creating a customized Start screen on a test computer and then export the layout to other devices.

Not all editions of Windows 10 support customizing Windows 10 Start and taskbar with Group Policy. These are shown in Table 1-10 as follows:

TABLE 1-10 Windows 10 Start and taskbar support

WINDOWS VERSION	SUPPORTED EDITION
Windows 10, version 1607	Windows 10 Enterprise and Windows 10 Education
Windows 10, version 1703	Windows 10 Pro, Windows 10 Enterprise, and Windows 10 Education

You can choose to export a layout that applies a full or partial Start layout.

- **Full Start layout** Users cannot pin, unpin, or uninstall apps from Start. Users cannot pin any apps to Start.
- **Partial Start layout** The contents of the specified tile groups cannot be changed. Users can move groups and can create and customize their own groups.

The Start layout is exported as a .xml file, which can then be deployed to devices using:

- Group Policy
- Windows Configuration Designer provisioning package
- Mobile device management (MDM)

On your test computer, you can customize the Start layout prior to exporting the layout. Customization can include:

- Pin apps to Start.
- Unpin the apps that you don't want to display.
- Drag the tiles on Start to reorder or group apps.
- Resize tiles.
- Create your own app groups.
- Name groups.

Once you have configured the desired Start layout, you use the Export-StartLayout Windows PowerShell cmdlet to export the Start layout to an .xml file using the following procedure.

1. Open Windows PowerShell.
2. Run the `Export-StartLayout –path <path><file name>.xml` cmdlet.
3. You can optionally edit the .xml file to add a taskbar configuration.

4. Copy the exported file to a shared folder.

5. Deploy the .xml file using any of the deployment methods.

If you use Group Policy, you must specify the .xml file in the GPO: User Configuration\ Policies\Administrative Templates\Start Menu and Taskbar\Start Layout. To do this, complete the following procedure.

1. Open Group Policy Management Console (GPMC) to configure a domain-based GPO.

2. Navigate to the appropriate AD DS container, such as your domain.

3. Open an existing GPO for editing or create a new GPO, link it to your chosen container, and open it for editing.

4. Navigate to the User Configuration\Policies\Administrative Templates\Start Menu And Taskbar folder and open the Start Layout GPO.

5. Enable the GPO and, in the Start Layout File text box, type the full UNC path name to your XML file, for example, **\\LON-SVR1\Marketing\Marketing.XML** as shown in Figure 1-20.

6. Click OK and close Group Policy Management.

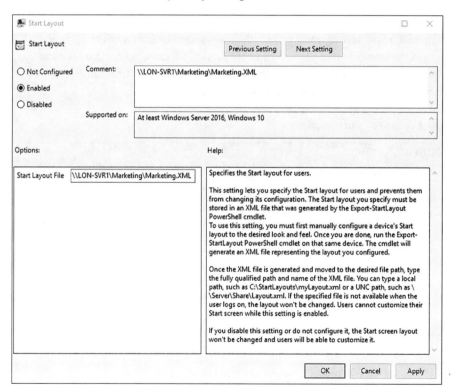

FIGURE 1-20 Deploy custom Start using Group Policy

For the policy to be effective, users must sign out and sign back in. Alternatively, you can issue a **Gpupdate.exe /force** command from an elevated command prompt to force GPO propagation.

To configure a partial Start screen layout, you should export the Start layout and then open the layout .xml file. You should then add **LayoutCustomizationRestrictionType="Only SpecifiedGroups"** to the **<DefaultLayoutOverride>** element as follows:

```
<DefaultLayoutOverride LayoutCustomizationRestrictionType="OnlySpecifiedGroups">
```

Then save the file and deploy the settings.

If you like, you can update an existing Start layout by replacing the .xml file that is specified in the Start Layout policy settings with an .xml file that has a newer timestamp.

NEED MORE REVIEW?   **MANAGE WINDOWS 10 START AND TASKBAR LAYOUT**

For more information about customizing Start and taskbar layout, visit the Microsoft website at *https://docs.microsoft.com/en-us/windows/configuration/customize-and-export-start-layout*.

In addition to the Start layout, you can control other aspects of Start with Group Policy. Table 1-11 shows the elements that you can control with GPOs and the respective values to use within GPOs. Unless otherwise noted, the path for these GPO settings is User Configuration\ Policies\Administrative Templates\Start Menu And Taskbar.

TABLE 1-11 Using Group Policy to configure Start

START ELEMENT	POLICY
User tile	Remove Logoff On The Start Menu
Most Used	Remove Frequent Programs List From The Start Menu
Suggestions	Computer Configuration\Policies\Administrative Templates\Windows Components \Cloud Content\Turn Off Microsoft Consumer Experiences
Power	Remove And Prevent Access To The Shut Down, Restart, Sleep, And Hibernate Commands
All Apps	Remove All Programs List From The Start Menu
Jump lists	Do Not Keep History Of Recently Opened Documents
Start size	Force Start To Be Either Full Screen Size Or Menu Size
All Settings	Prevent Changes To Taskbar And Start Menu Settings

CUSTOMIZE THE DESKTOP

In addition to customizing Start to your requirements, you can configure the desktop and related settings. To configure the desktop, click Start > Settings > Personalization.

From the Personalization Settings app, you can configure the following settings.

- **Background**   You can select and configure a desktop background color or picture image, or you can select a slideshow of images.
- **Colors**   On the Color tab, you can choose a color scheme and optionally configure the following options.
  - Enable transparency effects.
  - Show accent color on the following surfaces: Start, taskbar, Action Center, title bars, and window borders.
  - Choose the default app mode: Light or Dark.
  - Access the High Contrast Settings.
- **Lock Screen**   From the Lock Screen tab, as shown in Figure 1-21, you can select and configure a background image to display when your Windows 10 device is locked. A feature called Windows Spotlight allows you to display different background images on the lock screen each day and will occasionally suggest Windows 10 features that the user hasn't tried yet, such as Snap Assist. In addition, you can
  - Choose a lock screen background image.
  - Choose An App To Show Detailed Status (for example, Calendar).
  - Choose Apps To Show Quick Status (for example, Facebook, Mail, Calendar, or Alarms & Clock).
  - Configure Cortana Lock Screen Settings.
  - Show Lock Screen Background Picture On The Sign-In Screen.
  - Configure Screen Timeout Settings and Screen Saver Settings.

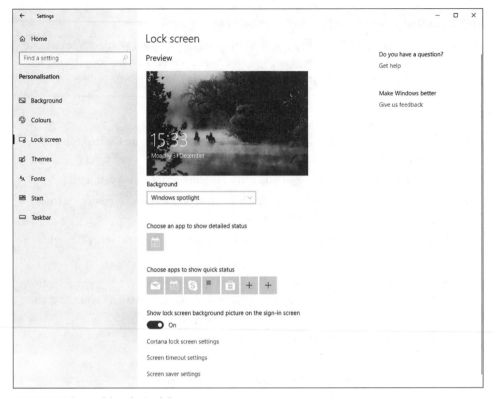

FIGURE 1-21 Customizing the Lock Screen

- **Themes** This setting enables you to configure and apply theme settings. Themes enable you to define combinations of background, color, sound, and mouse cursor settings. You can also configure desktop icon settings, such as whether to display the Recycle Bin on the desktop. You can download from the dozens of additional themes available free from the Microsoft Store, as shown in Figure 1-22.

- **Start** You can also configure Start settings, as previously discussed.

- **Taskbar** From this tab, among other settings, you can.

  - Lock the taskbar.

  - Automatically hide the taskbar when in Desktop or Tablet Mode.

  - Use small taskbar buttons.

  - Configure the way running tasks and apps combine on the taskbar.

  - Configure whether the Command Prompt will appear instead of Windows Power-Shell on Start; you can also configure whether the Command Prompt appears in the menu when the Windows key + X is pressed.

- Change the taskbar location.
- Customize the notification area.
- Turn system icons on or off.
- Customize the taskbar appearance when using multiple displays.
- Customize the People settings.

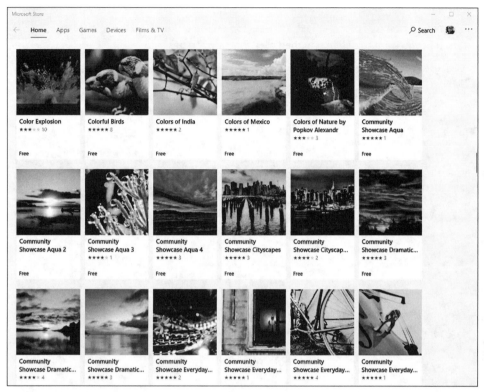

FIGURE 1-22 Additional themes

Multiple desktops

Windows 10 provides support for multiple desktops. This provides a simplistic multitasking view. Rather than running apps in multiple windows on the same desktop, you can create additional desktops for groups of apps or individual apps. Multiple desktops can be useful for keeping unrelated windows or projects organized; multiple desktops are also useful for quickly switching to a clean desktop before a meeting.

To add a new desktop, click the Task View button on the taskbar and then click New Desktop in the upper-left of the display. You can also add a new desktop by pressing Windows key + Tab on your keyboard, or you can swipe with one finger from the left of your screen if you have touch.

To switch between desktops, click the Task View button, press Windows key + Tab, or swipe with one finger from the left of your touchscreen. You can then select the appropriate desktop as shown in Figure 1-23.

To remove a desktop, click the Task View button on the taskbar and then hover over the desktop that you want to delete and then click the X on the desktop.

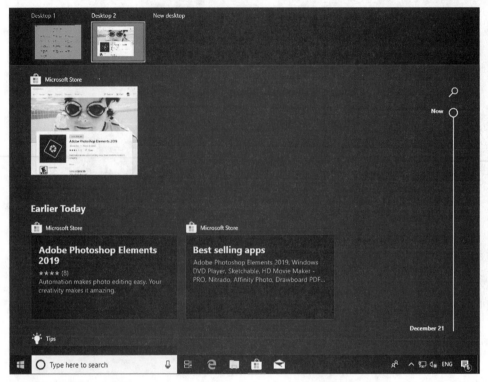

FIGURE 1-23 Virtual desktops

Configure Action Center and taskbar

In Windows 10, Microsoft introduces an improved Action Center, as shown in Figure 1-24. This is accessible by swiping from the right or by clicking the Notifications icon in the system tray.

FIGURE 1-24 The Action Center

Action Center includes the following elements:

- **Quick Action tiles** As shown at the bottom of Figure 1-24, the displayed tiles are configurable and dependent on your device.

- **Notifications area** You can configure how Windows notifies you of events.

CONFIGURE QUICK ACTION TILES

The Quick Action tiles are shortcuts to commonly used features of the Windows 10 operating system. The expanded view allows a larger number of tiles to become visible as shown in Figure 1-24. The specific tiles that appear in the expanded view will depend on your device type and orientation. For example, if your computer is not a tablet and is not capable of converting into a tablet, the Tablet Mode tile is not available. By default, in the expanded view, the following tiles are available.

- **Tablet Mode**   Enables you to switch between Tablet and Desktop Modes.
- **Rotation Lock**   Enables or disables the rotation lock. Normally, the display orients itself based on the orientation of your Windows 10 device, switching between landscape and portrait modes. Use this option to lock the orientation irrespective of physical orientation.
- **Airplane Mode**   Disables all internal radios in the device, including Wi-Fi and Bluetooth for use when you travel on an aircraft. This is also a convenient when you want to conserve battery power.
- **All Settings**   Provides a convenient shortcut to the Settings app.
- **Connect**   Enables you to find and connect to media servers. This includes Xbox and other devices running Windows that are sharing their media files. It can also include devices, such as TV set-top boxes.
- **Project**   Enables you to link your device to an external monitor or wireless display.
- **Battery Saver**   Only available when your device is running on battery alone; helps reduce power consumption. You can configure Power Options and Battery Saver in the Settings app.
- **VPN**   Switches to the VPN tab in the Network & Internet Settings app. From there, you can set up, configure, or connect to a VPN.
- **Bluetooth**   Enable or disable the Bluetooth radio.
- **Brightness**   Enables you to control display brightness. Click this tile to step through brightness levels in 25 percent increments.
- **Wi-Fi**   Enables or disables the Wi-Fi connection.
- **Focus Assist**   (Called Quiet Hours in earlier versions of Windows 10) allows you to avoid distracting notifications when you need to stay focused by reducing the notifications you receive.
- **Night Light**   Toggles your display to remove white light. You can configure Night Light in the Settings app.
- **Location**   Enables or disables location services. Many services use location to customize services, such as mapping apps, for your device.

You can modify which quick action tiles are displayed by clicking the Add Or Remove Quick Actions and rearrange the location of the tiles by dragging and dropping them within the Settings app, as shown in Figure 1-25.

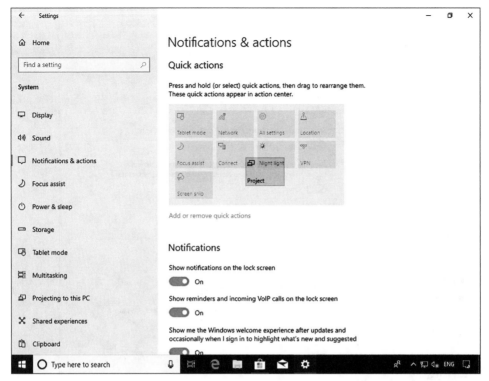

FIGURE 1-25 Windows 10 Quick Actions settings

CONFIGURE NOTIFICATIONS

When Windows 10 wants to inform you about something, it raises a notification. You can see and act on the notifications in a list shown in Action Center. To respond to a notification, click it. You can remove notifications by clicking Clear All at the top of the page.

Windows notifies you about a variety of operating system events and situations, including the need to obtain updates or perform an antivirus scan, and Windows also prompts you about which actions you want to take when a new device, such as a USB memory stick, has been detected.

As shown in Figure 1-26, you can configure which notifications you receive by opening Settings. Click System > Notifications & Actions. Under Notifications, you can configure the following options.

- Show Notifications On The Lock Screen.
- Show Reminders And Incoming VoIP Calls On The Lock Screen.
- Show Me The Windows Welcome Experience After Updates And Occasionally When I Sign In To Highlight What's New And Suggested.
- Get Tips, Tricks And Suggestions As You Use Windows.
- Get Notifications From Apps And Other Senders.

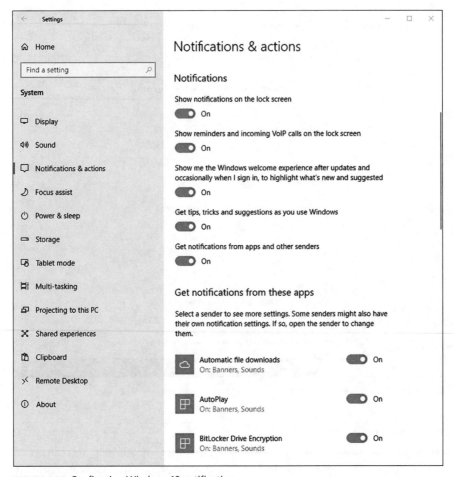

FIGURE 1-26 Configuring Windows 10 notifications

You can also configure notifications from individual apps. As shown in Figure 1-26, under the Get Notifications From These Apps heading, you can enable or disable notifications for each listed app. If you select an app from the list, such as for Microsoft Edge, as shown in Figure 1-27, you can fine tune the notifications for the application, including turning them on or off:

- Notifications
- Show Notification Banners
- Keep Notifications Private On The Lock Screen
- Show Notifications In Action Center
- Play A Sound When A Notification Arrives
- Number Of Notifications Visible In Action Center
- Priority Of Notifications In Action Center

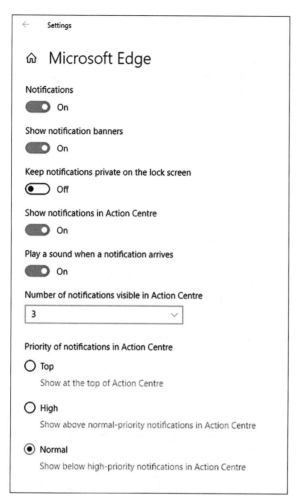

FIGURE 1-27 Configuring Windows 10 notifications for specific apps

EXAM TIP

You can remove the Notification & Action Center from the notification area on the taskbar using Group Policy. Notifications will pop up, but users won't be able to review any notifications they miss. Use the User Configuration\Policies\Administrative Templates\Start Menu And Taskbar node and enable the Remove Notifications And Action Center GPO.

CONFIGURE THE TASKBAR

You have seen how to configure the taskbar using the Settings app. The same functionality is available if you right-click the taskbar. Administrators can also pin additional apps to the taskbar and remove default pinned apps from the taskbar.

This is achieved by adding a **<TaskbarLayout>** section to a layout modification XML file used to configure the Start screen.

You can specify which apps are added the taskbar using the Application User Model ID (AUMID) or Desktop Application Link Path (the local path to the application). The easiest method to obtain the AUMID or Desktop Application Link Path is to extract the information from the **Export-StartLayout** cmdlet we saw earlier by following these steps:

1. Pin the required application to the Start menu on a reference or testing PC.
2. Open Windows PowerShell and run the **Export-StartLayout** cmdlet.
3. Open the generated XML file.
4. Identify the entry corresponding to the app you pinned.
5. Look for a property labeled **AppUserModelID** or **DesktopApplicationLinkPath**.

Once you have obtained the app information, you can configure the taskbar using these steps:

1. Create the XML file and include the **<CustomTaskbarLayoutCollection>** section.
2. Use the AUMID or Desktop Application Link Path to identify the apps to pin to the taskbar.
3. Add **xmlns:taskbar="http://schemas.microsoft.com/Start/2014/TaskbarLayout"** to the first line of the file, before the closing **>**.
4. Use **<taskbar:UWA>** and AUMID to pin Universal Windows Platform apps.
5. Use **<taskbar:DesktopApp>** and the Desktop Application Link Path to pin desktop applications.

The layout modification XML file can be applied to devices using Group Policy or a provisioning package created in Windows Configuration Designer.

NEED MORE REVIEW? **CONFIGURE WINDOWS 10 TASKBAR**

This Microsoft resource contains sample taskbar configuration XML files which can help you configure the taskbar and discusses how to remove default apps. Visit *https://docs.microsoft .com/windows/configuration/configure-windows-10-taskbar#sample-taskbar-configuration- added-to-start-layout-xml-file.*

CONFIGURE THE NOTIFICATION AREA

As shown in Figure 1-28, you can also configure taskbar options from the Personalization area of the Settings app. Open the Personalization area and then click the Taskbar tab. There are two headings under the Notification Area with options for each:

- Select Which Icons Appear On The Taskbar

Options include:

- Always Show All Icons In The Notification Area
- Power

- Network
- Volume
- Windows Security notification icon
- Microsoft OneDrive
- Location notification
- Turn System Icons On Or Off

Options include:

- Clock
- Volume
- Network
- Power
- Input Indicator
- Location
- Action Center
- Touch Keyboard
- Windows Ink Workspace
- Touchpad

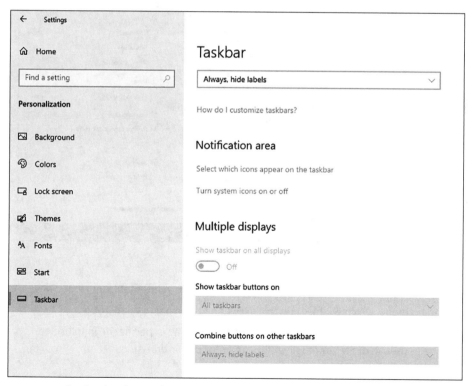

FIGURE 1-28 Configuring the Notification Area

Configure Microsoft Edge

Microsoft Edge, shown in Figure 1-29, is a web browser that provides a consistent interface across device types, such as Windows 10-based tablets, laptops, and smartphones. The interface is simple and touch-centric, making it the ideal browser for devices running Windows 10. Microsoft Edge is also available on Android and iOS devices.

For readers not familiar with Microsoft Edge, it is the default browser for all Windows 10 devices. Windows 10 ships with both Microsoft Edge for modern websites and Internet Explorer 11 for compatibility with enterprise web apps that use older web technologies like ActiveX.

Because Microsoft Edge supports only the latest web standards, it offers users a fast and safe browsing experience. Microsoft Edge is like Windows 10, in that it is regularly updated. Because it was first introduced with Windows 10, many new features and functionality have been added, including the ability to manage tabs, read e-books, write on webpages, and more.

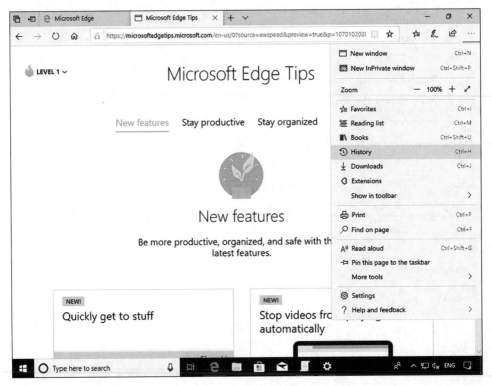

FIGURE 1-29 Microsoft Edge

Microsoft Edge includes a number of features not available in Internet Explorer 11. These are:

- Reading mode, which enables you to view webpages in a simplified layout.
- Kiosk mode, which allows only Microsoft Edge to display a specific site in full-screen mode as used in digital/interactive signage or for public browsing.

- The Hub, a feature that consolidates several items, including:
  - Favorites
  - Reading List
  - Books
  - Extensions
  - History
  - Downloads
- Web Notes, which enable you to use tools to make notes, draw, write, and highlight webpages.

It is important to know how to configure Microsoft Edge, including how to migrate web Favorites to this new browser, to support your organization's users. Microsoft Edge has streamlined settings that you can easily configure from the More Actions link in the browser, as shown in Figure 1-30.

FIGURE 1-30 Configuring settings in Microsoft Edge

From this window, you can access the following options:

- **New Window**   Enables you to open a new browser window.
- **New InPrivate Window**   Provides the same privacy options enabled by InPrivate browsing in Internet Explorer.
- **Zoom**   Enables you to zoom in or out on a webpage.
- **Favorites**   Opens your webpage favorites.
- **Reading List**   Opens your saved reading list items.
- **History**   Opens your webpage history.
- **Extensions**   Opens your browser add-ins and offers a list of suggested extensions.
- **Downloads**   Opens your download history.
- **Print**   Enables you to print the webpage.
- **Find On Page**   Searches for content on the current webpage.
- **Read Aloud**   Narrates the content on the current webpage.
- **Pin This Page To The Taskbar**   Enables you to pin frequently accessed webpages directly to the Taskbar.
- **More Tools**   Provides additional tools:
    - **Add Notes**   Uses OneNote to capture annotations, inking, and notes on a webpage
    - **Share This page**   Allows you to share the webpage to your contacts or create a link to the page
    - **Cast Media To Device**   Enables you to send content, such as a video, to wireless media devices
    - **Open With Internet Explorer**   Opens the current webpage in Internet Explorer 11
    - **Pin This Page To Start**   Enables you to pin frequently accessed webpages directly to your Start page
    - **Developer Tools**   Opens a new developer console

EXAM TIP

Microsoft Edge does not support ActiveX controls, Browser Helper Objects, VBScript, or other earlier technology. If your users access websites that rely on these features, you can configure Microsoft Edge to switch to Internet Explorer 11 automatically when these sites are accessed, enabling you to use Microsoft Edge as your default browser. To do this, enable and configure Enterprise Mode.

From the Settings Cog at the bottom of the window, you can access four submenus: General, Privacy and Security, Passwords and Autofill, and Advanced:

- **General** The general settings include:

  - **Choose A Theme** Enables you to choose between light and dark themes. The dark theme might display better in low-light situations.

  - **Open Microsoft Edge With** Enables you to specify what you see when you open Microsoft Edge, such as a specific webpage or multiple tabbed webpages.

  - **Open New Tabs With** Enables you to set how new tabs are displayed. You can configure it to match the Open With setting, or you can define another value.

  - **Transfer Favorites And Other Info** You can import your favorites and other information from another web browser, such as Internet Explorer.

  - **Show The Favorites Bar** You can enable a list of the sites on your Favorites bar.

  - **Show The Home Button** You can show or hide the Home button.

  - **Set your home page** You can configure the home page to be displayed when Microsoft Edge loads.

  - **Show Sites I Frequently Visit In "Top Sites"** You can configure Microsoft Edge to prioritize your most frequently visited sites.

  - **Show Definitions Inline For** You can turn on or off the display of dictionary definitions for words in Reading View, Books, and PDFs.

  - **Downloads** You can configure where you want Microsoft Edge to save downloads and if the user should be prompted each time.

  - **Account** You can view the Microsoft account that Microsoft Edge will use for sync.

  - **Sync Your Favorites, Reading List, Top Sites And Other Settings** Enables you to sync your Microsoft Edge settings to your other devices to provide a consistent browsing experience.

  - **About This App** Displays the current Microsoft Edge and Microsoft EdgeHTML versions.

- **Privacy And Security** Includes several options:

  - **Browsing Data**

    - Clear Browsing Data

    - Cookies

    - Media Licenses

  - **Privacy**

    - Send Do Not Track Requests

    - Search And Site Suggestions

- Show Search History
- Use Page Prediction

- **Security**
  - Block Pop-Ups
  - Windows Defender SmartScreen

- **Passwords And Autofill**   Includes several options:

- **Passwords**
  - Save Passwords
  - Manage Passwords

- **Autofill**
  - Save Form Data
  - Manage Forms
  - Save Cards
  - Manage Cards

- **Advanced Settings**   Includes several options:

- **Site Settings**
  - Adobe Flash: Use Adobe Flash Player
  - Media Autoplay
  - Website Permissions: Manage Permissions

- **Proxy Set-up**
  - Open Proxy Settings

- **Open Sites With Apps**
  - Choose Which Sites Open In Apps

- **Cortana**
  - Allow Cortana To Assist Me In Microsoft Edge

- **Address Bar Search**
  - Change Search Provider

Customize Microsoft Edge

One of the benefits of the integration between Windows 10 and Microsoft Edge is the extensive ability to customize Microsoft Edge for your organization. These settings cover every aspect of the modern browser including configuring default tabs, security settings, allowed extensions and browser experience preferences, and more.

A list of the configuration options relating to Microsoft Edge, together with a link to the Group Policy and Microsoft Intune reference webpage, can be found in Table 1-12.

TABLE 1-12 Microsoft Edge configuration options

CONFIGURATION AREA	DESCRIPTION & URL
Address bar	Configure Microsoft Edge to show search suggestions in the address bar. *https://docs.microsoft.com/microsoft-edge/deploy/group-policies/address-bar-settings-gp*
Adobe Flash	Configure Microsoft Edge to load Adobe Flash content automatically. *https://docs.microsoft.com/microsoft-edge/deploy/group-policies/adobe-settings-gp*
Books Library	Set up and use the books library, including creating a shared books folder for students and teachers. *https://docs.microsoft.com/microsoft-edge/deploy/group-policies/books-library-management-gp*
Browser experience	Customize browser settings, such as printing and saving browsing history. *https://docs.microsoft.com/microsoft-edge/deploy/group-policies/browser-settings-management-gp*
Developer tools	Configure Microsoft Edge for development and testing. *https://docs.microsoft.com/microsoft-edge/deploy/group-policies/developer-settings-gp*
Extensions	Configure Microsoft Edge to either prevent or allow users to install and run unverified extensions. *https://docs.microsoft.com/microsoft-edge/deploy/group-policies/extensions-management-gp*
Favorites	Provision a standard favorites list as well as keep the favorites lists in sync between IE11 and Microsoft Edge. *https://docs.microsoft.com/microsoft-edge/deploy/group-policies/favorites-management-gp*
Home button	Customize the home button or hide it. *https://docs.microsoft.com/microsoft-edge/deploy/group-policies/home-button-gp*
Interoperability and enterprise guidance	Use Microsoft Edge and Internet Explorer together. *https://docs.microsoft.com/microsoft-edge/deploy/group-policies/interoperability-enterprise-guidance-gp*
Deploy Microsoft Edge kiosk mode	Configure Microsoft Edge kiosk mode with assigned access. *https://docs.microsoft.com/microsoft-edge/deploy/microsoft-edge-kiosk-mode-deploy*
New Tab page	Configure the New Tab page in Microsoft Edge. *https://docs.microsoft.com/microsoft-edge/deploy/group-policies/new-tab-page-settings-gp*
Prelaunch Microsoft Edge and preload tabs in the background	Pre-launch Microsoft Edge to minimize the amount of time required to start up Microsoft Edge. *https://docs.microsoft.com/microsoft-edge/deploy/group-policies/prelaunch-preload-gp*

(Continued)

CONFIGURATION AREA	DESCRIPTION & URL
Search engine customization	Set the default search engine and configure additional ones. *https://docs.microsoft.com/microsoft-edge/deploy/group-policies/ search-engine-customization-gp*
Security and privacy	Keep your environment and users safe from attacks. *https://docs.microsoft.com/microsoft-edge/deploy/group-policies/ security-privacy-management-gp*
Start page	Configure the Start pages in Microsoft Edge. *https://docs.microsoft.com/microsoft-edge/deploy/group-policies/ start-pages-gp*
Sync browser settings	Prevent the "browser" group and users from syncing. *https://docs.microsoft.com/microsoft-edge/deploy/group-policies/ sync-browser-settings-gp*
Telemetry and data collection	Configure Microsoft Edge to collect certain data. *https://docs.microsoft.com/microsoft-edge/deploy/group-policies/ telemetry-management-gp*

If your organization uses Group Policy, you can locate the majority of the Microsoft Edge Group Policy settings in the following location:

Computer Configuration\Administrative Templates\Windows Components\Microsoft Edge

Microsoft Edge kiosk mode

If you are running Windows 10, version 1809, (Professional, Enterprise, and Education editions only) you can use Microsoft Edge in a kiosk environment using assigned access. The assigned access feature allows you to lock down a Windows 10 device to only run a single-app or multi-app, which can then be used in a public space, such as a kiosk.

Microsoft Edge in kiosk mode allows you to operate a digital signage for presentation in a public area or to deploy devices for members of the public to use for web browsing in InPrivate mode. You can configure the behavior of Microsoft Edge when it's running in kiosk mode by configuring the appropriate policy as shown in Table 1-13.

TABLE 1-13 Microsoft Edge kiosk mode policy

MANAGEMENT TOOL	POLICY
Group Policy	Configure Kiosk Mode
Microsoft Intune	ConfigureKioskMode

Microsoft Edge in kiosk mode supports four configuration types as shown in Table 1-14. The Group Policy settings are shown in Figure 1-31.

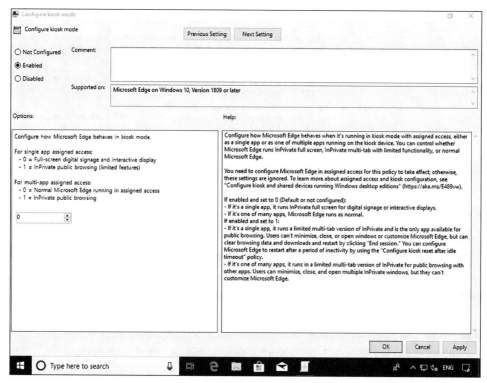

FIGURE 1-31 Microsoft Edge kiosk mode GPO

Microsoft Edge kiosk mode can be set up in various configurations depending on your requirements as listed in Table 1-14.

TABLE 1-14 Microsoft Edge kiosk mode configuration types

CONFIGURATION TYPE	DESCRIPTION

Single-app - Digital/interactive signage	■ Runs Microsoft Edge InPrivate displaying a single website running in full-screen mode for the following scenarios:
	  ■ **Digital signage** Rotating advertisement or menu requiring no user interaction.
	  ■ **Interactive signage** Allows user interaction, which is restricted to within the page, such as a building business directory or restaurant order/pay station.
	■ Prevents any other uses, such as browsing the Internet.
	■ Policy setting = Not configured (0 default)

Single-app - Public browsing	■ Runs a limited multi-tab version of Microsoft Edge. ■ Microsoft Edge is the only app users can use on the device—they can browse publicly or close Microsoft Edge using the End Session button. ■ The session will reset after five minutes of user inactivity, which will restart Microsoft Edge with a new session.

(Continued)

CONFIGURATION TYPE	DESCRIPTION
	■ Public browsing is useful within a public library or hotel concierge desk. ■ Policy setting = Enabled (1)
Multi-app - Normal browsing	■ Runs Microsoft Edge with all browsing features and preserves the user data and state between sessions. ■ With assigned access apps that have dependents may not work as expected. For example, if the Microsoft Store is not available then installing Microsoft Edge extensions will not work. ■ Policy setting = Not configured (0 default)
Multi-app - Public browsing	■ Runs a multi-tab version of Microsoft Edge InPrivate in full-screen mode. Users can open and close Microsoft Edge and launch other apps that have been allowed by assigned access. No "End session button" is shown and users close Microsoft Edge normally which clears their browsing session. ■ Policy setting = Enabled (1)

When you use Microsoft Edge in kiosk mode, the default experience includes:

- **Safer browsing**   Microsoft Edge in kiosk mode for public browsing runs Microsoft Edge InPrivate mode. This protects user data and deletes the browsing history, temporary Internet files, and cookies once the session has ended or is reset.

- **Automatic browser session reset**   Microsoft Edge kiosk mode has a built-in timer, which resets the browser session to the default URL after five minutes of idle time.

- **Default URLs**   You must configure the URL to load when the kiosk session launches. The URL sets the Home button, Start page, and New Tab page.

- **Assigned access required**   Configuring kiosk mode policy settings for Microsoft Edge are not applied unless Microsoft Edge is run using assigned access.

CONFIGURE KIOSK MODE

To set up a single-app device using Microsoft Edge kiosk mode follow these steps:

1. On the kiosk device, click Start, search for **kiosk,** and then select Set Up A Kiosk (Assigned Access).

2. On the Set Up A Kiosk page, click Get started.

3. Type a name to create a new kiosk local account and click Next.

4. On the Choose A Kiosk App page, select Microsoft Edge and then click Next.

5. Select how Microsoft Edge displays when running in kiosk mode:

   a. Digital Sign Or Interactive Display

   b. Public Browser

6. Select Next.

7. Type the URL to load when the kiosk launches.

8. Configure the idle time before Microsoft Edge resets and click Next.

9. On the Your Done! page, click Close.

10. Review the settings on the Set Up A Kiosk page.

11. Under Advanced Settings, you will see that if the device crashes, no error message will be displayed, and the device will automatically restart.

12. Restart the device for Microsoft Edge kiosk mode to run.

> **NOTE** **MICROSOFT EDGE KIOSK MODE FIRST RUN**
>
> The Welcome To The Best Windows Ever page will appear the first time you run Microsoft Edge kiosk mode. You should end this session by clicking the End Session button and then click Yes, which will restart Microsoft Edge and display the configured home page.

To end Microsoft Edge kiosk mode, you need to click Ctrl+Alt+Delete and then sign in to the device using another account. Once kiosk mode is enabled, the device will always automatically sign in and launch the configured app as a kiosk using assigned access.

To disable using Microsoft Edge as a kiosk using assigned access, you should follow these steps:

1. On the kiosk device click Ctrl+Alt+Delete.

2. On the sign in screen, sign in using another account.

3. Click Start, search for kiosk, and then select Set Up A Kiosk (Assigned Access). (If Search is not available you can access Set Up A Kiosk within the Settings app > Accounts > Family & Other Users.)

4. On the Set Up A Kiosk page, under Kiosk Info, select the kiosk username.

5. Click Remove Kiosk.

6. On the Remove Kiosk page, click Remove.

> **NEED MORE REVIEW?** **DEPLOY MICROSOFT EDGE KIOSK MODE**
>
> This Microsoft resource provides additional information relating to deploying and configuring Microsoft Edge kiosk mode using GPOs and Microsoft Intune including a comprehensive list of the Microsoft Edge policies that you can use to enhance the kiosk experience. Visit *https:// docs.microsoft.com/microsoft-edge/deploy/microsoft-edge-kiosk-mode-deploy*.

Microsoft Edge as a service

The Microsoft Edge web browser will have new features added on a regular basis, as has happened since the initial technical preview release in early 2015. Microsoft Edge is not available as a standalone download for Windows 10, though it is available as an app for Android and iOS devices through their respective app stores.

Microsoft Edge is updated through Windows Update, which will install security fixes, product feature enhancements, group policies and MDM settings for Microsoft Edge in a similar fashion to updates on Windows 10.

You can view the various update cadence in Table 1-15.

TABLE 1-15 Microsoft Edge update cadence

UPDATE	FREQUENCY / CONTENT
Quality updates (Security Enhancements)	Every second Tuesday of each month. Does not include new features; only issues relating to system stability and security are installed.
Out-of-band Quality updates	Ad hoc, outside of standard release schedule. Where devices must be updated immediately either to fix security vulnerabilities or to solve quality issues impacting many devices.
Cumulative updates	Minor feature updates, typically monthly.
Feature updates	Semi-annual basis. Twice per year, around March and September.

Enterprises can use several tools to manage the Microsoft Edge updates as part of the new Windows as a Service model, including:

- Windows Update (stand-alone)
- Windows Update for Business
- Windows Server Update Services (WSUS)
- System Center Configuration Manager

Every new update published includes all changes from previous updates, as well as new fixes; these updates are known as "latest cumulative update" (LCU) packages. A newly imaged device can simply become "up to date" by installing the most recent LCU.

When updates are available for download to Windows 10 using the Windows Update servicing engine, the operating system can scan the update and will automatically only install the updates that are needed by the device to become completely up to date.

Windows 10 users can expect new LCU packages to be published on the second Tuesday of each month (often referred to as Patch Tuesday), which is classified as a required security update and contains new security, non-security, and browser fixes.

You can check the installed version of Microsoft Edge by using the following steps:

1. Open the Microsoft Edge web browser.
2. Select the menu icon (...) and then choose Settings.
3. Scroll all the way down to the About This App section.
4. The versions of Edge and EdgeHTML are listed.

> **NOTE   MICROSOFT EDGE LONG TERM SERVICING CHANNEL**
>
> If you use the Long-Term Servicing Channel (LTSC) versions of Windows 10, you will not find Microsoft Edge installed. Because Microsoft Edge and its associated services are frequently updated with new functionality, it is not supported on systems running LTSC operating systems. The LTSC does support Internet Explorer 11.

Enterprise Mode

We have seen how Microsoft Edge offers safer browsing for modern websites and apps, but the majority of the web—including company intranet sites—is still using older versions of HTML, ActiveX controls, and unsupported third-party add-ins. Internet Explorer 11 is included with Windows 10 to allow users to continue to access these websites in a supported, safe, and secure way.

Enterprise Mode is a business-focused feature that allows you to operate a dual-browser experience, using Microsoft Edge as your default browser but automatically switch to Internet Explorer 11 when users need to access sites that cannot be viewed in Microsoft Edge.

It is unrealistic to expect enterprises to only permit viewing of websites and apps that can be viewed by Microsoft Edge. It is expected that newer development projects will be written using modern web standards, which will be supported by Microsoft Edge.

For widespread compatibility problems with your popular, or required, websites and apps opening in Microsoft Edge you can populate the Enterprise Mode site list with these sites, so that they seamlessly open in Internet Explorer 11. Once the user completes browsing the site, they can close the browser, or if they attempt to browse to another website, which is not on the site list, then Microsoft Edge will automatically launch to continue the browsing experience.

Using Enterprise Mode allows that you can continue to use Microsoft Edge as your default browser, while also ensuring that websites and apps needed by your users continue working.

Enterprise Mode includes the following features:

Web app and website compatibility   Allows many legacy web apps run unmodified on IE11.

Enterprise Mode Site List Manager   Provides a management tool for website lists.

Centralized Control   Specify the websites or web apps, which Enterprise Mode will manage and store this XML file on a website or network, or it can be stored locally.

Integrated Browsing   Once set up, users can browse the web normally, letting the browser change modes automatically.

Data Gathering   Enterprise Mode can be used to collect website compatibility issues from your users' browsing activity, which you can use to add URLs to your central site list.

CONFIGURE ENTERPRISE MODE

To enable and configure Enterprise Mode for Microsoft Edge, use the following steps:

1. Download and install the Enterprise Mode Site List Manager (schema v.2) tool for Windows 10 from *https://www.microsoft.com/download/confirmation.aspx?id=49974*.
2. Open the Enterprise Mode Site List Manager tool.
3. Add the URLs of websites that you want to direct to Microsoft Edge or Internet Explorer 11. (You don't need to include the http:// or https:// designation.)
4. For each URL, select None, IE11, or MSEdge to open the website.

5. Optionally, add any comments about the website into the Notes About URL box.

6. Click Save to validate your website and to add it to the site list.

7. Click File > Save To XML and save the file to a network share.

8. Open Group Policy Management Console (GPMC) to configure a domain-based GPO.

9. Navigate to the appropriate AD DS container, such as your domain.

10. Open an existing GPO for editing or create a new GPO, link it to your chosen container, and open it for editing.

11. Navigate to Computer Configuration\Policies\Administrative Templates\Windows Components\Microsoft Edge and enable the Configure The Enterprise Mode Site List policy.

12. In the Type The Location (URL) Of Your Enterprise Mode IE Website dialog box, type the location of the XML file you saved. For example, type **\\LON-SVR1\Marketing\Marketing. XML** as shown in Figure 1-32.

13. Click OK and close Group Policy Management.

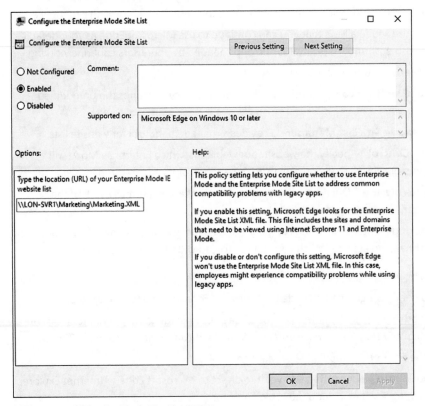

FIGURE 1-32 Enterprise Mode Site List GPO

Configure Internet Explorer

Although Microsoft Edge is suitable for most users when browsing modern websites, Internet Explorer 11 is included to provide backward compatibility for websites that require features currently not supported in Microsoft Edge. Because your users might use both browsers, it is important to know how to configure both Microsoft Edge and Internet Explorer.

Internet Explorer contains a number of security and privacy features that can help make browsing safer. Specifically, the Protected Mode, InPrivate Browsing, and InPrivate Filtering features help maintain user privacy, whereas the Windows Defender SmartScreen helps guard against malicious websites and software. To help your users get the best from Internet Explorer, it is important to know how to configure these and other settings.

To access Internet Explorer settings, open Internet Explorer and click the Tools menu (cog), as shown in Figure 1-33.

FIGURE 1-33 Accessing Internet Explorer settings

You can then choose from among the following options.

- **Manage Add-Ons**   Enable enhancements to some websites, such as providing toolbars and extensions, search providers, multimedia support, and enhanced content. Use this option to enable and disable add-ons.

- **Compatibility View Settings**   Most websites render as intended in Internet Explorer 11, but some sites use design standards for earlier versions of Internet Explorer. If you encounter websites that do not render correctly, you can use Compatibility View settings to force Internet Explorer to render the website as if it was using an earlier version of Internet Explorer. To render a website using an earlier version of Internet Explorer, from the Compatibility View Settings dialog box, enter the name of the website and click Add.

EXAM TIP

You can display all intranet sites in Compatibility View by selecting the Display Intranet Sites In Compatibility View check box in the Compatibility View Settings dialog box.

- **Internet Options**   To configure additional settings, click Internet Options. This opens the dialog box shown in Figure 1-34.

FIGURE 1-34 Configuring settings in Internet Explorer

The Internet Options dialog box has the following tabs.

- **General**   Available options are:
  - **Home Page**   Create home page tabs by entering addresses, each on its own line.
  - **Startup**   Choose Start With Tabs From The Last Session or Start With Home Page.
  - **Change How Webpages Are Displayed In Tabs**   Clicking the Tabs button opens the Tabbed Browsing Settings dialog box where you can control how tabbed browsing behaves, such as warning you when multiple tabs are closed at once, showing previews for individual tabs in the taskbar, and showing you how to deal with pop-ups.
  - **Browsing History**   This portion of the dialog box includes options to delete elements of browsing history, such as Temporary Internet Files, History and Caches And Databases.
  - **Appearance**   Four buttons—Colors, Languages, Fonts, and Accessibility—provide you with options for managing the appearance of websites.
- **Security**   Available options are
  - **Security Zone Settings** You can configure the four security zones' settings. The zones are Internet, Local intranet, Trusted Sites, and Restricted Sites. You can add or remove websites from these zones and configure the security settings for each zone. The Internet Zone is the default zone for all websites and has medium-high security settings, which allows users to perform most tasks.
  - **Enable Protected Mode**   Protected Mode makes it more difficult for malware to be downloaded, thereby helping to protect users from attack by running an IE process with greatly restricted privileges on Windows 10. It is enabled by default.
- **Privacy**   Available options are
  - **Sites**   This option enables you to define cookie handling on a per-site basis.
  - **Advanced**   This option enables you to define whether to accept, block, or prompt for first-party and third-party cookies.
  - **Never Allow Websites To Request Your Physical Location**   Select this option if you want to prevent sites from requesting your physical location.
  - **Turn On Pop-up Blocker**   This is enabled by default. The Settings button enables you to configure per-website settings for notification pop-up handling.
  - **Disable Toolbars And Extensions When In Private Browsing Starts**
- **Content**   Available options are
  - **Certificates**   This option enables you to view your certificates and trusted publishers.

- **AutoComplete**   This option enables you to define autocomplete options for the address bar, forms, and usernames and passwords. You can also delete autocomplete history here.
- **Feeds And Web Slices**   This option enables you to define the default schedule and frequency of when feeds and web slices from online content are updated.

- **Connections**   Available options are
    - **Dial-Up And Virtual Private Network**   These settings are for connecting to the Internet.
    - **LAN Settings**   This allows you to configure script settings and configuring IE to use a web proxy server.

- **Programs**   Available options are
    - **Define How Internet Explorer Opens**   This allows you to configure the default browser.
    - **Manage Add-Ons**   This allows you to enable or disable browser add-ons installed on your system.
    - **Configure HTML Editing**   This allows you to choose the program that you want Internet Explorer to use for editing HTML files.
    - **Internet Programs**   This allows you to select the programs you want to use for other Internet services such as email.
    - **Manage File Associations**   This allows you to the select file types that you want Internet Explorer to open by default.

- **Advanced**   Many options are available, enabling you to fine-tune Internet Explorer configuration and behavior. You can also reset Internet Explorer settings to their default condition.

Although you can manually configure these settings in Internet Explorer on each computer, you can also use more than 1,600 GPOs in an AD DS domain environment to configure the settings for computers at scale.

The GPO settings for Internet Explorer are located in the Computer Configuration\Policies\ Administrative Templates\Windows Components\Internet Explorer node.

There are 11 child nodes within the main Internet Explorer node as shown in Figure 1-35, including GPOs that control privacy, compatibility view, and security features. You can configure the same settings on the User Configuration node if necessary.

> **NEED MORE REVIEW?   GROUP POLICY AND INTERNET EXPLORER 11**
>
> To review further details about the GPO settings available for Internet Explorer 11, refer to the Microsoft website at *https://docs.microsoft.com/internet-explorer/ie11-deploy-guide/ group-policy-and-ie11.*

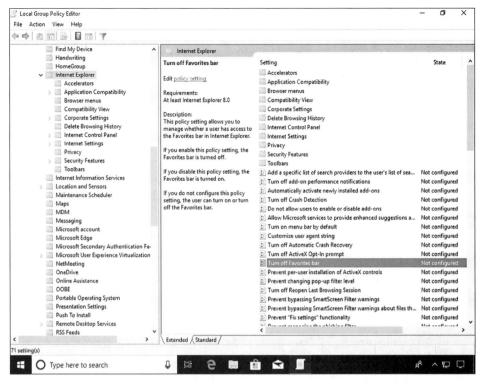

FIGURE 1-35 Internet Explorer Group Policy

Internet Explorer 11 will continue to receive security updates through its supported lifespan. Internet Explorer is a component of the operating system and follows the Lifecycle Policy of Windows 10. Internet Explorer 11 bugs will be evaluated by Microsoft on a case-by-case basis.

Microsoft recommends that users use Microsoft Edge as their default browser, and Microsoft supports Internet Explorer 11 for backward compatibility. The latest features and platform updates will only be available in Microsoft Edge.

Configure mobility settings

A priority for users of mobile devices, such as the Surface range of Windows 10 tablets and laptops, is to be able to conserve battery life so that extended device use is possible. Mobile devices are often used away from the office or home environment, and it is important to know how to configure power settings in Windows 10 to meet your users' needs.

Mobile devices can be used to display information, such as PowerPoint presentations during meetings, and enabling the presentation settings within Windows 10 can configure the device for a presentation and reduce distractions and interruptions.

Configure basic power options

You can control Windows 10 power settings in several ways. On a mobile device, you can configure basic power options by using the Power & Sleep tab in the System Settings app, as shown in Figure 1-36.

On the Power & Sleep tab, you can configure the following options.

- **Screen**   Available options are
    - **On Battery Power, Turn Off After**   Select a value or choose Never.
    - **When Plugged In, Turn Off After**   Select a value or choose Never.
- **Sleep**   Available options are
    - **On Battery Power, PC Goes To Sleep After**   Select a value or choose Never.
    - **When Plugged In, PC Goes To Sleep After**   Select a value or choose Never.
- **Network Connection**   Available options are
    - **When My PC Is Is Asleep And On Battery Power, Disconnect From The Network**   Select Always, Managed By Windows, or Never.

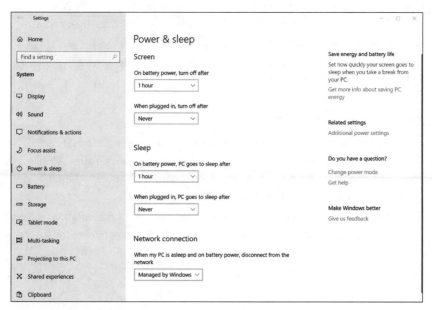

FIGURE 1-36 Power & Sleep options

You can configure additional power options by clicking the Battery tab, as shown in Figure 1-37, and set the following options.

- **Overview**   View estimated battery time remaining.
- **See Which Apps Are Affecting Your Battery Life**   View a report showing battery usage over the preceding 6 hours, 24 hours, or one week; also, you can filter by Apps with usage, All Apps and Always Allowed Apps.
- **Battery Notifications**   See notifications for battery life.
- **Battery Saver**   Configure when battery saver is enabled, implement battery saver until the next charge, and configure lower screen brightness while the device is using battery saver.
- **More Saving Options**   View battery saving tips and configure battery optimization settings for when watching films and playing video.

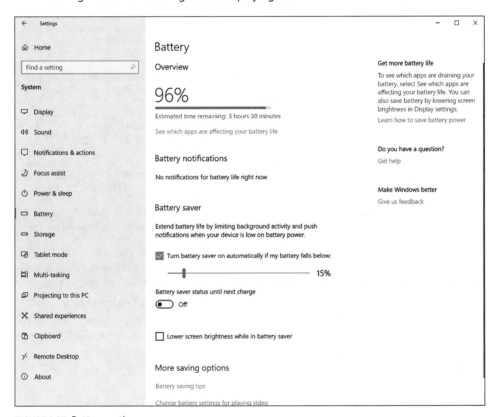

FIGURE 1-37 Battery options

Configure power plans

In addition to the battery settings available within the Settings app, Windows 10 provides a number of preconfigured power plans, as shown in Table 1-16. You can access these power plans from the Settings app, by clicking System, Power & Sleep, and then click the Additional Power Settings link.

TABLE 1-16 Power plans

PLAN	POWER CONSUMPTION	SCREEN	SYSTEM ACTIVITY
Power Saver	Low	By default, the display is powered off after five minutes of inactivity.	Saves energy by reducing system performance whenever possible.
Balanced	Medium	You can configure the plan to turn off the display after a specified amount of time.	Measures computer activity and continues to use full power to all system components currently in use.
High Performance	High	This sets the screen to 100% brightness.	Keeps the computer's drives, memory, and processors continuously supplied with power.
Ultimate Performance	High	This sets the screen to 100% brightness.	Keeps the computer's drives, memory, and processors continuously supplied with power. Forces processor state to be 100%. Not available on battery powered devices.

You can select from among existing power plans by clicking the desired power plan, or you can create a new power plan by clicking Create A Power Plan. Also, you can configure basic options, such as whether your device will prompt you for a password when it wakes up, and what the power buttons and lid do on your computer. To reconfigure a plan, click Change Plan Settings. Within the settings options, you can also choose Change Advanced Power Settings to configure detailed plan settings.

WINDOWS 10 PRO FOR WORKSTATIONS

If you're running Windows 10 Pro for Workstations, there is a new Ultimate Performance power plan scheme available, as shown in Figure 1-38. This is intended to be used on high-end workstation devices that demand increased performance. The policy implements fine-grained power management techniques that allow devices to run at maximum performance by removing the power management, performance, and efficiency tradeoffs that are normally present in Windows 10.

Unless you are using the Windows 10 Pro for Workstations edition the Ultimate Performance power plan will be hidden in Power Options. The plan is not available on battery powered devices.

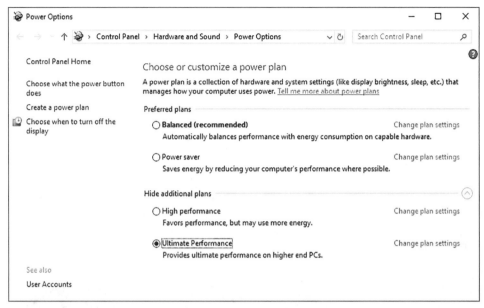

FIGURE 1-38 Ultimate Performance power plan

CONFIGURE POWER SETTINGS

You can exert more granular control over your computer's power settings by using the Additional Power Settings link in the Settings app or by opening the Power Options item in Control Panel. You can switch power plans, and you can also configure these options:

- **Choose What The Power Buttons Do** This allows you to specify the actions to be taken when the power button on the device is pressed.

- **Choose What Closing The Lid Does** This allows you to specify the actions to be taken when the device lid is closed.

- **Create A Power Plan** This allows you to create a new device power plan with custom settings.

- **Choose When To Turn Off The Display** This allows you to specify the idle time delay before the system automatically turns off the device display.

- **Change When The Computer Sleeps** This allows you to specify the idle time delay before the system automatically puts the device into sleep mode.

If you aren't already familiar with these features, take some time now to explore them. Make sure to create your own personal power plan by using the Create A Power Plan option because you might see something about that on the exam. You might also be asked to state how many minutes must pass for each of the three default plans (Balanced, High Performance, and Power

Saver) before the computer goes to sleep or turns off the display, when running on its battery, or when plugged in. Additionally, you'll need to know how to monitor battery usage from the Notification area of the Taskbar and how to change common mobility settings, such as the power plan type and display brightness.

USING POWERCFG.EXE

Powercfg.exe is a command-line tool you can use to configure and manage power settings. Using Powercfg.exe, you can view the power plans available and export power plans. Powercfg .exe can be useful when configuring a batch of devices, each with the same hardware specifications, such as a roll out of new laptops. You would create a custom power plan on one device, and then export the power management plan to a file using Powercfg.exe. You would then import the plan to the other devices either using Powercfg.exe or by using Group Policy.

To get a list of the available power plans using this command, type **powercfg.exe list** at a command prompt. If you haven't yet created any custom plans, you'll only see the three default plans that come with Windows 10, as shown in Figure 1-39. Choose the plan to export and note the GUID value. To export the policy, open an elevated command prompt, and run **powercfg.exe export** *power*.pow *GUID* (where the GUID value used is the plan that you want to export).

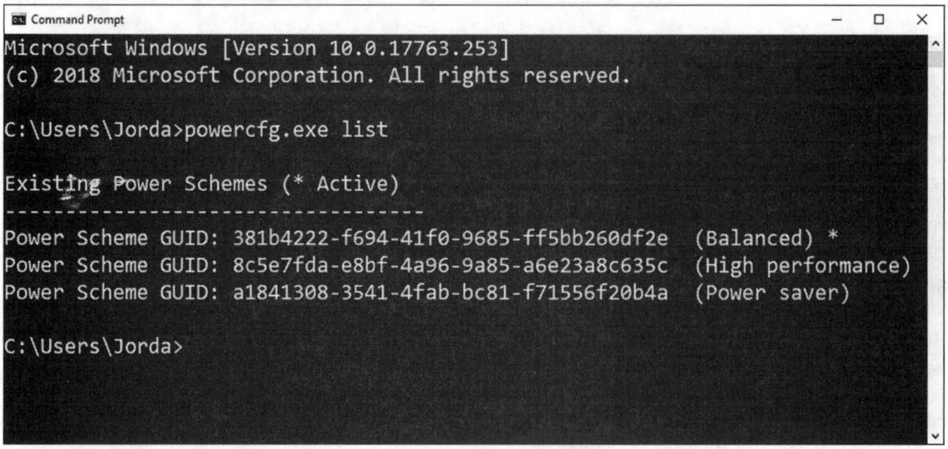

```
Command Prompt                                              —  □  ×
Microsoft Windows [Version 10.0.17763.253]
(c) 2018 Microsoft Corporation. All rights reserved.

C:\Users\Jorda>powercfg.exe list

Existing Power Schemes (* Active)
---------------------------------
Power Scheme GUID: 381b4222-f694-41f0-9685-ff5bb260df2e  (Balanced) *
Power Scheme GUID: 8c5e7fda-e8bf-4a96-9a85-a6e23a8c635c  (High performance)
Power Scheme GUID: a1841308-3541-4fab-bc81-f71556f20b4a  (Power saver)

C:\Users\Jorda>
```

FIGURE 1-39 The default Windows 10 power plans, as shown by Powercfg.exe

> *MORE INFO*   **POWERCFG COMMAND-LINE OPTIONS**
>
> For more information about Powercfg.exe command line options, visit *https://docs.microsoft. com/windows-hardware/design/device-experiences/powercfg-command-line-options*.

There are some other parameters you can use with Powercfg.exe. You should review these so that you are familiar with them.

- **changename**   This option modifies the name of a power scheme and optionally, its description.
- **-delete**   This option deletes the power scheme with the specified GUID.
- **-setactive**   This option makes the specified power scheme active on the system.
- **/deviceenablewake and /devicedisablewake**   This option enables and disables a device from waking the system from a sleep state.
- **/systempowerreport**   This option generates a diagnostic system power transition report.
- **/batteryreport**   This option generates a report of battery usage characteristics over the lifetime of the system.

Some of the modern reports, such as the battery usage or system power reports, are generated in HTML format and provide a huge amount of detail, which is invaluable if you are troubleshooting issues with battery life or device power consumption.

CREATING POWER POLICIES

You can use Group Policy to set policies related to the available power plans. Use the Group Policy Management Editor to navigate to Computer Configuration\Administrative Templates\ System\Power Management. When you expand Power Management in the left pane, you can see the additional containers: Button Settings, Energy Saver Settings, Hard Disk Settings, Notification Settings, Power Throttling Settings, Sleep Settings, and Video And Display Settings. In the right pane, you can see two options: Specify A Custom Active Power Plan and Select An Active Power Plan, as shown in Figure 1-40.

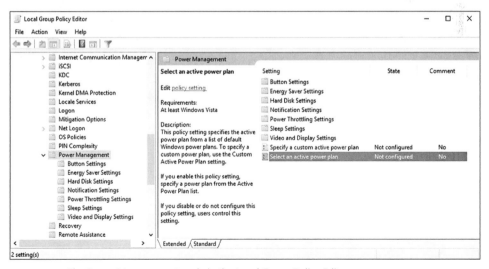

FIGURE 1-40 The Power Management node in the Local Group Policy Editor

When you click one of the seven nodes under Power Management, more options appear. You can control every aspect of power management here. For instance, in the Sleep Settings node, you can configure, enable, and disable the following (and more).

- **Specify The System Sleep Timeout (Plugged In)**   This policy setting allows you to specify the period of inactivity before the system is put into sleep mode while plugged into a power outlet.

- **Specify The System Sleep Timeout (On Battery)**   This policy setting allows you to specify the period of inactivity before the system is put into sleep mode while running on battery power.

- **Require A Password When The Computer Wakes (Plugged In)**   This policy setting specifies whether the user is prompted for a password when the system resumes from sleep while plugged into a power outlet.

- **Require A Password When The Computer Wakes (On Battery)**   This policy setting specifies whether the user is prompted for a password when the system resumes from sleep while running on battery power.

- **Allow Standby States (S1 S3) When Sleeping (Plugged In)**   This policy setting specifies whether a device can use standby states other than hibernate when putting the computer in a sleep state while plugged into a power outlet.

- **Allow Standby States (S1 S3) When Sleeping (On Battery)**   This policy setting specifies whether a device is able to use standby states other than hibernate when putting the computer in a sleep state while running on battery power.

You should review these policies in each node to familiarize yourself with the various options available.

VIEWING PROCESS POWER USAGE

A new feature within Task Manager allows you to view the instantaneous power usage of apps and services using your device's power.

Task Manager now includes two new columns in the Processes tab, as shown in Figure 1-41, to show energy impact of the running process on your system. This can be helpful to understand the levels of power that apps and services are using. Task Manager considers the processor, graphics, and disk drive power when calculating power usage. There are two columns available, as follows.

Power Usage   Provides an instantaneous view of apps and services using power.

Power Usage Trend   Provides a power usage trend over the previous two minutes for running apps and services.

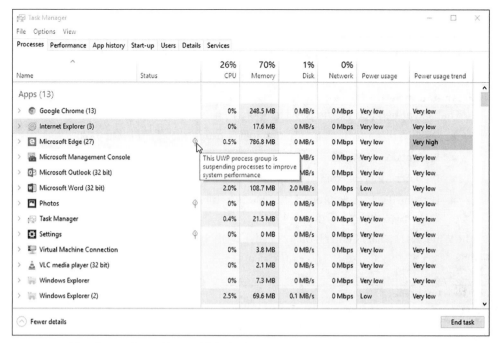

FIGURE 1-41 View Process Power Usage with Task Manager

Using Task Manager, you can also see if a process has been suspended. To view suspended apps, look in the Status column of the Processes tab for a leaf icon. You can see that the Photos, Microsoft Edge, and Settings apps have been suspended, as shown in Figure 1-41. You should also see that when the cursor is hovered over the leaf icon next to Microsoft Edge, a tooltip describing the status is displayed.

Configure presentation settings

Windows 10 includes a useful utility called the Windows Mobility Center, which can be used to configure various mobility settings, all from one location. Depending upon your system, some or all the following settings might be available on your mobile device, as shown in Figure 1-42.

Brightness Enables you to adjust the brightness of your display.

Volume Enables you to adjust the speaker volume of your device; also, you can select the Mute check box to silence the speaker.

Battery Status Lets you view how much charge is remaining on your battery and change the active power plan.

Screen Orientation   Lets you change the orientation of your device screen from portrait to landscape, or vice versa.

External Display   Enables connection to an additional monitor to your device.

Sync Center   Enables you to sync with external data sources, such as Offline Files.

Presentation Settings   Lets you turn on presentation settings during a presentation. Enabling presentation settings will temporarily have the following effects.

- Disables pop-ups and notifications area pop-ups (such as from Outlook)
- Prevents Windows from going into sleep mode
- Prevents Windows from turning the screen off
- Uses the display background and volume settings defined in the Presentation Settings, as shown in Figure 1-43

The Windows Mobility Center is only available on mobile devices, such as laptops and tablets.

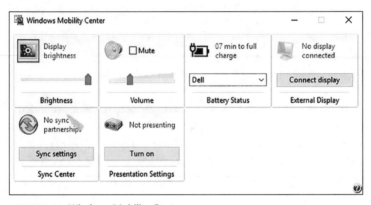

FIGURE 1-42   Windows Mobility Center

The Presentation Settings utility, as shown in Figure 1-43, can be used in association with the Windows Mobility Center to configure turning off the screen saver, controlling the volume, and selecting a background image to be displayed when you give a presentation.

You can access the Presentation Settings utility on a mobile device by clicking the Presentation Settings icon or by using these steps.

1. Click Start and search for Presentation Settings.
2. In the search results, select Adjust Settings Before Giving A Presentation Control Panel.
3. The Presentation Settings utility appears, as shown in Figure 1-43.

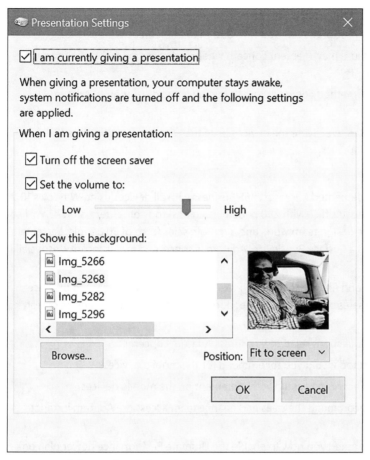

FIGURE 1-43 Adjust settings before giving a presentation

Thought experiments

In these thought experiments, demonstrate your skills and knowledge of the topics covered in this chapter. You can find the answers to these thought experiments in the next section.

Scenario 1

Adatum has 2,000 workstations running Windows 7. The company plans to implement Windows 10. Adatum management wants to minimize the effects of the changes and so it intends to roll out the new operating system over a weekend. All computers are less than two years old and must be running Windows 10 Enterprise at the end of the project.

As a consultant for Adatum, answer the following questions.

1. What is the most appropriate method for Adatum to implement Windows 10?
2. How can you reassure management concern whether devices meet the minimum system requirements?
3. What deployment method could you use to minimize the disruption to Adatum employees?
4. How would you plan to activate the devices once they are running Windows 10?

Scenario 2

Adatum has recently implemented Microsoft 365 Business with all devices using Windows 10 Pro. The company has a head office with 200 people using desktop computers, a branch office where 25 members of the design team work, and a remote sales force of 50 people. Each member of the sales team uses a Surface Pro device. Adatum is concerned about security, especially on the mobile devices.

Members of the sales and finance teams need to access the Adatum intranet to produce quotations and manage sales orders. The intranet does not display properly using Microsoft Edge.

Answer the following questions relating to address Adatum concerns.

1. What sign-on method would you recommend for the mobile devices?
2. What encryption technology could you implement on the mobile devices?
3. How would you recommend the sales and finance team access the Adatum intranet website?
4. Your manager has asked you how to enable the Ultimate Performance power plan on the design team desktop computers.

Thought experiment answers

This section provides the solutions for the tasks included in the Thought experiments section.

Scenario 1

1. An in-place upgrade from Windows 7 directly to Windows 10 is supported and recommended by Microsoft and could be performed in the timescale required.
2. Because all devices are less than two years old and currently run Windows 7, they already meet the minimum system requirements for running Windows 10.
3. By upgrading the devices directly to Windows 10 using an in-place upgrade, all user and application settings will be preserved. This will offer the least disruption to the users.
4. All devices would be automatically activated using the digital license present on the device if they were previously running a genuine version of Windows 7.

Scenario 2

1. The Surface Pro devices should be configured to use Windows Hello with users providing either facial recognition or their Microsoft 365 usernames and passwords for sign in.

2. The Surface Pro devices are running Window 10 Pro and therefore, they should be configured to use BitLocker Drive Encryption.

3. Adatum could implement Enterprise Mode so that the Adatum intranet website opens automatically in Internet Explorer 11. All other websites would be opened in Microsoft Edge, by default.

4. The design team desktop computers would need to be upgraded to the Windows 10 Pro for Workstations for them to use the Ultimate Performance power plan.

Chapter summary

- Windows 10 is available in many editions including Windows 10 Home, Windows 10 Pro, Windows 10 Pro for Workstations, Windows 10 Enterprise, and Windows 10 Education.

- Windows 10 in S mode is a special edition of Windows 10 that is a limited, locked down version of the operating system.

- Some features of Windows 10 require special hardware or additional configuration, such as biometric sensors or TPM.

- You cannot perform an in-place upgrade from a 32-bit version of Windows to the 64-bit version of Windows 10.

- There are multiple methods of implementing Windows 10, including clean installs and upgrading a prior version of Windows.

- You can choose between three upgrade strategies: in-place, side-by-side, and wipe-and-load.

- You can use a number of tools in Windows ADK, including the Windows Configuration Designer, to customize, and distribute Windows 10 settings for deployment throughout your organization.

- Windows Configuration Designer generates provisioning packages with the .ppkg file extension, which can customize Windows 10.

- You can migrate user and application settings from one device to another, using the USMT.

- USMT uses ScanState and LoadState to migrate data and can use compression or encryption during the migration process.

- Windows 10 can be configured with additional language features including the display language, text-to-speech, speech recognition, and handwriting support.

- You can use the Lpksetup command-line tool to implement silent-mode language pack installations.

- Windows 10 requires activation, which can be performed manually or automatically.
- Microsoft provides a number of ways to manage Windows 10 volume activation.
- Microsoft provides the Activation Troubleshooter, which can identify issues experienced with activating Windows 10.
- Windows Hello is a two-factor biometric authentication mechanism built into Windows 10.
- Dynamic Lock allows you to pair a Bluetooth device, such as a smartphone, to your Windows 10 device, which will automatically lock the device when the Bluetooth device is moved away from the PC.
- You can customize the Start menu, desktop, taskbar, and notification settings individually or by using Group Policy, provisioning packages, or using mobile device management.
- To customize the Start layout using XML templates and GPOs requires Windows 10 Pro, Windows 10 Enterprise, or Windows 10 Education.
- Microsoft Edge is a cross-platform web browser for Windows 10 that supports touch devices, inking, reading mode, and secure browsing.
- Microsoft Edge kiosk mode allows Microsoft Edge to display a specific site in full-screen mode as used in digital/interactive signage or for public browsing.
- Enterprise Mode allows you to configure Microsoft Edge to be the default browser and allow selected websites to open in Internet Explorer 11 for web app and website compatibility.
- Windows 10 provides several ways to manage power settings, including creating custom power policies, thereby extending the battery life of your users' devices.
- Desktop computers running Windows 10 Pro for Workstations can use the Ultimate Performance power plan scheme, which allows the device to run at maximum performance.
- You can import and export power plans by using the Powercfg.exe command-line tool.

Manage Devices and Data

The MD-100 Windows 10 exam focuses on how to manage devices within an enterprise environment, such as a Microsoft 365 subscription. Once you have installed or upgraded devices with Windows 10, you need to understand how to join devices to Azure Active Directory.

Users need to access data stored on file servers, NAS drives, and on other PCs. Also, you need to know how to manage and protect data by using file-and folder-level data protection. You'll be expected to know how to configure Windows security and use Windows Defender Firewall to safeguard Windows 10.

Skills covered in this chapter:

- Skill 2.1: Manage local users, local groups, and devices
- Skill 2.2: Configure data access and protection
- Skill 2.3: Configure devices by using local policies
- Skill 2.4: Manage Windows security

Skill 2.1: Manage local users, local groups, and devices

In this skill, you will review how to manage local users and local groups on Windows 10 devices. If you have experience of an earlier version of Windows, you might be familiar with configuring local users and local groups as these operations are largely unchanged. Before you use Windows 10 on a device, you must sign in with the credentials for a user account. In an enterprise environment, the device and the user are often used to provide, control, and audit access to resources. Groups may be used for simplifying administration, allowing entities to share a common function or role or require the same set of privileges. You need to understand how local users, local groups, and devices form a key component in Windows security.

> **This skill covers how to:**
> - Manage local users
> - Manage local groups
> - Manage devices in directories

Manage local users

A user account is required to log on to a Windows 10 computer, and to secure the device, it should have a password. You need to understand the default user accounts that are created automatically when you install Windows 10 and how to create new user accounts so that users can log on to machines and access resources. In this skill, you will focus on local accounts that are created and operate only on the local device.

Configure local accounts

Local accounts, as the name suggests, exist in the local accounts database on your Windows 10 device; they can only be granted access to local resources and, where granted, exercise administrative rights and privileges on the local computer.

When you first install Windows 10, you are prompted to sign in using a Microsoft account or Work Account, such as a Microsoft 365 account that is connected to Azure Active Directory. If neither of these options are available or are suitable to your requirements, you can choose an offline account and create a local account to sign in. Thereafter, you can create additional local user accounts as your needs dictate.

Default accounts

In Windows 10, there are three default local user accounts on the computer in the trusted identity store. This store is a local list of users and groups and is stored as the Security Accounts Manager (SAM) database in the registry. The three accounts are the Administrator account, Default Account, and Guest account.

The default Administrator account cannot be deleted or locked out, but it can be renamed or disabled. When the default administrator account is enabled, it requires a strong password. Another local account called the HelpAssistant account is created and enabled when a Windows Remote Assistance session is run. The HelpAssistant account provides limited access to the computer to the person who provides remote assistance. The HelpAssistant account is automatically deleted if there are no Remote Assistance requests pending.

When you install Windows 10 using a local account, you can create additional user accounts and give these accounts any name that is valid. To be valid, the username

- Must be from 1 to 20 characters
- Must be unique among all the other user and group names stored on the computer
- Cannot contain any of the following characters: / \ [ ] : ; | = , + ? < > " " @
- Cannot consist exclusively of periods or spaces

The initial user account created at installation is a member of the local Administrators group and therefore can perform any local management task on the device. You can view the installed accounts, including the default accounts, by using the Computer

Management console, as shown in Figure 2-1. If you cannot find the Local Users And Groups section within Computer Management, then you are probably running Windows 10 Home Edition, which does not have the Local Users And Groups Microsoft Management Console (MMC) snap-in.

You can also use the net user command-line tool and the **get-wmiobject -class win32_ useraccount** Windows PowerShell cmdlet to list the local user accounts on a device.

EXAM TIP

In Windows 10 Home edition, you must use the User Accounts applet in Control Panel, and you cannot create or manage groups as the Local Users And Groups Console snap-in is not present.

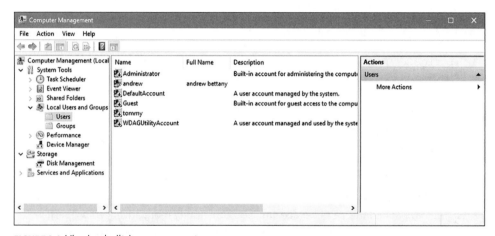

FIGURE 2-1 Viewing built-in user accounts

Managing local user accounts

You can manage local user accounts by using Computer Management (except with Windows 10 Home edition), Control Panel, the Settings app, and Windows PowerShell.

USING COMPUTER MANAGEMENT

To manage user accounts by using Computer Management, right-click Start and then click Computer Management. Expand the Local Users And Groups node and then click Users. To create a new user, right-click the Users node and click New User.

In the New User dialog box, configure the following properties, as shown in Figure 2-2, and then click Create.

FIGURE 2-2 Adding a user with Computer Management

- User Name
- Full Name
- Password
- User Must Change Password At Next Logon
- User Cannot Change Password
- Password Never Expires
- Account Is Disabled

After you have added the new user account, you can modify more advanced properties by double-clicking the user account. On the General tab, you can change the user's full name and description and password-related options. On the Member Of tab, you can add the user to groups or remove the user from groups. The Profile tab, shown in Figure 2-3, enables you to modify the following properties:

- **Profile Path** This is the path to the location of a user's desktop profile. The profile stores the user's desktop settings, such as color scheme, desktop wallpaper, and app settings (including the settings stored for the user in the registry). By default, each user who signs in has a profile folder created automatically in the C:\Users*Username* folder. You can define another location here, and you can use a Universal Naming Convention (UNC) name in the form of *Server**Share**Folder*.

- **Logon Script** This is the name of a logon script that processes each time a user signs in. Typically, this will be a .bat or .cmd file. You might place commands to map network drives or load apps in this script file. It is not usual to assign logon scripts in this way. Instead, Group Policy Objects (GPOs) are used to assign logon and startup scripts for domain user accounts.

- **Home Folder** This is a personal storage area where users can save their personal documents. By default, users are assigned subfolders within the C:\Users*Username* folder for this purpose. However, you can use either of the following two properties to specify an alternate location:

- **Local Path** A local file system path for storage of the user's personal files. This is entered in the format of a local drive and folder path.

- **Connect** A network location mapped to the specified drive letter. This is entered in the format of a UNC name.

FIGURE 2-3 Modifying the profile properties for a user

USING CONTROL PANEL

You can manage user accounts from Control Panel by opening Control Panel, clicking User Accounts, and then clicking User Accounts again. From here, you can:

- **Make Changes To My Account In PC Settings** Launches the Settings app to enable you to make user account changes.

- **Change Your Account Type** Enables you to switch between Standard and Administrator account types.

- **Manage Another Account** Enables you to manage other user accounts on this computer.

- **Change User Account Control Settings** Launches the User Account Control Settings dialog box from Control Panel.

If you are an administrator and you select another local user, you can perform these tasks:

- **Change The Account Name** Enables you to change your account name.

- **Change The Password** You can change the password for the user and provide a password hint.

- **Change Your Account Type** Enables you to switch between Standard and Administrator account types.

- **Delete The Account** Allows you to delete the user account and optionally any files associated with their account.

- **Manage Another Account** Enables you to manage other user accounts on this computer.

You cannot add new accounts from the Control Panel. If you want to add a new local account, use Computer Management, Windows PowerShell, or click the Add A New User In PC Settings link to open the Family And Other Users section of the Settings app.

USING THE SETTINGS APP

The preferred way to manage local accounts in Windows 10 is by using the Settings app. From Settings, click Accounts. As shown in Figure 2-4, on the Your Info tab, you can modify your account settings, including:

- **Sign In With A Microsoft Account Instead** You can sign out and sign in using a Microsoft account.

- **Create Your Picture** You can browse for an image or take a selfie if your device has a webcam.

- **Create A Microsoft Account** You can create a new Microsoft account using this option.

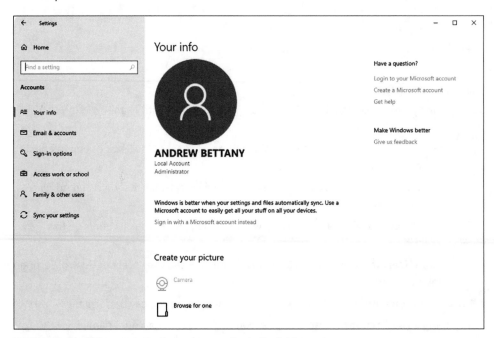

FIGURE 2-4 Modifying your user account properties in the Settings app

If you need to add a new local user account, click the Family & Other Users section and then click Add Someone Else To This PC.

Windows 10 requires you to then enter that person's email address, typically the address they use to sign in to Office 365, OneDrive, Skype, Xbox, or Outlook.com.

If you do not have the recipient's email address, you can still add a local account by using the following procedure:

1. In the Settings app, click Accounts.

2. On the Family & Other Users tab, under Other Users, click Add Someone Else To This PC.

3. In the How Will This Person Sign In dialog box, click I Don't Have This Person's Sign-In Information.

4. In the Create Account dialog box, click Add A User Without A Microsoft Account.

5. On the Create An Account For This PC page, type the user name, type a new password twice, provide answers to the three security questions, and then click Next to create the local account.

6. The account is listed under Other Users.

USING WINDOWS POWERSHELL

You can view local user accounts using Windows PowerShell, but to add or modify local accounts, you will need to run the cmdlets with elevated privileges.

You can use the following cmdlets to manage local user accounts.

- **Get-LocalUser** Gets local user accounts
- **New-LocalUser** Creates a local user account
- **Remove-LocalUser** Deletes local user accounts
- **Rename-LocalUser** Renames a local user account
- **Disable-LocalUser** Disables a local user account
- **Enable-LocalUser** Enables a local user account
- **Set-LocalUser** Modifies a local user account

For example, to add a new local user account called User 03 with a password, run the following cmdlets.

```
$Password = Read-Host -AsSecureString
<<Enter Password>>
New-LocalUser "User03" -Password $Password -FullName "Third User" -Description "User 3 "
```

> **NEED MORE REVIEW?** **LOCAL ACCOUNTS CMDLETS**
>
> To review further details about using Windows PowerShell to manage local accounts, refer to the Microsoft PowerShell reference at *https://docs.microsoft.com/powershell/module/microsoft.powershell.localaccounts/?view=powershell-5.1*

Manage local groups

There are a number of built-in groups with Windows 10, which provide an easy way for users to be granted the same permissions and rights as other group members. Assigning permissions to groups is usually more efficient than applying them to individual users.

You use the Computer Management console, or if you are an administrator, you can create a custom Microsoft Management Console (MMC) and add the Local Users And Groups Snap-in as shown in Figure 2-5 to create and manage local groups.

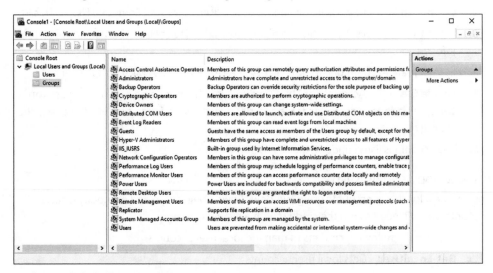

FIGURE 2-5 Default groups in Windows 10

In Figure 2-5, you can see the default built-in local groups (such as Administrators and Device Owners) and a description for each. These built-in groups already have the necessary permissions associated to them to accomplish specific tasks.

If you select the Users or Administrators groups, you should see members that you recognize. Administrators have complete and unrestricted access to the computer, whereas users are unable to make accidental or intentional system-wide changes, but they can run most applications that have already been installed on a device.

BUILT-IN LOCAL GROUPS

You can add your own groups, change group membership, rename groups, and delete groups. It is best practice to use the built-in groups wherever possible because these already have the appropriate permissions and are familiar to other administrators. Some of the built-in local groups are special groups that Windows 10 system requires (and cannot be managed).

Some of the following local groups that are created on Windows 10 devices together with their uses are shown in Table 2-1.

TABLE 2-1 Built-in Local Groups

LOCAL GROUP	DESCRIPTION
Access Control Assistance Operators	Members of this group can remotely query authorization attributes and permissions for resources on the computer.
Administrators	The Administrators group has full permissions and privileges on a Windows 10 device. Members can manage all the objects on the computer. The Administrator and initial user accounts are members of the Administrators local group.
Backup Operators	Backup Operators group members have permissions to back up and restore the file system regardless of any NTFS permissions. Backup Operators can access the file system only through the Backup utility.
Cryptographic Operators	The Cryptographic Operators group has access to perform cryptographic operations on the computer.
Device Owners	Members of this group can change system-wide settings to the computer.
Distributed COM Users	The Distributed COM Users group can launch and run Distributed COM objects on the computer.
Event Log Readers	Event Log Readers group members can read the event log on the local computer.
Guests	The Guests group has very limited access to the computer. In most cases, administrators disable guest access because guest access can pose a potential security risk; instead, most administrators prefer to create specific users. By default, the Guest user account is a member of the Guests local group.
Hyper-V Administrators	Members of this group have complete and unrestricted access to all features of Hyper-V if this feature has been installed.
IIS_IUSRS	The IIS_IUSRS group is used by Internet Information Services (IIS). By default, the NT AUTHORITY\IUSR user account, used by IIS, is a member of the IIS_IUSRS group.
Network Configuration Operators	Members of the Network Configuration Operators group can manage the computer's network configuration.
Performance Log Users	The Performance Log Users group can access and schedule logging of performance counters and create and manage trace counters on a device.
Performance Monitor Users	The Performance Monitor Users group can access and view performance counter information on a device. Members of this group can access performance counters both locally and remotely.
Power Users	The Power Users group is included in Windows 10 for backward compatibility only. Power Users was a group used on computers running Windows XP and granted members limited administrative rights.
Remote Desktop Users	The Remote Desktop Users group members can log on remotely using the Remote Desktop service.
Remote Management Users	Members of this group can access WMI resources over management protocols (such as WS-Management via the Windows Remote Management service). This applies only to WMI namespaces that grant access to the user.

(Continued)

LOCAL GROUP	DESCRIPTION
Replicator	The Replicator group supports directory replication, which is a feature used by domain controllers.
System Managed Accounts Group	Members of this group are managed by the system.
Users	The Users group is used for end users who require very limited system access. On a fresh copy of Windows 10, members of the Users group are unable to compromise the operating system or program files. By default, all users who have been created on a device, except Guest users, are members of the Users local group.

In Table 2-1, you saw that Administrators group members have full permissions and privileges on a Windows 10 device. A member of the Administrators local group can perform the following tasks:

- Access any data on the computer
- Assign and manage user rights
- Backup and restore all data
- Configure audit policies
- Configure password policies
- Configure services
- Create administrative accounts
- Create administrative shares
- Increase and manage disk quotas
- Install and configure hardware device drivers
- Install applications that modify the Windows system files
- Install the operating system
- Install Windows updates, service packs, and hot fixes
- Manage disk properties, including formatting hard drives
- Manage security logs
- Modify groups and accounts that have been created by other users
- Modify system wide environment variables
- Perform a system restore
- Re-enable locked-out and disabled user accounts
- Remotely access the Registry
- Remotely shut down the system
- Stop or start any service
- Upgrade the operating system

CREATE AND DELETE GROUPS

Only members of the Administrators group can manage users and groups. When creating a new group, the group name is required to be unique on the local computer and cannot be the same as a local username that exists on the computer.

You should make the group name descriptive, and wherever possible, you should include a description of the new group's function. Group names can have up to 256 characters in length and include alphanumeric characters including spaces, but the backslash (\) character is not allowed.

To create a new group, follow these steps:

1. Right-click Start and select Computer Management.
2. Open the Local Users And Groups console.
3. Right-click the Groups folder and select New Group from the context menu.
4. In the New Group dialog box, enter the group name. (Optionally, you can enter a description for this group.)
5. To add group members, click the Add button.
6. In the Select Users dialog box, type the username then click OK.
7. In the New Group dialog box, you will see that the user has been added to the group.
8. To create the new group, click the Create button.

To delete a group from the Local Users And Groups console in Computer Management, right-click the group name and choose Delete from the context menu. You will see a warning that deleting a group cannot be undone, and you should click the Yes button to confirm the deletion of the group.

When a group is deleted, all permissions assignments that have been specified for the group will be lost.

SPECIAL IDENTITY GROUPS

There are a number of special identity groups (sometimes known as special groups) that are used by the system or by administrators to allocate to resources. Membership in special groups is automatic, based on criteria, and you cannot manage special groups through the Local Users And Groups console. Table 2-2 describes the special identity groups that are built in to Windows 10.

TABLE 2-2 Built-in Special Identity Groups

SPECIAL IDENTITY GROUP	DESCRIPTION
Anonymous Logon	When a user accesses the computer through an anonymous logon, such as via special accounts created for anonymous access to Windows 10 services, they become members of the Anonymous Logon group.
Authenticated Users	This is a useful group because it includes all users who access Windows 10 using a valid username and password.
Batch	This group includes users who log on as a batch job operator to run a batch job.

(Continued)

SPECIAL IDENTITY GROUP	DESCRIPTION
Creator Owner	The creator owner is the account that created or took ownership of an object, such as a file, folder, printer, or print job. Members of the Creator Owner group have special administrator-level permissions to the resources over which they have ownership.
Dialup	This group includes users who log on to the network from a dial-up connection.
Everyone	This group includes anyone who accesses the computer. This includes all users, including Guest accounts and all users that are within a domain or trusted domains. Members of the Anonymous Logon group are not included as a part of the Everyone group.
Interactive	This group includes all users who use the computer's resources locally and those who are not using the computer's resources remotely via a network connection.
Network	This group includes users who access the computer's resources over a network connection.
Service	This group includes users who log on as a user account that is used to run a service.
System	When Windows 10 needs to access internal functions, it can perform actions as a system user. The process being accessed by the operating system becomes a member of the System group.
Terminal Server User	This group includes users who log on through Terminal Server applications.

Manage devices in directories

Microsoft has designed Windows 10 to be managed using cloud-based tools such as Microsoft Intune and Microsoft 365 Device Management. As more businesses migrate away from traditional on-premises domain environments to the cloud, you will need to understand how to configure devices to register them in Azure Active Directory.

In this section, you will learn how to register a device so that it can be managed by a work or school using cloud-based services. You will see how to enable device registration and the process of joining devices to Azure Active Directory.

Understand Device Management

Once devices are managed by Azure Active Directory (Azure AD), you can you ensure that your users are accessing your corporate resources from devices that meet your standards for security and compliance. To protect devices and resources using Azure AD, users must be allowed to have their Windows 10 devices managed by Azure AD.

Azure AD is a cloud-based identity authentication and authorization service that enables your users to enjoy the benefits of single sign-on (SSO) for cloud-based applications, such as Office 365. Users can easily join their devices to your organization's Azure AD once you have enabled device joining in the Azure Active Directory Admin Center.

When joining devices to an on-premises domain environment, the types of devices that you can join to the domain are quite restrictive; devices, for example, must be running a supported operating system. This means that any users that have devices running Windows 10 Home editions cannot join the company's on-premises domain. However, Azure AD is less restrictive in this respect; you can add to Azure AD almost any tablet, laptop, smartphone, and desktop computer running a variety of platforms. When you enable users to add their devices to Azure AD, you will manage their enrolled devices by using a mobile device management solution, such as Microsoft Intune, which allows you to manage and provision your users' devices.

Devices can be managed by Azure AD using two methods:

- Joining a device to Azure AD
- Registering a device to Azure AD

AZURE AD–JOINED DEVICE

Joining a Windows 10 device to Azure AD is similar to registering a device with Azure AD, but it allows enhanced management capabilities. Once a device has been joined to Azure AD, the local state of a device changes to allow your users to sign in to the device using the work or school account instead of a personal account.

An enterprise will typically join its work-owned devices to Azure AD to allow for cloud-based management of the devices and to grant access to corporate apps and resources.

Bulk joining of devices to Azure AD and Windows AutoPilot deployment are outside the scope of the MD-100 Windows 10 exam, though you should expect to find these topics covered in the MD-101 Managing Modern Desktops exam.

Organizations of any size can deploy Azure AD Join. Azure AD Join works well in a cloud-only (no on-premises infrastructure) environment. When Azure AD Join is implemented in a hybrid environment, users gain access to both cloud and on-premises apps and resources.

Azure AD–joined devices allow your users to access the following benefits:

- **Single-Sign-On (SSO)** Allows users simplified access to Azure managed SaaS apps, services, and work resources.
- **Enterprise-compliant roaming** User settings can be roamed across joined devices using their Azure AD–joined devices (without the need to sign in using a Microsoft account).
- **Access to Microsoft Store for Business** Users can access a Microsoft Store populated with apps chosen by your organization.
- **Windows Hello** Devices can be secured using the enterprise features of Windows Hello.
- **Restriction of access** Devices will only be able to access apps that meet the organizational compliance policy.
- **Seamless access to on-premises resources** Hybrid Azure AD–joined devices can access on-premises resources when connected to the domain network.

Organizations that already have Office 365 or other SaaS apps integrated with Azure AD have the necessary components in place to have devices managed in Azure AD instead of being managed in Active Directory.

AZURE AD–REGISTERED DEVICES

Once a device is registered into management, it is known to Azure AD, and information relating to the device is stored in Azure AD. Effectively, the device is given an identity with Azure AD. You can create conditional access rules to determine whether access to resources from your devices will be granted.

Azure AD–registered devices allow users to use personally owned devices to access your organization's resources in a controlled manner. Azure AD supports Bring Your Own Device (BYOD) scenarios for multiple types of devices, including Windows 10, iOS, Android, and macOS.

With an Azure AD–registered device, the user will gain access to resources using a work or school Azure AD account at the time they access the resources. All corporate data and apps will be kept separate from the personal data and apps on the device. If the personal computer, tablet, or phone that is registered with Azure AD does not meet your corporate standards for security and compliance—for example, if a device is not running a supported version of the operating system, or it has been jail broken—then the access to the resource will be denied.

Device Registration enables you to facilitate a single sign-on (SSO) experience for users, removing the need for them to repeatedly enter credentials to access resources.

The main reasons to implement Device Registration are

- To enable access to corporate resources from nondomain-joined or personally owned devices
- To enable SSO for specific apps and/or resources managed by Azure AD

After you enable Device Registration, users can register and enroll their devices in your organizational tenant. After they have enrolled their devices

- Enrolled devices are associated with a specific user account in Azure AD.
- A device object is created in Azure AD to represent the physical device and its associated user account.
- A user certificate is installed on the user's device.

Configure Device Management

Device management requires configuration to ensure that when your users attempt device registration, the process will not fail. By default, the setting is enabled, and it allows all Windows 10 devices that present valid credentials to be managed by your Azure AD.

The Azure portal provides a cloud-based location to manage your devices. To allow registration of devices into Azure AD follow these steps:

1. Sign in as an administrator to the Azure portal at *https://portal.azure.com*.
2. On the left navigation bar, click Azure Active Directory.

3. In the Manage section, click Devices.

4. Click Device Settings.

5. On the Device Settings blade, ensure that the Users May Join Devices To Azure AD setting is configured to All, as shown in Figure 2-6. If you choose Selected, then click the Selected link and choose the users who can join Azure AD. You can select both individual users and groups of users.

6. Click Save.

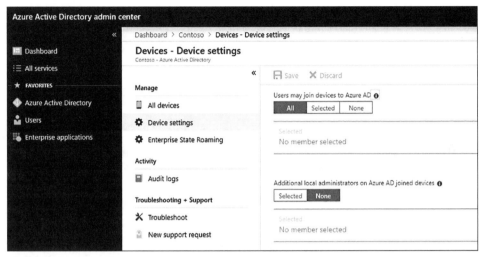

FIGURE 2-6 Enabling Azure AD join

Within the Azure AD portal, you can fine-tune the process of registering and joining devices by configuring the device settings as listed in Table 2-3.

TABLE 2-3 Azure AD device configuration settings

DEVICE SETTING	DESCRIPTION
Users May Join Devices To Azure AD	The default is All. The Selected option allows you to select users who can join Windows 10 devices to Azure AD.
Additional Local Administrators On Azure AD Joined Devices	You can select the users who are granted local administrator rights on a device and added to the Device Administrators role in Azure AD. By default, global administrators in Azure AD and device owners are granted local administrator rights. Requires an Azure AD Premium P1 or P2 license.
Users May Register Their Devices With Azure AD	Required to allow devices to be registered with Azure AD by users. Options include: ■ None Prevents devices from being registered with Azure AD. ■ ALL Automatically configured if Enrollment with Microsoft Intune or Mobile Device Management (MDM) for Office 365 is configured and requires registration.

(Continued)

DEVICE SETTING	DESCRIPTION
Require Multi-Factor Auth To Join Devices	Choose whether users are required to use multifactor authentication to join their devices to Azure AD. The default setting is No. This setting is only applicable to Azure AD Join on Windows 10 and BYOD registration for Windows 10, iOS, and Android.
Maximum Number Of Devices	By default, all users can have a maximum of 20 devices in Azure AD. Once this quota is reached, they are not be able to add additional devices until one or more of the existing devices are removed. The device quota is across both Azure AD–joined and Azure AD–registered devices.
Users May Sync Settings And App Data Across Devices	By default, this setting is set to NONE, but you can enable this for specific users or groups. The ALL setting allows all the user's settings and app data to sync across their Windows 10 devices. Requires Azure AD Premium P1 or a P2 license.

EXAM TIP

Each device must be able locate the Internet to allow you to authenticate using your Azure AD credentials. If a device cannot locate the cloud-based identity service, then there will be a problem accessing resources managed by Azure AD.

DEVICE MANAGEMENT TASKS

Once devices have been registered or joined to Azure AD, they appear in the list within the All Devices section of the Azure Active Directory Admin Center. Devices managed by another management authority, such as Microsoft Intune, are also listed.

To locate a device, you can search using the device name or device ID. Once you have located a device, you can perform additional device management tasks including:

- **Update devices**—You can enable or disable devices. You need to be a global administrator in Azure AD to perform this task, which prevents a device from being able to authenticate with Azure AD and thus, prevents the device from accessing any Azure AD resources.

- **Delete devices**—When a device is retired, or it no longer requires access to your corporate resources, it should be deleted in Azure AD. Deleting a device requires you to be a to be a global administrator in Azure AD or an Intune administrator. Once deleted, all details stored in Azure AD relating to the device— for example, BitLocker keys for Windows devices—are removed. If a device is managed elsewhere, such as in Microsoft Intune, you should ensure that the device has been wiped before deleting the device in Azure AD.

- **View device ID**   Each device has a unique device ID that can be used to search for the device; the unique device ID can be used as a reference if you need to use PowerShell during a troubleshooting task.

- **View device BitLocker key** Windows devices managed by Azure AD can have their BitLocker recovery keys stored in Azure AD. You can access this key if the encrypted drive needs to be recovered. To view or copy the BitLocker keys, you need to be either the owner of the device or have one of the following roles assigned: Global Administrator, Helpdesk Administrator, Security Administrator, Security Reader, or Intune Service Administrator.

> **NOTE** **USE POWERSHELL TO BACK UP THE BITLOCKER RECOVERY KEY TO AZURE AD**
>
> For Azure AD–joined computers, the BitLocker recovery password should be stored in Azure AD. You can use the PowerShell cmdlets **Add-BitLockerKeyProtector**, **Get-BitLockerVolume**, and **BackupToAAD-BitLockerKeyProtector** to add a recovery password and back it up to Azure AD before enabling BitLocker.

Connect devices to Azure AD

Once the pre-requisites have been configured to allow device registration service to take place, you are able to connect devices to Azure AD.

There are three ways to connect a Windows 10 device to Azure AD as follows:

- Join a new Windows 10 device to Azure AD
- Join an existing Windows 10 device to Azure AD
- Register a Windows 10 device to Azure AD

In this section, you will learn the steps required for each method of connecting Windows 10 to Azure AD.

JOIN A NEW WINDOWS 10 DEVICE TO AZURE AD

In this method, we will take a new Windows 10 device and join the device to Azure AD during the first-run experience. The device could have been previously prepared using an enterprise deployment method, or it could have been distributed by the original equipment manufacturer (OEM) directly to your employees.

If the device is running either Windows 10 Professional or Windows 10 Enterprise, the first-run experience will present the setup process for company-owned devices.

> **NOTE** **JOINING A DEVICE TO ACTIVE DIRECTORY DURING THE FIRST-RUN EXPERIENCE**
>
> Joining an on-premises Active Directory domain is supported in Windows 10 during the Windows out-of-box experience. If you need to join a computer to an AD domain, during setup, you should choose the option to Set Up For An Organization and then select the Domain Join Instead link. You then need to set up the device with a local account, then join the domain from the Settings app on your computer. For the MD-100 Windows 10 exam, you should expect that devices will be cloud- or hybrid cloud–enabled.

To join a new Windows 10 device to Azure AD during the first-run experience, use the following steps:

1. Start the new device and allow the setup process.

2. On the Let's Start With Region. Is This Correct? page, select the regional setting that you need and click Yes.

3. On the Is This The Right Keyboard Layout? page, select the keyboard layout settings and click Yes.

4. On the Want To Add A Second Keyboard Layout? page, add a layout or select Skip.

5. The computer should automatically connect to the Internet, but it if it does not, you will be presented with the Let's Connect You To A Network page where you can select a network connection.

6. On the How Would You Like To Set Up? Page, choose Set Up For An Organization and click Next.

7. On the Sign In With Microsoft page, enter your Organization or school account and password and click Next.

8. On the Do More Across Devices With Activity History page, choose whether to enable the Timeline feature.

9. On the Do More With Your Voice page, choose whether to enable the Speech Recognition feature and click Accept.

10. On the Let Microsoft And Apps Use Your Location page, choose whether to enable the location-based features and click Accept.

11. On the Find My Device page, choose whether to enable the Find My Device feature and click Accept.

12. On the Send Diagnostic Data To Microsoft page, choose Full or Basic diagnostic data transfers and click Accept.

13. On the Improve Inking & Typing page, choose Yes or No and click Accept.

14. On the Get Tailored Experiences With Diagnostic Data page, choose Yes or No and click Accept.

15. On the Let Apps Use Advertising ID settings page, choose the privacy settings that you require and click Accept.

16. Depending on organizational settings, your users might be prompted to set up Windows Hello. By default, they will be prompted to set up a PIN. When prompted to set up a PIN, click Set Up PIN.

17. On the More Information Required page, click Next, provide the additional security verification information, and click Next again.

18. You should now be automatically signed in to the device, joined to your organization or school Azure AD tenant, and presented with the desktop.

JOIN AN EXISTING WINDOWS 10 DEVICE TO AZURE AD

In this method, we will take an existing Windows 10 device and join it to Azure AD. You can join a Windows 10 device to Azure AD at any time. Use the following procedure to join the device:

1. Open the Settings app and then click Accounts.

2. In Accounts, click the Access Work Or School tab.

3. Click Connect.

4. On The Set Up A Work Or Education Account page, under Alternative Actions, click Join This Device To Azure Active Directory, as shown in Figure 2-7.

FIGURE 2-7 Joining a device to Azure AD

5. On The Let's Get You Signed In page, enter your Work or Education username and click Next.

6. On the Enter Password page, enter your password and click Sign In.

7. On the Make Sure This Is Your Organization page, confirm that the details on screen are correct and click Join.

8. On the You're All Set! page, click Done.

9. To verify that your device is connected to your organization or school, your Azure AD email address will be listed under the Connect button indicating that it is connected to Azure AD.

If you have access to the Azure Active Directory portal, then you can validate that the device is joined to Azure AD by following these steps:

1. Sign in as an administrator to the Azure portal at *https://portal.azure.com*.

2. On the left navigation bar, click Azure Active Directory.

3. In the Manage section, click Devices > All Devices.

4. Verify that the device is listed as shown in Figure 2-8.

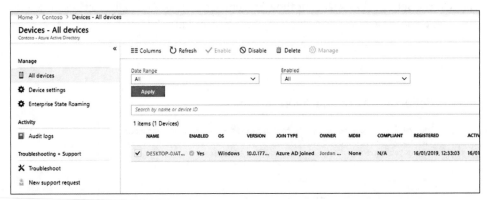

FIGURE 2-8 Viewing All devices in Azure AD

REGISTER DEVICES TO AZURE AD

You connect a Windows 10 device to Azure Active Directory using the Add Work or School Account feature found in the Settings app. Device registration is used to allow devices to be known by both Azure AD and MDM solutions.

In this method, we will take an existing Windows 10 device and register it to Azure AD. Use the following procedure to register the device:

1. Open the Settings app and then click Accounts.

2. In Accounts, click the Access Work Or School tab.

3. Click Connect.

4. On The Set Up A Work Or Education Account page, enter your work or education email address, click Next, and complete the wizard.

To verify that a device is registered to your organization or school Azure AD tenant, users can use these steps:

1. Open the Settings app and then click Accounts.

2. In Accounts, click the Access Work Or School tab.

3. On the Access Work Or School page, verify that your organization or school Azure AD email address is listed under the Connect button.

Enroll devices into Microsoft 365

Microsoft 365 is a bundled subscription including Office 365, Windows 10, and Enterprise Mobility + Security. Microsoft 365 comes in three primary bundles:

- **Microsoft 365 Business** For small- and medium-sized organizations up to 300 users
- **Microsoft 365 Enterprise** For organizations of any size
- **Microsoft 365 Education** For educational establishments

With Microsoft 365, you use Azure Active Directory for your identity and authentication requirements, and you can (and should) enroll Windows 10 into device management, so that your users can gain access to corporate resources. Once devices are joined to your Microsoft 365 tenant, Windows 10 becomes fully integrated with the cloud-based services offered by Office 365 and Enterprise Mobility + Security. Microsoft 365 supports other platforms including Android and iOS, which can also be managed as mobile devices. However, only Windows 10 devices can be joined to Azure AD.

ENROLL DEVICES INTO MICROSOFT 365 BUSINESS

When you enroll Windows devices into Microsoft 365 Business, they must be running Windows 10 Pro, version 1703 (Creators Update) or later. If you have any Windows devices running Windows 7 Professional, Windows 8 Pro, or Windows 8.1 Pro, the Microsoft 365 Business subscription entitles you to upgrade them to Windows 10 Pro.

Microsoft 365 Business includes a set of device-management capabilities powered by Microsoft Intune. Microsoft 365 Business offers organizations a simplified management console that provides access to a limited number of device management tasks, including

- Deploy Windows with Autopilot
- Remove company data
- Factory reset
- Manage Office deployment

To enroll a brand-new device running Windows 10 Pro into Microsoft 365 Business, known as a "user-driven enrollment", follow these steps:

1. Go through Windows 10 device setup until you get to the How Would You Like To Set Up? Page, as shown in Figure 2-9.

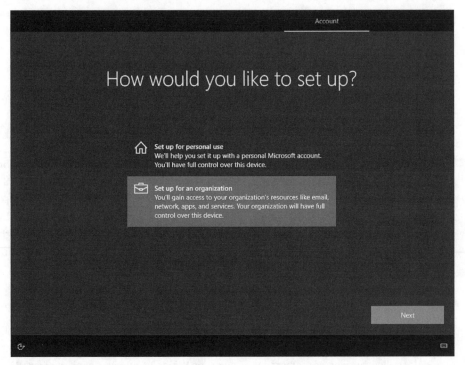

FIGURE 2-9 Windows 10 device setup

2. Choose Set Up For An Organization and then enter your username and password for your Microsoft 365 Business subscription (the new user account not the tenant admin account).

3. Complete the remainder of the Windows 10 device setup.

4. The device will be registered and joined to your organization's Azure AD, and you will be presented with the desktop.

5. You can verify the device is connected to Azure AD by opening the Settings app and clicking Accounts.

6. On the Your Info page, click Access Work Or School.

7. You should see that the device is Connected to your organization. Click your organization name to expose the Info and Disconnect buttons.

8. Click Info to see that your device is managed by your organization and to view your device sync status.

9. To verify that the device has been granted a Windows 10 Business license, click the Home icon, click System, and then click About.

10. Within Windows specifications, the Windows 10 Edition shows Windows 10 Business, as shown in Figure 2-10.

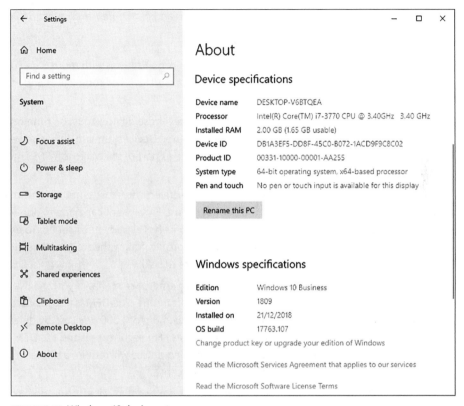

FIGURE 2-10 Windows 10 device setup

Although there is no link to Microsoft Intune within the Microsoft 365 Business Admin Center, the subscription includes the use of the full Intune capabilities for iOS, Android, MacOS, and other cross-platform device management. To access the Microsoft Intune console in Microsoft Azure, launch a browser and sign in with your Microsoft 365 Business credentials at *https://portal.azure.com*.

Follow these steps to access Intune App Protection in the Azure portal and view the app protection settings for managed Windows 10, Android, and iOS devices.

1. Sign into the Microsoft 365 Device Management portal at *https://devicemanagement .microsoft.com* with your Microsoft 365 Business admin credentials.

2. In the left navigation bar, select Client Apps.

3. In the Client Apps blade, select App Protection Policies.

4. You can now select Create Policy from the menu and configure App Protection Policies.

ENROLL DEVICES INTO MICROSOFT 365 ENTERPRISE

Microsoft 365 Enterprise plans can be chosen by larger organizations with more than 300 users or businesses of any size that require access to the increased levels of compliance and security management over Microsoft 365 Business.

When enrolling devices into Microsoft 365 Enterprise, those devices must be running Windows 10 Enterprise, version 1703 (Creators Update) or later. Devices running an earlier version of Windows can be upgraded to Windows 10 Enterprise as part of the Microsoft 365 Enterprise licensing.

Users can perform an Azure AD join using the user-driven enrollment method shown in the previous section to enroll their devices into management. Enrollment can happen during the Out-of-Box Experience (OOBE) or after a Windows profile has already been set up. To enroll a device once a user has already set up a Windows user profile, follow the steps outlined in the "Join a new Windows 10 device to Azure AD" section of this skill.

If you want to enroll a large number of devices in an enterprise scenario, you can use the Device Enrollment Manager (DEM) account in Microsoft Intune. The DEM is a special account in Microsoft Intune that allows you to enroll up to a maximum of 1,000 devices. (By default, standard users can manage and enroll up to five devices.) For security reasons, the DEM user should not also be an Intune administrator. Each enrolled device will require a single Intune license, but the DEM user does not require an Intune license.

By default, there is no device enrollment account user present in Microsoft Intune. You can create a device enrollment account by performing the following steps:

1. Sign into the Microsoft 365 Device Management portal at *https://devicemanagement.microsoft.com* with your Microsoft 365 Enterprise admin credentials.

2. In the left navigation bar, select Device Enrollment, and then under Manage, choose Device Enrollment Managers.

3. Select Add.

4. On the Add User blade, enter the username for the DEM user and select Add. The user is promoted to the DEM role.

5. Close the Add User blade.

6. The list of Device Enrollment Managers now contains the new user, as shown in Figure 2-11.

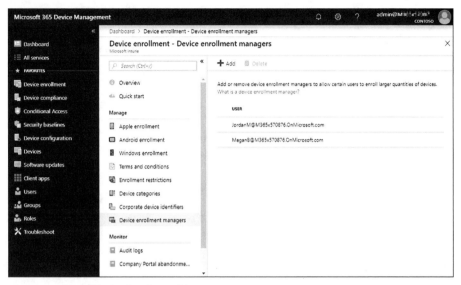

FIGURE 2-11 List of Device Enrollment Managers

> **MORE INFO** **ENROLL DEVICES USING DEVICE ENROLLMENT MANAGER**
>
> For more information on the DEM in Microsoft Intune, including example scenarios and limitations of devices that are enrolled with a DEM account, visit *https://docs.microsoft.com/intune/device-enrollment-manager-enroll*.

View and manage devices in Microsoft 365

Microsoft 365 Business subscription administrators can manage their enrolled devices directly from the Microsoft 365 Business Admin Center Home screen using the Enroll Devices tile, as shown in Figure 2-12. Also, enrolled devices can be managed in the Microsoft 365 Device Management portal.

On the Microsoft 365 Business Admin portal Home screen, both the Device Enrollment link on the Enroll Devices tile and the Device Management option (under Admin Centers) will open the standalone Microsoft 365 Device Management portal. This portal can also be accessed at *https://devicemanagement.microsoft.com*.

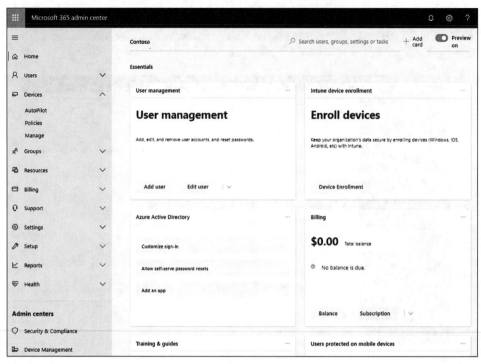

FIGURE 2-12 Microsoft 365 Business Admin portal Home screen

> **NOTE** **MICROSOFT 365 ADMIN PORTAL PREVIEW**
>
> At the time of writing, the Microsoft 365 Admin portal is available in a preview mode. This provides administrators with a portal with a new, cleaner look and feel. The Preview On toggle to swap between the old Admin Center and Preview Admin Center is located in the top-right corner of the Admin Center home page, as shown in Figure 2-12.

You can perform the following device-related actions on devices from within the Devices section on the navigation bar.

- **AutoPilot** Including adding new devices to be deployed with the Windows Autopilot service and managing Windows Autopilot profiles that can be applied to devices.
- **Policies** Including managing existing policies and assigning policies to groups. Add new application policies to Android, iOS, and Windows 10 devices, and add new device configuration polices to Windows 10 devices.
- **Manage** Including view device details, Factory Reset, Remove Company Data, and Remove Device.

Organizations with a Microsoft 365 Enterprise subscription cannot view or manage devices from the Microsoft 365 Enterprise Admin Center and will need to use the following locations:

- **Azure Active Directory** *https://aad.portal.azure.com*
- **Intune in the Azure portal** *https://portal.azure.com*
- **Microsoft 365 Device Management** *https://devicemanagement.microsoft.com*

From these views, you can manage and interact with the devices enrolled into your Azure AD tenant, including retiring or wiping a device. Also, you can perform remote tasks, such as retiring, wiping, or restarting the device, as shown in Figure 2-13.

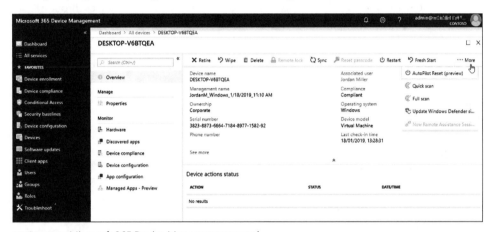

FIGURE 2-13 Microsoft 365 Device Management portal

Skill 2.2: Configure data access and protection

Being able to access your data from anywhere is a key feature of Windows 10, whether in a small workgroup, in a large enterprise across a LAN, or when mobile using the Internet. This skill discusses multiple methods of sharing configuration and setting access permissions on the share so that you are in control of who can see or edit the data. You review how to troubleshoot data access issues and stay informed of your usage status when using a metered connection.

> **This skill covers how to:**
> - Configure NTFS permissions
> - Configure shared permissions

Configure NTFS permissions

Most users are familiar with using the File Explorer tool to view and manage files and folders. When administrating shared files and folders over a network, File Explorer is still the primary tool to configure file- and folder-level permissions. Although permissions have been part of NTFS and earlier versions of Windows, you need to ensure that you are familiar with NTFS and the changes offered in Windows 10.

Understand NTFS

NTFS is the native file system Windows 10 uses, which is widely used across most Windows operating systems. It offers you the ability to protect and secure folders and files through file- and folder-level security permissions to control access. NTFS offers the following characteristics:

- File-level compression
- Per-user volume quotas
- Symbolic links and junction points
- Volume sizes up to 256 TB
- Support for large volumes—up to 2^{32}-1 files per volume
- Maximum implemented file size is 256 TB minus 64 KB or 281,474,976,645,120 bytes
- Support for extended-length paths
- Support for long file names, with backward compatibility
- Enterprise-level file and folder encryption
- Support for BitLocker Drive Encryption
- Metadata transactional logging to ensure that file structure can be repaired
- Limited self-healing capabilities

Use File Explorer to manage files and folders

The most common tool used to manage files and folders is File Explorer, which is located on the taskbar and on the Start screen. Typical functions provided through File Explorer include:

- Creating new folders and files
- Viewing and accessing files and folders
- Searching for files and information contained in files
- Managing properties of files and folders
- Previewing contents or thumbnails of files and folders

The Quick Access area is new in Windows 10 and appears at the uppermost left area of the File Explorer navigation pane; it includes pinned shortcuts for frequently used files and folders including the Desktop, Downloads, Documents, Pictures, and Music. As you browse and access files in other folders on your computer, folder shortcuts for these items appear in the right navigation pane under Frequent Folders or Recent Files. You can modify the behavior of Quick Access by right-clicking Quick Access and selecting Options, as shown in Figure 2-14.

On a shared computer, you might want to clear the check boxes for Show Recently Used Files In Quick Access and Show Frequently Used Folders In Quick Access.

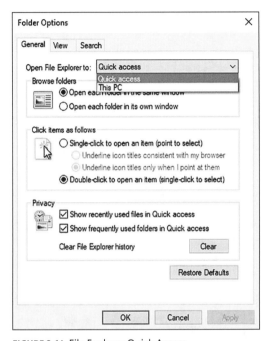

FIGURE 2-14 File Explorer Quick Access

Set file and folder permissions

Volumes formatted using either NTFS or the newer ReFS enable you to configure file and folder permissions. NTFS permissions are robust, reliable, and effective, and they enable you to configure granular permissions on both files and folders that determine how individual users and groups can use the objects.

The creator of the resource, such as a file or folder, is automatically assigned the special status of creator-owner, and the creator can grant or deny permissions to it. Administrators and anyone given the Full Control permission also can modify permissions for that file or folder.

To modify permissions to a file or folder, access the Security tab in the object's properties, as shown in Figure 2-15.

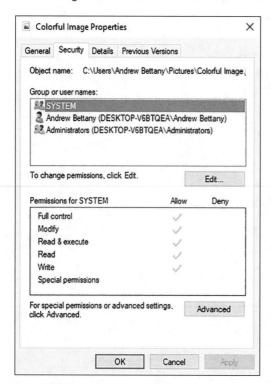

FIGURE 2-15 Security permissions for a file

If a user leaves the organization or the account is deleted, an Administrator can take ownership of the files and folders to modify permissions by changing the Owner principal found in the Advanced settings in Properties.

If you have the permission to modify the security settings in the access control list (ACL), you can add or remove users or groups and then grant or deny a specific permission level. In organizations, you assign permissions to groups rather than to multiple users because this minimizes administrative effort.

Review the acronyms relating to objects that you might use when applying security permissions, as shown in Table 2-4.

TABLE 2-4 Security Permission acronyms

NAME	ACRONYM	DESCRIPTION
Access control list	ACL	A list of trustees (users and groups) with permissions for the object.
Access control entry	ACE	Identifies specific permissions granted to a user or group. Each ACE identifies the trustee and specifies the access rights allowed, denied, or audited for that trustee.
Discretionary access control list	DACL	Specifies which trustees are allowed or denied access to an object.
System access control list	SACL	Specifies which users and groups will be audited when they perform actions, such as creating, modifying, or deleting objects.

When configuring permissions for files and folders, you can configure basic or advanced permissions. Unless you are seeking a very fine degree of control to a resource, you typically work with basic permissions and assign them to groups and users, as shown in Table 2-5.

TABLE 2-5 Basic file and folder permissions for NTFS and ReFS

FILE PERMISSION	DESCRIPTION
Full Control	Complete authority and control of all file or folder permissions.
Modify	Ability to read a file, write changes to it, and modify permissions.
Read & Execute	Ability to see folder content, read files and attributes, and start programs.
Read	Ability to read a file but not make any changes to it.
Write	Ability to change folder or file content and create new files.
Special Permissions	Indication of whether additional advanced permissions have been configured for the file or folder.

> *NOTE* **BASIC AND ADVANCED PERMISSIONS**
>
> If you are familiar with older versions of Windows, you might notice that Windows 10 uses the modern naming for permissions as follows: Standard Permissions has been changed to Basic Permissions, and Special Permissions has been changed to Advanced Permissions.

Basic permissions are easier to manage and document. Under the hood, a basic permission is made from a combination of individual advanced special permissions. Consider that permissions for folders can have a different effect on files, as described in Table 2-6.

TABLE 2-6 Basic NTFS file and folder permissions

BASIC PERMISSION	DESCRIPTION: WHEN APPLIED TO A FOLDER	DESCRIPTION: WHEN APPLIED TO A FILE
Full Control	Permits reading, writing, changing, and deletion of files and subfolders. Allows the modification of permissions on folders.	Permits reading, writing, changing, and deletion of the file. Allows modification of permissions on files.
Modify	Permits reading, writing, changing, and deletion of files and subfolders. Does not allow changes to permissions on folders.	Permits reading, writing, changing, and deletion of the file. Does not allow changes to the permissions on files.
Read & Execute	Allows the content of the folder to be accessed and executed.	Allows the file to be accessed and executed (run).
List Folder Contents	Allows the contents of the folder to be viewed.	Does not apply to files.
Read	Allows content to be read.	Allows access to the contents. Does not allow files to be executed.
Write	Allows addition of files and subfolders to the folder.	Allows a user to modify but not delete a file.

Behind the basic permissions is a matrix of 13 advanced permissions that can also be applied to files and folders. Each basic permission is a collection of one or more advanced permissions, as shown in Table 2-7.

TABLE 2-7 Basic and advanced permissions

ADVANCED PERMISSION	FULL CONTROL	MODIFY	READ & EXECUTE	LIST FOLDER CONTENTS	READ	WRITE
Traverse Folder/ Execute File	X	X	X	X		
List Folder/Read Data	X	X	X	X	X	
Read Attributes	X	X	X	X	X	
Read Extended Attributes	X	X	X	X	X	
Create Files/Write Data	X	X				X
Create Folders/Append Data	X	X				X
Write Attributes	X	X				X
Write Extended Attributes	X	X				X
Delete Subfolders And Files	X					

(Continued)

ADVANCED PERMISSION	FULL CONTROL	MODIFY	READ & EXECUTE	LIST FOLDER CONTENTS	READ	WRITE
Delete	X	X				
Read Permissions	X	X	X	X	X	X
Change Permissions	X					
Take Ownership	X					

It is recommended to use basic permissions unless there is a clear requirement for setting advanced permissions; otherwise, they can become complex and difficult to troubleshoot. If you do use the advanced permissions, it is best practice to document any modifications so that you can review the configuration and, if necessary, reverse the settings.

Many inexperienced users who configure NTFS permissions can complicate the settings on files by setting advanced permissions (frequently using deny permissions) and setting permissions for individual users instead of setting permissions for groups. There is a strict canonical order or hierarchy of how Deny and Allow permissions can interoperate, and the general rule is that a Deny setting prevents an Allow setting.

EXAM TIP

Remember the principle of least administration when applying NTFS or ReFS permissions. If you want to prevent a user or group from having any access to a resource, you could set no permissions. If neither Allow nor Deny permission is explicitly configured or inherited on a resource, users are prevented from accessing the file or folder.

Review Table 2-8 to understand the relationship between Deny and Allow settings and how the behavior changes, depending on how the setting is applied.

TABLE 2-8 Allow and Deny NTFS permissions

PERMISSION TYPE	DESCRIPTION	CHECK BOX STATUS
Explicit Deny	The user is denied the permission on the file or folder.	The check box is selected.
Explicit Allow	The user is allowed the permission on the file or folder.	The check box is selected.
Inherited Deny	Deny permission is applied to the file or subfolder by permissions given to the parent folder.	The check box is dimmed but selected.
Not configured	When no permissions are assigned, the user has no permission to access the file or folder.	The check box is cleared.
Inherited Allow	Allow permission is applied to the file or subfolder by permissions given to the parent folder.	The check box is dimmed but selected.

Although most administrators will use File Explorer to set individual ACLs for files and folders, you can also use Windows PowerShell or the ICACLS command-line utility.

Windows PowerShell offers two cmdlets that you can use to manage file and folder permissions: Get-Acl and Set-Acl. For additional information and examples of how to use these cmdlets, type **Get-Help Get-Acl**, or **Get-Help Set-Acl**.

ICACLS enables you to configure and view permissions on files and folders on a local computer. Some of the most common ICACLS parameters and permission masks are shown in Table 2-9.

TABLE 2-9 Common ICACLS parameters and permission masks

PARAMETER/ PERMISSION MASK	DESCRIPTION
/grant	Grants specific user access rights. Permissions replace previously granted explicit permissions.
/deny	Explicitly denies specified user access rights. An explicit Deny ACE is added for the stated permissions, and the same permissions in any explicit grant are removed.
/reset	Replaces ACLs with default inherited ACLs for all matching files.
F	Full access.
M	Modify access.
RX	Read and execute access.
R	Read-only access.
W	Write-only access.
(OI)	Object inherit.
(NP)	Do not propagate inherit.

To grant a permission, use the **/grant** switch, as the following example on an existing file called My New Files within the C:\Working Folder shows.

1. Open File Explorer.
2. Navigate to the folder on which you want to set permissions.
3. Click File and then click Open Windows PowerShell As Administrator.

4. Type the following command.

```
Icacls 'My new files.rtf' /grant 'Demo:(OI)(M)'
```

5. Type **Icacls** '**My new files.rtf**' to view the permissions.

> **NEED MORE REVIEW?**   **ICACLS**
>
> This Microsoft resource provides additional information for you to review relating to ICACLS.
> Visit *https://docs.microsoft.com/windows-server/administration/windows-commands/icacls*.

Understand NTFS inheritance

Setting NTFS permissions on hundreds of files and folders would take a long time, especially if each setting were configured manually. Fortunately, you don't need to because, by default, NTFS and ReFS security permissions are inherited from their parent folder. In this way, permissions will "flow" from top to bottom and follow the folder hierarchy. By default, inheritance is enabled because this facilitates more efficient administration. NTFS enables you to disable inheritance from flowing from a parent folder to the child.

You can review the inheritance status of a file or folder in File Explorer by following these steps.

1. Open File Explorer.

2. Navigate to the folder whose inheritance settings you want to review.

3. Right-click the file or folder, and choose Properties > Advanced.

4. On the Permissions tab, review the permission entries and notice the Inherited From column, as shown in Figure 2-16.

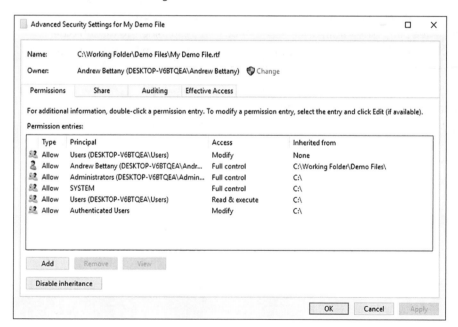

FIGURE 2-16 NTFS inheritance

Figure 2-16 shows a Disable Inheritance button. If you select this button, you are presented with two choices as shown in Figure 2-17.

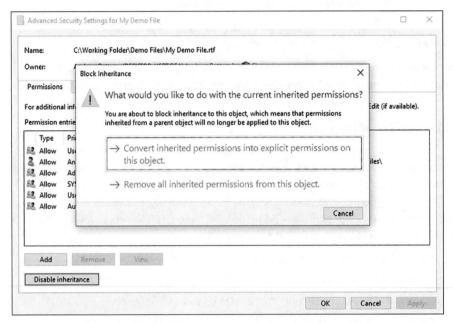

FIGURE 2-17 Blocking Inheritance

In the Block Inheritance dialog box, there are two options, as follows:

- **Convert Inherited Permissions Into Explicit Permissions On This Object** Prevents inherited permissions from being able to "flow" from top folders to the subfolders. Current inherited permissions are changed by the system from implicit permissions to explicit permissions. This can result in hundreds or thousands of inherited permissions being changed into explicit permissions.

- **Remove All Inherited Permissions From This Object** Removes all permissions and gives you a folder structure with no permissions set. Care needs to be taken with this option because it is very easy to remove all access—even system access—to the file structure.

The option to convert inherited permissions to explicit permissions on this object stops inheritance from flowing from the parent folders and changes the permissions on all child items from implicit permissions to explicit permissions. You can then modify the permissions.

If you choose the second option, Remove All Inherited Permissions From This Object, you completely remove all permissions. This provides you with a folder structure with no permissions at all.

Both options are powerful and can have far reaching effects. Best practice recommends employing inheritance wherever possible, to ease administration. You should also document and test your outline folder structure before it becomes too large. A big change on a small structure is simple to put in place, whereas modifying a large, established file structure could be cumbersome.

Understanding move, copy, and permissions inheritance

When you need to move or copy a folder from one location to another, you need to under-stand how NTFS will perform the task with respect to how permissions on the resource are modified. Table 2-10 shows the behavior that NTFS adopts when copying files from one folder to another folder, and between partitions.

TABLE 2-10 Resultant effect of moving or copying NTFS files

ACTION	EFFECT
Copy or Move a file or folder to a different volume	Inherits the permissions from the destination (new location) folder.
Copy or Move a file or folder within the same NTFS volume	Inherits the permissions from the new parent folder, and explicitly assigned permissions are retained and merged with the inherited permissions.
Copy a file or folder to a non-NTFS volume	The copy of the folder or file loses all permissions.

> **NOTE WHAT HAPPENS WHEN YOU MOVE A NTFS-PROTECTED FILE TO A FAT VOLUME?**
>
> If you're moving a file or folder from NTFS to a non-NTFS partition, such as a FAT volume, all NTFS file and folder permissions will be lost because FAT does not support NTFS file and folder permissions. Only Creator Owners and users with the Modify permission (and administrators) can perform this task because they have permission to move files and folders. When moving files to a FAT volume, the process involves saving the object onto the new file system, losing the original NTFS permissions in the process, and then deleting the original object.

When you copy a file or folder within the same volume or between volumes, the user must have Read permission for the source folder and Write permission for the destination folder.

When you move a file or folder within the same volume or between volumes, you need to have both Write permission for the destination folder as well as Modify permission for the source file or folder. This is because Windows 10 will move the resources (Write) and then delete (Modify) the resources from the source folder once it has completed the copy to the destination folder.

View Effective Access

You might be required to calculate the access that a user has to a resource. Within the Advanced options of an object's Security settings, you will find the Effective Access tab (previously called Effective Permissions) as shown in Figure 2-18. When setting permissions in a corporate environ-ment you should verify that NTFS permissions are applied correctly and use the Effective Access feature to ensure that the results are as expected.

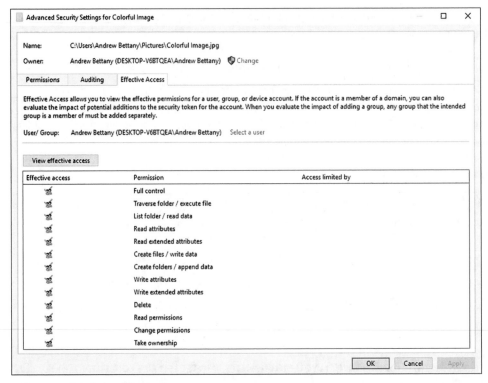

FIGURE 2-18 Calculating Effective Access

For example, for a resource, if you assign a user the Read permission and assign the Modify permission to a group that the same user is a member of, the effective access permissions are a combination of the Read permission and Modify permission, which is Modify permission.

When you combine permissions that include Deny permissions, NTFS will evaluate the Deny permissions before the Allow permissions that are set on the same resource with explicit Deny taking precedence over all Allow permissions.

If Deny and Allow permissions are set at different levels within a folder structure, or nested within each other—for example, if Deny is set at the top-level folder and an Allow permission is set at its subfolder—Allow can take precedence and override Deny because the Allow permission is explicit and not implicit.

When assigning permissions to several groups, remember that the security settings have a cumulative effect; you should review the effective permissions obtained for the user by following these steps.

1. Open Windows Explorer.
2. Navigate to the file or folder whose effective permissions you want to view.
3. Right-click the file or folder, click Properties, and click the Security tab.

4. Click Advanced and then click the Effective Access tab.

5. Next to the User/Group, click Select A User.

6. On the Select User Or Group dialog box, click in the Enter The Object Name To Select (Examples) box, enter the name of a user or group, and then click OK.

7. Click View Effective Access.

   You should now see the detailed effective permissions of the user or group for that file or folder.

Be careful when using the Effective Access tool and reviewing permissions on folders that you own since the permissions given to the Creator Owner of the object are not taken into account.

Take ownership of resources

It is possible to remove access to a particular user or group on an object, such as a folder. Sometimes, this happens accidentally when configuring permissions, but typically, it will happen when the user who originally created the resource leaves the organization and the resource is then said to be "orphaned."

In the Advanced Security Settings dialog box for an object, you will find the Effective Access tab and at the top of this screen, as shown in Figure 2-18, is an option to change the object owner. So long as you have administrative privileges, you can take ownership of the object and allocate it to another user or group. You can reset the permissions of all the folders, files and subfolders using the command-line tool **icacls <file name> /reset,** using an elevated command prompt.

Resolve NTFS permission issues

The type of security that can be configured on Windows 10 is determined by the file system in place. NTFS is the default underlying file system and it offers several security options, but you may also encounter removable drives or legacy systems that use FAT16, FAT32, or exFAT, which offer less security.

It has been several years since NTFS was established as the default file system of choice for all recent Windows client and server operating systems. NTFS file permissions offer administrators a very powerful tool for granting, controlling, auditing, and denying access to resources. Unlike share-level permissions, NTFS operates at the file level, which means NTFS permissions are applicable to resources shared over a network or accessed locally.

When troubleshooting resource access issues, you need to determine the following:

1. Is the file system in NTFS?

2. Are the files and folders being accessed locally or over the network?

It is easy to test if the file system is using NTFS by checking to see if there is a security tab on the volume on which the resource resides, as shown in Figure 2-19. The Security tab relates to NTFS permissions.

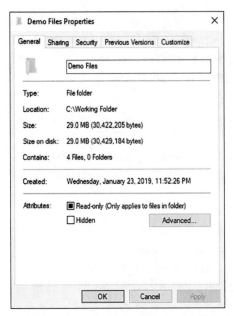

FIGURE 2-19 An NTFS formatted volume will display a Security tab

NTFS permissions can be complex and sometimes difficult to manage, especially for a junior or inexperienced administrator. Often the most challenging environment is one in which a newly hired administrator must adopt an enterprise, which has an existing problematic NTFS permission infrastructure in place that has very little documentation. Required small changes can sometimes have unintended consequences, which pose security risks. The role of the system administrator is to optimize data security, and to make sure that data is accessible to the right users. If users are denied access to files to which they have rights or given access to privileged files, it is a major problem that needs immediate remediation.

> **NOTE   NEW VERSUS LEGACY FOLDER STRUCTURE**
>
> Sometimes when adopting an existing NTFS permission infrastructure, it is better to design and recreate the file and folder permission structure rather than adopt a legacy environment.

NTFS permissions are cumulative, which means a user may have been given various group memberships as well as explicit permissions to resources that they are able to access. If a user has not been given any implicit or explicit permissions, they will not have access. If a combination of permissions for a resource has been set, you'll need to calculate the cumulative effect of all permissions.

Faced with an issue resulting from lack of access or over privilege, you need to start troubleshooting the problem by determining the effective permissions for the files or folders in question. Establish the scope. For example, who does this problem affect, and is it confined to a single user or a group of users? Establishing the effective permissions will allow you to quickly determine permissions that apply and provide you with a starting point.

User-effective permissions are based on the total of all permissions that they have been granted or denied. Take special care to look for any Deny permissions because these are infrequently set. However, when Deny permissions are set, they are very powerful because any explicit Deny permission will have precedence over Allow entries.

EXAM TIP

The Sharing tab shown in Figure 2-20 will only be visible if you are viewing the effective permissions for a shared folder.

REAL WORLD   DOCUMENT ALL CHANGES

The best practice when configuring NTFS permissions is to document a plan for how the NTFS permissions will be applied to the predefined users, groups, and folders. Ensure that all new users, groups, and folders are created according to the plan, and then apply NTFS permissions to this structure. Once the NTFS plan has been created, repeat for the Share permissions. Once permissions have been configured, continue to the testing phase where you perform tests for selected users to establish whether their effective access to resources matches the intended objectives of the plan. Over time, your NTFS change log will extremely useful when trouble-shooting NTFS access issues.

Configure shared permissions

Data is often shared in an organization, perhaps within a team for project work or between you and your boss. You must know how this can be achieved in Windows 10 within a networked environment, whether that is at home or in a larger workplace network. You must be able to manage shared files and printers.

File and printer sharing is disabled by default, and it is automatically turned on when you share the first folder on a Windows 10 device. If you want to configure this setting manually, you can do so in the advanced sharing settings in the Network And Sharing Center in Control Panel.

Another consideration is that when sharing is enabled, the Windows Defender Firewall is automatically configured to allow users to access shares on a computer in the network. This is a potential security risk. Although the firewall settings are configured automatically when you first share a folder, they are not returned to their default status even if you remove all shared folders.

Configure folder shares

When you share a folder, other users can connect to the shared folder and its contents across the network. Shared folders available on the network are no different from normal folders, and they can contain applications, corporate data, or private data. Be careful when creating a network share, to ensure that you do not accidentally provide access to a user or group of users who should not have access. By default, everyone on the network is given read access to the share, although you can change this setting.

Normally, a shared folder is located on a file server, but in a small network environment, the sharing can be located on a Windows 10–based computer or network-attached storage (NAS) device. When choosing the device or server, the resources should be available whenever the users need them and, often, this means the server is always on.

By providing a central location for shared folders to reside on, you enable the following features.

- Simplification of management
- User familiarity
- Ease in backing up data
- Consistent location and availability

When a user tries to use resources accessed on a shared folder, the access permissions are determined by taking into consideration both the share permission and the NTFS security permissions. The most restrictive set of permissions prevail to the user.

Ensure that you do not create shared folders where the share permissions (SMB) become the primary access security mechanism. They are more restrictive than the NTFS permissions because users gaining access to the resource locally or by logging on through Remote Desktop would completely bypass SMB permissions. It is therefore essential for NTFS permissions to be configured independently to protect the resource.

To allow access to a locally stored folder across a network, first share the folder. Files contained in folders are also shared, but files cannot be specifically shared independently, except from within a user profile.

SERVER MESSAGE BLOCK

Shares are provided by the Server Message Block (SMB) application-layer network protocol and not by NTFS. You can see what version of SMB your Windows 10 operating system is using by following these steps.

1. Sign in to your computer by using an administrative user account.

2. Open File Explorer and navigate to a shared or mapped folder on the network so that the shared files are visible in the right navigation pane.

3. On the File Explorer menu, click File and then click Open Windows PowerShell As Administrator.

4. Accept UAC if prompted.

5. Type the Windows PowerShell cmdlet **Get-SmbConnection**.

   Windows PowerShell should report the SMB version (dialect) in use, as shown in Figure 2-20.

```
Administrator: Windows PowerShell                                          –  □  ×
PS Z:\> Get-SmbConnection

ServerName    ShareName UserName      Credential                    Dialect NumOpens
---------     --------- --------      ----------                    ------- --------
192.168.1.92  4tb       DESKTOP\andrew MicrosoftAccount\▒▒▒▒▒▒▒▒▒▒  1.5     9
81RTM         down      DESKTOP\andrew MicrosoftAccount\▒▒▒▒▒▒▒▒▒▒  3.0.2   9


PS Z:\>
```

FIGURE 2-20 Windows 10 SMB version

NEED MORE REVIEW? **SMB 3.0 OVERVIEW**

This Microsoft resource, although focused on Windows Server 2016 and SMB 3.0, is useful to obtain more information relating to the benefits of using the latest version of SMB compared to previous versions. Visit *https://docs.microsoft.com/windows-server/storage/file-server/file-server-smb-overview.*

CONFIGURE NETWORK DISCOVERY

The network discovery feature was introduced in Windows Vista and uses a new layer 2-level protocol called Link Layer Topology Discovery (LLTD). It allows Windows to identify other devices present on the local subnet and, when possible, establish the quality of service (QoS) bandwidth capabilities of the network.

Knowing what is on the network increases the communication between devices. One downside of this increased awareness capability is that the firewall security settings are slightly relaxed. This means that not only does your computer see other network computers and devices, it also becomes discoverable on the network by other Windows clients.

EXAM TIP

Administrators working in a domain environment can manage the settings of the two network discovery settings, LLTD Mapper (LLTDIO) and Responder (RSPNDR), in Group Policy settings. The Group Policy settings can be found here: Computer Configuration\Policies \Administrative Templates\Network\Link Layer Topology Discovery.

Network discovery is tightly linked to network location profiles and to Windows Defender Firewall configuration. As we have seen, by default, network discovery is enabled for devices connecting to networks that are assigned the Domain or Private network location profile, but network discovery is disabled on public networks.

To change network discovery settings, from the Network And Sharing Center, click Change Advanced Sharing Settings. As shown in Figure 2-21, you can then configure network discovery for each network location profile.

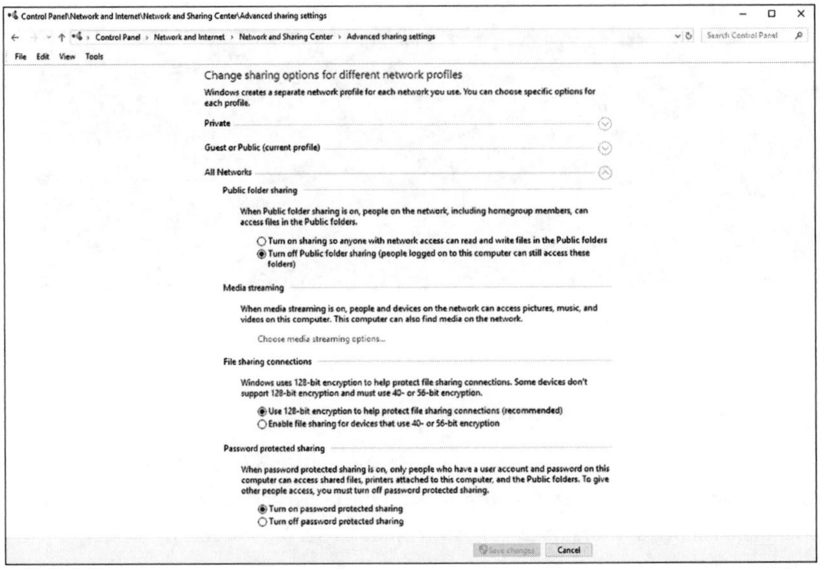

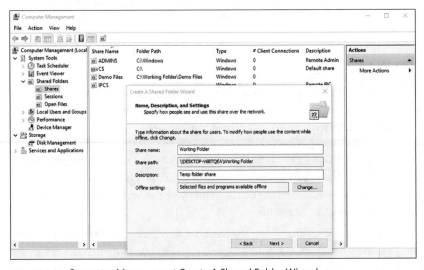

FIGURE 2-21 Advanced Sharing Settings

CREATE A SHARE BY USING THE SHARED FOLDERS SNAP-IN

You can create and manage file shares centrally on your computer by using the Shared Folders snap-in, which can be loaded into an empty Microsoft Management Console (MMC), or the snap-in found in Computer Management.

When you create a new share in the Shared Folders snap-in, the Create A Shared Folder Wizard appears and guides you through specifying the folder path, share name, description, and other settings, as shown in Figure 2-22.

FIGURE 2-22 Computer Management Create A Shared Folder Wizard

By default, the share name will be the same as the folder name, and permissions for the share are set at read-only access for the Everyone group, but you can choose other options or full customization by completing the underlying Share Permissions discretionary access control list (DACL) page.

The Shared Folders snap-in enables you to view existing shares and modify their properties, including settings such as offline file status, share permissions, and even the NTFS security permissions.

EXAM TIP

To launch the Create A Shared Folder Wizard directly from a command prompt, use Shrpubw.exe.

SHARE FOLDERS BY USING FILE EXPLORER

There are multiple methods of sharing a folder using File Explorer including

- Use the Share With option, found on the Share tab on the ribbon bar (also called Network File And Folder Sharing).

- Select Advanced Security from the Share tab on the ribbon bar.

- Use the Sharing tab in the Properties dialog box.

- Use the Give Access To context menu by right-clicking a folder to be shared.

All the methods present you with slightly different GUIs and wizards from which to choose the sharing options. Although they all result in sharing folders that can be accessed across the network, the main difference between each method is the speed and simplicity that some offer the novice.

In practice, most home users and small businesses prefer to use the sharing wizards found on the ribbon bar, but more experienced users seek the advanced level of control that can be gained through the Sharing tab in the Properties dialog box.

EXAM TIP

Review the options for configuring shares and pay attention to the limitations of the wizard-based methods. The wizards configure the file system permissions automatically, based on the limited choices they present.

The Share tab in File Explorer enables you to launch the File Sharing Wizard and provides the same functionality as the Share With shortcut menu. Next to this is Advanced Security, which enables you to fine-tune the sharing beyond the limitations of the File Sharing Wizard.

When you configure basic sharing permissions, you have one of two simplified options.

- **Read**   Users and groups can open but cannot modify or delete files.

- **Read/Write**   Users and groups can open, modify, or delete a file and modify permissions.

After you create a share, all users see the share name over the network. Only users who have at least the Read permission can view its content.

> **NOTE** **ADMINISTRATORS CAN SHARE FILES AND FOLDERS**
>
> To share a file or folder across the network in Windows 10, you must be a member of the Administrators group or provide UAC credentials for an administrator.

SHARE FOLDERS FROM THE COMMAND PROMPT

The command prompt enables you to share a folder by using the net share command. To create a simple share, you would use the following example.

```
net share MyShareName=c:\Temp\Data /remark:"Temp Work Area"
```

This command shares the C:\Temp\Data folder with the share name MyShareName and includes a description of Temp Work Area.

You must have administrative privileges to create a shared folder by using Net Share.

Review the additional command-line options that you can use with Net Share, as shown in Table 2-11.

TABLE 2-11 Net Share command-line options

OPTION	DESCRIPTION
/Grant:user permission	Enables you to specify Read, Change, or Full Share permissions for the specified user
/Users:number	Enables you to limit the number of users who can connect to the share concurrently (default and maximum for Windows 10 is 20 users)
/Remark:"text"	Enables you to add a description to the share
/Cache:option	Enables you to specify the offline files caching options for the share
sharename /Delete	Enables you to remove an existing share

> **NOTE** **SHARING CAUTION**
>
> The Net Share command will not create a folder and share it. You can only share folders that already exist on the computer.

SHARE FOLDERS BY USING WINDOWS POWERSHELL

If you need to script the creation of shares, Windows PowerShell is the most appropriate choice and provides several cmdlets that enable you to manage shares in Windows 10. Windows PowerShell offers more in both scope and functionality than Net Share and will continue to expand in the future.

An example command for creating a share is:

```
New-SmbShare -Name MyShareName -Path c:\Temp\Data
```

Other Windows PowerShell cmdlets used in the administration of shares are shown in Table 2-12.

TABLE 2-12 Windows PowerShell Share cmdlets

CMDLET	DESCRIPTION
Get-SmbShare	Lists the existing shares on the computer
Get-SmbShareAccess	Lists the access control list of the SMB share
New-SmbShare	Creates a new SMB share
Set-SmbShare	Modifies the properties for an existing share
Remove-SmbShare	Deletes an existing share
Grant-SmbShareAccess	Sets the share permissions on an existing share
Get-SmbShareAccess	Lists the current share permissions for a share

> **NOTE MULTIPLE SHARES**
>
> Sometimes you might want to provide different groups access to the same shared resources. You can share the same folder multiple times and use a different share name and share permission settings for each instance. Each group should only be able to access the share that they have permission for.

SHARE FILES BY USING FILE EXPLORER

Files typically cannot be shared without first sharing the parent folder. In Windows 10, files that reside in the user profile, such as Documents, Downloads, and Pictures folders, can be shared. To do this, follow these steps.

1. Sign in to your computer using an administrative user account.

2. Open File Explorer and navigate to the user profile.

3. Right-click a file, such as Pictures, in the user's profile.

4. Select Give Access To Specific People, as shown in Figure 2-23.

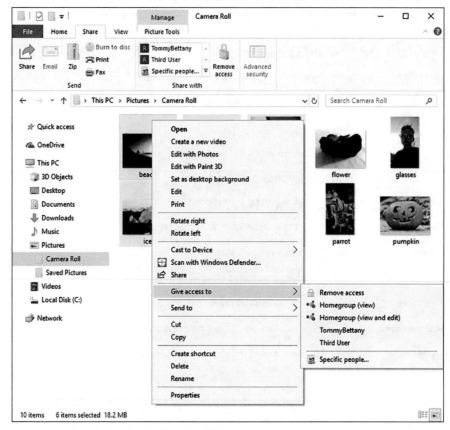

FIGURE 2-23 Share, using the sharing wizard

5. In the Choose People To Share With dialog box, type a user or group and click Add.

6. Set Permission Level to Read or Read/Write and click Share.

7. Note that you are sharing. The File Sharing Wizard completes, and the files are shared.

8. Optionally, you can use the links in the File Sharing Wizard to send someone the links to the shares.

9. Click Done.

You can also share a file using the Share icon on the Share ribbon bar. Select the file or multiple files and then click Share on the ribbon bar, as shown in Figure 2-24.

FIGURE 2-24 Sharing files from Windows Explorer

The Share option is also available within other apps including Microsoft Edge. The set of targets, including contacts and other apps will depend on which apps are installed on your device and offer a simplified method of sharing files quickly and with minimum effort.

Configure shared folders permissions

Permissions that are set on the share determine the level of access a user has to the files in the share. They can be set on FAT or later file systems. When you use the NTFS file system, be careful not to restrict access at the share level, because this might affect the effective permissions. You can configure the permissions when you share a folder and set a level that the user or group will have when they connect to the folder through the share across the network.

Sharing permissions have three options:

- **Read**   Users and groups can view the files, but they cannot modify or delete them.
- **Change**   Users and groups can open, modify, delete, and create content, but they cannot modify file or folder permissions; the Change permission incorporates all Read permissions.
- **Full**   Users and groups can perform all actions, including modifying the permissions; the Full permission incorporates all Change permissions.

Unlike in earlier versions of Windows, there is no longer a visual icon or indicator in File Explorer to distinguish whether a folder is shared. All shared folders on your device appear in the Shared Folders node of the Computer Management console. You can also view the shared folders that exist on your device by using the **Get-SmbShare** Windows PowerShell cmdlet or by typing **net view \\localhost /all** at the command prompt.

After a user has found the share in File Explorer, they can access the files directly. Another common way that users can connect to a shared folder over the network is by using the shares Universal Naming Convention (UNC) address. UNC addresses contain two backward slashes (\\) followed by the name of the computer that is sharing the folder and the shared folder name; for example, the UNC name for the Marketing shared folder on the LON-DC1 computer in the Fabrikam.com domain would be:

```
\\LON-CL1.Fabrikam.com\Marketing
```

TROUBLESHOOT SHARE PERMISSION ISSUES

Share permissions can cause many problems when troubleshooting access to files and folders. You need to remember that Share permissions work together with NTFS permissions and that the most restrictive permission will apply. Another common cause of confusion is that Share permissions only affect shared resources over the network.

If your file system is configured with FAT or FAT32, there is no option to configure NTFS permissions. If no Security tab is available in the resource Properties dialog box, we know that it cannot be formatted with NTFS, and the file system is likely to be FAT/FAT32, as shown in Figure 2-25.

FIGURE 2-25 A FAT32 formatted volume will not display a Security tab

If you need to confirm the file system in use, you can view the properties of the drive by following these steps:

1. Open File Explorer and right-click the drive that is under review.

2. Select Properties.

3. On the General tab, view the File System.

4. Click OK to close the dialog box.

COMBINE NTFS AND SHARE PERMISSIONS

Within a corporate environment, administrators share files over the network, using Share permissions. If the volume is formatted with NTFS, there are likely to be NTFS permissions configured on the shared file as well. To fully understand the effects of these two sets of permissions, you will need to combine them.

When combining share and NTFS permissions, restricting access to resources across the network can be easy. By accepting the default share permissions, you provide standard users with read-only access even if NTFS permissions are less restrictive.

Unfortunately, there is no wizard to diagnose which restrictions are in effect, but you can use the Effective Permissions feature in NTFS to determine the permissions being applied to a specific user or group (Principal).

NTFS is all about rules, and they are applied thoroughly by the file system. Wrongly applied settings, often combined with default inheritance, can instantly spread an incorrectly configured setting across hundreds of files. Unlike most computer operations, there is no undo option.

When troubleshooting access, always look for the most restrictive permission that has been set and evaluate whether this is being applied. If necessary, you can view the effective permissions. If the most restrictive permission is not being applied when the resource is being accessed, you need to determine the problem. Some other permission must be overlapping and affecting the resource; perhaps the user is a member of the Administrators group or another group that has full control permissions? You can also test what permissions are effective both at the local access level as well as when accessing the resource over the network share.

Often, the cause of many permission-based issues when troubleshooting file and folder access is that the Share permissions being applied on the share are too restrictive. It is preferable to use the more powerful NTFS permissions because these will always be effective, regardless of how they are accessed (over the network share or locally).

RESET SHARE AND NTFS PERMISSIONS

If you simply cannot decipher which NTFS settings are creating the problems, or if the problems are too complex or widespread, you can try to reset the file and folder permissions by using the ICACLS command-line utility.

This is especially useful if you get locked out of files and folders because of incorrect or deleted NTFS permissions.

To reset permissions using ICACLS, follow these steps.

1. Sign in to your computer using an administrator user account.
2. Open File Explorer and navigate to the folder that is giving you the problems.
3. On the File Explorer menu, click File > Open Windows PowerShell As Administrator.
4. Accept the UAC prompt, if prompted.
5. Type **icacls * /RESET /T /C /Q**.

The process of resetting files and folders to their default settings is very quick. After the original operating system defaults have been applied, you can configure the desired settings.

Skill 2.3: Configure devices by using local policies

In this section, you review how the Windows 10 registry can be used to configure computer settings that may not be available within the Settings app or Control Panel.

Group Policy is a key technology designed to help manage and control how users use Windows 10–based computers. Local Group Policy is the local implementation of these policies and you need to understand how to configure local settings on your computer using polices.

Finally, in this skill, you will review how to troubleshoot group policies on a computer to identify what policies are effective and how to resolve issues. Some of the tools used to fix policy issues on a local computer can be directly applied to domain joined devices, and this knowledge is valuable if you must apply the same type of settings to thousands of computers in a domain environment.

> **This skill covers how to:**
> - Configure local registry
> - Implement local policy
> - Troubleshoot group policies on devices

Configure Local Registry

All settings within Windows 10 are ultimately stored in the Windows Registry. This is a database that contains details of all Windows settings, installed software, device drivers, and much more. Without the registry, Windows would not work.

Every reference to working the registry always stipulates that you should take great care when working with or editing the registry. An incorrect registry change can prevent your system from booting and can result in you needing to completely reinstall the operating system. You should always take care and create a system backup before editing the registry.

Understanding the registry structure

The registry is a database that is split into multiple separate files known as hives, together with associated log and other support files.

You can find the registry files located in the %systemroot%\System32\Config\ though you will need to be an administrator to access this folder. Within this system folder, you should find several binary format "files" that the registry uses:

- SAM (Security Accounts Manager used to store local passwords)
- SECURITY
- SOFTWARE
- SYSTEM
- DEFAULT
- USERDIFF (used only for Windows upgrades)

In addition to the system files the user-specific settings are stored within the user profile and are loaded into system memory when a user signs in. These registry files are located in the following locations:

- %userprofile%\ntuser.dat
- %userprofile%\AppData\Local\Microsoft\Windows\UsrClass.dat

Other notable registry files include the Boot Configuration Data (BCD) store which stores its own file on the boot drive. The local services are located in %SystemRoot%\ServiceProfiles\LocalService and network services are stored in %SystemRoot%\ServiceProfiles\NetworkService.

The vast majority of changes to the hive files are made automatically by Windows whenever you install an application, or change a setting or configuration by using the Settings app or Control Panel.

The main hives, or subtrees which store settings for Windows 10 are shown in Table 2-13.

TABLE 2-13 Registry Hives

HIVE	DESCRIPTION
HKEY_CLASSES_ROOT	This hive relates to file association information relating to applications installed in the device. For example, it defines that the application for .docx files is Microsoft Word. This hive contains application information from derived from the settings that are stored in the HKEY_LOCAL_MACHINE\Software\Classes and HKEY_CURRENT_USER\Software\Classes hives.
HKEY_CURRENT_USER	This hive contains information for the signed-in user. Personalized settings such as background image, Windows color scheme, and font settings are stored in this hive.

(*Continued*)

HIVE	DESCRIPTION
HKEY_LOCAL_MACHINE	This hive stores computer-related configuration settings.
HKEY_USERS	This hive contains user-related configuration settings for all users who have signed in locally to the computer, including the currently signed-in user. The HKEY_CURRENT_USER hive is a subkey of HKEY_USERS. Edits to this hive will affect the user settings for the currently signed-in user.
HKEY_CURRENT_CONFIG	This hive contains current hardware profile information for the local computer.

Should you need to make a manual change, create a new entry, or modify an existing registry entry, these will typically take place in the following two hives:

- HKEY_LOCAL_MACHINE
- HKEY_CURRENT_USER

The primary tool for managing and editing the registry is the built-in registry editor.

Within the hives, settings containing values are stored in subtrees, keys and subkeys. The hierarchical nature of the registry makes it easy to locate a registry value. An example of a key, subkeys, and value would be

```
Computer\HKEY_CURRENT_USER\Control Panel\Mouse
```

This key holds many subkeys, which Windows uses to store settings for the mouse.

The mouse settings can be modified in the registry, as shown in Figure 2-26, or by using the Mouse item within the Control Panel. If you enable mouse pointer trails in the Control Panel, the registry subkey for MouseTrails is modified to have a value of 7.

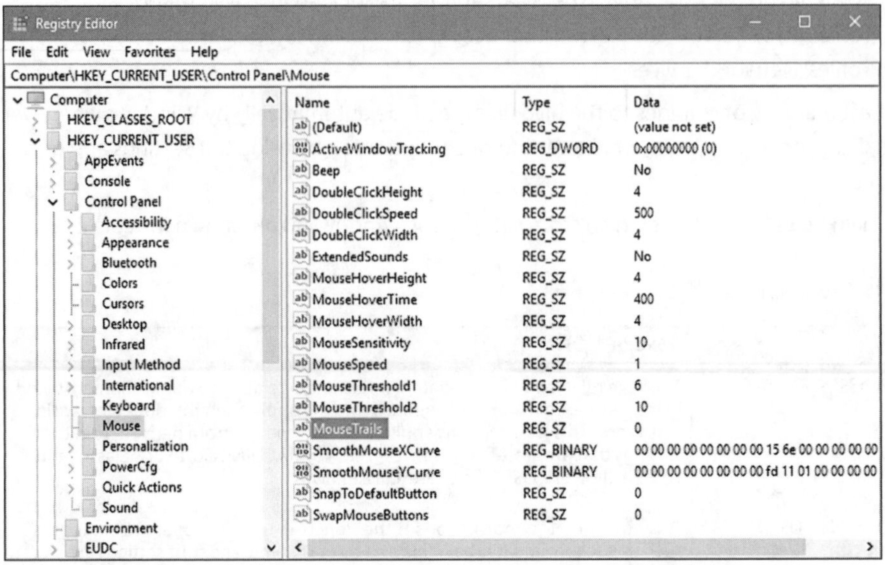

FIGURE 2-26 Registry keys

Values are stored within each key and subkey that are used to configure the operating system. There are several value types which are used to store information such as numerical data, text, and variables such as file paths. Often a value is empty or not defined as shown in the (Default) subkey in Figure 2-26. Table 2-14 lists more common types of registry values.

TABLE 2-14 Registry Value Types

VALUE TYPE	DATA TYPE	DESCRIPTION
REG_BINARY	Binary	Raw binary data. Values are normally displayed in hexadecimal format. Hardware information is often stored in these values.
REG_DWORD	DWORD	4-byte numbers (a 32-bit integer). Device-driver and service-related values are stored in these values.
REG_SZ	String	A fixed-length text string. Most of the values listed in the \HKEY_CURRENT_USER\Control Panel\Mouse keys are REG_SZ values.
REG_EXPAND_SZ	Expandable string	A variable length text string. Windows uses REG_EXPAND_SZ values to contain variables, such as file system paths.
REG_MULTI_SZ	Multiple strings	Multiple string values. These values are typically used when multiple values are required.

Understanding the Registry Editor

The built-in Registry Editor (Regedit.exe) allows you to view, search, and modify the registry's contents. Some of the common tasks that administrators can perform using the Registry Editor tool include

- Search the registry for a value, value name, subkey, or key
- Create, delete, and modify keys, subkeys, and values
- Import entries into the registry from an external (.REG) file
- Export entries from the registry into an external (.REG) file
- Back up the entire registry
- Manage the HKEY_LOCAL_MACHINE and HKEY_USERS registry hives on a remote computer

You can also import registry keys and values directly into the registry using a text file with the .REG extension.

All .REG files will use the following syntax for Registry Editor to understand them:

```
Windows Registry Editor Version 5.00
[<Hive name>\<Key name>\<Subkey name>]
"Value name"=<Value type>:<Value data>
```

Because .reg files are associated with the registry, executing a .REG file will merge it with—or import it to—the local Windows Registry. The contents of the .REG file will add, delete, or modify one or more keys or values in the registry. Depending on the changes contained within the .REG file, you might need to restart your computer after the changes have been made.

You can also use the import option on the file menu within the Registry Editor to import the settings, or you can use the command line with a script similar to the following example:

```
regedit /s C:\\Registry\\regsetting.reg \> nul
```

Using PowerShell to manage registry settings

The registry can be accessed directly using Windows PowerShell. The registry provider within PowerShell displays the registry like a file system, displaying the keys and subkeys as subfolders within a registry hive.

Windows PowerShell uses the abbreviated form of the hive nomenclature where the HKEY_LOCAL_MACHINE hive becomes HKLM and HKEY_LOCAL_USER becomes HKLU.

To view the registry using Windows PowerShell, open an elevated Windows PowerShell command prompt and then type the following, pressing Enter after each line.

```
Get-ChildItem -Path hklm:
Dir
```

You can also obtain a richer output by using this PowerShell command:

```
Get-Childitem -ErrorAction SilentlyContinue | Format-Table Name, SubKeyCount, ValueCount -AutoSize
```

To create a new registry key, you can first use the **Set-Location** cmdlet to change to the appropriate registry subtree and key as shown here:

```
Set-Location "HKCU:\Software"
```

Alternatively, you can use the full path to the registry key in the cmdlet as follows:

```
New-Item -Path HKCU:\Software -Name "Demonstration" –Force
```

Use the following cmdlet to assign the new registry key a value of "demo":

```
Set-Item -Path HKCU:\Software\Demonstration -Value "demo"
```

To validate that the key value has been stored correctly, view the key in the registry, or type:

```
Get-Item -Path HKCU:\Software\Demonstration
```

Implement local policy

Local Security Policy allows you to configure various security policies on a local computer. The computer may or may not be domain joined. When used in a domain-based environment, local policies can be used to affect all computers in the domain. Only the Windows 10 Pro,

Enterprise, and Education editions provide access to the Local Security Policy console. For Windows 10 Home edition, the settings and rights are predefined and unchangeable.

With Local Security Policy, you create rules so that you can manage users' computers. You can apply configuration settings that can affect a single device when deployed using the Local Group Policy Editor. When settings are configured using Group Policy within a domain environment, the settings can be deployed from one to thousands of targeted devices. When a policy has been configured, standard users cannot modify a managed policy setting.

Local Security Policy is a subset of the Local Group Policy Object Editor (gpedit.msc). You can also see the same settings by using the dedicated tool called Local Security Policy Editor, as shown in Figure 2-27. To launch the tool, follow these instructions:

1. Log onto Windows 10 with administrative privileges.
2. Click Start and search for **Secpol.msc**.
3. Click the Secpol.msc link to open the Local Security Policy Editor.
4. Expand both Account Policies and Local Policies.

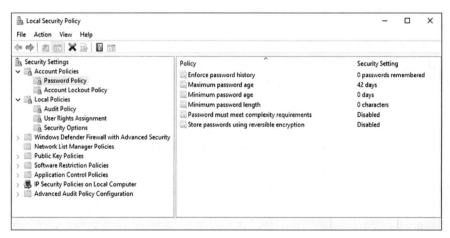

FIGURE 2-27 Local Security Policy

Within Local Security Policy, you can find the following sections:

- **Account Policies**   These include local account Password Policy and Account Lockout Policy. These allow you to configure the device password history, maximum and minimum password age, password complexity, and password length. You can also configure what action will be taken when a user enters an incorrect password during logon.

- **Local Policies**   These include Audit Policy, User Rights Assignment, and Security Options, and they allow you to enable/disable auditing, configure user rights (including the ability to log on locally to the device), access the computer from the network, and have the right to shut down the system. In this section, you will also find settings to configure many security settings, such as interactive logon settings, User Account Control settings, and shutdown settings.

- **Windows Defender Firewall with Advanced Security**   These are used to configure the local firewall settings.
- **Network List Manager Policies**   These enable you to configure whether users can configure new network properties, including the network name, location, and icon.
- **Public Key Policies**   These allow you to configure settings for Certificate Auto-Enrollment and the Encrypting File System (EFS) Data Recovery Agents.
- **Software Restrictions Policies**   These are used to identify and control which applications can run on the local computer.
- **Application Control Policies**   These are used to configure AppLocker.
- **IP Security Policies on Local Computer**   These allow you to create, manage, and assign Internet Protocol Security (IPsec) policies.
- **Advanced Audit Policy Configuration**   These allow you to provide additional fine tuning and control when using audit policies.

Configuring a password policy

On a local device, if you want to ensure that all users use secure passwords and that the passwords are changed after a set number of days, you can configure a password policy as follows:

1. Log onto Windows 10 with administrative privileges.
2. Click Start and search for **Secpol.msc**.
3. Click the Secpol.msc link to open the Local Security Policy Editor.
4. Expand Account Policies and click Password Policy.
5. Double-click Enforce Password History. You can now enter a value that represents the number of unique new passwords that a user account must have used before an old password can be reused.
6. Enter **5** and click OK to set this policy.
7. Double-click Maximum Password Age. The default setting is 42, which allows a user can use their password over a 42-day period before they are forced to change it. The best practice is to have passwords expire every 30 to 90 days.
8. Enter **90** and click OK.
9. Double-click Minimum Password Age. The default setting is 0 days, which allows users to change their passwords whenever they like. A setting of 14 days prevents users from changing their password in rapid succession to bypass the password history setting.
10. Enter **14** and click OK.

11. Double-click Minimum Password Length. The default is set to 0 characters. A setting of 8 would require that a password must be at least 8 characters long.

12. Enter **8** and click OK.

13. Double-click Password Must Meet Complexity Requirements. This setting is disabled by default. Once set to enabled, all passwords need to be complex.

14. Double-click Store Passwords Using Reversible Encryption. The default is disabled. If you enable this policy, all passwords are stored in a way that all applications are able access the password, which also makes them vulnerable to hackers to access.

15. Close the Local Security Policy editor.

The changes relating to local passwords become effective immediately once the policy is configured. Users with existing passwords can continue to use them until they need to be changed. The next time a user changes his or her password, the new password will need to conform with the settings in the Password Policy.

> *NOTE* **PASSWORD MUST MEET COMPLEXITY REQUIREMENTS**
>
> When the Password Must Meet Complexity Requirements policy is enabled, passwords must meet the following minimum requirements:
>
> - Must not contain the user's account name or parts of the user's full name that exceed two consecutive characters
> - Must be at least six characters in length
> - Must contain characters from three of the following four categories:
>   - English uppercase characters (A through Z)
>   - English lowercase characters (A through Z)
>   - Base 10 digits (0 through 9)
>   - Nonalphabetic characters (for example, !, $, #, %)
>
> Complexity requirements are enforced when passwords are changed or created.

Configuring an account lockout policy

When you implement a strong password policy, it is recommended that you also configure account lockout policy, which helps to protect accounts from password-cracking tools, which can attempt thousands of different passwords every hour in the hope that they succeed. Within a local environment, even an employee can try to guess a password to gain access to a system.

This brute-force attack on a system cannot be prevented. However, you can implement measures within the Account Lockout Policy that monitor incorrect attempts to log in to a local device. If a brute-force attack is suspected (for example, five incorrect passwords are entered in quick succession), then the account can be locked for a period of time.

To define that lockout policy, use the following steps:

1. Log onto Windows 10 with administrative privileges.
2. Click Start and search for **Secpol.msc**.
3. Click the Secpol.msc link to open the Local Security Policy Editor.
4. Expand Account Policies and click Account Lockout Policy.
5. Double-click Account Lockout Threshold, enter **3**, and click OK.
6. When the Account Lockout Threshold has been set, Windows suggests two other settings:
   - **Account Lockout Duration**   This setting specifies how long, in minutes, the user account will remain locked once the threshold has been reached.
   - **Reset Account Lockout Counter After**   This setting specifies how long, in minutes, before the count of incorrect passwords entered is set back to zero.
7. Leave these settings as recommended and click OK.

Configuring local policy

Local policies are used to control users once they have logged on and gained access to a system. You can configure policies that implement auditing, specify user rights, and set security options.

Audit Policy

Audit policies are used to track specified user actions on a device. These actions are recorded as a success or failure, such as accessing a file or being blocked from printing a document. Auditing is costly because system resources are required to constantly monitor a system and record actions to the audit logs. Audit settings can generate many log items, and this may impede a computer's performance. Therefore, you should use auditing on selective actions and turn off the feature when it is no longer required.

Auditing allows you to create a history of specific tasks and actions, such as file access (Audit Object Access policy), user account deletion (Audit Account Management) or successful logon attempts (Audit Account Logon Events). Often, auditing is used to identify security violations that arise; security violations could include, for example, when users attempt to access system management tasks or files within File Explorer for which they do not have permission. In this example, failed attempts to access resources will be logged in the audit log, with details of the user account, time, and details of the resources for which access was denied because of insufficient privileges.

Configuring audit policy involves three components:

- Enable auditing within Local Policies for success or failure (or both) for specific events or actions.
- For object access, such as file system files and folders, enable auditing on the objects to be audited.
- Use Event Viewer to view the results of the audit in the security log.

To view the various settings that can be configured using audit policy, view the audit policy options in Table 2-15.

TABLE 2-15 Audit policy options

POLICY DESCRIPTION	DESCRIPTION
Audit Account Logon Events	Tracks user logon activity on his local device or to a domain (if domain auditing is enabled).
Audit Account Management	Tracks user and group account management including creation, deletion, and password changes.
Audit Directory Service Access	Tracks access to Active Directory objects by a user within a domain.
Audit Logon Events	Audits events related to local account activity, such as running a logon script, accessing a member server, or a device that uses a local account to generate a logon event.
Audit Object Access	Enables auditing of access to the file system and registry objects, including files, folders, printers, hives, and values.
Audit Policy Change	Tracks any changes to user rights assignment policies, audit policies, or trust policies, such as assigning, removal, creation, changing, starting, or stopping policies.
Audit Privilege Use	Tracks each instance of when a user exercises a user right that has been assigned to her user account.
Audit Process Tracking	Tracks events whenever a program is activated, a new process is created or exited, or if a user attempts to install a service.
Audit System Events	Tracks system events, such as when a user shuts down or restarts his computer and when an event occurs that affects either the system security or the security log.

To configure an audit policy to monitor account logon events, use these steps:

1. Log onto Windows 10 with administrative privileges.
2. Click Start and search for **Secpol.msc**.
3. Click the Secpol.msc link to open the Local Security Policy Editor.
4. Expand Local Policies and click Audit Policy.

5. Double click the Audit Account Logon Events policy and check the Success and Failure boxes.

6. Click OK.

7. Log off the device and attempt to log back on as an Administrator, but use an incorrect password. Allow the logon to fail.

8. Log on as an administrator using the correct password.

9. Click Start and search for Event Viewer.

10. Click the Event Viewer app to open the Event Viewer.

11. Expand Windows Logs and select the Security log.

12. You should see the audited events listed with an Event ID of 4776 and a Task Category of Credential Validation, as shown in Figure 2-28.

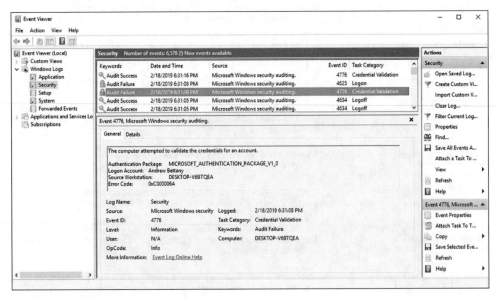

FIGURE 2-28 Review audited events within the Security Log

User Rights Assignment

The user rights policies are used to determine what rights a user or group of users have on a device. Often, there is confusion between rights and permissions, and you should be clear that user rights, or privileges, apply to the system and relate to activities or tasks that the user can perform.

Some of the activities that you can grant to a user include:

- Add Workstations To Domain
- Allow Log On Locally

- Allow Log On Through Remote Desktop Services
- Back Up Files And Directories
- Change The System Time
- Deny Log On Locally
- Shut Down The System
- Take Ownership Of Files Or Other Objects

To configure a user to have the right to perform a backup of a device, use the following steps:

1. Log onto Windows 10 with administrative privileges.
2. Click Start and search for **Secpol.msc**.
3. Click the Secpol.msc link to open the Local Security Policy Editor.
4. Expand Local Policies and click User Rights Assignment.
5. Double-click the user right Back Up Files And Directories.
6. Click the Add User Or Group button. The Select Users Or Groups dialog box appears.
7. Type the name of the user or group to which you want to grant the right or click the Advanced button and then select Find Now. Select the user or group of users within the list.
8. Click OK.
9. Click OK in the Select Users Or Groups dialog box.
10. In the Back Up Files And Directories Properties dialog box, click OK.

> **NOTE** **USER RIGHTS ASSIGNMENT**
>
> A user may be given a right that could contradict any existing permissions. For example, if when a user is given the right to Back Up Files And Directories, the user can back up files and folders even if the user does not have specific NTFS-level permissions to the files or folders.

Remember, a right authorizes a user to perform specific actions on a device, such as logging on to a computer interactively or backing up files and directories on a system. Before leaving this section, you should review the list of user rights policies, which can be found within the User Rights Assignment node of the Local Policies.

Security Options

The Security Options section of the local policies includes many options, which are used to allow or restrict activities on the device.

Some of the activities that you can configure with Security Options include:

- **Accounts**   Block Microsoft Accounts
- **Interactive Logon**   Do Not Require CTRL+ALT+DEL
- **Interactive Logon**   Don't Display Username At Sign-In
- **User Account Control**   Admin Approval Mode For Built-In Administrator Account

Nearly all the several dozen settings have their default settings set to Not Defined. Once configured, a setting can be have the following statuses:

- **Enabled** or **Disabled**
- **Text entry**   (For example, a user account name, or a system path.)
- **Value**   (For example, the number of previous logons to cache for when a domain controller is not available.)

One area of the Security Options that you should pay attention to are the User Account Control (UAC) settings. We will cover UAC in detail in the next skill, but you should note that you can configure UAC using policy settings in this area of Local Policy.

EXAM TIP

For the exam, you should know how to set local group policies and understand the purpose of account policies and local policies. Work through the examples showing how to configure password policies and account lockout policies. Review the various audit policies, user rights assignments, and security options that are available.

Troubleshoot group policies on devices

Diving deep into Group Policy would double the size of this book, but you should understand how to perform basic troubleshooting of Group Policies on Windows 10 devices.

Generally, when we refer to Group Policy, we are referring to Group Policy Objects (GPO) containing GPO settings that are created by IT administrators and pushed over the network to affect devices within a domain environment. Local policy, or Local Group Policy, refers to policy settings that are locally administered and configured.

Whatever the source of a GPO setting or group policy, sometimes, these can fail to apply. There can be many reasons for these failures, including incorrect GPO settings, poor network connection, or failure of the Group Policy Client service.

Troubleshooting Tools

You can use many tools to investigate GPO-related issues, including the Resultant Set of Policy (RSoP.msc) tool within the GUI and Group Policy Result (GPResult) from the command line.

CONNECTION ISSUES

There are several preliminary troubleshooting areas that you should verify before proceeding to use the specialist GPO tools. These relate to the essential services, network connection, and time synchronization.

- **Group Policy Client Service**   Before troubleshooting group policy, you should verify the status of the required services for GPO. Check that the Group Policy Client service has the status of Running or Automatic within the Services utility.

- **Network Connection**   Verify the network connection and configuration. This can be achieved by running the Network Adapter troubleshooter within the Settings app to find and fix issues automatically. Without a reliable network connection, your device will not be able to connect to the domain controller and obtain group policy.

- **Time**   The device time needs to be within five minutes of the time on the server. If there is more than a five-minute time difference, then problems with Active Directory synchronization can occur, which can then affect GPO delivery.

RESULTANT SET OF POLICY TOOL

The Resultant Set of Policy (RSoP) tool is a diagnostic tool that is used to check and troubleshoot group policy settings. RSoP is built into Windows 10 and can be used to view the policies being applied to users and devices, and it can identify where the policy settings are coming from. It can also be used to simulate GPO settings for planning purposes.

There are two modes in which RsoP can be run: Logging Mode and Planning Mode.

- **Logging Mode**   Generates a report on policy settings for users and computers and is used to verify and troubleshoot group policy settings.

- **Planning Mode**   Used for "what if" scenarios, such as: If a user or computer is moved to a different Active Directory AD group, will they still receive the expected GPOs?

To run RSoP to determine computer and user policy settings, perform these steps:

1. Log onto Windows 10 with administrative privileges.

2. Click Start and type **rsop.msc**.

3. Click the rsop.msc link to open the Resultant Set of Policy tool.

4. RSoP will run and generate a report for the user and computer policy settings.

5. Review the policy settings that have been applied to the system by any Group Policy Objects that are in effect.

6. To verify that the policies that you have linked are being applied, you should compare the system results to those that are expected.

To simulate GPO policy settings, you can use the planning mode of the Resultant Set Of Policy tool. You would open the RSoP tool from Microsoft Management Console and add the Resultant Set Of Policy snap-in, follow the wizard, and select Generate Rsop Data while in Planning Mode.

GPRESULT

The GPResult command line tool provides a powerful method of verifying what group policy objects are applied to a user or computer. The tool creates a report that displays what GPOs have been applied to a system and separates the results into the user and computer settings.

Follow these steps to display all GPOs that have been applied to a system:

1. Log on to Windows 10 with administrative privileges.

2. Right-click Start and select Windows PowerShell (Admin).

3. Confirm the User Account Control warning, if prompted.

4. Type **gpresult /r** and press Enter. You should see the RSoP data for your logged-in user and device.

The output of the **gpresult /r** command will display information, including:

- The applied GPOs name(s)

- Order of GPO application

- GPO details and the last time group policy was applied

- Domain and domain functional level

- Which domain controller issued the GPO

- Network speed link threshold

- Which security groups the user and computer are a member of

- Details of GPO filtering

You can fine tune the report to select only the user or computer GPOs by limiting the command scope as follows:

- If you don't want to see both User and Computer GPOs, then you can use the scope option to specify a user or computer.

- To display GPOs applied to a specific user:

  gpresult /r /scope:user

- To display GPOs applied to a specific computer:

  gpresult /r /scope:computer

- To display GPOs applied on a remote computer, you can use the command:

  gpresult /s Laptop123 /r

- To generate an HTML report of the GPResult, as shown in Figure 2-29, you can use the command:

  gpresult /h c:\GPOreport.html

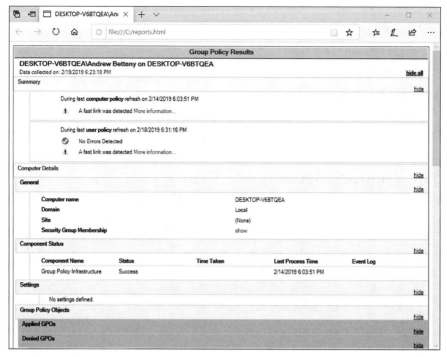

FIGURE 2-29 Generate an HTML report using GPResult

Skill 2.4: Manage Windows security

In this section, you review how to keep Windows 10 secure by using features built into Windows. Devices and users need to be protected while online, and they rely on the built-in defense features, which provide resilience against ever-increasing threats.

You will review the Windows Security features and options that help maintain your device's health and manage threat-protection settings.

You will also review how to use User Account Control (UAC) to help you control administrative privilege elevation in Windows 10 to reduce security risks.

Windows Defender Firewall provides a significant security barrier that helps isolate and protect Windows from external threats, and you will need to understand how to configure and maintain the firewall.

Finally, as a method of protecting data, you need to understand the various encryption methods available with Windows 10 and when to use encrypting file system and BitLocker.

Configure Windows Security

The Windows Security feature is an app accessible from within the Settings app that provides a single portal for users to control and view their device security, health, and online safety. The Windows Security section within the Settings app, as shown in Figure 2-30, contains an overview of the status of Windows security features, as well as links to other settings and support.

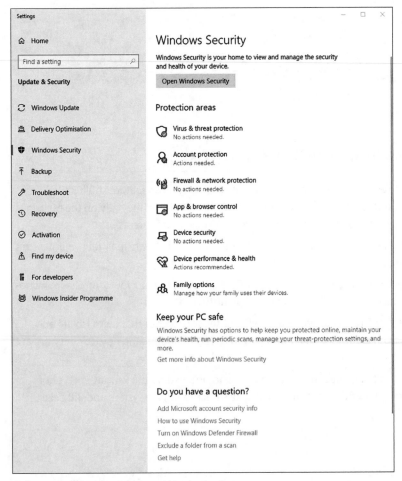

FIGURE 2-30 Windows Security within the Settings app

The Windows Security page in the Settings app provides a status report covering seven areas of security.

- **Virus & Threat Protection**   Monitor threats to your device, run scans, and get updates to help detect the latest threats.
- **Account Protection**   Access sign-in options and account settings, including features such as Windows Hello and Dynamic Lock.
- **Firewall & Network Protection**   Manage firewall settings and monitor network and Internet connections.
- **App & Browser Control**   Review and update settings for Windows Defender Smart-Screen and configure exploit protection settings.
- **Device Security**   Review built-in security options that use virtualization-based security to help protect your device from attacks by malicious software.
- **Device Performance & Health**   View the status information about your device's performance health.
- **Family Options**   Use features, such as Parental controls, that allow you to keep track of your kids' online activity.

From the summary portal, you can review the color-coded status icons, which indicate the level of safety of the system:

- **Green**   The device is sufficiently protected, and there aren't any recommended actions.
- **Yellow**   There is a safety recommendation that should be reviewed.
- **Red**   This is a warning indicating that something needs immediate attention.

From within the Settings app, you can launch the individual security elements, or launch the standalone Windows Security app by clicking the Open Windows Security button, shown previously in Figure 2-30.

NOTE WINDOWS DEFENDER SECURITY CENTER

In previous versions of Windows 10, Windows Security is called Windows Defender Security Center.

When a Windows Security item requires action from the user, such as to update the virus and threat protection definitions, the shield icon within the notification area of the taskbar will show a red cross to indicate action is required.

The Windows Security app collects the status from each of the included security features and allows you to perform some configuration. As updates are collated by the Windows Security app, they will also trigger notifications through the Action Center.

It is possible to customize the view of the Settings app. Administrators can add support information about your organization in a contact card to the Windows Security app, as shown in Figure 2-31, and admins can hide entire sections of the app by using Group Policy. Hidden sections will not appear on the home page of the Windows Security app, and its icon will not be shown on the navigation bar on the side of the app.

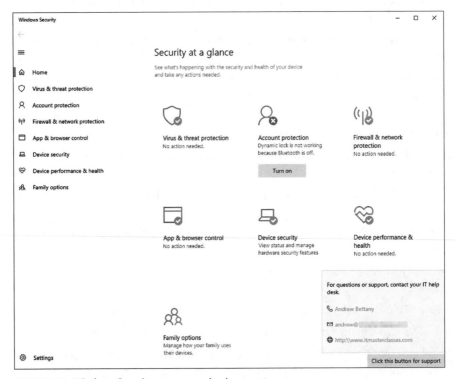

FIGURE 2-31 Windows Security app customized support

NEED MORE REVIEW? **THE WINDOWS SECURITY APP**

To review further details about configuring the Windows Security app, refer to the Microsoft website at *https://docs.microsoft.com/windows/security/threat-protection/windows-defender-security-center/windows-defender-security-center*.

Configure User Account Control

Once a user has gained access to the operating system following successful sign-on, the Windows 10 feature called *User Account Control* (UAC) prevents unauthorized changes to the system.

Systems that suffer from malware attacks can easily be compromised if the malware can effectively use administrative access and wreak havoc on the system. This creates extra work for the help desk, increases support costs, and reduces productivity. UAC has been very successful in preventing users and malware from using administrative credentials to harm a system.

With Windows 10, administrators no longer have "always on" full access to the system. Rather than enabling administrators to implement system-wide changes, UAC presents administrators with a challenge pop-up prompt to force them to confirm their actions. Similarly, a standard user who attempts to change system settings will receive a UAC prompt, which requires administrative credentials to be provided. If the proper admin credentials are not provided, the user is denied the ability to make the requested changes.

Since the introduction of UAC in Microsoft Vista, Microsoft has fine-tuned the UAC process with the aim of making the use of UAC less frustrating for all users by reducing the number of application and system tasks that require elevation.

UAC offers various layers of protection, with the UAC prompt being the most visible to the user. The following features complement UAC:

- File and Registry Redirection
- Installer Detection
- UAC prompt
- ActiveX Installer Service
- Secure Desktop
- Application Information Service

NOTE **ACCESS DENIED**

For UAC to function properly, the Application Information Service component must be running. If this service is stopped or disabled, applications that require administrative access will not be able to request UAC elevation and therefore will not launch, resulting in Access Denied errors.

Standard users

Except for administrators, all users are standard users with few privileges and limited ability to make changes to the system, such as installing software or modifying the date and time. Standard user accounts are described as "operating with least privilege." The list of system tasks that a standard user can perform include:

- Change the desktop background and modify display settings
- View firewall settings
- Change the time zone
- Add a printer
- Change their own user account password
- Configure accessibility options
- Configure power options
- Connect to a wireless or LAN connection

- Install drivers, either from Windows Update or those that are supplied with Windows 10
- Install updates by using Windows Update
- Use Remote Desktop to connect to another computer
- Pair and configure a Bluetooth device with the device
- Perform other troubleshooting, network diagnostic, and repair tasks
- Play CD/DVD media
- Restore own files from File History
- View most settings, although the elevated permissions will be required when attempting to change Windows settings

UAC prevents you from making unauthorized or hidden (possibly malware-initiated) changes to your system that require administrator-level permissions. A UAC elevation prompt is displayed to notify you, as follows:

- **Prompt For Consent** This is displayed to administrators in Admin Approval Mode whenever an administrative task is requested. Click Yes to continue if you consent.
- **Prompt For Credentials** This is displayed if you are a standard user attempting to perform an administrative task. An administrator needs to enter her password into the UAC prompt to continue.

When an administrator provides permissions to a standard user via a UAC prompt, the permissions are only temporarily operative, and the permissions are returned to a standard user level once the isolated task has finished.

Standard users can become frustrated when they are presented with the UAC prompt, and Microsoft has reduced the frequency and necessity for elevation. Following are some common scenarios wherein a standard user would be prompted by UAC to provide administrative privileges. You will see that they are not necessarily daily tasks for most users:

- Add or remove a user account
- Browse to another user's directory
- Change user account types
- Change Windows Defender Firewall settings
- Configure Windows Update settings
- Install a driver for a device not included in Windows or Windows Update
- Install ActiveX controls
- Install or uninstall applications
- Modify UAC settings
- Move or copy files to the Program Files or Windows folders
- Restore system backup files
- Schedule Automated Tasks

Administrative users

Administrative users need to be limited to authorized personnel within the organization. In addition to the ability to perform all tasks that a standard user can perform, they also have the following far-reaching permissions:

- Read/Write/Change permissions for all resources
- All Windows permissions

From this, it looks like administrators have considerable power, which can potentially be hijacked by malware. Thankfully, by default, administrators are still challenged with the UAC prompt, which pops up when they perform a task that requires administrative permissions. However, they are not required to re-enter their administrative credentials. This is known as Admin Approval Mode.

A user who signs on to a system with administrative permissions will be granted two tokens:

- The first token enables him or her to operate as a standard user.
- The second token can be used when the administrator performs a task that requires administrative permissions.

Just as with the standard user, after the task is completed using elevated status, the account reverts to a standard-user privilege.

> **NOTE TURNING OFF UAC IS NOT RECOMMENDED**
>
> UAC helps prevent malware from damaging PCs and should not be turned off. If UAC is turned off, all Universal Windows Platform apps will stop working.

Types of elevation prompts

UAC has four types of dialog boxes, as shown in Table 2-16. The Description column explains how users need to respond to the prompt.

TABLE 2-16 UAC elevation prompts

TYPE OF ELEVATION PROMPT	DESCRIPTION
A Windows 10 setting or feature needs your permission to start.	This item has a valid digital signature that verifies that Microsoft is the publisher of this item, and it is usually safe to use the application.
A non-Windows 10 application needs your permission to start.	This application has a valid digital signature, and it is usually safe to use the application.
An application with an unknown publisher needs your permission to start.	This application does not have a valid digital signature from its publisher. Use extra caution and verify that the application is safe before using. Search the Internet for the program's name to determine whether it is a known trustworthy application or malware.
You have been blocked by your system administrator from running this application.	This application has been blocked because it is known to be untrusted. To run this application, you need to contact your system administrator to remove the restriction, if appropriate.

Within large organizations, nearly all users will be configured to sign in to their computer with a standard user account. On a managed system that has been provisioned and deployed by the IT department, standard user accounts should have little need to contact the help desk regarding UAC issues. They can browse the Internet, send email, and use applications without an administrator account. Home users and small businesses that lack a centralized IT resource to provision and manage their devices are often found to use administrative user accounts.

As with previous versions of Windows, an administrator can determine when the UAC feature will notify you if changes are attempted on your computer.

To configure UAC, use the following procedure.

1. Log onto Windows 10 with administrative privileges.

2. Click Start and type **UAC**.

3. Click Change User Account Control Settings to be shown the User Account Control Settings screen where you can adjust the UAC settings, as shown in Figure 2-32.

FIGURE 2-32 Changing User Account Control Settings

You need to review the information on this dialog box by moving the slider to each position in order to determine how the UAC feature will behave with each setting. The default is Notify Me Only When Applications Try To Make Changes To My Computer.

Table 2-17 shows the four settings that enable customization of the elevation prompt experience.

TABLE 2-17 User Account Control Settings

PROMPT	DESCRIPTION
Never notify	UAC prompting is disabled.
Notify me only when applications try to make changes to my computer (do not dim my desktop)	When an application makes a change, a UAC prompt appears. However, if the user makes a change to system settings, the UAC prompt is not displayed. The desktop does not dim.
Notify me only when applications try to make changes to my computer (default)	When an application makes a change, a UAC prompt appears. However, if the user makes a change to system settings, the UAC prompt is not displayed. Secure desktop feature is active.
Always notify	The user is always prompted when changes are made to the computer by applications or by the user.

The settings enable changes to the UAC prompting behavior only, and do not elevate the status of the underlying user account.

> **NEED MORE REVIEW?** **USER ACCOUNT CONTROL**
>
> To review further details about configuring UAC, refer to the Microsoft website at *https:// docs.microsoft.com/windows/security/identity-protection/user-account-control/user-account-control-overview.*

In addition to the UAC settings within the GUI, there are many more UAC security settings that can be configured via Group Policy. These can be found here: Computer Configuration\ Windows Settings\Security Settings\Local Policies\Security Options.

> **EXAM TIP**
>
> You need to take time to review the UAC settings configurable by Group Policy, with attention to the settings that feature Admin Approval Mode.

Secure Desktop

When UAC prompts the user for consent or elevated credentials, it first switches to a feature called Secure Desktop, which focuses only on the UAC prompt. In addition, Secure Desktop prevents other applications (including malware) from interacting with the user or influencing the user response to the UAC prompt.

While it is possible for malware to generate a screen that imitates the look of Secure Desktop (and even re-create the visual UAC prompt), it is not possible for malware to actually provide UAC with the correct credentials. If a system was infected with malware, it could try to bypass the UAC security setting—using a bogus credential prompt to harvest usernames and passwords from unsuspecting users—and then use these credentials on genuine UAC prompts. Therefore, it is important that administrators are vigilant against potential malware attacks, and all devices are set to ensure that their malware protection is configured to automatically update.

Configure Windows Defender Firewall

After you connect a computer to a network, you might expose the computer to security risks. To mitigate these possible risks, you can implement several network security features in Windows 10, including Windows Defender Firewall.

Windows Defender Firewall blocks or allows network traffic based on the properties of that traffic. You can configure how Windows Defender Firewall controls the flow of network traffic by using configurable rules. In addition to blocking or allowing network traffic, Windows Defender Firewall can filter traffic, implement authentication and apply encryption to this filtered traffic.

The way in which you configure Windows Defender Firewall and your network location profiles can have a significant effect on file and printer sharing, and it can affect the discoverability of your device on connected networks.

Configure Firewall and Network Protection

Within the Windows Security app is the Firewall and Network Protection page. This page provides a unified interface for accessing firewall and network protection features, and consolidates several firewall-related components that are found within the Windows Defender Firewall in the Control Panel.

To access the Firewall and Network Protection page as shown in Figure 2-33, open Windows Security, and on the Home tab, click Firewall & Network Protection.

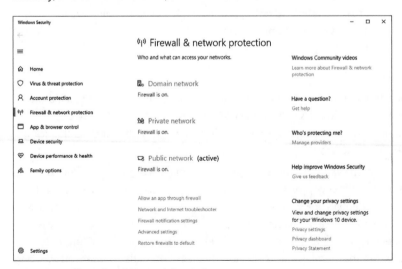

FIGURE 2-33 Firewall and Network Protection

On the Firewall & network protection page, you can view the current Windows Defender Firewall status and access links to enable you to configure firewall behavior. Much of the functionality is duplicated between the Firewall & Network Protection page and Windows Defender Firewall. You can choose to perform the configuration and monitoring task outlined in this chapter using either tool. Eventually, the Windows Defender Firewall located within the Control Panel will be deprecated.

Configure Windows Defender Firewall

Windows Defender Firewall is a software-based firewall built into Windows 10 that creates a virtual barrier between a computer and the network to which it is connected. Windows Defender Firewall protects the computer from unwanted incoming traffic and protects the network from unwanted outgoing traffic.

To access the Windows Defender Firewall, click Start, type **Firewall**, and then click Windows Defender Firewall.

A firewall allows specific types of data to enter and exit the computer while blocking other data; settings are configured by default (but they can be changed). This type of protection is called filtering. The filters are generally based on IP addresses, ports, and protocols. A description for each filter type includes:

- IP addresses are assigned to every computer and network resource connected directly to the network. The firewall can block or allow traffic based on an IP address of a resource (or a scope of addresses).

- Port numbers identify the application that is running on the computer. For example

  - Port 21 is associated with the File Transfer Protocol (FTP).

  - Port 25 is associated with Simple Mail Transfer Protocol (SMTP).

  - Port 53 is associated with DNS.

  - Port 80 is associated with Hypertext Transfer Protocol (HTTP).

  - Port 443 is associated with HTTPS (HTTP Secure).

- Protocols are used to define the type of packet being sent or received. Common protocols are TCP, Telnet, FTP, HTTP, Post Office Protocol 3 (POP3), Internet Message Access Protocol (IMAP), HTTPS, and User Datagram Protocol (UDP). (You should be familiar with the most common protocols before taking the exam.)

Although there are many rules already configured for the firewall, you can create your own inbound and outbound rules based on ports, protocols, programs, and more to configure the firewall to suit your exact needs.

Monitor the Windows Defender Firewall

You can monitor the state of the Windows Defender Firewall from either the Firewall & Network Protection area or the Windows Defender Firewall. It's easy to tell from here if the firewall is on or off and which is the active network.

To make basic changes to the state of the firewall within the Firewall & Network Protection area, select the network and choose to turn the Windows Defender Firewall on or off. On the left pane of Windows Defender Firewall, click Turn Windows Defender Firewall On Or Off. From there, you can change settings for both private and public networks. There are two options for each:

- Turn On Windows Defender Firewall (selected by default)
  - Block All Incoming Connections, Including Those In The List Of Allowed Apps
  - Notify Me When Windows Defender Firewall Blocks A New App (selected by default)
- Turn Off Windows Defender Firewall (not recommended)

You can also use the links on the page to allow an app or feature through the firewall and the links to the advanced settings options.

Allow an app through the Windows Defender Firewall

Some data generated with and by specific apps is already allowed to pass through the Windows Defender Firewall. You can see the list of which apps are allowed by clicking Allow An App Or Feature Through Windows Defender Firewall in the left pane of the Windows Defender Firewall window in Control Panel. As you scroll through the list, you'll see many apps (some you recognize and some you don't), including Candy Crush Saga, Cortana, Groove Music, and of course, Microsoft Edge.

You can modify which firewall profile apps can use by clicking the Change Settings button and providing administrator approval to the UAC prompt. The list will be editable. You will notice from the list that not all apps listed are enabled by default, including Windows Media Player Netlogon Service, Windows Remote Management, and Remote Shutdown. The list of apps and settings may vary depending upon your existing configurations.

If you don't see the app you want to allow or block, click Allow Another App. You can then browse to the app executable and select the app from the list of applications in the Add An App dialog box, as shown Figure 2-34. You can configure the app to allow or stop it from communicating through the appropriate network profile by selecting the network type option in the dialog box. For existing apps, you can choose the network profile within the Allow An App Or Feature Through Windows Defender Firewall dialog box. There are two checkbox options for each app: Private and Public.

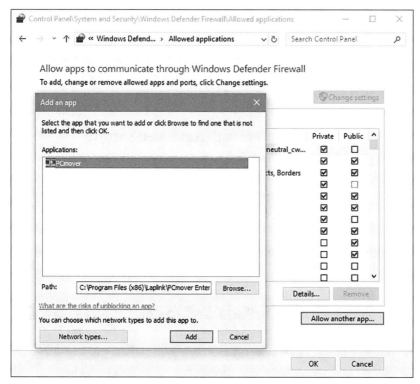

FIGURE 2-34 Adding an app through Windows Defender Firewall

You can also configure Windows Defender Firewall by using either the command line tool Netsh.exe or by using Windows PowerShell. For example, to configure an app exception in Windows Defender Firewall with Netsh.exe, run the following command.

```
netsh firewall add allowedprogram C:\Program Files (x86)\MyApp\MyApp.exe "My Application"
ENABLE
```

> **NEED MORE REVIEW?** **USING NETSH.EXE TO CONFIGURE WINDOWS DEFENDER FIREWALL**
>
> To find out more about controlling Windows Defender Firewall with Netsh.exe, refer to the Microsoft Support website at *https://support.microsoft.com/kb/947709*.

There are a significant number of Windows PowerShell cmdlets that you can use to configure and control Windows Defender Firewall. For example, to allow a new app through the firewall, you can use the following command.

```
New-NetFirewallRule -DisplayName "Allow MyApp" -Direction Inbound -Program "C:\Program
Files (x86)\MyApp\MyApp.exe" -RemoteAddress LocalSubnet -Action Allow
```

Configure Windows Defender Firewall with Advanced Security

Although you can configure a few options in the main Windows Defender Firewall window, you can perform more advanced firewall configurations by using the Windows Defender Firewall With Advanced Security management console snap-in, as shown in Figure 2-35. To access the snap-in, from Windows Defender Firewall, click the Advanced Settings link on the Firewall & Network Protection page within Windows Security or from the Windows Defender Firewall.

The Windows Defender Firewall With Advanced Security configuration is presented differently. Traffic flow is controlled by rules, and there is a Monitoring node for viewing the current status and behavior of configured rules.

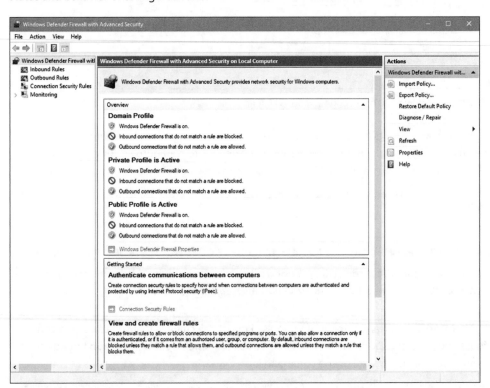

FIGURE 2-35 Windows Defender Firewall with Advanced Security

Once opened, there are several options and terms with which you need to be familiar.

- In the left pane, your selection determines which items appear in the middle and right panes.

  - **Inbound Rules**   Lists all configured inbound rules and enables you to double-click any item in the list and reconfigure it as desired. Some app rules are predefined and can't be modified, although they can be disabled. Explore the other nodes as time allows. You can also right-click Inbound Rules in the left pane and create your own custom rule. Rule types include Program, Port, Predefined, and Custom. They are detailed later in this section.

  - **Outbound Rules**   Offers the same options as Inbound Rules, but these apply to outgoing data. You can also right-click Outbound Rules in the left pane and create your own custom rule.

- **Connection Security Rules**   Connection security rules establish how computers must authenticate before any data can be sent. IP Security (IPsec) standards define how data is secured while it is in transit over a TCP/IP network, and you can require a connection to use this type of authentication before computers can send data. You'll learn more about connection security rules in the next section.

  - **Monitoring**   Offers information about the active firewall status, state, and general settings for both the private and public profile types.

- In the right pane, you'll see the options that correspond to your selection in the left pane.

  - **Import/Export/Restore/Diagnose/Repair Policies**   Enables you to manage the settings you've configured for your firewall. Polices use the WFW extension.

  - **New Rules**   Enables you to start the applicable Rule Wizard to create a new rule. You can also do this from the Action menu.

  - **Filter By**   Enables you to filter rules by Domain Profile, Private Profile, or Public Profile. You can also filter by state: Enabled or Disabled. Use this to narrow the rules listed to only those you want to view.

  - **View**   Enables you to customize how and what you view in the middle pane of the Windows Defender Firewall With Advanced Security window.

When you opt to create your own inbound or outbound rule, you can choose from four rule types. A wizard walks you through the process, and the process changes depending on the type of rule you want to create. The rules are as follows:

- **Program**   A program rule sets firewall behavior for a specific program you choose or for all programs that match the rule properties you set. You can't control apps, but you can configure traditional EXE. Once you've selected the program for which to create the rule, you can allow the connection, allow the connection only if the connection is secure and has been authenticated using IPsec, or block the connection. You can also choose the profiles to which the rule will be applied (domain, private, or public) and name the rule.

- **Port**   A port rule sets firewall behavior for TCP and UDP port types and specifies which ports are allowed or blocked. You can apply the rule to all ports or only ports you specify. As with other rules, you can allow the connection, allow the connection only if the connection is secured with IPsec, or block the connection. You can also choose the profiles to which the rule will be applied (domain, private, public) and name the rule.

- **Predefined**   This sets firewall behavior for a program or service that you select from a list of rules that are already defined by Windows.
- **Custom**   This is a rule you create from scratch, defining every aspect of the rule. Use this if the first three rule types don't offer the kind of rule you need.

EXAM TIP

You might encounter questions regarding how to create a rule on the exam. Therefore, you should spend a few minutes working through the wizard a few times, selecting different rule types each time, to become familiar with the process.

With Windows Defender Firewall With Advanced Security selected in the left pane and using the Overview section of the middle pane, click the Windows Defender Firewall Properties link to see the dialog box shown in Figure 2-36. From here, you can make changes to the firewall and the profiles, even if you aren't connected to the type of network you want to configure.

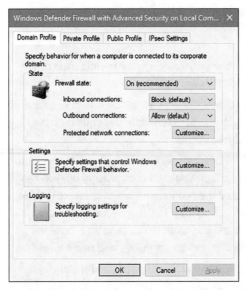

FIGURE 2-36 Viewing the Windows Defender Firewall properties

In Figure 2-36, the Domain Profile tab is selected. If you want, you can configure the firewall to be turned off when connected to a domain network. Additionally, you can strengthen the settings for the Public Profile and customize settings for the Private Profile. Finally, you can customize IPsec defaults, exemptions, and tunnel authorization on the IPsec Settings tab. Make sure to explore all areas of this dialog box and research any terms with which you are not familiar.

Configure connection security rules with IPsec

By default, Windows 10 does not always encrypt or authenticate communications between computers (there are exceptions). However, you can use Windows Defender Firewall With Advanced Security connection security rules to apply authentication and encryption to network traffic in your organization.

You can use IPsec network data encryption to ensure confidentiality, integrity, and authentication in data transport across channels that are not secure. Though its original purpose was to secure traffic across public networks, many organizations have chosen to implement IPsec to address perceived weaknesses in their own private networks that might be susceptible to exploitation.

If you implement IPsec properly, it provides a private channel for sending and exchanging potentially sensitive or vulnerable data, whether it is email, FTP traffic, news feeds, partner and supply-chain data, medical records, or any other type of TCP/IP-based data. IPsec provides the following functionality:

- Offers mutual authentication before and during communications
- Forces both parties to identify themselves during the communication process
- Enables confidentiality through IP traffic encryption and digital-packet authentication

Connection security rules are used to force authentication between two peer computers before they can establish a connection and transmit secure information. To secure traffic with IPsec using a connection security rule, you must allow the traffic through the firewall by creating a firewall rule. Connection security rules do not apply to programs and services. Instead, they apply only between the computers that are the two endpoints.

EXAM TIP

Connection security rules specify how and when authentication occurs, but they do not allow those connections. To allow a connection, you must create an inbound or outbound rule. During the inbound or outbound rule creation, you choose the required conditions for the connection, including requiring that the connections have been authenticated by using IPsec. When you do, connections will be secured using the settings in the IPsec properties and rules in the Connection Security Rule node.

Windows Defender Firewall with Advanced Security uses IPsec to enforce the following configurable rules:

- **Isolation**   An isolation rule isolates computers by restricting connections based on credentials, such as domain membership or health status. Isolation rules allow you to implement an isolation strategy for servers or domains.

- **Authentication Exemption**   You can use an authentication exemption to designate connections that do not require authentication. You can designate computers by a specific IP address, an IP address range, a subnet, or a predefined group, such as a gateway.

- **Server-To-Server**   This type of rule usually protects connections between servers. When you create the rule, you specify the network endpoints between which communications are protected. You then designate requirements and the authentication that you want to use.

- **Tunnel**   This rule allows you to protect connections between gateway computers. It is typically used when you are connecting across the Internet between two security gateways.

- **Custom**   There might be situations in which you cannot configure the authentication rules that you need by using the rules available in the New Connection Security Rule Wizard. However, you can use a custom rule to authenticate connections between two endpoints.

> **NEED MORE REVIEW?   LAYERING SECURITY USING WINDOWS DEFENDER FIREWALL WITH ADVANCED SECURITY**
>
> To find out more about using and configuring Windows Defender Firewall with Advanced Security refer to the Microsoft website at *https://docs.microsoft.com/windows/security/ threat-protection/windows-firewall/windows-firewall-with-advanced-security*.

Creating Firewall rules

To create a rule, from within the Windows Defender Firewall With Advanced Security management console, first select the appropriate node and then click New Rule from the Actions pane. You can then complete the wizard to create your rule. As an example, to create a new inbound rule to enable network traffic for a program, perform the following procedure.

1. Click Inbound Rules and then click New Rule in the Action pane.
2. On the Rule Type page, click Program and then click Next.
3. On the Program page, click This Program Path, browse and select the program executable, and then click Next.
4. On the Action page, choose Allow The Connection and click Next.

5. On the Profile page, select which network location profiles are affected by the rule and click Next.

6. Provide a name and description for your rule and click Finish.

EXAM TIP

To configure port-based or custom rules properly, you might need to know about the TCP and UDP ports that common networking apps use. For further information, visit the following website at *https://www.iana.org/assignments/service-names-port-numbers/service-names-port-numbers.xhtml*.

In addition to using the Windows Defender Firewall With Advanced Security management console, you can also use the following Windows PowerShell cmdlets to configure and manage firewall settings and rules.

- **Get-NetFirewallRule** Displays a list of available firewall rules
- **Enable-NetFirewallRule** Enables an existing firewall rule
- **Disable-NetFirewallRule** Disables an existing firewall rule
- **New-NetFirewallRule** Creates a new firewall rule
- **Set-NetFirewallRule** Configures the properties of an existing firewall rule

NEED MORE REVIEW? **USING WINDOWS POWERSHELL TO CONFIGURE WINDOWS DEFENDER FIREWALL WITH ADVANCED SECURITY**

To find out more about controlling Windows Defender Firewall with Advanced Security Administration with Windows PowerShell, refer to the Microsoft website at *https:// docs.microsoft.com/en-us/windows/security/threat-protection/windows-firewall/ windows-firewall-with-advanced-security-administration-with-windows-powershell*.

Implement Encryption

There are two encryption technologies available for Windows 10 devices: Encrypting File System (EFS) and BitLocker. Both tools are available for use on all Windows 10 editions except for Windows 10 Home. While both technologies offer robust methods of encryption, you need to understand how to implement each method as well as the use case for each, so that you can decide the most appropriate tool to use in a given scenario. Just because BitLocker is more modern, you should not assume it is better or worse than EFS. Both provide Windows 10 users with very strong encryption.

Implement Encrypting File System

The built-in Encrypting File System (EFS) is a very powerful method of restricting access to files within a NTFS environment. Although EFS has been available since Windows 2000, very few organizations routinely implement file- and folder-level encryption. Most organizations requiring encryption will choose to use BitLocker Drive Encryption, which encrypts complete drives.

Where EFS is utilized, most issues reported to the help desk relating to EFS often result from an over-enthusiastic member of staff encrypting some of their own files. By default, they have permission to encrypt their own files because they have the Creator Owner special identity.

The best way to ensure that EFS is not inadvertently used, potentially causing problems later, is to implement some or all the following measures:

- Stand-alone computers that are not domain-joined should backup their encryption keys to ensure they can be used for recovery purposes later.
- Explain the (strict) usage criteria of EFS in the staff handbook / policy.
- Train IT staff on the use of EFS and the potential implications of unauthorized usage.
- Plan and document where EFS will be applied and who will apply it.
- Sufficient restrictions placed across the domain to prevent unauthorized use of EFS.
- Implementation of an EFS Data Recovery Agent (DRA) so that if EFS is misused, then an Administrator within the organization can recover any encrypted files.
- Implement employee-leaving procedures and scan for encrypted files to ensure all encrypted files are decrypted or ownership transferred.
- Disable, rather than delete, user accounts for a fixed time period in case the user account needs to be reactivated in order to remove EFS from corporate resources.

It's necessary to ensure that selected users and members of IT departments appreciate that EFS is an extremely secure method of protecting files and often, this level of protection is not necessary. Only the original file owner who applied the encryption can access the file and remove the encryption.

If an organization does not have a DRA in place, one needs to be created as soon as possible. Doing so will enable subsequent files encrypted with EFS to be decrypted by the DRA, if needed.

The process for creating a DRA certificate in Windows 10 for a device that is not domain joined can be performed using this procedure:

1. Open a PowerShell window, or a command prompt window. (This does not require administrative privilege.)
2. Navigate to the location where you want to store your DRA certificate.
3. Type **cipher /r: file name** and press Enter.
4. Provide a password to protect the DRA certificate. (This can be null.)

To install the DRA so that a user can use it, follow these steps:

1. Sign in with the user credentials of the user for whom you want to create access to the DRA.
2. In the search box, type **secpol.msc** and press Enter.

3. In the left pane of Local Security Policy, double-click Public Key Policies, right-click Encrypting File System, and then click Add Data Recovery Agent.

4. In the Add Recovery Agent Wizard, click Next.

5. Browse to the location of the DRA recovery certificate. (It will have a .cer file extension.)

6. Select the certificate, and then click Open.

7. When you are asked if you want to install the certificate, click Yes > Next > Finish.

8. In the right pane of Local Security Policy, scroll across and note that the Intended Purposes for the certificate is File Recovery.

9. Open a Command Prompt window, type **gpupdate**, and press Enter to update Group Policy.

Once the DRA has been created, all EFS encrypted files can be recovered by the DRA.

The encrypted files that are already encrypted are not automatically updated when a DRA is created. Existing encrypted files cannot be recovered by the DRA unless they are opened and closed by the resource owner, which causes the DRA to update the file. To update all encrypted files on a local drive, you can type **cipher.exe /u** in an elevated command prompt on the system containing the encrypted files.

ENCRYPT FILES AND FOLDERS BY USING ENCRYPTING FILE SYSTEM

When used with a Data Recovery Agent (DRA), Encrypting File System (EFS) is a very secure method to protect sensitive data by encrypting files and folders. Because EFS was first introduced in Windows 2000, EFS often suffers from being dismissed as being old or obsolete. Many people pass over EFS in favor of BitLocker Drive Encryption or BitLocker To Go. Don't be fooled, though. EFS offers functionality that BitLocker does not, and despite EFS having been available for many years, it still offers an incredibly secure method of enterprise-grade encryption.

It is important to use EFS and a DRA together. Without a DRA available within your organization, you may never regain access to an EFS-encrypted resource. The DRA will help to recover data if the encryption key is deleted or if the machine has been lost or compromised.

EFS offers encryption at a file and folder level, and it cannot be used to encrypt an entire hard disk. Instead, you would use BitLocker (covered later in this section) to encrypt an entire drive. Users can encrypt any file or folder they have created on an NTFS-formatted hard disk by right-clicking the resource and selecting Properties from the context menu that appears. In the Advanced Attributes dialog box (shown in Figure 2-37) select the option to Encrypt Contents To Secure Data.

FIGURE 2-37 Enabling EFS encryption

Encryption should not be used without prior planning and establishing some safeguards to secure the encryption keys that are used. EFS protects data from unauthorized access, and it is especially effective as a last line of defense from attacks, such as physical theft.

EFS uses Windows Public Key Infrastructure (PKI) and a fast encryption algorithm to protect files. The public and private keys generated during encryption ensure that only the user account that encrypted the file can decrypt it. Encrypted data can be decrypted only if the user's personal encryption certificate is available, which is generated through the private key. Unless exported by the user, this key cannot be used by anyone else, and EFS prevents any access to the data. EFS will prevent attempts to copy or move encrypted data by anyone except users who have the proper credentials. If the user deletes his account or leaves the company, any encrypted resources will not be accessible, which could lead to data being lost. The only way to prevent data loss is to ensure that a DRA has previously been created, so that an administrator can use the DRA to decrypt the resource.

Here are some key points you need to learn about EFS:

- The process of encryption and decryption happens behind the scenes and is not visible to users.
- Encryption occurs when you close files; decryption occurs when you open them.
- EFS is available only on NTFS volumes.
- EFS keys aren't assigned to a computer; they are assigned to a specific user.
- If a hacker gains access to the user's PC while he is signed in, they will be able to access and open EFS-protected files.
- The file owner can move or copy an EFS-protected file.
- You can't use EFS and compression together. It's one or the other.

- If the file owner moves an EFS-protected file to a volume that does not support EFS (such as FAT32), the file will be decrypted.

- Encrypted files and folders are no longer colored green in File Explorer; now they include a padlock icon on each file, as shown in Figure 2-38.

- EFS uses Advanced Encryption Standard (AES), which uses a 256-bit key algorithm, which is a very credible industry standard of encryption.

- EFS is only available on Windows 10 Pro, Enterprise, and Education editions.

By default, any user can use EFS to encrypt any file of which they have ownership. Unless company policy requires EFS, you should consider disabling EFS within Group Policy until a DRA is created.

It is very important that a DRA is in place before EFS is enabled. Without a DRA, even an administrator is unable to recover EFS-protected files and folders. For the exam, you need to be able to configure a DRA using the command-line tool Cipher.exe.

Once you have created a DRA, you should update the encryption of each currently encrypted file to have the new DRA applied by using **cipher /u.** You can continue to encrypt your files and folders within File Explorer using the Encrypt Contents To Secure Data option shown later in Figure 2-38.

> *NOTE* **DRA AND EFS: THE SEQUENCE IS IMPORTANT**
>
> Only encrypted files that are created after the DRA has been created can be recovered using the DRA.

PERFORM BACKUP AND RECOVERY OF EFS-PROTECTED FILES

Built into Windows is a wizard for users who want to use EFS to create a file encryption certificate and key and back up these files. After you first encrypt files or folders, you will see the EFS pop-up notification in the notification area of the desktop asking you to back up your encryption key.

You can use the following steps to start the wizard and complete the process to configure an EFS certificate.

1. Open Control Panel and select User Accounts.

2. Click Manage Your File Encryption Certificates to open the Encrypting File System Wizard.

3. Click Next. The wizard asks for your file encryption certificate; you can select your existing certificate, or you can create a new certificate.

4. Click Create A New Certificate, and then click Next.

5. On the Create A Certificate page, select Make A New Self-Signed Certificate And Store It On My Computer and click Next.

6. Provide a backup location and password and click Next.

7. On the Update Your Previously Encrypted Files page, select All Logical Drives and click Next.

8. On the Your Encrypted Files Have Been Updated page, click Close.

In addition to the Cipher.exe command-line tool, you can also use the Certificates MMC (CertMgr.msc) to manage or back up your personal EFS certificate. You can also import your certificates to a new computer that doesn't already contain your certificate. In the event of your certificate being lost, perhaps due to a failed computer or corrupted profile, you can import the DRA certificate onto a new computer, which would allow recovery of the encrypted files.

To import your EFS certificate into your personal certificate store via the Certificate Import Wizard, you should follow these steps:

1. Open Certificates MMC, by typing **CertMgr.msc** into the search box, and then press Enter.

2. Select the Personal folder.

3. Click Action > All Tasks > Import.

4. Work through the Certificate Import Wizard to import the .pfx certificate.

> **NEED MORE REVIEW?**   **CIPHER.EXE**
>
> For more information about Cipher.exe, refer to https://docs.microsoft.com/windows-server/administration/windows-commands/cipher.

Some of the most common parameters used with the Cipher.exe command include:

- **/c**   Displays information about an encrypted file
- **/d**   Decrypts specified files and directories
- **/s:<directory>**   Performs the specified operation on all subdirectories in the specified directory
- **/u**   Updates all encrypted files on the local drives (useful if you need to update previously encrypted files with a new recovery certificate)
- **/u /n**   Finds all encrypted files on a local drive
- **/?**   Displays help
- **/x**   Backs up the EFS certificate and keys to the specified file name
- **/r:<FileName>**   Generates an EFS recovery agent key and certificate, based on the user account, then writes them to a .pfx file (Personal Information Exchange file, which contains a certificate and private key) and a .cer file (Security Certificate file, which contains only the certificate)

After you have encrypted your first file or folder, Windows 10 will prompt you to make a backup of the EFS certificate and key, as shown in Figure 2-38. This reminder will appear in the notification area and it will re-appear on a regular basis until you back up the EFS certificate and key or choose to Never Back Up the files. You need to ensure you do take a backup and store this safely in a separate location from that of the files.

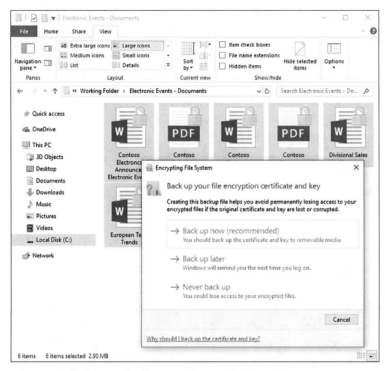

FIGURE 2-38 Backing up the file encryption certificate and key

TROUBLESHOOT ENCRYPTING FILE SYSTEM

When users report that they are unable to use EFS to encrypt files, you need to verify that all the four statements are correct:

- A recovery agent policy has been defined, which prevents the use of EFS unless a DRA has been created.
- The file volume is NTFS; EFS is only supported on NTFS.
- The file is not compressed. NTFS allows files to be encrypted or compressed, not both.
- You have Write access to the file. You need to be able to save the encrypted file.

Other examples of help desk EFS issues include the following scenarios and possible answers:

- **I can't open files I have encrypted**   Only users with the correct EFS certificate and private key for the file can open EFS-protected files. Has the user account been deleted/recreated since the file was created? Use a DRA to recover the file and have the user encrypt the file again.

- **Will I get a warning that I will lose the EFS protection on my file when I copy my file to a FAT32 USB drive?** There is no warning if the user has the necessary NTFS permissions to move or copy the file, and then Windows will carry out the operation without error or warning. Encrypted data copied to a drive not formatted with NTFS will lose the EFS protection.

- **I saved a file that is protected using Windows Information Protection (WIP) to a FAT32 USB drive. The file looks like it is encrypted using EFS. Is this correct?** WIP is supported in Windows 10 to protect files. Protected files look and behave like EFS files, but they do not use EFS. The file is an encrypted PFILE that stores the Enterprise Data Protection metadata, which can be stored on a FAT32 drive.

- **I can't open an EFS file after upgrading from a previous version of Windows** You can still recover the files by importing the EFS certificate and key from your old computer into your new computer.

- **My anti-virus check program runs but I get "Access Denied" error messages** An anti-virus check program can only read your encrypted files. If the device is a shared computer and other users have encrypted files on the hard disk, the anti-virus tool will not be able to access these files. Other users need to perform a virus check for files by signing in on the device.

Configure BitLocker

BitLocker Drive Encryption enables you to encrypt an entire hard disk, which can be the Windows operating system drive or a data drive. Only the Windows 10 Pro, Enterprise, and Education editions support BitLocker in both x86 and x64-bit varieties. During the encryption process, BitLocker Drive Encryption will configure the drive that contains the operating system to have a system partition and an operating system partition.

EXAM TIP

Two partitions are required to run BitLocker because pre-startup authentication and system integrity confirmation must occur on a separate partition from the drive that is encrypted.

If these partitions are not present the process will automatically modify the partitions as required.

EXAM TIP

You can enable BitLocker before you deploy the operating system. When you do, you can opt to encrypt used disk space only or encrypt the entire drive.

Many modern computers now ship with a Trusted Platform Module (TPM), which is a microchip that is used to securely store cryptographic information, such as the encryption keys that BitLocker uses. BitLocker supports versions 1.2 and 2.0 of the TPM specification, and information contained on the TPM is more secure from external software attacks and physical theft. If a device has been tampered with—for instance, a hard drive has been removed from the original computer—BitLocker will prevent the drive from being unlocked. BitLocker will seek remediation from the user by entering BitLocker recovery mode and requiring the user to enter a 48-digit recovery key. While a TPM is the most secure option, BitLocker technology can also be used on devices without a TPM by configuring a GPO to require that BitLocker obtains the required cryptographic information from a USB flash drive. This information must be presented to unlock the volume.

> ***MORE INFO*** **OVERVIEW OF BITLOCKER DEVICE ENCRYPTION IN WINDOWS 10**
>
> For more information about Windows BitLocker, visit *https://docs.microsoft.com/ en-us/windows/security/information-protection/bitlocker/bitlocker-device-encryption- overview-windows-10*.

When configuring BitLocker, you must consider the following:

- **The requirements for hardware and software**   This includes TPM versions, BIOS configuration, firmware requirements, drive size, and so on.

- **How to tell if your computer has a TPM**   An administrator might opt to type **TPM.msc** into Search and click Enter. An end user might opt to access Control Panel, All Items, open BitLocker Drive Encryption, and see if he can turn on BitLocker. If a TPM isn't found, you'll have to configure the Group Policy setting called Require Additional Authentication At Startup, which is located in Computer Configuration\Administrative Templates\Windows Components\BitLocker Drive Encryption\Operating System Drives. You need to enable this policy and then select the Allow BitLocker Without a Compatible TPM check box.

- **What credentials are required to configure BitLocker?**   Only Administrators can manage fixed data drives, but Standard users can manage removable data drives. (The latter can be disabled in Group Policy.) Standard users can also change the PIN or password on operating system drives to which they have access via BitLocker.

- **How to automate BitLocker deployment in an enterprise**   One way is to use the command-line tool Manage-bde.exe. Manage-bde command-line tools you might use in your own work are detailed later in this section. There are other ways to automate BitLocker deployment in an enterprise, including using Windows Management Instrumentation (WMI) and Windows PowerShell cmdlets.

- **The reasons why BitLocker might start in recovery mode**   Reasons include disabling the TPM, making changes to the TPM firmware, making changes to the master boot record, and faults on the drive, motherboard, or TPM.

- **How to manage recovery keys**   Recovery keys let you access a computer in the event that BitLocker doesn't permit access. There are many ways to store these keys for fixed drives, including saving them to a folder or your Microsoft account online, printing them, and storing the keys on multiple USB drives.

UNDERSTAND BITLOCKER KEY PROTECTORS

BitLocker offers users several protection options. Administrators can choose which type of protection users should adopt to unlock a BitLocker-encrypted drive. BitLocker supports multi-factor authentication for operating system drives, allowing you to require additional authentication, such as adding a smart card or a USB drive with a startup key on it or requiring a PIN on start up. These are called key protectors.

BitLocker offers multiple key protectors that can be used to unlock a protected system. These are as follows:

- **TPM + startup PIN + startup key**   This is the most secure combination. The encryption key is stored on the TPM chip. The user might find this option cumbersome because it requires multiple authentication tasks.

- **TPM + startup key**   The encryption key is stored on the TPM chip. The user needs to insert a USB flash drive that contains a startup key.

- **TPM + startup PIN**   The encryption key is stored on the TPM chip. The user needs to enter a PIN to unlock the device.

- **Startup key only**   The user needs to insert a USB flash drive with the startup key on it. The device doesn't need to have a TPM chip. The BIOS must support access to the USB flash drive before the operating system loads.

- **TPM only**   The encryption key is stored on the TPM chip, and no user action is required.

With all the BitLocker authentication methods, the drive is encrypted until unlocked. When the BitLocker encrypted drive is in recovery mode, you can also unlock the drive by using either the recovery password or recovery key.

- **Recovery password**   This is a 48-digit number typed on a regular keyboard, or by using the function keys (F1–F10) to input the numbers.

- **Recovery key**   This is an encryption key created when BitLocker is first employed and is used for recovering data encrypted on a BitLocker volume. Often, the encryption key is stored on removable media.

Because the TPM chip together with BitLocker protects the hard drive, administrators can also configure BitLocker to operate without additional unlock steps; provided the device (and TPM) recognize the drive, then it will be unlocked.

With BitLocker enabled, the drive is no longer susceptible to data theft. On a system that is not encrypted, simply removing the drive from the PC, and attaching it as a slave to another PC allows the data to be read, which bypasses all NTFS security.

EXAM TIP

Administrators can fine-tune within Group Policy the settings for BitLocker, and you would do well to review the available GPOs in detail because they are likely to appear on the exam. Review the GPOs located in Computer Configuration\Policies\Administrative Templates\ Windows Components\BitLocker Drive Encryption.

ENABLE BITLOCKER WITHOUT A TPM

By default, a modern Windows device such as a Surface Pro will contain a TPM, and BitLocker Drive Encryption will be already enabled when shipped. When the user signs onto the device for the first time with a Microsoft account, the recovery key is saved to their Microsoft account.

If a TPM isn't found, click Cancel on the BitLocker Drive Encryption, and follow the displayed instructions to configure the Require Additional Authentication At Startup GPO located in Computer Configuration\Administrative Templates\Windows Components\BitLocker Drive Encryption\Operating System Drives. Enable this GPO and select the Allow BitLocker Without A Compatible TPM check box, as shown in Figure 2-39.

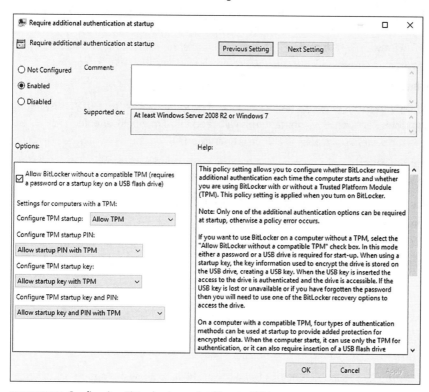

FIGURE 2-39 Configuring BitLocker to work without a TPM

> **NOTE BITLOCKER IS MORE SECURE WITH A TPM**
>
> Although BitLocker is fully supported and can be enabled on a Windows 10 device without a TPM present, you should fully understand that the most secure implementation of BitLocker is with a TPM present. The TPM also provides pre-operating system startup system integrity verification, which will not take place otherwise. Additionally, if you store the decryption key on a USB flash drive, you should protect the key with a PIN.

A new GPO is included with Windows 10 and can be found at Computer Configuration\Policies\ Administrative Templates\Windows Components\BitLocker Drive Encryption\Operating System Drives\Configure Pre-boot Recovery Message And URL. This GPO enables administrators to configure a custom recovery message and to replace the existing URL that is displayed on the pre-boot recovery screen when the operating system drive is locked. This allows administrators to provide information to the user, such as help desk support contact information.

CONFIGURE BITLOCKER

To use BitLocker to encrypt the operating system drive on a supported Windows 10 device, the drive must be formatted as NTFS. Perform these steps to encrypt the drive using BitLocker:

1. Launch Control Panel, click System and Security, and then click BitLocker Drive Encryption.

2. Select the operating system drive and click Turn On BitLocker. (If you receive an error that the device can use a TPM chip, either enable the TPM within the BIOS or Unified Extensible Firmware Interface (UEFI) settings or enable the Require Additional Authentication At Startup Group Policy setting, which is referred to earlier in this section.)

3. On the BitLocker Drive Encryption Setup page, click Next.

4. On the Preparing Your Drive for BitLocker page, if prompted, click Next. (If your system has a Windows Recovery Environment, this will need to be manually enabled and moved to the system drive after the drive is encrypted.)

5. If you are presented a warning message regarding the Windows Recovery Environment, click Next.

6. Choose how to unlock your drive at startup. (Enter A Password is used in this example.)

7. Enter the password, re-enter to confirm and then click Next.

8. On the How Do You Want To Back Up Your Recovery Key page, select one of the options, then click Next and back up your key. (Optionally, you can choose to back up the key in a secondary location.)

9. On the Choose How Much Of Your Drive To Encrypt page, select to encrypt either the used disk space or the entire drive and click Next.

10. On the Choose Which Encryption Mode To Use page, select either the newest encryption mode or the compatible mode and click Next.

11. On the Are You Ready To Encrypt This Drive page, chose to allow the option BitLocker system check to take place (default), or deselect the option and then click Continue.

12. Restart the PC, enter the BitLocker password and allow the drive to be encrypted in the background.

13. In the taskbar notification area, there should be an icon indicating that BitLocker Drive Encryption is in progress.

> **NOTE** **BITLOCKER IS IMMEDIATELY ENFORCED**
>
> When BitLocker Drive Encryption starts to encrypt the device, the drive is protected, and it will require unlocking during startup, even if the encryption process has not fully completed encrypting every file.

From within the BitLocker Drive Encryption page in the Control Panel, you can review the BitLocker status and perform additional tasks, including suspending protection, backing up your recovery key, changing the BitLocker password, removing the password, and turning off BitLocker.

> **NOTE** **USED DISK SPACE ONLY**
>
> An improvement to BitLocker enables administrators to choose whether to encrypt only the used disk space or encrypt the entire drive during the initial deployment of Windows. Choosing the first option significantly reduces the time to deploy and requires less administrative effort, though purists will tell you this is slightly less secure.

CONFIGURE BITLOCKER USING COMMAND-LINE TOOLS

Administrators can also manage BitLocker Drive Encryption using the command-line tool Manage-bde.exe or by using the Command Prompt, PowerShell, and WMI. Managing recovery keys is discussed later.

There are many parameters that can be used with Manage-bde to manage BitLocker, as listed in Table 2-18.

TABLE 2-18 Manage-bde command line tool parameters

PARAMETER	DESCRIPTION
Manage-bde -status	Provides information about all drives on the computer, regardless of whether they are BitLocker-protected.
Manage-bde -on	This encrypts the drive and turns on BitLocker. Use the UsedSpaceOnly switch to set the encryption mode to Used Space Only encryption.
Manage-bde -off	This decrypts the drive and turns off BitLocker. All key protectors are removed when decryption is complete.
Manage-bde -pause & Manage-bde -resume	Use with a drive letter to pause or resume encryption or decryption.

(Continued)

PARAMETER	DESCRIPTION
Manage-bde -lock & manage-bde -unlock	Use with a drive letter to lock and unlock access to BitLocker-protected data.
Manage-bde -autounlock	Manages automatic unlocking of a data drive.
Manage-bde -protectors	Manages protection methods for the encryption key.
Manage-bde -changepassword	Modifies the password for a data drive.
Manage-bde -changepin	Modifies the PIN for an operating system drive.
Manage-bde - forcerecovery	Forces a BitLocker-protected drive into recovery mode on restart.
Manage-bde -changekey	Modifies the startup key for an operating system drive.
Manage-bde -WipeFreeSpace	Wipes the free space on a drive.
Manage-bde -help or -h	Displays complete Help at the command prompt.

MORE INFO **MANAGE-BDE COMMAND-LINE TOOL**

More information on using the manage-bde command-line tool is available in this article at *https://docs.microsoft.com/windows-server/administration/windows-commands/manage-bde*.

Windows 10 offers built-in support for BitLocker PowerShell cmdlets, as listed in Table 2-19. You can also use **Get-help <BitLocker cmdlet>,** such as **Get-Help Enable-BitLocker -examples**.

NOTE **POWERSHELL HELP**

You may need to use the **update-help** cmdlet to allow PowerShell to display the most current help files and examples, which may assist your understanding.

TABLE 2-19 BitLocker PowerShell cmdlets

CMDLET	DESCRIPTION
Add-BitLockerKeyProtector	Adds a key protector for a BitLocker volume
Backup-BitLockerKeyProtector	Saves a key protector for a BitLocker volume in Active Directory Domain Services (AD DS)
Clear-BitLockerAutoUnlock	Removes BitLocker automatic unlocking keys
Disable-BitLocker	Disables BitLocker encryption for a volume
Disable-BitLockerAutoUnlock	Disables automatic unlocking for a BitLocker volume
Enable-BitLocker	Enables encryption for a BitLocker volume

(Continued)

CMDLET	DESCRIPTION
Enable-BitLockerAutoUnlock	Enables automatic unlocking for a BitLocker volume
Get-BitLockerVolume	Gets information about volumes that BitLocker can protect
Lock-BitLocker	Prevents access to encrypted data on a BitLocker volume
Remove-BitLockerKeyProtector	Removes a key protector for a BitLocker volume
Resume-BitLocker	Restores BitLocker encryption for the specified volume
Suspend-BitLocker	Suspends BitLocker encryption for the specified volume
Unlock-BitLocker	Restores access to data on a BitLocker volume

> **MORE INFO   CONFIGURE BITLOCKER USING POWERSHELL CMDLETS**
>
> For more information about how to configure BitLocker using PowerShell cmdlets, visit this reference article at *https://docs.microsoft.com/powershell/module/bitlocker/?view=win10-ps*.

Using PowerShell, you can obtain very detailed information from systems, including status, key protectors used, encryption method, and type. If you run the **Get-BitLockerVolume | format-list** cmdlet to provide information about an encrypted drive without first unlocking the drive, the amount of information obtained will be restricted.

UPGRADE A BITLOCKER-ENABLED COMPUTER

BitLocker is designed to protect your computer from pre-boot changes, such as updating the BIOS or UEFI. If you upgrade your computer, for example, with a BIOS firmware upgrade, this can cause the TPM to perceive it is under attack. In order to prevent Windows 10 from entering BitLocker recovery mode, it's recommended that some precautions are taken while upgrading a BitLocker-enabled computer. Prior to updating the BIOS, you should carry out the following steps:

1. Temporarily suspend BitLocker by opening the BitLocker Drive Encryption in Control Panel and selecting Suspend Protection on the operating system drive, which places it in disabled mode.

2. Upgrade the system or the BIOS.

3. BitLocker protection will be automatically turned back on following a reboot, but if this default behavior has been modified, you should turn BitLocker on again by opening Bit-Locker Drive Encryption in Control Panel and select Resume Protection on the operating system drive.

Forcing BitLocker into disabled mode keeps the data encrypted, with the volume master key encrypted with a clear key. The availability of this unencrypted key disables the data protection that BitLocker offers, but it ensures that the subsequent computer startup will succeed without further user input. After the BIOS upgrade, BitLocker is re-enabled so that the unencrypted key is erased from the disk and BitLocker protection is functional again. The encryption key will be resealed with the new key that has been regenerated to incorporate new values of the measured components that may have changed during the system upgrade.

> ***NOTE*** **THROUGHOUT SUSPENSION, DATA IS ENCRYPTED**
>
> **Although BitLocker is suspended, the drive remains encrypted and all new data written to the disk is still encrypted. Suspension prevents BitLocker from validating system integrity at startup and is a security risk; therefore, the protection status should be resumed at the earliest opportunity.**

MOVE A BITLOCKER-ENCRYPTED DRIVE TO ANOTHER COMPUTER

Moving a BitLocker-encrypted drive to another BitLocker-enabled computer requires that you turn off BitLocker temporarily (by using the Suspend Protection option). After the move is complete, you need to re-enable BitLocker, which will then resume BitLocker protection.

The PowerShell command for suspending BitLocker encryption on the system drive is:

```
Suspend-BitLocker -MountPoint "C:"
```

Sometimes a system change can cause the BitLocker system integrity check on the operating system drive to fail. This prevents the TPM from releasing the BitLocker key to decrypt the protected operating system drive and requires the user to enter recovery mode. Examples of system changes that can result in a BitLocker system integrity check failure include:

- Moving the BitLocker-protected drive to a new computer
- Installing a new motherboard with a new TPM
- Turning off, disabling, or clearing the TPM
- Making changes to any boot configuration settings
- Making changes to the BIOS, UEFI firmware, master boot record, boot sector, boot manager, option ROM, or other early boot components or boot configuration data

When Windows 10 upgrades itself from one version to another, such as 1803 to 1809, there should be no issues with BitLocker because the system will automatically perform the suspend and resume actions during the process.

CONFIGURE STARTUP KEY STORAGE AND RECOVERY OPTIONS

You know that without access to the encryption key contained in the TPM or stored in the startup key, you are unable to unlock a BitLocker-encrypted drive.

You should ensure that you're familiar with BitLocker-related terminology:

- **Recovery password and recovery key** When you first configure BitLocker, it will create a recovery key and prompt you to store it safely. You'll need to provide this recovery key if the TPM is unable to validate that the drive hasn't been tampered with or if the startup key, password, or PIN have not been supplied during boot time.

- **Password** A password or passphrase is created to protect fixed, removable, and operating system drives with or without a TPM. The password length can be set in Group Policy and can consist of eight to 255 characters.

- **PIN** When you use a TPM, you can configure BitLocker with a PIN that the user must type during the initial startup of the device to allow Windows 10 to start. The PIN can consist of between 4 to 20 digits, and the length can be set in the Configure Minimum PIN Length For Startup Group Policy setting.

- **Enhanced PIN** This enables administrators to force the use of a complex PIN, just like a password or passphrase (including spaces), by configuring the Allow Enhanced PINs For Startup GPO setting. This policy is applied when you turn on BitLocker and is configurable only for operating system drives.

- **Startup key** This is stored on a USB flash drive and can be used with or without a TPM. To use this method of unlock, the USB flash drive must be inserted every time the computer starts. The USB flash drive can be formatted by using NTFS, FAT, or FAT32.

- **TPM Lockout** By default, TPM 2.0 will lock the user out for two hours whenever the TPM is under attack. (TPM 1.2 lockout duration varies by manufacturer.)

CONFIGURE BITLOCKER TO GO

A portable version of BitLocker, BitLocker To Go, is aimed at protecting removable USB devices and uses the same technology as BitLocker Drive Encryption, but it does not require use of a TPM. BitLocker To Go can protect flash drives, Secure Digital (SD) cards, and removable hard disks formatted with NTFS, FAT16, FAT32, or exFat file systems. BitLocker To Go is available for users with Windows 10 Pro, Windows 10 Enterprise, or Windows 10 Education.

To create a BitLocker To Go drive, follow these steps:

1. Insert a removable drive.
2. Open Windows Explorer (though it may open automatically).
3. Right-click the removeable drive and select Turn BitLocker On.
4. After the BitLocker Drive Encryption wizard initializes, choose how to unlock the drive and click Next.
5. On the How Do You Want To Back Up Your Recovery Key? Page, choose an option and then once the password is saved, click Next.
6. On the Choose How Much Of Your Drive To Encrypt page, select to encrypt either the used disk space or the entire drive and click Next.
7. On the Choose Which Encryption Mode To Use page, select either the newest encryption mode or the compatible mode and click Next.
8. On the Are You Ready To Encrypt This Drive page, click Start Encrypting.
9. The encryption process will commence. Once complete, you can close the wizard.

If the option to encrypt the drive is not available, you need to check to ensure you are using a supported version of Windows and that the feature has not been disabled by Group Policy.

Once a removable drive has been encrypted, each time you insert the removable drive into a device, you will need to unlock it with one of the following methods:

- A recovery password or passphrase. (This complexity can be set within Group Policy.)
- A smart card.
- Always auto-unlock this device on this PC.

The last option is very useful for users who frequently use removable drives because it reduces the likelihood of frustration of entering the password every time they use their removable drives. If the removable drive is used on other devices once the user unlocks the removable drive, it can also be configured to auto-unlock if required.

Standard users can turn on, turn off, or change configurations of BitLocker on removable data drives. They are also able to change their own password for encrypted drives via BitLocker Drive Encryption in Control Panel. However, if a user loses or forgets the password for the data or removable drive, you need to have access to the BitLocker recovery key to recover the data and unlock the drive.

 EXAM TIP

It is important to remember that a TPM is *not* required for BitLocker To Go. The encryption keys are secured using a password or passphrase or smart card, and not by a TPM.

The following GPOs are available within the BitLocker To Go settings found at Computer Configuration\Policies\Administrative Templates\Windows Components\BitLocker Drive Encryption\Removable Data Drives:

- Control use of BitLocker on removable drives.
- Configure use of smart cards on removable data drives.
- Deny Write access to removable drives not protected by BitLocker.
- Configure use of hardware-based encryption for removable data drives.
- Enforce drive-encryption type on removable data drives.
- Allow access to BitLocker-protected removable data drives from earlier versions of Windows.
- Configure use of passwords for removable data drives.
- Choose how BitLocker-protected removable data drives can be recovered.

Users of Windows 10 Home cannot encrypt removable data drives, but they can access BitLocker To Go enabled data drives and have read-only access to the data, if they provide the correct recovery password, passphrase, or smart card.

UNDERSTAND BITLOCKER AND BITLOCKER TO GO DATA RECOVERY

You need to support users who have devices that will not boot into Windows because of BitLocker-related issues during boot time. There are several situations in which BitLocker will enter into BitLocker recovery mode because of a perceived threat to the system, such as one of the following:

- Repeatedly failing to provide the startup password.
- Changing the startup boot order to boot another drive in advance of the hard drive.
- Changing the NTFS partition table, such as creating, deleting, or resizing a primary partition.
- Entering the PIN incorrectly too many times so that the anti-hammering logic of the TPM is activated.
- Turning off, disabling, deactivating, or clearing the TPM.
- Upgrading critical early startup components, such as a BIOS or UEFI firmware upgrade, causing the related boot measurements to change.
- Adding or removing hardware (for example, inserting a new motherboard or video card into the computer).
- You can also force a BitLocker-protected device into recovery mode by pressing the F8 or F10 key during the boot process.

> **MORE INFO**   **BITLOCKER RECOVERY GUIDE**
>
> The following article provides a useful list of examples of specific events that will cause BitLocker to enter recovery mode when attempting to start the operating system drive at *https://docs.microsoft.com/windows/device-security/bitlocker/bitlocker-recovery-guide-plan*.

When the device has entered the BitLocker recovery mode, you need to recover the drive by using one of these methods:

- Supply the 48-digit recovery password.
- Allow a domain administrator to obtain the recovery password from Active Directory, which may or may not use Microsoft BitLocker Administration and Monitoring (MBAM) Tool version 2.0. MBAM is included in the Microsoft Desktop Optimization Pack (MDOP) for Microsoft Software Assurance.
- Allow an administrator to obtain the recovery password from Azure Active Directory.
- Run a script to reset the password, using PowerShell or VBScript, which uses the key package.

For standalone and small-business users, the BitLocker recovery key is stored in the user's Microsoft account at *https://onedrive.live.com/recoverykey*. You will need to use the keyboard number or function keys to enter the number to unlock the drive. Once the operating system has started, users can then re-create a new startup key; otherwise, the BitLocker recovery mode will remain in place.

For corporate users, there are several settings that can be configured in Group Policy that will define the recovery methods that require Windows to save BitLocker recovery information to Active Directory. The GPOs found in the subfolders of Computer Configuration\Administrative Templates\Windows Components\BitLocker Drive Encryption are as follows:

- Choose how BitLocker-protected operating system drives can be recovered
- Choose how BitLocker-protected fixed drives can be recovered
- Choose how BitLocker-protected removable drives can be recovered

For each of these GPOs, you can also enable the Do Not Enable BitLocker Until Recovery Information Is Stored In Active Directory check box to keep users from enabling BitLocker unless the device is connected to the domain and the backup of BitLocker recovery information to Active Directory has succeeded.

Once BitLocker recovery information has been saved in Active Directory, the recovery information can be used to restore access to a BitLocker-protected drive by using the **Manage-bde** command-line tool introduced earlier.

> **NOTE** **BITLOCKER FAQ**
>
> You need to take some time to review BitLocker. It is an important feature that pro-
> tects against data loss. Read the BitLocker FAQ at *https://docs.microsoft.com/windows/*
> *device-security/bitlocker/bitlocker-frequently-asked-questions.*

In an Azure Active Directory environment, you can locate the BitLocker key within the Azure Active Directory Admin Center. Locate the device, and if the Windows 10 machine has been encrypted, you can use the BitLocker recovery key or provide it to the user to recover his or her device.

To view or copy the BitLocker keys within Azure Active Directory, you need to be either the device owner or have one of the following roles assigned.

- Global Administrator
- Helpdesk Administrator
- Security Administrator
- Security Readers
- Intune Service Administrator

Thought experiments

In these thought experiments, demonstrate your skills and knowledge of the topics covered in this chapter. You can find the answers to these thought experiments in the next section.

Scenario 1

Adatum has 3,000 workstations currently running Windows 10. Most of the users belong to the Active Directory domain, but 50 research engineers in the R&D department do not. The research engineers need to access special 3D printing hardware that is located within their secure area. Adatum needs to ensure that only the research engineers can use the specialized printing devices.

As a consultant for Adatum, answer the following questions:

1. What type of group will you use for the research engineers?
2. How will you ensure that only the research engineers are able to print to the 3D printer?
3. You find that a user has been using the 3D printer for personal use outside of normal office hours. How would you investigate this matter?

Scenario 2

You have recently implemented a new network-shared storage facility for your organization. This storage is formatted using NTFS and has been shared to groups containing users within Active Directory. Users of the design department will use the local storage to store CAD drawings in two folders: Current Projects and New Projects. The files within the New Projects folder are confidential. You notice that users who are not part of the design department are able to access the CAD files.

You must ensure that the network-shared storage facility is accessed by the design department personnel only.

Answer the following questions for your manager:

1. How will you ensure that only design department personnel can access the storage?
2. What share-level permissions should you grant on the storage?
3. You need to confirm to your manager that members of the organization who are not in the design department do not have access to the files contained in the storage. How will you reassure your manager?
4. You need to provide an audit trail of the access to the New Projects folder. How will you proceed?

Scenario 3

Your organization wants to use Group Policy to configure power settings on the sales department laptops. All laptops are identical. You add a new Group Policy to remove the sleep feature on the laptops. Some members of the sales department report that they can still put their laptops into sleep mode. You access one of the sales departmental laptops and confirm the GPO has not been applied.

Answer the following questions for your manager:

1. What GUI tool could you use to verify whether the GPO is being delivered to the laptop?

2. Some members of the sales department work out of the office, often in rural locations. How could location affect the effectiveness of the GPO?

3. How could you ensure that all members of the sales department receive the GPO?

4. What command line tool could you use to verify what GPOs have been delivered to the laptop?

Scenario 4

Adatum Corporation uses Microsoft 365 and has an IT security policy in place that requires company laptop devices to be encrypted at all times. Many of the remote workers operate from home, and the IT policy allows these users to choose a corporate-owned device from an authorized device list. Employees selected various devices, including the Surface laptop, which comes pre-installed with Windows 10 Home.

All company data is stored in Microsoft 365 cloud-based storage, such as OneDrive for Business and SharePoint Online. The sales department often needs to leave customers with USB thumb drives that contain presentations, which include sensitive information.

How will you respond to the security manager, who has raised the following concerns?

1. The Surface laptops do not currently support EFS or BitLocker Drive Encryption. What should you do first?

2. You need to recommend an encryption solution for the company data stored on the sales department laptop devices so that they comply with the IT security policy. What should you recommend?

3. How will your encryption solution be deployed to the remote staff?

Thought experiment answers

This section provides the solutions for the tasks included in the Thought experiments section.

Scenario 1

1. Create a Research Engineers Local Group.

2. Add only the research engineers to the Research Engineers Local Group and grant print permissions for the 3D printer to the research engineers local group.

3. Investigate the logs within the Event Viewer, and look for instances in which a print job has been sent to the 3D printer outside of normal office hours. You could enable logging within the Microsoft-Windows-PrintService Operational logs.

Scenario 2

1. Create a design department security group, add all the design department personnel to the group, and give the design department group NTFS access to the storage.

2. You should give full-access, share-level permissions for the design department group.

3. You should use the Effective Access feature to verify the NTFS permissions in place. In the Advanced Security settings for the shared folders, evaluate the effective access permissions for a user or group that is not a member of the design department group.

4. Enable Auditing for success and failure in Group Policy, and then enable auditing on the New Projects folder to track both successful access to the folder and failed attempts.

Scenario 3

1. Use the Resultant Set of Policy (RSoP) tool to diagnose and troubleshoot group policy settings.

2. The GPOs are only delivered once the user connects to and logs into the Active Directory Domain. If members are unable to connect their laptops to the organization, such as by using a VPN or via a wired or a Wi-Fi network, they might be using cached credentials, and therefore, they will not receive the new GPO.

3. Ask the members of the sales department to connect to the corporate network using a VPN or via the internal wired or Wi-Fi network. Once connected, they should then log on so that they can receive the new GPO.

4. Use the GPResult tool to display a report of the GPOs that have been applied to a system.

Scenario 4

1. You need to upgrade the device license on the Surface Laptops to Windows 10 Pro or Windows 10 Enterprise before encryption can be used.

2. You could ensure that devices use BitLocker Drive Encryption. In this way, all data stored on the device will be encrypted.

3. The Surface Laptops can be joined to Azure Active Directory by the user or by using Windows Autopilot. Once joined, they can be auto-enrolled into Microsoft Intune. Once managed by Intune, they will receive device policies to enforce encryption.

Chapter summary

- Local accounts are local to the Windows 10 device, and the password is stored in the SAM database.

- Most settings are configured within the Settings app and not the Control Panel.

- The Administrator has full permissions and privileges on a Windows 10 device and can manage all the objects on the computer.

- The Creator Owner is a special identity that has special administrator level permissions to the resources over which they have ownership.

- Azure Active Directory (Azure AD) is a cloud-based identity authentication and authorization service.

- Devices can be joined or registered to Azure AD.

- Azure AD supports registering of Bring Your Own Device (BYOD) scenarios for multiple types of devices, including Windows 10, iOS, Android, and macOS.

- Only Windows 10 devices can be joined to Azure AD.

- Existing Windows 10 devices can be joined to Azure AD using the Accounts section of the Settings app.

- The Device Enrollment Manager (DEM) account in Microsoft Intune is a special account that allows you to enroll up to a maximum of 1,000 devices.

- Windows 10 supports NTFS as the default file system.

- The Quick Access area is new in Windows 10 and appears at the uppermost left area of the File Explorer navigation pane. It shows the frequently used files and folders.

- Effective Permissions is useful to determine the permissions a particular user would have through NTFS permissions.

- Windows 10 NTFS uses 6 Basic Permissions and 13 Advanced Permissions for securing files and folders.

- When applying permissions to groups, an explicit Allow setting will override an implicit Deny permission.

- Use the ICACLS command line tool to configure and view permissions on files and folders on a local computer and reset them to defaults.

- Inheritance of permissions can be useful when applying permissions to a large environment because the permissions will be automatically propagated based on the default inheritance setting.

- You can use the Effective Access feature to ensure that your NTFS permissions are as expected.

- If you have administrative privileges, you can take ownership of an object, such as a file, and allocate it to another user or group.

- You can reset the permissions of all the folders, files, and subfolders using the command-line tool icacls <file name> /reset.

- Only files stored on a NTFS-formatted hard drive have a Security tab in their File properties.

- Windows 10 uses a feature called Network Discovery, which uses a new layer two protocol called Link Layer Topology Discovery (LLTD) to identify other devices present on the local subnet.

- Share permissions can be Read, Change, or Full.

- The registry is a database, which is split into multiple separate files known as hives.

- You use the built-in Registry Editor (Regedit.exe) tool to view, search, and modify the registry's contents.

- Local Security Policy allows you to configure security policies, such as a password or audit policy, on a local computer.

- User rights policies are used to determine what rights a user or group of users have on a device and relate to activities or tasks that the user can perform.

- User Rights Assignments policies affect what users can do to a system, and Security Permissions affect which access permissions a user has.

- Use the Resultant Set of Policy (RSoP) tool to check and troubleshoot group policy settings.

- Use the GPResult command line tool to verify what group policy objects have been applied to a user or computer.

- The Windows Security app collects and displays the security status of your device and will trigger notifications through the Action Center.

- User Account Control (UAC) helps protect the operating system from unauthorized configuration changes and app installations.

- UAC elevation prompts can be prompts for consent or prompts for credentials.

- Whenever UAC prompts the user for consent, it uses a feature called Secure Desktop to focus the activity only on the UAC prompt and prevents malware from interacting with the UAC process.

- Windows 10 is protected by the Windows Defender Firewall, which acts as a network barrier.

- You can Allow an app through the Windows Defender Firewall or create connection security rules using Windows Defender Firewall with Advanced Security.

- Windows 10 supports two encryption technologies: Encrypting File System (EFS) and BitLocker.

- Windows 10 Home does not support encryption.

- You should always create a Data Recovery Agent (DRA) whenever EFS is used within an enterprise, so that encrypted files can be recovered.

- EFS can be managed though the GUI or by using the command line tool cipher.exe.

- BitLocker Drive Encryption enables you to encrypt an entire hard disk.

- Devices with a Trusted Platform Module (TPM) can securely store the encryption keys that BitLocker uses.

- BitLocker supports versions 1.2 and 2.0 of the TPM specification.

- BitLocker offers users several key-protection options, including storing the key protectors on a TPM, smart card, or a USB drive with a startup key on it. BitLocker also allows you to require a PIN on start up.

- On a modern Windows device, BitLocker Drive Encryption will be already enabled when shipped. When the user signs in to the device for the first time with a Microsoft account, the recovery key is saved to his or her Microsoft account.

- For personal and small-business users, a BitLocker recovery key is stored in their Microsoft accounts at https://onedrive.live.com/recoverykey.

- On devices without a TPM, you can configure the Require Additional Authentication At Startup GPO setting to allow BitLocker to be used without a compatible TPM.

- Before upgrading your computer—for example, performing a BIOS firmware upgrade—you should suspend BitLocker Drive Encryption. By default, after a reboot, protection will be automatically resumed.

- If a device enters BitLocker recovery mode, you will need to recover the drive by supplying the 48-digit recovery password.

- The BitLocker recovery password can be stored in Active Directory or Azure Active Directory.

CHAPTER 3

Configure Connectivity

Computing devices do not typically work in isolation. Usually, devices are connected to networks to enable users to access services and resources. Sometimes, remote connectivity is required to enable a user's connection to these services and resources. This chapter explores how to set up and configure networking and remote connectivity in Windows 10.

Skills covered in this chapter:

- Skill 3.1: Configure networking
- Skill 3.2: Configure remote connectivity

Skill 3.1: Configure networking

The ability to connect devices running Windows 10 to both wired and wireless networks is important, whether this is a home network or your organization's network infrastructure. To configure networking settings correctly, you must understand fundamental IP settings and know how to configure name resolution. It is also important to know how to configure virtual private networks (VPNs) to enable remote connectivity to your organization's network infrastructure. In addition, the *MD-100 Windows 10* exam also covers network troubleshooting issues, and it is, therefore, important to know how to use Windows 10 networking tools to investigate and resolve network-related problems.

> **This skill covers how to:**
> - Configure client IP settings
> - Configure mobile networking
> - Configure VPN client
> - Troubleshoot networking
> - Configure Wi-Fi profiles

Configure client IP settings

Before you can configure any other network settings, such as name resolution or firewall settings, you must have a grasp of the underlying fundamentals of networking and how to configure both Internet Protocol version 4 (IPv4) and Internet Protocol version 6 (IPv6) network settings.

Overview of IPv4

IPv4 is a mature networking protocol and is widely used on almost all Internet-connected client devices. Each client on an IPv4 network is assigned a unique IPv4 configuration that identifies that client device. This configuration is based on a number of elements.

- **An IPv4 address** IPv4 uses a 32-bit binary address, which is divided into four octets (or groups of eight digits), each of which is converted to a decimal number. Thus: 11000000101010000001000100000001 becomes 11000000.10101000.00010001.00000001 and converts to: 192.168.17.1.

- **A subnet mask** A subnet mask is also a 32-bit binary string, entered as four decimal digits; it is used to indicate the client's unique identity, known as the host ID, and the subnet where the client resides, known as the network ID.

- **A default gateway address** To facilitate communications between network segments, or subnets, each client device is assigned the IPv4 address of a router in the local network that is used to forward network traffic destined for devices in other subnets.

- **A Domain Name System (DNS) server address** DNS enables the client computer to resolve names into IPv4 or IPv6 addresses.

> **NEED MORE REVIEW?** **IPV4 ADDRESSING**
>
> To review further details about IPv4 addressing fundamentals, refer to the Microsoft website at *https://docs.microsoft.com/en-us/previous-versions/windows/it-pro/windows-server-2008-R2-and-2008/dd379547(v=ws.10)*.

Subnets

A subnet is a network segment. One or more routers separate the subnet from other subnets. Each subnet on an internet has a unique ID, just as each host within a subnet has a unique ID. You must use the 32 bits of an IPv4 address to define both the host's ID and the subnet ID in which that host resides.

SIMPLE NETWORKS

Remember that each 32-bit IPv4 address is divided into four octets. In simple IPv4 subnetting, whole octets are reserved for defining the subnet portion of the IPv4 address, as shown in Figure 3-1; consequently, the remaining whole octets are available for defining the host portion of the address.

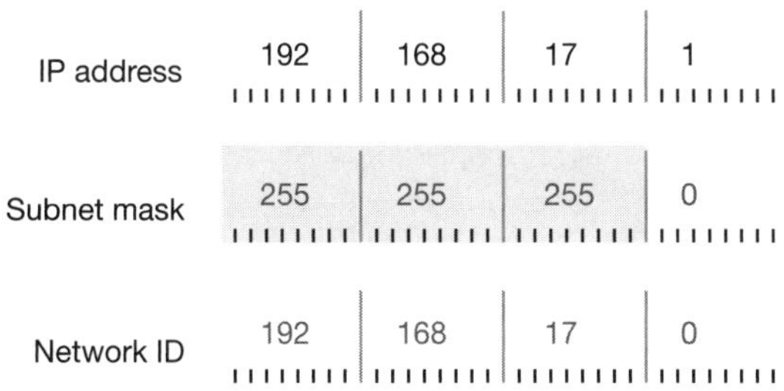

| IP address | 192 | 168 | 17 | 1 |

| Subnet mask | 255 | 255 | 255 | 0 |

| Network ID | 192 | 168 | 17 | 0 |

FIGURE 3-1 An IPv4 address using a simple Class C network addressing scheme

This simple subnetting is referred to as classful addressing, by which the address class, A, B, or C, defines the number of octets reserved for host and subnet IDs. Table 3-1 shows how this works.

TABLE 3-1 Characteristics of the default IPv4 address classes

CLASS	FIRST OCTET	DEFAULT SUBNET MASK	NUMBER OF NETWORKS	NUMBER OF HOSTS PER NETWORK
A	1 to 127	255.0.0.0	126	16,777,214
B	128 to 191	255.255.0.0	16,384	65,534
C	192 to 223	255.255.255.0	2,097,152	254

> **NOTE OTHER ADDRESS CLASSES**
>
> There are also class D and class E addresses. Class D addresses are used for multicasting when a client device is part of a group. Class E addresses are reserved and are not used for hosts or subnets.

COMPLEX NETWORKS

For some situations, using a classful addressing scheme can be ideal. But for many situations, it might be important to have more flexibility over the number of bits allocated to the subnet address portion of an IPv4 address. For example, instead of using 8, 16, or 24 bits for the subnet, you can use 12 or 18.

Bear in mind that the more bits you allocate to subnetting, the fewer bits remain for the host portion of the IPv4 address. That is, you can have more subnets, each containing fewer hosts, or you can have few subnets, each containing many hosts. Figure 3-2 shows how changing the subnet mask changes the subnet ID without changing the octets that define the whole IPv4 address. This scheme is often referred to as classless addressing, or Classless Interdomain Routing (CIDR).

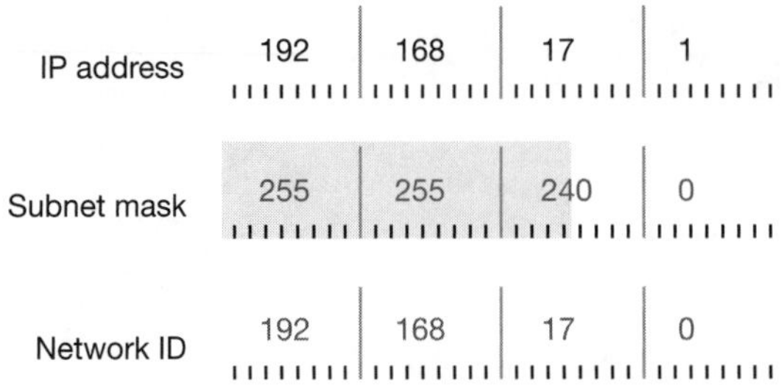

IP address	192	168	17	1
Subnet mask	255	255	240	0
Network ID	192	168	17	0

FIGURE 3-2 An IPv4 address using a classless network addressing scheme

In Figure 3-2, notice how changing the subnet mask from 255.255.255.0 to 255.255.240.0 shifts the device from subnet 192.168.17.0 to 192.168.16.0. In this case, by shifting the mask to the left, we have allocated more bits to describe hosts in each subnet, with correspondingly fewer subnets. You can see that to express a host's IPv4 configuration properly, not only must you state the IPv4 address, but you must also state the subnet mask. For example, in Figure 3-2, this host has an IPv4 configuration of 192.168.17.1/255.255.240.0.

EXAM TIP

You will often see devices with IPv4 configurations shown as 192.168.17.1/20. The number after the slash denotes the number of sequential binary 1s in the subnet mask (20 in this instance). If the mask were 255.255.248.0, that would be represented as /21.

NEED MORE REVIEW? **IPV4 ROUTING**

To review further details about IPv4 subnetting and routing, refer to the Microsoft website at *https://docs.microsoft.com/en-us/previous-versions/windows/it-pro/windows-server-2008-R2-and-2008/dd379495(v=ws.10)*.

Public and private addressing

Devices that connect directly to the Internet require a unique public IPv4 configuration. However, because of the limitation of the 32-bit addressing scheme of IPv4, there is a limit to the number of hosts that can be connected to the Internet using a public configuration. To alleviate this potential but significant problem, many organizations use private IPv4 configurations for their network clients, only using public IPv4 configurations for Internet-facing devices, such as routers.

The Internet Assigned Numbers Authority (IANA) has defined the address ranges shown in Table 3-2 as being available for private use. A technology, such as network address translation (NAT), is used to enable devices using private IPv4 configurations to communicate with the Internet.

TABLE 3-2 Private IPv4 address ranges

CLASS	MASK	RANGE
A	10.0.0.0/8	10.0.0.0–10.255.255.255
B	172.16.0.0/12	172.16.0.0–172.31.255.255
C	192.168.0.0/16	192.168.0.0–192.168.255.255

Configuring an IPv4 connection

Devices running Windows 10 are configured to obtain an IPv4 configuration automatically by default, as shown in Figure 3-3.

FIGURE 3-3 The Internet Protocol Version 4 (TCP/IPv4) Properties dialog box

Typically, Windows 10-based devices obtain their IPv4 configurations from a Dynamic Host Configuration Protocol (DHCP) service, perhaps running on a Windows Server 2019 server computer or provided as a service on a device such as a router or wireless access point (wireless AP).

EXAM TIP

If a Windows 10-based device fails to obtain an IPv4 configuration from a DHCP server, it reverts to using an Automatic Private IP Address (APIPA). If your computer has an IPv4 address that starts with 169.254.*X.Y*, it is using an APIPA address. APIPA enables only local, subnet-based communications at best. You can override this behavior by opening the Alternative Configuration tab, shown in Figure 3-3, choosing User Configured, and specifying the IPv4 configuration to use when DHCP is unavailable.

To view or configure the IPv4 settings on your computer, perform the following procedure.

1. Right-click the network icon in the system tray and then click Open Network Internet Settings.

2. Click Change Adapter Options.

3. Right-click the appropriate network adapter and then click Properties.

4. Double-click Internet Protocol Version 4 (TCP/IPv4).

You can then configure the IPv4 settings. Click Use The Following IP Address and then specify the following: IP Address, Subnet Mask, Default Gateway, Preferred DNS Server, and Alternative DNS Server (Optional).

You can also configure a number of options from the Advanced TCP/IP Settings dialog box. From the Internet Protocol Version 4 (TCP/IPv4) Properties dialog box, click Advanced to open the dialog box, shown in Figure 3-4.

Configure the options on the following tabs.

- **IP Settings**   Enables you to configure additional IPv4 addresses and default gateways manually for this network interface.

- **DNS**   You can define additional DNS server addresses for name resolution and additional DNS suffix processing options.

- **WINS**   The Windows Internet Name Service (WINS) is an older name resolution service used by earlier versions of Windows and Windows Server. Generally, you do not need to configure anything here.

FIGURE 3-4 The IP Settings tab of the Advanced TCP/IP Settings dialog box

CONFIGURING IPV4 FROM THE COMMAND LINE AND BY USING WINDOWS POWERSHELL

In addition to configuring IPv4 settings from the user interface, you can also use the Netsh.exe command-line tool and Windows PowerShell cmdlets. You can use the Netsh.exe command-line tool to reconfigure many network-related settings. For example, the following command reconfigures the IPv4 settings.

```
Netsh interface ipv4 set address name="Ethernet" source=static addr=192.168.17.1
mask=255.255.240.0 gateway=192.168.31.254
```

There are numerous Windows PowerShell cmdlets that you can use to view and configure network settings, some of which are shown in Table 3-3.

TABLE 3-3 Windows PowerShell IPv4 networking-related cmdlets.

CMDLET	PURPOSE
Get-NetIPAddress	Displays information about the IP address configuration
Get-NetIPv4Protocol	Displays information about the IPv4 protocol configuration
Set-NetIPAddress	Changes the IP address configuration
Set-NetIPv4Protocol	Changes the IPv4 protocol configuration

For example, to change the IPv4 configuration for a network connection with Windows PowerShell, use the following cmdlet.

```
Set-NetIPAddress -InterfaceAlias Ethernet -IPAddress 192.168.17.1
```

Overview of IPv6

It is still the case that almost all computers and other devices connect to the Internet by using an IPv4 configuration. However, some network services and devices do require an IPv6 configuration, so it is important to understand the IPv6 fundamentals, including how to configure IPv6. There are a number of reasons to consider IPv6. These include:

- **Some services require IPv6**   Services, such as DirectAccess, use IPv6 to facilitate remote connections.

- **Larger address space**   IPv6 uses a 128-bit address space, providing a vast increase in the availability of addresses for devices on the Internet.

- **Hierarchical addressing**   IPv6 uses a structured address space, which is more efficient for routers, helping to optimize network communications.

- **Support for stateless and stateful autoconfiguration**   You can configure your IPv6 devices to use DHCPv6 to obtain a stateful configuration, or you can rely on router discovery to use a stateless configuration, simplifying the process of enabling IPv6 on your network devices.

IPv6 addressing

As mentioned, IPv6 uses a 128-bit addressing scheme. This is usually written in hexadecimal.

The following is an example of an IPv6 address.

`2001:CD8:1F2D::2BB:FF:EF82:1C3B`

IPv6 uses the following three address types.

- **Unicast addresses**   Packets are delivered to a single interface.
- **Multicast addresses**   Packets are delivered to multiple interfaces.
- **Anycast addresses**   Packets are delivered to multiple interfaces that are the closest in routing distance.

Unlike IPv4, IPv6 does not use broadcast messages. Instead, unicast and anycast addresses in IPv6 can have the following scopes.

- **Link-local**   IPv6 hosts on the same subnet
- **Site-local**   IPv6 hosts in the same organization, also known as private site addressing
- **Global**   IPv6 Internet addresses

Configuring an IPv6 connection

Configuring IPv6 is almost identical to the process of configuring IPv4. By default, Windows 10 uses automatic IPv6 configuration. If a DHCPv6 server is available, it obtains its configuration from that service; otherwise, it will use stateless autoconfiguration. As with IPv4, you can use either the Windows user interface to configure IPv6, as shown in Figure 3-5, or you can use Netsh.exe or Windows PowerShell.

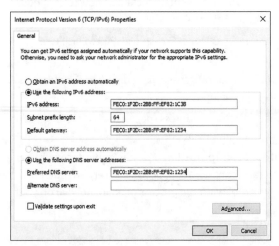

FIGURE 3-5 The Internet Protocol Version 6 (TCP/IPv6) Properties dialog box

To view or configure the IPv6 settings on your computer, perform the following procedure.

1. Right-click the network icon in the system tray and then click Open Network Internet Settings.

2. Click Change Adapter Options.

3. Right-click the appropriate network adapter and then click Properties.

4. Double-click Internet Protocol Version 6 (TCP/IPv6).

There are numerous Windows PowerShell cmdlets that you can use to view and configure IPv6 network settings, some of which are shown in Table 3-4.

TABLE 3-4 Windows PowerShell IPv6 networking-related cmdlets

CMDLET	PURPOSE
Get-NetIPAddress	Displays information about the IP address configuration
Get-NetIPv6Protocol	Displays information about the IPv6 protocol configuration
Set-NetIPAddress	Changes the IP address configuration
Set-NetIPv6Protocol	Changes the IPv6 protocol configuration

For example, to change the IPv6 configuration for a network connection with Windows PowerShell, use the following cmdlet.

```
Set-NetIPAddress -IPAddress 2001:CD8:1F2D::2BB:FF:EF82:1C3B -PrefixLength 64
```

Configure name resolution

Devices running Windows 10 communicate over networks by using names rather than IPv4 or IPv6 network addresses. A service on the Windows 10–based device, known as a client resolver, resolves names into IPv4 or IPv6 addresses. To configure Windows 10 networking, you must know how to configure name resolution.

Although IP addressing is not especially complex, it is generally easier for users to work with host names rather than with the IPv4 or IPv6 addresses of hosts, such as websites, to which they want to connect. When an application, such as Microsoft Edge, references a website name, the name is converted to the underlying IP address by using a process known as name resolution. Windows 10–based devices can use two types of names. These are:

- **Host names** A host name, up to 255 characters in length, contains only alphanumeric characters, periods, and hyphens. A host name is an alias combined with a fully qualified domain name (FQDN). For example, the alias *computer1* is prefixed to the domain name contoso.com to create the host name, or FQDN, of *computer1*.contoso.com.

- **NetBIOS names** Less relevant today, NetBIOS names use a nonhierarchical structure based on a 16-character name. The sixteenth character identifies a particular service running on the computer named by the preceding 15 characters. Thus, LON-SVR1[20h] is the NetBIOS server service on the computer called LON-SVR1.

The way a client computer resolves names varies based on its configuration but is typically resolved as shown in Figure 3-6.

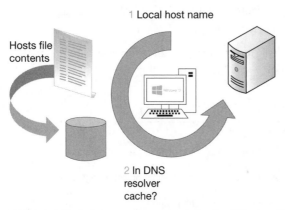

FIGURE 3-6 Typical stages of name resolution in a Windows 10 client

The following process identifies the typical stages of name resolution for Windows 10–based devices.

1. Determine whether the queried host name is the same as the local host name.

2. Search the local DNS resolver cache for the queried host name. The cache is updated when records are successfully resolved. In addition, the contents of the local Hosts file are added to the resolver cache.

3. Petition a DNS server for the required host name.

 EXAM TIP

Windows 10 devices also use Link-Local Multicast Name Resolution for networks that do not provide DNS. You can find out more on the Microsoft Press Store website at *https://www. microsoftpressstore.com/articles/article.aspx?p=2217263&seqNum=8.*

NEED MORE REVIEW? IPV4 NAME RESOLUTION

To review further details about IPv4 name resolution, refer to the Microsoft website at *https: //docs.microsoft.com/en-us/previous-versions/windows/it-pro/windows-server-2008-R2-and-2008/dd379505(v=ws.10).*

CONFIGURE DNS SETTINGS

To configure DNS settings for either IPv4 or IPv6, perform the following procedure.

1. Right-click the network icon in the system tray and then click Open Network Internet Settings.

2. Click Change Adapter Options.

3. Right-click the appropriate network adapter and then click Properties.

4. Double-click either Internet Protocol Version 4 (TCP/IPv4) or Internet Protocol Version 6 (TCP/IPv6).

5. Click Use The Following DNS Server Addresses and then enter a valid IPv4 or IPv6 address for a DNS server that is accessible to the client.

You can also configure DNS settings by using Netsh.exe, as follows.

```
netsh interface ip set dns name="Ethernet" static 192.168.16.1
```

Alternatively, you can use Windows PowerShell to configure the DNS client settings.

```
Set-DNSClientServerAddress –interfaceIndex 12 –ServerAddresses ('192.168.16.1')
```

CONFIGURE ADVANCED DNS SETTINGS

In addition to configuring the basic DNS client settings, you can configure advanced DNS settings, as shown in Figure 3-7. To configure these settings, from either the Internet Protocol Version 4 (TCP/IPv4) Properties dialog box or from the Internet Protocol Version 6 (TCP/IPv6) Properties dialog box, click Advanced and then click the DNS tab.

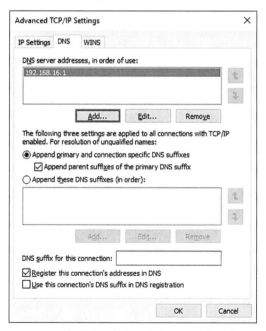

FIGURE 3-7 The DNS tab of the Advanced TCP/IP Settings dialog box

The advanced DNS settings are:

- **Append Primary And Connection Specific DNS Suffixes**   This option controls how the DNS resolver on the local client appends the DNS suffixes during queries. For example, if you query **www** and your computer's primary suffix is **contoso.com**, the microsoft.com suffix is appended to your query to make **www.contoso.com**.

- **Append Parent Suffixes Of The Primary DNS Suffix**   In this example, the parent suffix of **contoso.com** is **com**. This option determines whether, after attempting **www.contoso.com**, the DNS resolver tries **www.com**.

- **Append These DNS Suffixes (In Order)**   This option enables you to define suffixes and order them for queries.

- **DNS suffix For This Connection**   You can define a DNS suffix for each network interface card installed in your device.

- **Register This Connection's Address In DNS**   Windows-based devices can register their IPv4 addresses with DNS servers that support dynamic updates of host records, such as the DNS server role service in Windows Server 2016.

- **Use This Connection's DNS Suffix In DNS Registration**   This option determines whether the IP addresses and the connection-specific domain name of this connection are registered with DNS.

Configure mobile networking

Setup Windows 10 for a cellular data plan

Some devices with Windows 10 installed can support connectivity by using cellular networks. This is useful for users who cannot always connect to Wi-Fi networks, but still need access to corporate services and resources.

To enable and configure cellular remote access in Windows 10 you must obtain a cellular data plan from a telecom provider. Microsoft can provide this service.

> **NEED MORE REVIEW?**   **GET ONLINE WITH PAID CELLULAR DATA**
>
> To find out more about getting online with Microsoft cellular data packages, refer to the Microsoft website at *https://support.microsoft.com/en-us/help/4027933/windows-10-get-online-with-paid-cellular-data*.

Typically, your telecom provider must provide you with a suitable SIM card for your Windows 10 device. The SIM size might vary depending on the vendor of the device you intend to use. For example, if you or your users are intending to connect using a Microsoft Surface Pro device, you must obtain a Nano SIM from your telecom provider. Note that you can use the SIM card from your cellphone for this, but it must be the right size. Some hardware vendors, including Microsoft, support a built-in SIM, or Embedded SIM (eSIM). This enables you to use cellular data without obtaining a separate, physical SIM from a telecom provider. You can also combine the use of an external SIM and an eSIM, effectively creating a device that has two data plans; perhaps one for business and one for personal use—much like some users use their cellphones with dual-SIM.

After you have installed the SIM into your Windows device, you must configure Windows 10 to connect using cellular data. If you use a Microsoft data plan, you can configure network access simply by running the Mobile Plans app. This app is built-in to Windows 10. The app detects your eSIM (or SIM) and then guides you through the setup process. To set up cellular network access, use the following procedure:

1. Connect to the Internet using a wired or wireless connection.

2. Select the Network symbol on the taskbar, look for Get Connected beneath the name of your mobile operator, and then click Connect With A Data Plan. This will open the Mobile Plans app.

3. In Mobile Plans, do one of the following, depending on what your computer displays on the screen:

   ■ On the Connect Your Device page, enter your cellphone number, and then click Find My Mobile Operator. This enables you to determine if your telecom provider offers any plans.

      ■ If they do, click Continue. A webpage opens on your telecom provider's website. Sign in (using your existing mobile account details) or create a new account if needed, and then follow the steps to add your device to your account.

      ■ If your provider doesn't offer plans, click Choose From A List Of Mobile Operators. Choose a new provider, and then click Continue to go to the telecom provider's website to set up a new account and plan.

   ■ On the Select A Mobile Operator To Get Online Now page, select a telecom provider, click Continue to go to their site, sign in, and then choose a plan.

When you want to use your mobile data connection, use the following procedure to connect:

1. Click the Network icon in the system tray.

2. In the list of available networks, choose the mobile network.

If you experience any problems with your cellular connections, use the following procedure to troubleshoot your connection:

1. Open the Settings app.

2. Click Network & Internet.

3. Assuming you have an eSIM or compatible SIM, you should see a Mobile tab on the left. Select the Mobile tab.

4. If you have multiple SIMs, then select whichever SIM you want to use for a given data plan, and click Use This SIM For Mobile Data.

5. Open the Mobile Plans app and choose a mobile operator from those listed.

6. Follow the instructions above to set up a plan with your telecom provider.

Setup Windows 10 as a mobile hotspot

Windows 10 devices are becoming lighter and more mobile. Often, users have multiple connected devices, including laptops, tablets, and cellular phones. Virtually ubiquitous Internet connectivity enables users to adopt an "always on" lifestyle. When users face situations where traditional connections, such as corporate Wi-Fi or Ethernet, are not available, they will look for other forms of connectivity, such as Wi-Fi hotspots; they also might use their mobile devices to connect to the Internet.

Broadband tethering, referred to as a Windows 10 Mobile hotspot, enables users to share their own Internet connections with others by enabling the device to function as a wireless "hotspot." Similarly, users can connect to other users' shared personal "hotspots," provided they have the necessary credentials.

To connect to a shared mobile hotspot connection, follow these steps:

1. In Settings, click Network & Internet.
2. As shown in Figure 3-8, click the Mobile Hotspot tab.
3. In the Share My Internet Connection From list, choose the appropriate network connection.
4. Click Edit and enter a Network name and Network password. These are used by other users who connect to your device.
5. Finally, enable the Share My Internet Connection With Other Devices option.

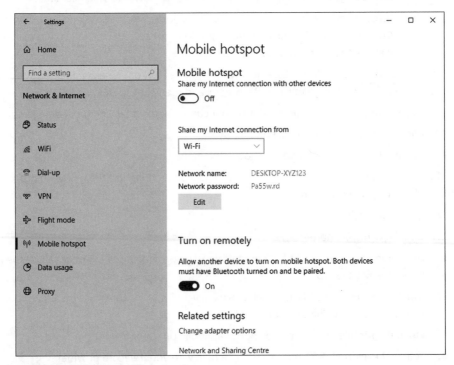

FIGURE 3-8 Enabling a mobile hotspot

Configure VPN client

In Windows 10, creating a VPN enables data to be transferred through a virtual private network via a secured connection (tunnel) over a public network, such as the Internet, as shown in Figure 3-9.

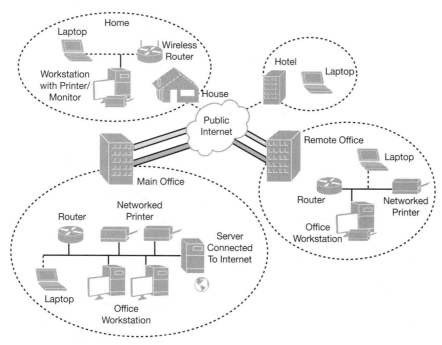

FIGURE 3-9 Using a VPN to connect locations securely over the Internet

Except in a few specialized scenarios, nearly all dial-up remote connections have been replaced by broadband-enabled VPN communications. Windows 10 still supports Point-to-Point Protocol (PPP), which can be used with a dial-up connection. This is an old protocol, but because it creates a direct connection and maintains a dedicated link between the two points, it is used as the starting point for most dial-up and PPP connections.

For the exam, you will be required to understand the different types of VPN protocol that Windows 10 supports and when each protocol should be used.

VPN protocols

Windows 10 supports four commonly used VPN protocols. Each protocol offers different characteristics and age. Typically, the newest protocol will be the most secure.

- **Point-to-Point Tunneling Protocol (PPTP)** The oldest and what is considered one of the least secure of all supported VPN protocols. However, it can be used successfully in low-security scenarios because it is very easy to set up and still offers more protection than using PPP over the Internet. PPTP creates the tunnel and then can use several authentication methods, including the Microsoft Challenge Handshake Authentication

Protocol versions 1 and 2 (MS-CHAP v1 and MS-CHAP v2), Extensible Authentication Protocol (EAP), and Protected Extensible Authentication Protocol (PEAP). If EAP is used, certificates can be used with PPTP; otherwise, they are not necessary

- **Layer 2 Tunneling Protocol (L2TP)**   This protocol uses the IP security extensions (IPsec) for encryption and encapsulation. L2TP encapsulates the messages with IPsec, and then encrypts the contents using the Data Encryption Standard (DES) or Triple DES (3DES) algorithm. The encryption keys are provided by IPsec using Internet Key Exchange (IKE). L2TP/IPsec can use pre-shared keys or certificates for authentication. Using a pre-shared key is useful during testing and evaluation, but should be replaced with a certificate in a production environment.

- **Secure Socket Tunneling Protocol (SSTP)**   This is a recent protocol introduced with Windows Server 2008 and supported on Vista SP1 or later. It encapsulates PPP traffic using the Secure Sockets Layer (SSL) protocol, which is widely supported on the Internet and passes through TCP port 443, which is the same as SSL. Using the Extensible Authentication Protocol-Transport Layer Security (EAP-TLS) authentication protocol together with certificates makes SSTP a very versatile and widely used protocol.

- **Internet Key Exchange, Version 2 (IKEv2)**   IKEv2 is most useful for mobile users and is the default protocol for Windows 10 and Windows 8.1 when trying to connect to remote access servers. This protocol is partially supported on Windows 7 and later versions of Windows and provides support for IPv6 traffic and the IKEv2 Mobility and Multi-homing (MOBIKE) protocol through the Windows VPN Reconnect feature, which allows automatic reconnection if a VPN connection is lost. Authentication is offered using EAP, PEAP, EAP-MSCHAPv2, and smart cards. IKEv2 will not support older authentication methods, such as Password Authentication Protocol (PAP) and Challenge-Handshake Authentication Protocol (CHAP), which offer low protection.

Authenticating remote users

Windows users authenticate using Kerberos when accessing the local network, but for remote authentication, this is not suitable; a separate protocol, which protects against network intrusion, must be used. During the initial negotiation sequence (using PPP) when a client connects to the remote computer, each party must agree on a shared authentication protocol to use. By default, Windows 10 will use the strongest protocol that both parties have in common.

In the Add A VPN Connection Wizard, Windows 10 offers three sign-in options when configuring a VPN, such as:

- User name and password
- Smart card
- One-time password

In addition to these options, you can also configure Windows 10 to use the common authentication protocols:

- **EAP-MS-CHAPv2**   This is a protocol that uses Extensible Authentication Protocol (EAP), which offers the default and most flexible authentication option for Windows 10 clients.

It offers the strongest password-based mechanism for the client side, with certificates being used on the server side. Authentication can be negotiated based on certificates or smart cards, and EAP-MS-CHAPv2 is likely to be further extended and developed as technology advances. Windows 10 will aim to use this method for authentication connections where possible. IKEv2 connections must use EAP-MS-CHAPv2 or a certificate.

- **PAP**   This is the least secure protocol as it uses plaintext passwords. It is not considered secure and should only be used whenever other authentication methods cannot be negotiated.

- **CHAP**   Used for down-level client compatibility and has been surpassed by MS-CHAP v2. This protocol uses a pre-shared key between the client and server to enable encryption to take place.

- **MS-CHAP v2**   Stronger than the CHAP protocol, with significantly improved security when partnered with EAP to enable encryption of the password.

Creating a VPN connection in Network And Sharing Center

To create a VPN in Windows 10, from the Network And Sharing Center, under Change Your Network Settings, click Set Up A New Connection Or Network and then click Connect To A Workplace.

To configure your VPN connection, in the Connect To A Workplace Wizard, provide the following information.

- **How Do You Want To Connect?**   You can connect by using an existing Internet connection or by dialing directly to your workplace.

- **Internet Address**   This is the name or IP address of the computer that you connect to at your workplace, as shown in Figure 3-10. Typically, this is an FQDN, such as remote .adatum.com.

- **Destination Name**   This is the name of this VPN connection.

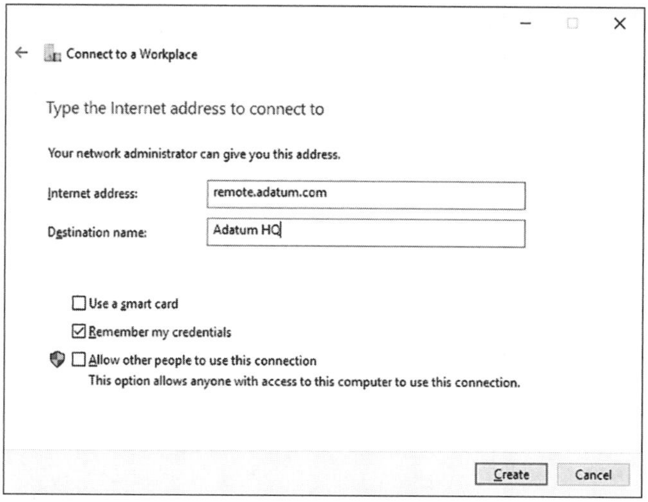

FIGURE 3-10 The Connect To A Workplace Wizard

After you have created the VPN connection, from the Network And Sharing Center, click Change Adapter Settings, right-click your VPN connection, and click Properties. As shown in Figure 3-11, you can then configure additional options as required by your organization's network infrastructure.

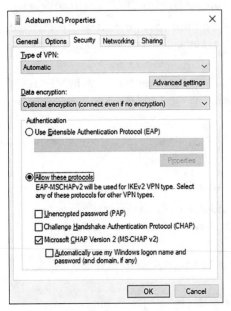

FIGURE 3-11 The Security tab of a VPN connection

These settings must match the remote access device that your device connects to, and includes the following options

- **Type Of VPN** Point-to-Point Tunneling Protocol (PPTP), Layer Two Tunneling Protocol with IPsec (L2TP/IPsec), Secure Socket Tunneling Protocol (SSTP), or Internet Key Exchange version 2 (IKEv2).
- **Data Encryption** None, Optional, Required, or Maximum Strength

Under Authentication, you choose either Use Extensible Authentication Protocol (EAP) or Allow These Protocols. If you choose to use EAP, you then configure one of the following.

- Microsoft: EAP-AKA (Encryption Enabled)
- Microsoft: EAP-SIM (Encryption Enabled)
- Microsoft: EAP-TTLS (Encryption Enabled)
- Microsoft: Protected EAP (PEAP) (Encryption Enabled)
- Microsoft: Secured Password (EAP-MSCHAP v2) (Encryption Enabled)
- Microsoft: Smart Card Or Other Certificate (Encryption Enabled)

If you choose Allow These Protocols, you then configure the following options.

- Unencrypted Password (PAP)
- Challenge Handshake Authentication Protocol (CHAP)
- Microsoft CHAP Version 2 (MS-CHAP v2)
    - Automatically Use My Windows Log-on Name And Password (And Domain, If Any)

EXAM TIP

You can use the Connection Manager Administration Kit (CMAK) to create and deploy VPN profiles for remote access. This kit can be installed as a Windows 10 feature from Control Panel. Find out more from the Microsoft website at *https://docs.microsoft.com/en-us/previous-versions/windows/it-pro/windows-server-2008-R2-and-2008/cc726035(v=ws.11).*

Using the Settings app to create and configure a VPN

You can also use the Settings app to create and configure VPN connections. Use the following procedure:

1. Click Start and then click Settings.
2. In Settings, click Network & Internet.
3. Select the VPN tab, and then, in the details pane, click Add A VPN Connection.
4. On the Add A VPN Connection page, enter the following information:
    - VPN Provider: Windows (Built-In)
    - Connection Name
    - Server Name Or Address
    - VPN Type: Automatic (Default). You can also choose PPTP, L2TP/IPsec With Certificate, L2TP/IPsec With Pre-Shared Key, SSTP, or IKEv2.
    - Type Of Sign-In Info: User Name And Password, Smart Card, One-Time Password, or Certificate.
    - User Name And Password, although these options are only configurable if you selected User Name Or Password as the Type Of Sign-In Info.
5. Click Save.

After you have created the VPN, you can manage it from Network Connections in Control Panel. Alternatively, on the VPN page in the Network & Internet node in Settings, you can click the VPN and then choose Advanced Options. From there, you can reconfigure the VPN's settings.

VPN profiles

Although manually configuring VPN connections is relatively simple, completing the process on many computers, with the same or similar settings, is very time-consuming. In these circumstances, it makes sense to create a VPN profile and then distribute the profile to your users' computers.

When you use VPN profiles in Windows 10, you can take advantage of a number of advanced features. These are:

- **Always On** This feature enables Windows to automatically connect to a VPN. The Always On feature can be triggered by sign-in when the desktop is unlocked, and on network changes. When the Always On profile is configured, VPN remains always connected unless the user disconnects manually or logs off the device. The profile is optimized for power and performance, and the profiles can be pushed and managed on devices using mobile device management (MDM) tools.

- **App-Triggered VPN** You can configure the VPN profile to respond to a specific set of apps; if a defined app loads, then the VPN initiates.

- **Traffic Filters** To protect the server from a remote attack, an administrator can configure policies on a Windows 10 device to inspect and, if necessary, filter VPN traffic before it is enabled to travel over the VPN. There are two types of Traffic Filter rules available:

  - **App-based rules** An app-based rule will only enable VPN traffic originating from applications that have been marked as being allowed to traverse the VPN interface.

  - **Traffic-based rules** Enterprise-level traffic-based rules enable fine-tuning of what type of traffic is allowed. By using the industry-standard rules covered by five tuple policies (protocol, source/destination IP address, source/destination port), administrators can be very specific on the type of network traffic that is allowed to travel over the VPN interface.

  An administrator can combine both app-based rules and traffic-based rules.

- **LockDown VPN** The LockDown VPN profile is used to enforce the use of the VPN interface. In this scenario, the device is secured to only allow network traffic over the VPN, which is automatically always on and can never be disconnected. If the VPN is unable to connect, then there will be no network traffic allowed. The LockDown profile overrides all other VPN profiles and must be deleted before other profiles can be added, removed, or connected.

EXAM TIP

You can find out more about VPN profile options in Windows 10 from the Microsoft website at *https://docs.microsoft.com/en-gb/windows/security/identity-protection/vpn/vpn-profile-options*.

You can create and distribute Windows 10 VPN profiles with these advanced settings by using Microsoft Intune and/or Configuration Manager.

NEED MORE REVIEW?   **VPN CONNECTIONS IN MICROSOFT INTUNE**

To review further details about VPN connections in Microsoft Intune, refer to the Microsoft website at *https://docs.microsoft.com/intune/vpn-settings-configure.*

NEED MORE REVIEW?   **HOW TO CREATE VPN PROFILES IN CONFIGURATION MANAGER**

To review further details about creating VPN Profiles in Configuration Manager, refer to the Microsoft website at *https://docs.microsoft.com/en-us/sccm/mdm/deploy-use/create-vpn-profiles.*

Troubleshoot networking

Windows 10 is a reliable and robust operating system, and the networking technologies built into it are tried and tested. However, networking is an inherently complex area, and problems might occur on your network. When you are facing a networking problem, use an appropriate procedure for troubleshooting the issue. This procedure might include the following steps.

1. Determine the scope of the problem. Knowing how many users are affected can help you determine possible causes.

2. Determine the IP configuration. Verify that the network configuration of affected devices is correct.

3. Determine the network's hardware configuration. Determine whether there are problems with the networking hardware or device drivers for that hardware.

4. Test communications. Perform a series of tests that help you pinpoint the nature of the problem. Tests might include

   - Verifying basic communications
   - Checking the routing and firewall configuration of your network
   - Testing name resolution
   - Testing connectivity to specific applications on servers

It is important that you know how to troubleshoot network-related problems that occur on your network to minimize disruption to your users.

Network troubleshooting tools

Windows 10 provides a number of tools that you can use to diagnose and resolve many network-related issues. These tools are identified in Table 3-5.

TABLE 3-5 Windows 10 network troubleshooting tools

TOOL	PURPOSE
Event Viewer	Windows collects information about system activity into event logs. For example, the System log stores information about IP conflicts and network-related service failures.
Windows Network Diagnostics	You can use Diagnose Connection Problems to help you diagnose and repair a network issue. Windows Network Diagnostics presents possible descriptions of the issue and suggests a potential solution. You can access this tool by clicking Troubleshoot Problems In Network And Sharing Center.
IPConfig	Use this command-line tool to display the current TCP/IP configuration of your Windows 10–based device. You can use the command with the following switches. **ipconfig /all** View detailed configuration information. **ipconfig /release** Release the leased configuration back to the DHCP server. **ipconfig /renew** Renew the leased configuration. **ipconfig /displaydns** View the DNS resolver cache entries. **ipconfig /flushdns** Purge the DNS resolver cache. **ipconfig /registerdns** Register or update the client's host name with the DNS server.
Ping	This command-line tool can be used to verify connectivity to a target computer system by sending a series of network packets to that target system. Consider that many firewalls block the ICMP packets Ping uses, so you might receive false negatives. Type **ping www.contoso.com**.
Tracert	Use this tool to determine the path that packets take to a designated target computer system, which helps you diagnose routing-related problems.
NSLookup	Use this tool to troubleshoot name resolution.
Pathping	This traces a network route similar to how the Tracert tool works but provides more statistics on the hops through the network.
Windows PowerShell	In addition to the configuration cmdlets referred to earlier, there are also a number of Windows PowerShell cmdlets you can use to troubleshoot and test network connectivity. For example, the **test-connection** cmdlet behaves in a way similar to Ping.exe. Type **test-connection www.contoso.com**.
Network Troubleshooter	You can use the Network Troubleshooter tool from within Network & Internet in the Settings app. On the Status tab, click Network Troubleshooter. A wizard starts that scans the network configuration for problems, and where possible, makes suggestions about fixes. This is very similar to the Windows Network Diagnostics tool mentioned earlier.
Network Reset	You can use the network reset tool from within Network & Internet in the Settings app. On the Status tab, click Network Reset. Note that you should use Network Reset as a last resort. This is because it removes and then reinstalls your network adapters and related settings. This can help restore your Internet connection, but it might result in additional configuration work after the reset has been performed.

Troubleshoot name resolution

Many network failures can be caused by a failure in name resolution, such as when the wrong server IP address is returned or a service has not registered itself with a DNS server correctly (or at all). When troubleshooting name resolution issues, use a suitable procedure, which might consist of the following steps.

1. Clear the DNS resolver cache. Use the **Ipconfig /flushdns** command from an elevated command prompt. This ensures that all subsequent name resolution attempts are performed rather than being satisfied from DNS resolver cache. You can also use the **Clear-DnsClientCache** Windows PowerShell cmdlet to achieve the same thing.

2. Attempt to verify basic connectivity by using an IP address. Use the **Ping** command, or the **test-connection** Windows PowerShell cmdlet, to verify communications to an IP address; for example, type **test-connection 172.16.16.1**.

3. Attempt to verify connectivity to a host name. Using the same tools, check whether you can communicate with a host by using its name, for example, **test-connection LON-DC1**. If this is successful, it is likely that your problem is not related to name resolution.

4. If the test is not successful, edit the Hosts file. Add the correct IP address and name to your hosts file. For example, add the line **172.16.16.1 LON-DC1.adatum.com** to C:\Windows\System32\Drivers\Etc\Hosts. Repeat the procedure to verify connectivity to a host name. Name resolution should now be successful.

5. Display the resolver cache. Use the **Get-DnsClientCache** cmdlet (or use **IPConfig /displaydns**) to verify that the entry appears in a resolved cache. You have proven that the problem is likely a name resolution issue. Remove the entry from the hosts file and clear the resolver cache.

6. Test the name server. Test the name server by performing a query against it by using the **Resolve-dnsname lon-DC1.adatum.com**. cmdlet. Alternatively, use the **NSLookup .exe -d2 LON-cl1.adatum.com**. command. You can see the partial output from the **Resolve-dnsname** cmdlet in Figure 3-12.

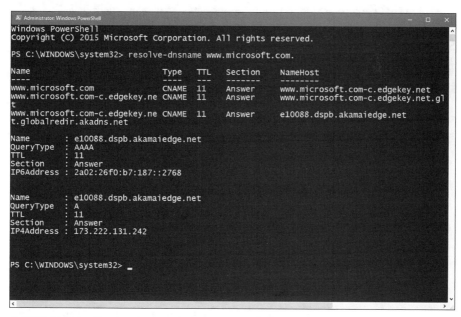

FIGURE 3-12 Using Resolve-dnsname to test name resolution

The information returned from the name server test shows IP addresses of the server you queried against. It also shows which name servers provided the response. It is important to know how to interpret this returned information to diagnose any failures or faults properly.

> **NEED MORE REVIEW?   DIAGNOSING NAME RESOLUTION PROBLEMS**
>
> To find out more about troubleshooting name resolution, refer to the Microsoft website at *https://technet.microsoft.com/library/cc959340.aspx.*

Configure Wi-Fi profiles

You can configure wireless networks by using one of several modes to suit your requirements and using one of a number of standards to secure the network and achieve compatibility between your wireless devices.

Modes

Wireless networking can be configured in one of three modes.

- **Ad-hoc**   This setting enables you to configure a wireless connection between devices in a peer-to-peer manner without requiring a wireless access point (AP).
- **Wi-Fi Direct**   This setting is a wireless networking standard that you can use to connect your wireless devices without a wireless AP. Similar to ad hoc wireless networking, it is typically used to connect to peripherals such as printers and media players.
- **Infrastructure**   Based on wireless APs, infrastructure networks consist of wireless local area networks to enable communications between wireless client devices.

Standards

To ensure compatibility between wireless networked devices, a number of standards have evolved. The 802.11x wireless standards are described in Table 3-6.

TABLE 3-6 802.11 wireless standards

STANDARD	DEFINITION
802.11a	Provides up to 54 megabits per second (mbps) and uses the 5 gigahertz (GHz) range. Not compatible with 802.11b.
802.11b	Provides 11 mbps and uses the 2.4 GHz range.
802.11e	Defines Quality of Service and multimedia support.
802.11g	For use over short distances at speeds up to 54 mbps. Backward compatible with 802.11b and uses the 2.4 GHz range.
802.11n	Increases data throughput at speeds up to 100 mbps, and it uses both 2.4 GHz and 5 GHz ranges.
802.11ac	Builds on 802.11n to achieve data rates of 433 mbps. 802.11ac uses the 5 GHz frequency range.

Security

It is comparatively easy to gain access to a wireless network, so it is important to secure network traffic on your wireless network infrastructure. A number of wireless security standards exist that can help, as shown in Table 3-7. When choosing a security method, ensure that your wireless devices and infrastructure support that method.

TABLE 3-7 Wireless security standards

STANDARD	EXPLANATION
Wired Equivalent Privacy (WEP)	WEP is an old wireless security standard, and a number of documented security issues surround it. Use WEP only if there is no choice.
Wi-Fi Protected Access (WPA)	WPA has two variations. WPA-Personal. Easier to implement than WPA Enterprise and, therefore, ideal for smaller networks. Authentication is based on a password. The password and the network Service Set Identifier (SSID) generate encryption keys for each wireless device. WPA-Enterprise. Designed for larger networks and requires the use of a Remote Authentication Dial-In User Service (RADIUS) server to provide for authentication.
WPA2	An improved version of WPA that is the de facto Wi-Fi security standard. It employs larger encryption key sizes than WPA.

Configure wireless settings

After you have selected the appropriate wireless infrastructure components and chosen your wireless security standard, you must set up and configure your wireless network in Windows 10.

CONNECT TO A WIRELESS NETWORK

To connect to a wireless network, in the system tray, click the network icon to see a list of available wireless networks. Click the appropriate network and then click Connect. Enter the required security information as shown in Figure 3-13 and click Next.

FIGURE 3-13 Connecting to a wireless network

CONFIGURE EXISTING WIRELESS NETWORKS

To review or edit your existing wireless networks, from Settings, click Network & Internet. On the Wi-Fi tab, shown in Figure 3-14, you can configure the following options.

- **Show Available Networks** Enables you to view the currently available Wi-Fi networks within range of your device

- **Hardware Properties** Enables you to view the properties of your Wi-Fi connection, including SSID, Protocol, Security type, Network band, Network channel, IPv4 and IPv6 configuration, and details about your Wi-Fi adapter

- **Manage Known Networks** Enables you to view, configure, or forget any Wi-Fi networks to which your device has connected. To forget a Wi-Fi connection, click it, and then click Forget. To configure a Wi-Fi network, click it, and then click Properties. You can then view or configure the following:

  - Connect Automatically When In Range

  - Network Profile: Public Or Private. This option is only available when you are connected to the specific Wi-Fi network.

  - Set As Metered Connection

- **Random Hardware Address** Enables your computer to use a different hardware address for each network to which it connects. This can help secure your device by making it harder to track your device's location.

- **Hotspot 2.0 Networks** Under this heading, you can enable the following options:

  - Let Me Use Online Sign-Up To Get Connected

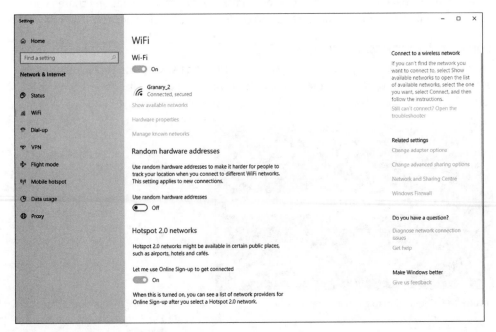

FIGURE 3-14 Managing Wi-Fi settings

HOTSPOT 2.0 NETWORKS

For connecting to public Wi-Fi networks, Windows 10 supports the Hotspot 2.0 wireless 802.11u Wi-Fi standard. This should make connecting to hotspots in public places, such as airports, or coffee shops, easier and more secure.

Your device will attempt to connect you to available public hotspots automatically, in a similar fashion to cellular-style "roaming."

There are several benefits to using Hotspot 2.0:

- Public Hotspots become easier and more secure—your device will detect which Wi-Fi network is authentic and connect automatically.

- Network Providers can partner with other providers. This will allow great network coverage and allow cellular-style "roaming."

- Encryption is enforced and utilizes enterprise-grade WPA2 encryption.

When you attempt to join a Hotspot 2.0 network for the first time, Windows 10 presents an "Online Sign-Up" screen with a list of available network providers. After you have set up an account with one of the providers, your device will be able to connect to other Hotspot 2.0 networks automatically in the future.

ENABLE VPN RECONNECT

VPN Reconnect uses the IKEv2 protocol with the MOBIKE extension to automatically re-establish a lost VPN connection without user intervention. For mobile users, the prevalence of dropped Wi-Fi or LTE connections can be frequent because of volatile signal strength. It is best to use and configure VPN Reconnect for your mobile users because this will reduce the frustration of having to reconnect manually, and it will also increase productivity.

The network outage time can be configured from five minutes up to an interruption of eight hours. To enable VPN Reconnect, follow these steps:

1. On the taskbar, in the search box, type **VPN**.
2. Click VPN Settings from the returned list.
3. In the Settings app, click Change Adapter Options.
4. Select the appropriate VPN adapter, and then click Change Settings Of This Connection, as shown in Figure 3-15.
5. Click the Security tab in the VPN Properties dialog box, and click Advanced Settings.
6. In the Advanced Properties dialog box, check the Mobility option on the IKEv2 tab.
7. Modify the Network Outage Time as necessary.
8. Click OK twice.

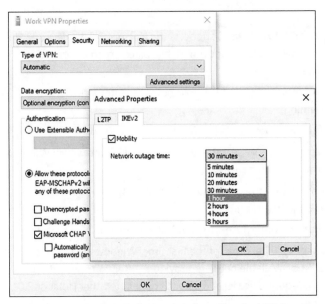

FIGURE 3-15 Configuring the Network Outage Time for VPN Reconnect

ADVANCED SETTINGS

To configure advanced wireless settings, from the Network And Sharing Center, under View Your Active Networks, click the wireless network you want to configure, as shown in Figure 3-16. Then, in the Wi-Fi Status dialog box, click Wireless Properties. You can then view the security settings for your wireless network connection.

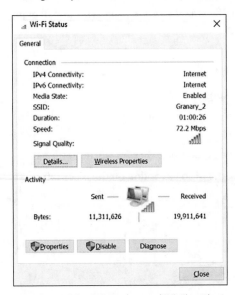

FIGURE 3-16 Managing advanced Wi-Fi settings

You can also manage wireless networks by using Netsh.exe. For example, to list the wireless network profiles on your computer, type:

```
Netsh wlan show profile
```

> **NEED MORE REVIEW?** **USING NETSH.EXE TO MANAGE WIRELESS NETWORKS**
>
> To find out more about managing Wi-Fi settings by using Netsh.exe, refer to the Microsoft website at *https://docs.microsoft.com/en-us/previous-versions/windows/it-pro/windows-server-2008-R2-and-2008/dd744890(v=ws.10)*.

CONFIGURING WI-FI DIRECT

Wi-Fi Direct is a standard developed with the Wi-Fi Alliance, is fully supported by Windows 10, and enables Wi-Fi Direct devices to connect seamlessly to one another. This can be achieved using Miracast over Infrastructure, which uses Ethernet if a network access point or secure ad hoc Wi-Fi network is available, or over a private ad hoc wireless network as and when required.

Wi-Fi Direct enables you to interact with other hardware, for example, print to a wireless printer or send your PowerPoint presentation to an external display.

Devices that are utilizing Wi-Fi Direct include mobile phones, cameras, printers, TVs, PCs, and gaming devices, such as Xbox One.

Wi-Fi Direct is very similar to Bluetooth, but only 10x faster. (Wi-Fi Direct transfers data at up to 250 Mbps, whereas Bluetooth 4.0 transfers data at up to 25 Mbps.)

As the technology continues to mature, Microsoft has upgraded and enhanced the application program interface (API) support with Windows 10 for developers to use when writing their software. Original equipment manufacturer (OEM) vendors are gradually incorporating Wi-Fi Direct into their devices, such as printers utilizing Wi-Fi Direct. Unlike Bluetooth, only one device needs to support Wi-Fi Direct, though they will still pair in much the same way as Bluetooth. For example, Miracast enables a Windows device to wirelessly display on to a projected screen, such as a TV or projector. Miracast is ideal for enabling screens that do not have built-in support for Wi-Fi Direct because it uses a High-Definition Multimedia Interface (HDMI) adapter, which plugs into the remote screen. Windows 10 can wirelessly connect to the Miracast adapter.

To use the Wi-Fi Direct technology, a user will turn on or enable the Wi-Fi Direct device, such as a Miracast adapter or printer, and Windows 10 will locate the device wirelessly and connect. Once connected, application files that are required for the user interface, such as display or printer dialog screens, are received directly from the Wi-Fi Direct device.

Some characteristics of Wi-Fi Direct are listed below:

- **Distance between devices (ad hoc Wi-Fi)** Compared to Bluetooth, which creates a Personal Area Network of just a few feet, Wi-Fi Alliance states that Wi-Fi Direct devices can reach each other over a maximum distance of up to 656 feet.

- **Security**   Wi-Fi Direct uses either WPA2-PSK or WPA2-Enterprise security, which uses AES 256-bit encryption with a key-based encryption and authentication method.
- **Speed**   Wi-Fi Direct claims device-to-device transfer speeds of up to 250 Mbps.
- **Services**   Wi-Fi Direct Send, Wi-Fi Direct Print, Wi-Fi Direct for DLNA, Miracast, and Miracast over Infrastructure are the five services that currently utilize the Wi-Fi Direct standard.

To set up Wi-Fi Direct in Windows 10, you need a compatible network adapter. Type **ipconfig /all** at the command line and verify that one of the network adapters listed returns the Description value Microsoft Wi-Fi Direct Virtual Adapter, as shown in Figure 3-17.

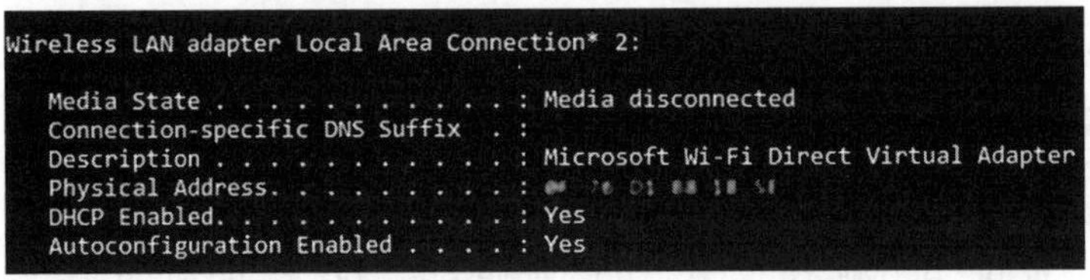

```
Wireless LAN adapter Local Area Connection* 2:

   Media State . . . . . . . . . . . : Media disconnected
   Connection-specific DNS Suffix  . :
   Description . . . . . . . . . . . : Microsoft Wi-Fi Direct Virtual Adapter
   Physical Address. . . . . . . . . : ## 7# D1 88 18 5#
   DHCP Enabled. . . . . . . . . . . : Yes
   Autoconfiguration Enabled . . . . : Yes
```

FIGURE 3-17 Viewing available network adapters with Ipconfig

After you have checked that your wireless network adapter supports Wi-Fi Direct, use the Netsh.exe command-line tool to set up your Wi-Fi Direct network. You can use the following command to start the process of enabling Wi-Fi Direct.

```
netsh wlan set hostednetwork mode=allow ssid=Wi-Fidirect key=passphrase
```

Use the following command to start Wi-Fi Direct.

```
netsh wlan start hostednetwork
```

To stop the Wi-Fi Direct network, use:

```
netsh wlan stop hostednetwork
```

Skill 3.2: Configure remote connectivity

When you have a large number of computers to manage or a workforce that uses their devices in a number of locations, you must know how to enable and configure remote connectivity. It is also important to be able to manage those computers by using remote management tools.

This skill covers how to:
- Configure remote management
- Configure remote desktop access
- Enable PowerShell Remoting

Configure remote management

Windows 10 provides a number of tools that you can use to manage your organization's computers remotely. These include Remote Assistance, Remote Desktop, Windows PowerShell remoting, and many management console snap-ins. Knowing which tools to use to support a given situation helps you address your users' needs more quickly.

Remote management tools in Windows 10

You can use a variety of tools to manage Windows 10 devices remotely. Table 3-8 shows the available remote management tools in Windows 10.

TABLE 3-8 Windows 10 remote management tools

TOOL	PURPOSE
Remote Assistance	A built-in tool that provides for interaction with the remote user. By using Remote Assistance, you can view or take remote control of the user's computer and perform remote management of it. You can also use a text-based chat facility to interact with the user.
Quick Assist	A built-in Microsoft Store app that enables you to offer or receive assistance quickly. As with Remote Assistance, you can view or take remote control of the user's computer and perform remote management of it. To initiate a session, participants exchange a 6 digit security code.
Remote Desktop	A built-in tool that you can use to access a computer remotely over the Remote Desktop Protocol (RDP). In the past, users often accessed their computers from other locations by using Remote Desktop. Security concerns and the adoption of mobile devices have made this a less common use of this tool. However, you can also use Remote Desktop to manage a remote computer. It does not provide for user interaction and requires the user of the computer to sign out before you can access the computer remotely.
Windows PowerShell	Windows PowerShell is a powerful command-line management tool and scripting environment. You can use it to perform virtually any management function in Windows 10. You can also use Windows PowerShell to manage remote computers. This is known as Windows PowerShell remoting.
Microsoft Management Console	Microsoft Management Console (MMC) is an extensible interface for management applications in both Windows clients and Windows Server. To perform management by using MMC, a specific tool for the management task, known as a snap-in, is loaded into the console. For example, to perform management of disks and attached storage, you add the Disk Management snap-in to MMC. You can use MMC snap-ins to manage Windows 10 devices remotely by targeting the remote computer from the MMC interface.

Selecting the appropriate remote management tool

Given that a variety of tools are available, it is important to know which one to use in a given situation. When considering the appropriate tool, use the guidance in Table 3-9 to help you make your choice.

TABLE 3-9 Selecting the appropriate Windows 10 remote management tool

SCENARIO	TOOL
User requires help and guidance. For example, you must help the user perform a specific task in an application such as printing, using the appropriate settings.	Remote Assistance or Quick Assist
You must perform a single remote management task on a single computer and require no user interaction.	Remote Desktop or MMC
You must perform the same management task on several or many remote computers.	Windows PowerShell
You must perform a remote management task that you have performed many times in the past and expect to perform again in the future.	Windows PowerShell
You are unsure of the nature of a problem a user is experiencing on her computer and wish to investigate computer settings.	Remote Desktop
You want to be able to perform the same management task, using the same management tool on any computer.	MMC

You can see from Table 3-9 that you can sometimes use several methods to address a specific remote management scenario. It is, therefore, a question of choosing the most appropriate method. Generally, if you know you will be required to perform the same management task again, on the same or a different computer, it is worth considering Windows PowerShell remoting. If you need to provide user interaction, choose Remote Assistance or Quick Assist. After that, it's probably a personal preference of whether you use an MMC snap-in remotely or Remote Desktop.

Configure remote management settings

Depending on the remote management tool you have decided to use, it is almost certain that you must configure the target computer (the one you wish to manage) and possibly the local management computer (the one you are using) to enable the selected remote management tool. For example, it is common to have to enable the appropriate feature through Windows Defender Firewall to allow for management of a remote Windows 10–based device.

CONFIGURING WINDOWS DEFENDER FIREWALL TO ENABLE REMOTE MANAGEMENT

To enable remote management through Windows Defender Firewall on a target computer, open Control Panel and complete the following procedure.

1. In Control Panel, click System And Security and then click Windows Defender Firewall.

2. In Windows Defender Firewall, click Allow An App Or Feature Through Windows Defender Firewall.

3. In Allowed Applications, click Change Settings.

4. In the Allowed Apps And Features list, scroll down and select the appropriate management feature.

For example, as shown in Figure 3-18, select Remote Assistance. This enables the selected management feature on the Private network location profile. If you also wish to allow the remote management feature on Public networks, select the Public check box.

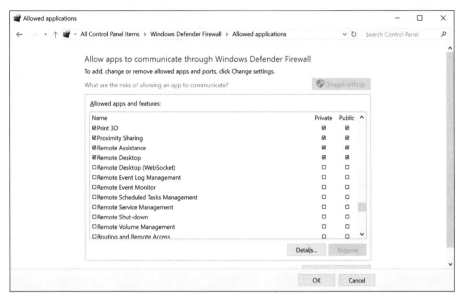

FIGURE 3-18 Allowing Remote Assistance through Windows Defender Firewall

5. Click OK. The available remote management features are

- Remote Assistance
- Remote Desktop
- Remote Event Log Management
- Remote Event Monitor
- Remote Scheduled Tasks Management
- Remote Service Management
- Remote Shutdown
- Remote Volume Management
- Virtual Machine Monitoring
- Windows Defender Firewall Remote Management
- Windows Management Instrumentation (WMI)
- Windows Remote Management
- Windows Remote Management (Compatibility)

It is not always feasible, or especially desirable, to reconfigure these settings manually on each computer to enable the appropriate remote management feature. Instead, in an Active

Directory Domain Services (AD DS) environment, you can use Group Policy Objects (GPOs) to configure the desired firewall settings.

ENABLING REMOTE MANAGEMENT THROUGH SYSTEM PROPERTIES

Both Remote Assistance and Remote Desktop can be enabled through the System Properties dialog box, as shown in Figure 3-19. To access these settings, open the Settings app and follow these steps.

1. Click System and then click About.

2. In the details pane, under Related Settings, click System Info.

3. Click Remote Settings.

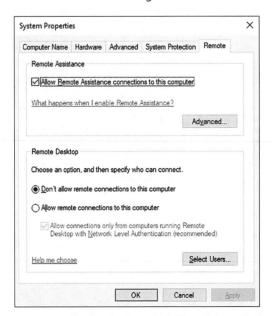

FIGURE 3-19 Configuring Remote Settings through System Properties

ENABLING REMOTE ASSISTANCE

To enable Remote Assistance, on the Remote tab of the System Properties dialog box, select the Allow Remote Assistance Connections To This Computer check box. Then, optionally, click Advanced. As shown in Figure 3-20, you can then configure the following additional settings.

- **Allow This Computer To Be Controlled Remotely** This setting enables you to determine whether the person providing remote support can take remote control of the computer or only view the computer desktop. This setting is enabled by default when Remote Assistance is enabled.

- **Set The Maximum Amount Of Time Invitations Can Remain Open** One way of initiating a Remote Assistance session is for the user to invite the support person to connect. This setting defines the validity period of the invitations. The default is 6 hours.

- **Create Invitations That Can Only Be Used From Computers Running Windows Vista Or Later**   Windows Vista and later versions of Windows use a superior method of encrypting Remote Assistance network traffic. It is advised to select this option if you are using Windows Vista and later on all support computers.

FIGURE 3-20 Configuring Remote Assistance advanced settings

ENABLING REMOTE DESKTOP

To enable Remote Desktop, on the Remote tab of the System Properties dialog box, select the Allow Remote Connections To This Computer check box. Then, optionally, select Only Allow Connections From Computers Running Remote Desktop With Network Level Authentication (Recommended), shown in Figure 3-19. This setting improves the security of the Remote Desktop network traffic between the management computer and the target computer.

Click Select Users. As shown in Figure 3-21, you can then add the users or groups that you want to have remote access to this computer by using Remote Desktop. You can also enable Remote Desktop by opening the Settings app, selecting System, and then selecting the Remote Desktop tab.

FIGURE 3-21 Configuring Remote Desktop users

EXAM TIP

When you enable Remote Assistance or Remote Desktop by using these methods, the corresponding Windows Defender Firewall setting is automatically configured to allow the selected app.

Configure Remote Assistance

After you have enabled Remote Assistance, you can configure and use this tool to help your users to administer and manage their computers remotely. There are two fundamental ways of initiating a Remote Assistance session: one is for the user to request assistance, and the other is for the support person to offer it.

REQUESTING HELP USING REMOTE ASSISTANCE

If a user is experiencing problems with her computer, she can request assistance from support personnel by using the Request Assistance feature of Remote Assistance. This is known as solicited remote assistance. To request assistance, the user must open Control Panel, select System And Security, and then click Launch Remote Assistance.

As shown in Figure 3-22, you can then choose between:

- **Invite Someone You Trust To Help You**   Choose this option if you require assistance.
- **Help Someone Who Has Invited You**   Choose this option if you can provide assistance.

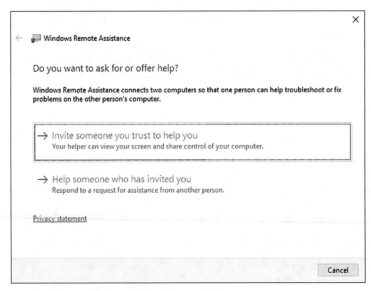

FIGURE 3-22 Requesting Windows Remote Assistance

To request help, click Invite Someone You Trust To Help You. You can then choose from among three options, as shown in Figure 3-23. These are:

- **Save This Invitation As A File**   Choose this option to create an RA Invitations file. These have a .msrclIncident file extension. You are prompted to save the request file. Store this file in a location that is accessible to the user from whom you are requesting help. Typically, this location will be a file server shared folder. After you have defined a save location, a dialog box appears with the password for the remote assistance session. Share this password with your helper. When your helper double-clicks the file you saved, she is prompted for the password, and then the Remote Assistance session begins.

- **Use Email To Send An Invitation**   If you choose this option, your default email program is opened by Remote Assistance, and the invitation file is automatically attached to an email message. You must enter the email address of the person you want to invite. When you send the message, the same dialog box appears containing the session password. Again, share this password with your helper. When your helper double-clicks the attached file in the email you sent, she is prompted for the password, and then the Remote Assistance session begins.

- **Use Easy Connect**   Easy Connect enables you to establish a Remote Assistance session without the need to use an invitation file. After you have established an Easy Connect session, you can save the name of the helper for future use, enabling you to receive remote assistance without the need to exchange a password.

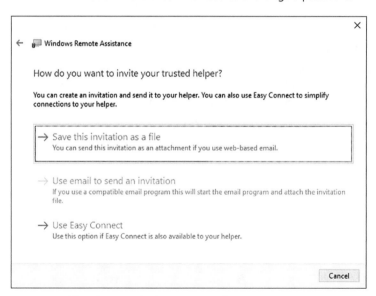

FIGURE 3-23 Choosing a method to request assistance

EXAM TIP

Easy Connect only works if both computers are running Windows 7 or later and if both computers have access to the global peer-to-peer network. This network can sometimes be inaccessible to users of computers that are placed behind network routers that do not support the Peer Name Resolution Protocol. This protocol is used to transfer Remote Assistance invitations over the Internet.

EXAM TIP

You can open the Windows Remote Assistance tool by running **Msra.exe** from the command line or the Windows Run dialog box.

OFFERING HELP WITH REMOTE ASSISTANCE

A user might not be in a position to request assistance. In these circumstances, an administrator can offer assistance. This is known as unsolicited remote assistance. To offer remote assistance, run **Msra.exe** and choose Help Someone Who Has Invited You. Then, on the Choose A Way To Connect To The Other Person's Computer page, click Advanced Connection Option For Help Desk, as shown in Figure 3-24.

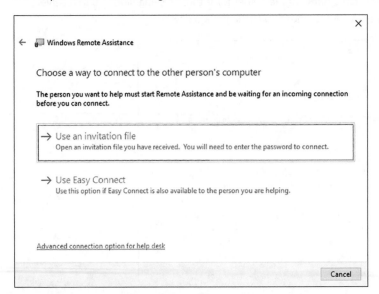

FIGURE 3-24 Offering Remote Assistance

On the Who Do You Want To Help page, in the Type A Computer Name Or IP Address box, as shown in Figure 3-25, type the relevant computer name or IP address of the computer that you want to send the offer of help to and then click Next.

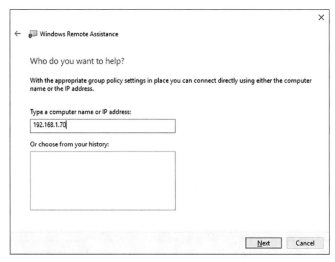

FIGURE 3-25 Offering Remote Assistance

The user on the target computer must accept your offer, and then the remote assistance session is initiated. This is often a useful way to start a remote assistance session, especially when you are attempting to support novice users.

CONFIGURING REMOTE ASSISTANCE WITH GPOS

Although you can configure the necessary settings for Remote Assistance manually on each computer, in an AD DS domain environment, it is easier to use GPOs to distribute the required settings. Table 3-10 shows the settings you can configure for Remote Assistance by using GPOs. To configure these settings, open Group Policy Management and locate the appropriate GPO. Open the GPO for editing and navigate to Computer Configuration > Policies > Administrative Templates > System > Remote Assistance.

TABLE 3-10 Configuring Remote Assistance with GPOs

POLICY SETTING	EXPLANATION
Allow Only Windows Vista Or Newer Connections	Enables Remote Assistance to generate invitations with more secure encryption. This setting does not affect Remote Assistance connections initiated by unsolicited offers or Remote Assistance.
Turn On Session Logging	Enables session logging. Logs are stored in the user's Documents folder in the Remote Assistance folder.
Turn On Bandwidth Optimization	Provides performance improvements in low-bandwidth situations. Adjust from No Optimization through Full Optimization.
Configure Solicited Remote Assistance	Enables solicited Remote Assistance on a computer. If you disable this setting, it prevents users from asking for Remote Assistance. You also can use this setting to configure invitation time limits and whether to allow remote control.
Configure Offer Remote Assistance	Enables unsolicited Remote Assistance on this computer.

USING REMOTE ASSISTANCE TO MANAGE A COMPUTER REMOTELY

After you have configured the desired settings and established a Remote Assistance session, you can perform the following tasks.

- **Request Control** Enables you to ask the remote user for permission to take remote control of their computer. They must allow you to do this. Remember also that the ability to gain remote control is a configurable option.

- **Chat** Enables you to open a chat window to communicate with the remote user. You can use this to explain what you are doing, or the remote user can use chat to discuss the details of their computer problem.

Using Microsoft Management Console (MMC) to manage remote computers

With both Remote Desktop and Remote Assistance, you use RDP to connect to a remote computer. After you establish a connection, you can perform any management task interactively just as if you were sitting at the remote computer. This is not the case with either MMC or Windows PowerShell remoting.

With MMC, you must enable the necessary remote management feature that you wish to exploit by modifying the Windows Defender Firewall configuration. Then you can use the appropriate management console snap-in and target the desired remote machine.

It is very easy to use MMC snap-ins to manage remote computers. Some management snap-ins enable you to specify additional computers to connect to from the console. As shown in Figure 3-26, you can right-click the uppermost node in the navigation pane and then click Connect To Another Computer.

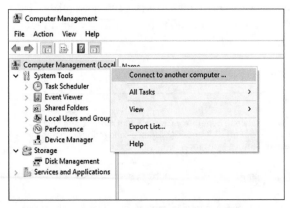

FIGURE 3-26 Connecting to another computer with MMC

If the management snap-in you want to use does not enable you to connect to additional computers, you can create a new management console by running **mmc.exe** and adding the appropriate snap-in to the empty console. When prompted, specify Another Computer, as shown in Figure 3-27.

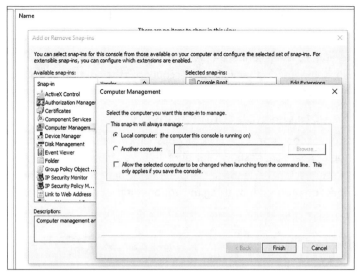

FIGURE 3-27 Connecting remotely with MMC

It is important to realize that the remote computer must recognize you. This means that you must authenticate your connection by using a username and password that have the necessary management rights on the target computer. This is simple in an AD DS domain environment because you can use domain admin credentials. However, in workgroup environments, this is trickier. Generally, you must be able to provide credentials of a member of the target computer's local Administrators group.

In addition to authentication, the necessary Windows Defender Firewall feature must be enabled. The available remote management features are

- Remote Assistance
- Remote Desktop
- Remote Event Log Management
- Remote Event Monitor
- Remote Scheduled Tasks Management
- Remote Service Management
- Remote Shut-down
- Remote Volume Management
- Virtual Machine Monitoring
- Windows Defender Firewall Remote Management
- Windows Management Instrumentation (WMI)
- Windows Remote Management
- Windows Remote Management (Compatibility)

After you have enabled the required remote management feature in Windows Defender Firewall and modified your MMC to connect to a remote computer using appropriate credentials, performing remote management is no different from performing local management.

Configure remote desktop access

After Remote Desktop is enabled on a computer, you can use the Remote Desktop Connection program to connect to the computer. When connected, you can use the computer as if locally signed in and perform all management tasks that your user account has the rights to perform. This makes using Remote Desktop particularly useful.

Creating and editing Remote Desktop connections

To create a Remote Desktop connection, from Start, click All Apps, click Windows Accessories, and then click Remote Desktop Connection. As shown in Figure 3-28, you must then specify the computer that you want to connect to. Use either a computer name or an IP address. You can configure additional connection properties by using the options discussed in Table 3-11.

TABLE 3-11 Configurable Remote Desktop Connection options

TAB	SETTINGS
General	■ Logon Settings: ■ Computer ■ Username ■ Allow Me To Save Credentials ■ Connection Settings: ■ Save ■ Save As ■ Open
Display	■ Display Configuration: ■ Small > Large ■ Use All My Monitors For The Remote Session ■ Colors: ■ Choose The Color Depth Of The Remote Session ■ Display The Connection Bar When I Use Full Screen
Local Resources	■ Remote Audio: ■ Remote Audio Playback: ■ Play On This Computer ■ Do Not Play ■ Play On Remote Computer ■ Remote Audio Recording: ■ Record From This Computer ■ Do Not Record ■ Keyboard, Apply Windows Key Combinations: ■ Only When Using The Full Screen ■ On This Computer ■ On The Remote Computer ■ Local Devices And Resources: ■ Printers ■ Clipboard

(Continued)

TAB	SETTINGS
	■ Smart Cards ■ Ports ■ Drives ■ Other Supported Plug And Play (Pnp) Devices
Experience	■ Performance: ■ Modem (56 kbps) ■ Low-Speed Broadband (256 Kbps–2 Mbps) ■ Satellite (2 Mbps–16 Mbps With High Latency) ■ High-Speed Broadband (2Mbps–10 Mbps) ■ WAN (10 Mpbs Or Higher) ■ Detect Connection Quality Automatically ■ Persistent Bitmap Caching ■ Reconnect If The Connection Is Dropped
Advanced	■ Server Authentication, If Server Authentication Fails: ■ Connect And Don't Warn Me ■ Warn Me ■ Do Not Connect ■ Connect From Anywhere: ■ Connection Settings: ■ Automatically Detect RD Gateway Server Settings ■ Use These RD Gateway Server Settings ■ Do Not Use An RD Gateway Server ■ Log-on Settings: ■ Username ■ Use My RD Gateway Credentials For The Remote Computer

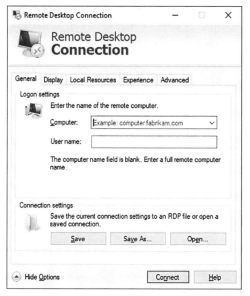

FIGURE 3-28 Creating a Remote Desktop connection

When you have finished configuring the connection, from the General tab, click Connect. You can also choose to save your configuration to a .rdp file for subsequent use.

Customizing Remote Desktop settings from the command line

You can open the Remote Desktop Connection app by running Mstsc.exe from the command line or the Windows Run dialog box. The **Mstsc.exe** command also enables administrators to launch the tool, with several parameters configured.

The default firewall port that Remote Desktop uses is 3389, and this needs to allow RDP traffic through for Remote Desktop to work. If an administrator changes the firewall port for RDP traffic, the revised port number must be specified in the command-line tool **Mstsc.exe** when launching the application.

The syntax for mstsc is

```
mstsc [<connection file>] [/v:<server[:port]>] [/admin] [/f[ullscreen]] [/w:<width>]
[/h:<height>] [/public] | [/span] [/multimon] [/edit "connection file"]
[/restrictedAdmin] [/remoteGuard] [/prompt] [/shadow:sessionID> [/control]
[/noConsentPrompt]] [/?]
```

The list of command-line parameters for Remote Desktop Connection are shown in Table 3-12.

TABLE 3-12 Command-line parameters for Remote Desktop Connection

PARAMETER	DESCRIPTION
<connection file>	Specifies the name of a .rdp file for the connection.
/v:<Server[:<Port>]	Specifies the remote computer to which you want to connect.
/admin	This parameter is used to connect you to a session for the administration of a Remote Desktop Session Host server (The RD Session Host role service must be installed on the remote server).
/edit <"connection file">	Opens the specified .rdp file for editing.
/f	Starts Remote Desktop Connection in full-screen mode.
/w:<Width>	Specifies the width of the Remote Desktop window.
/h:<Height>	Specifies the height of the Remote Desktop window.
/public	Runs the Remote Desktop in public mode where passwords and bitmaps are not cached.
/span	This enables the Remote Desktop width and height to be matched with the local virtual desktop, spanning across multiple monitors if necessary.
/multimon	Configures the Remote Desktop session monitor layout to render it identical to the client configuration.

(Continued)

PARAMETER	DESCRIPTION
/restrictedAdmin	Connects to the remote PC or server in Restricted Administration mode, which prevents login credentials being sent to the remote PC or server. Functionality and or compatibility may be impacted as the connection is made as local administrator.
/remoteGuard	Utilizes Remote Guard to protect the connection. No credentials are sent to the remote device; however, full access is provided.
/shadow:sessionID	Allows you to specify the SessionID to which you wish to connect.
/control	Allows control of the remote session.
/noConsentPrompt	Allows the connection to continue without user consent.
/?	Lists the available parameters.

Configuring Remote Desktop with GPOs

Just as with Remote Assistance, although you can configure Remote Desktop settings manually on each computer, in an AD DS domain environment, it makes sense to configure these settings with GPOs. Table 3-13 contains the configurable GPO settings for Remote Desktop. To configure these settings, open Group Policy Management and locate the appropriate GPO. Open the GPO for editing and navigate to Computer Configuration \ Policies \ Administrative Templates \ Windows Components \ Remote Desktop Services.

TABLE 3-13 Configuring Remote Desktop with GPOs

POLICY SETTING	EXPLANATION
Remote Desktop Connection Client \Do Not Allow Passwords To Be Saved	Determines whether users can save passwords on this computer from Remote Desktop Services clients.
Remote Desktop Connection Client \Prompt For Credentials On Client Computer	If enabled, a user is prompted to provide credentials for a remote connection to a Remote Desktop server on their client computer rather than on the Remote Desktop server.
Remote Desktop Session Host\Connections \Allow Users To Connect Remotely By Using Remote Desktop Services	If enabled, users that belong to the Remote Desktop Users group on the target computer can connect remotely to the target computer, using Remote Desktop Services.
Remote Desktop Session Host \Device And Resource Redirection	You use these settings to specify whether to allow or prevent data redirection from local devices (such as audio and clipboard) to the remote client in a Remote Desktop Services session.
Remote Desktop Session Host\Security \Set Client Connection Encryption Level	If enabled, all communications between clients and Remote Desktop servers is encrypted, using the encryption method specified. By default, the encryption level is set to High.
Remote Desktop Session Host \Session Time Limits	These policies control session time limits for disconnected, idle, and active sessions and whether to terminate sessions when specified limits are reached.

Troubleshooting Remote Desktop Connections

Remote Desktop is a powerful tool for administrators that enables them to manage PCs and servers within the enterprise. Some common problems encountered when trying to connect to a remote PC using Remote Desktop, and their resolution, are listed in Table 3-14.

TABLE 3-14 Troubleshooting Remote Desktop Connections

PROBLEM	POSSIBLE RESOLUTION
The remote PC can't be found.	<ul><li>Make sure you have the correct PC name.</li><li>Try using the IP address of the remote PC.</li></ul>
There's a problem with the network.	<ul><li>Ensure that the router is turned on (home networks only).</li><li>Make sure that the Ethernet cable is plugged into your network adapter (wired networks only).</li><li>See that the wireless switch on the PC is turned on (devices using wireless networks only).</li><li>Make sure your network adapter is functional.</li></ul>
The Remote Desktop port might be blocked by a firewall.	<ul><li>Contact your system administrator to check that Remote Desktop is not blocked.</li><li>Allow the Remote Desktop application through Windows Firewall.</li><li>Make sure the port for Remote Desktop (usually 3389) is open.</li></ul>
Remote connections might not be set up on the remote PC.	<ul><li>In the System Properties dialog box, under Remote Desktop, select the Allow Remote Connections To This Computer button.</li></ul>
The remote PC might only enable PCs that have Network Level Authentication set up to connect.	<ul><li>Upgrade to Windows 7, Windows 8 or Windows 8.1, or Windows 10, which support Network Level Authentication.</li></ul>
The remote PC might be turned off.	<ul><li>You can't connect to a PC that's turned off, asleep, or hibernating.</li><li>Turn on the remote PC.</li></ul>

Enable PowerShell Remoting

Although using Windows PowerShell cmdlets can sometimes seem daunting, they do offer a convenient and quick way of configuring many machines more quickly than by using a graphical tool. In addition, through the use of scripting, you can use Windows PowerShell to complete frequently performed management tasks.

Using Windows PowerShell to manage remote computers is referred to as *Windows PowerShell remoting*, but before you can use Windows PowerShell remoting, you must know how to enable and configure it.

Windows PowerShell is ubiquitous across the Windows platform, appearing in both Windows 10 and Windows Server. Therefore, using Windows PowerShell to perform management tasks on both local and remote computers makes sense because you can transfer those skills to other management and administration situations.

Many cmdlets in Windows PowerShell can be used with a **-ComputerName** parameter, making the use of the command remotely no more complex than specifying the name of the computer you want to run the command against. For example, to determine the IP configuration of a computer, you can run the following command.

```
Get-NetIPConfiguration -computername LON-CL1
```

However, not all cmdlets accept the **-ComputerName** parameter, and for these, you must enable and configure Windows PowerShell remoting. The function of Windows PowerShell remoting is to enable you to connect to one or several remote computers and execute one or more cmdlets or scripts on those remote computers and return the results to your local computer.

Although Windows PowerShell remoting is enabled by default on Windows Server 2016, you must manually enable it on Windows 10. To do this, complete one of the following procedures.

- If necessary, start the Windows Remote Management service. You must also enable Windows Remote Management through the Windows Defender Firewall. As shown in Figure 3-29, you can do this by running the **winrm quickconfig** command at an elevated command prompt. When prompted, press **Y** and Enter twice.

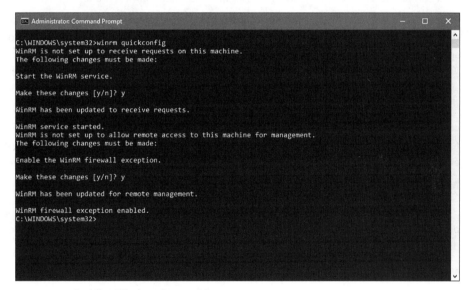

FIGURE 3-29 Enabling Windows Remote Management

> **NOTE** **WINRM QUICKCONFIG AND THE PUBLIC NETWORK LOCATION PROFILE**
>
> If one of your network connections is assigned the Public network location profile, this command fails, and you must manually configure the Windows Defender Firewall exceptions.

- Alternatively, to enable Windows PowerShell remoting, you can run the **enable-PSremoting -force** cmdlet from a Windows PowerShell (Admin) window.

EXAM TIP

Windows Remote Management uses HTTP. By default, both Windows Remote Management and Windows PowerShell remoting use TCP port 5985 for incoming unencrypted communications and TCP port 5986 for incoming encrypted communications.

NEED MORE REVIEW? **ENABLE-PSREMOTING**

To review further details about enabling Windows PowerShell remoting, refer to the Microsoft website at *https://docs.microsoft.com/en-gb/powershell/module/Microsoft.PowerShell.Core/ Enable-PSRemoting?view=powershell-5.1.*

Using Windows PowerShell to manage remote computers

After you have enabled Windows PowerShell remoting, you can use Windows PowerShell cmdlets and scripts to manage the remote computer in virtually the same way that you manage local computers. However, you must first establish a connection with the remote computer.

After you have established a connection, you can run any cmdlets or scripts against the remote machine. When you connect to the remote computer and run a remote command against it, the command is transmitted across the network and run on the remote computer. The results are sent back to your local computer and displayed in your Windows PowerShell window.

One way to establish a remote connection and run a command is to use the **invoke-command** cmdlet. You can also use the **Invoke-command** cmdlet to establish a temporary remote connection. For example, the following command retrieves the contents of the system event log from the remote computer LON-CL1.

```
Invoke-Command -ComputerName LON-CL1 -ScriptBlock {Get-EventLog -log system}
```

If you intend to run several cmdlets, or to run more complex scripts, it is useful to establish a persistent connection to the remote computer. Use the **New-PSWorkflowSession** cmdlet to do this. For example:

```
$s = New-PSWorkflowSession -ComputerName LON-CL1
```

You can now use the **Enter-PSSession** command to establish the persistent connection.

```
Enter-PSSession $s
```

You will now have a Windows PowerShell prompt that looks like this.

```
[LON-CL1]: PS C:\>
```

Any commands that you run in this session run on the LON-CL1 computer. The session remains active until you close with the **exit-PSSession** command.

You can also use these commands to establish remote connections with multiple computers. For example, to connect simultaneously to computers called LON-CL1 and LON-CL2, use the following command.

```
$s = New-PSSession -ComputerName LON-CL1, LON-CL2
```

Next, run the remote Windows PowerShell cmdlets against the new session.

```
Invoke-Command -Session $s -ScriptBlock { Get-EventLog -log system }
```

You can run any Windows PowerShell command remotely in this way.

> **NEED MORE REVIEW?** **AN INTRODUCTION TO POWERSHELL REMOTING: PART ONE**
>
> To review further details about using Windows PowerShell remoting, refer to the Microsoft website at *https://blogs.technet.microsoft.com/heyscriptingguy/2012/07/23 /an-introduction-to-powershell-remoting-part-one/.*

Thought experiments

In these thought experiments, demonstrate your skills and knowledge of the topics covered in this chapter. You can find the answers to these thought experiments in the next section.

Scenario 1

You have been hired to deploy Windows 10 at a new office for Adatum Corporation. The office was a greenfield site with no computer infrastructure and has just had all the network cabling and wireless infrastructure installed by a contractor. You must help plan and implement networking services at the new location and verify that all equipment is working on the network.

As a consultant for Adatum, answer the following questions about networking.

1. You connected a number of devices to the wireless APs in the new building. They seem to be connected, but you want to verify that they can communicate with each other. Is it true that the **Test-Connection** Windows PowerShell cmdlet is the equivalent of the **Ping** command-line tool?

2. You want to be able to view the current network configuration of the installed laptops in the new building. Which of the following commands enable you to do this?

   A. Ping

   B. Tracert

   C. NSlookup

   D. IPconfig

   E. Get-NetIPAddress

   F. Netsh

3. You are troubleshooting name resolution to the LON-DC1 domain controller. You suspect a problem might reside with the configured DNS server that was just installed at the site. If you create an entry for LON-DC1 in the local hosts file of a test computer running Windows 10, which is used first, the DNS server or the local resolver cache?

4. You have been asked to set up a VPN solution for some users who want to work from home. Which VPN tunneling protocols can you use with Windows 10?

5. You notice that one of your computers has an IPv4 address that starts 169.254. What could this mean?

Scenario 2

You work in support at Adatum Corporation. Many of your users work in small branch offices. Some work from home, using work laptops. It is important for you to be able to manage these users' computers remotely. As a consultant for Adatum, answer the following questions about remote management in the Adatum organization.

1. One of your users telephones the help desk, requiring assistance with an application. They need to know how to perform a grammar check with Microsoft Word 2016. They are not very experienced and, despite your best efforts and explanation of how the process works, they are still confused. What remote management tool might you consider using in this situation?

2. Another user calls the help desk. They've lost a file and need you to locate it. They're due to leave the office for a conference this afternoon, and they tell you that's the best time for you to resolve the issue. What remote management tool would you use?

3. You try to connect to this user's computer later that afternoon, but despite knowing that the necessary Windows Firewall settings are configured, you cannot connect. Why?

4. You want to use Windows PowerShell remoting. You try to connect to a remote machine but are unsuccessful. What steps must you perform on the remote machine before Windows PowerShell remoting can work?

Thought experiment answers

This section provides the solutions for the tasks included in the thought experiment.

Scenario 1

1. Yes, the **Test-Connection** Windows PowerShell cmdlet is the equivalent of the Ping command-line tool.

2. The **IPconfig**, **Get-NetIPAddress**, and **Netsh** commands enable you to view the network configuration of computers running Windows 10.

3. The DNS resolver cache is checked before a DNS server is petitioned.

4. You can use the following VPN tunneling protocols: Point-to-Point Tunneling Protocol (PPTP), Layer Two Tunneling Protocol with IPsec (L2TP/IPsec), Secure Socket Tunneling Protocol (SSTP), or Internet Key Exchange version 2 (IKEv2).

5. It means that the device is configured to obtain an IPv4 address automatically and has been unable to obtain an IPv4 configuration from a DHCP server. This might be because the DHCP server is offline or because an insufficient number of addresses are available on the server.

Scenario 2

1. Using Remote Assistance would enable you to demonstrate how to perform the grammar check. You could take remote control of the user's computer and show them the procedure.

2. Remote Desktop is the most suitable tool. Remote Assistance requires the interaction of the user to accept your connection request and, initially, to invite you to help. Remote Desktop requires no invitations and does not require the remote user to assist you in connecting.

3. The most likely reason you can't connect is that Remote Desktop users must be granted access in addition to the Windows Firewall configuration changes being made.

4. You must start the Windows Remote Management service and reconfigure the Windows Firewall, and then Windows PowerShell remoting must be enabled. You can perform these steps by running either **winrm quickconfig** or by running **enable-PSremoting**.

Chapter Summary

- Each device on a network requires a unique IPv4 and, optionally, IPv6 configuration.

- Windows 10-based network devices use name resolution to change names in IP addresses for network communications.

- Windows 10 supports four commonly used VPN protocols. These are Point-to-Point Tunneling Protocol (PPTP), Layer 2 Tunneling Protocol (L2TP), Secure Socket Tunneling Protocol (SSTP), and Internet Key Exchange, Version 2 (IKEv2).

- Windows 10 uses common authentication protocols including EAP-MS-CHAPv2, PAP, CHAP and MS-CHAP v2.

- VPN Reconnect is a feature supported when using IKEv2, which enables VPN connections to be automatically re-established if they are broken. VPN Reconnect uses the IKEv2 tunneling protocol with the MOBIKE extension.

- Always On, App-triggered VPN, and LockDown VPN profiles are new VPN features in Windows 10 that enable administrators to implement enterprise-grade VPN requirements.

- Wi-Fi Direct enables Windows 10 devices to interact with other hardware, such as printers, TVs, PCs, and gaming devices, such as Xbox One.
- Windows 10 provides a number of tools that you can use to help troubleshoot networking issues.
- You can choose from a number of management tools to perform remote management.
- To configure and enable remote management settings, you must first modify the Windows Firewall configuration.
- Remote Assistance and Quick Assist can be used to view or take remote control of a remote user's computer.
- Both Remote Desktop and Remote Assistance can be configured manually or by using GPOs.
- Windows PowerShell remoting enables you to perform remote management of any Windows 10-based computer with Windows PowerShell.
- Management console snap-ins support both local and remote connections.

CHAPTER 4

Maintain Windows

After you have deployed computers within your organization, it is necessary for you to maintain those computers. If users experience problems with their computers, you might be required to perform system recovery. If users have lost files, you might be called upon to recover those missing files.

Computers typically do not remain in the same state throughout their use. In most organizations, computers are updated periodically. With the new Windows as a Service model for feature updates, you must be aware of how and when Windows Updates are applied. You might also need to know how to manage updates, and in certain circumstances, troubleshoot the application of updates.

Finally, even in normal circumstances, it is necessary to monitor your users' computers. This might be to help to ensure the ongoing reliable use of those computers. This chapter covers those aspects of the *MD-100 Windows 10* exam that relate to Windows 10 monitoring and maintenance.

Skills covered in this chapter:

- Skill 4.1: Configure system and data recovery
- Skill 4.2: Manage updates
- Skill 4.3: Monitor and manage Windows

Skill 4.1: Configure system and data recovery

In this section, you review how to configure system and data recovery options for Windows 10. If you have experience with an earlier version of Windows, you might be familiar with many of the options because some are included in Windows 10. To prepare for the exam, it is recommended that you work through all the wizards and tools to ensure that you're comfortable with each process, paying particular attention to the newer features, tools, and options.

> **This skill covers how to:**
> - Perform file recovery
> - Recover Windows 10
> - Troubleshoot the startup process

Perform file recovery

Windows 10 provides a number of tools that you or your users can use to recover files. These tools include:

- Windows Backup and Restore (Windows 7)
- WBAdmin
- File History
- Previous Versions

Use Windows Backup And Restore

Windows 10 includes the Backup And Restore (Windows 7) tool, which allows the creation of backups of your data. This backup feature was not included in Windows 8, but it has returned in Windows 10 to enable users who might have upgraded from Windows 7 to this version to restore data contained in Windows 7 system image backups.

In addition to restoring files and folders, you can also use this tool to create backups of files contained in folders, libraries, and whole disk volumes.

You cannot save your backups to the disk on which Windows 10 is installed, so you must provide another location, such as an external USB drive, network drive, or non-system local disk. To launch the Backup And Restore (Windows 7) tool in the GUI, open the System And Security section of Control Panel or use the Backup And Restore (Windows 7) item listed in the Settings app.

To create a backup of your files and folders and a system image, follow these steps:

1. Open the Settings app, and then click Update & Security.
2. In the navigation pane, click Backup, and in the details pane, click Go To Backup And Restore (Windows 7).
3. In the Backup And Restore (Windows 7) window, click Set Up Backup.
4. On the Select Where You Want To Save Your Backup page, choose the location and click Next.
5. On the What Do You Want To Back Up page, click Let Windows Choose (Recommended) and click Next.
6. On the Review Your Backup Settings page, click Change Schedule.
7. On the How Often Do You Want To Back Up page, leave the Run Backup On A Schedule (Recommended) check box selected and, if necessary, modify the backup schedule.
8. Click OK.
9. On the Review Your Backup Settings page, click Save Settings And Run Backup.

The backup begins, and you see the progress bar as shown in Figure 4-1. The first backup takes the longest time because it is a full backup. Subsequent backups are incremental and can take only a few minutes to complete.

When the backup is complete, use the links on the Backup And Restore (Windows 7) page to see the size of the backup on disk, edit the schedule, and manage the disk space the Backup And Restore (Windows 7) tool uses.

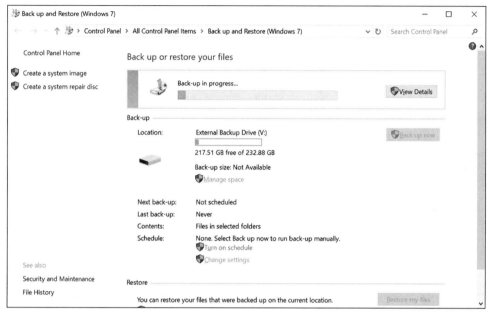

FIGURE 4-1 Backup and Restore (Windows 7)

When backing up your system, you can opt for the recommended settings, which create a backup of all files and folders in your user profile (including libraries) as well as a system image. The system image files are large, likely to be approximately 10 GB in size. You can specify the frequency and time when Windows 10 performs backups or retain the default backup schedule of Sunday at 7 PM every week.

If you require more specific scheduling, you can modify the triggers in the AutomaticBackup job in Task Scheduler after you have enabled scheduled backups. Available options to trigger a scheduled backup include:

- On A Schedule
- At Logon
- At Startup
- On Idle
- On An Event

- At Task Creation/Modification

- On Connection/Disconnect To A User Session

- On Workstation Lock/Unlock

If you want to choose specific libraries and folders for the backup manually, select Let Me Choose on the What Do You Want To Back Up page when initially setting up the backup. Although you cannot select individual files for backup, you can clear the check box to include a system image of the drive.

The Backup And Restore (Windows 7) tool uses the Volume Shadow Copy Service (VSS) to create the backups. The initial backup creates a block-level backup of the files to the backup file and uses the virtual hard disk (.vhdx) file format. VSS greatly enhances the performance of the backup operation because subsequent backups only copy the data that has changed since the previous backup, which is typically a smaller amount of data, thus creating the incremental backup much faster.

Each time you run a backup, the Backup And Restore (Windows 7) tool creates a new restore point, which the Previous Versions feature in File Explorer can use (and is covered later in this chapter).

> **NOTE BACKUP NTFS ONLY**
>
> The Backup And Restore (Windows 7) tool can only be used to back up data that is stored on file system volumes formatted as NTFS.

To restore libraries, folders, or files from a backup, you can use the Restore My Files link in the lower-right of the Backup And Restore (Windows 7) screen. You can select which backup set to use and restore items to their original locations or to different locations. To restore data from a backup, use these steps.

1. On the Backup And Restore (Windows 7) page, click Restore My Files.

2. The Restore Files dialog box presents you with access to the latest backup. If you want to choose an alternative backup, click Choose A Different Date, select the correct backup, and click OK.

3. Locate the files or folders you intend to restore by using one of the three options for you to find your files to recover.

   - **Search**   Type part of the name of the file you intend to restore. Click the file or Select All to restore all the found files. Click OK. (The search speed is very fast.)

   - **Browse For Files**   Click the backup name with the correct date and time stamp and browse to the folder that contains the items you want. Select the items and click Add Files.

   - **Browse For Folders**   Click the backup name with the correct date and time stamp and browse to the folder that you want. Select the folder and click Add Folder.

   You can choose multiple files and folders and use any of the three options or combinations of the options to locate the items you want.

4. Click Next.

5. On the Where Do You Want To Restore Your Files page, choose to restore to the original location or browse and select a different location.

6. If you restore an item to a location that contains the same item name, you are prompted to choose one of the following.

   - **Copy And Replace** The item restored from the backup overwrites the item in the destination location.

   - **Don't Copy** Nothing changes, and no item is restored.

   - **Copy, But Keep Both Files** The original items remain as is, and the file name of the restored item is modified to show it is a version of the same item.

   - **Do This For All Conflicts** If you're restoring multiple items, you can apply the same choice to each conflict.

7. When the restoration is complete, the Your Files Have Been Restored page appears, and you can click the link to View Restored Files.

8. Click Finish.

Perform a backup and restore with WBAdmin

In addition to the Backup And Restore (Windows 7) tool, Windows 10 includes another backup tool, the Windows Backup tool, which you can use from a command line. This tool is also found in Windows Server and is useful if you need to automate or create a backup job on several computers. Use the **WBAdmin.exe** command to create, configure, and restore backup jobs. In this section, you review some of the commonly used applications for WBAdmin.

BACKING UP USING WBADMIN

The Windows 10 version of WBAdmin is a simplified version of the utility that is available with the Microsoft Server operating systems and offers some of the low-level features such as the generation of index listings of all files and folders within an image data file. To perform a recovery using WBAdmin, you must be a member of the Backup Operators group or the Administrators group, or you must have been delegated the appropriate permissions. You must also run **WBAdmin** from an elevated command prompt. A number of the subcommands are not supported in Windows 10, and you must boot to Windows RE to perform a restore operation of data that was created using the WBAdmin Start Backup subcommand.

Table 4-1 lists the command-line syntax of WBAdmin.exe.

TABLE 4-1 WBAdmin.exe command-line syntax

COMMAND	DESCRIPTION
Wbadmin get versions	Lists the details of backups available from the local computer or from a specified computer.
Wbadmin enable backup	Configures and enables a regularly scheduled backup.
Wbadmin start backup	Runs a one-time backup; if used with no parameters, it uses the settings from the daily backup schedule.
Wbadmin get items	Lists the items included in a backup.
Wbadmin start recovery	Runs a recovery of the volumes, applications, files, or folders specified. Supported only in a Windows Recovery Environment (RE).

> **NEED MORE REVIEW?** **WBADMIN COMMAND LINE REFERENCE**
>
> You can find additional detailed information relating to WBAdmin by typing **WBAdmin /?**
> at the command prompt. The content provided in this section should be sufficient for your
> exam preparation, and if required, you can find additional WBAdmin resources on the
> Windows IT Pro Center at *https://docs.microsoft.com/en-us/windows-server/administration/*
> *windows-commands/wbadmin*.

For example, if you connect a removable hard drive to your computer that uses the drive
letter E, the following examples guide you through the process of performing a backup and
restore using the WBAdmin command-line tool.

To back up the entire contents of the C drive to a backup drive located on E, follow these
steps.

1. Open an elevated command prompt.

2. Type the following command.

   ```
   WBAdmin start backup -BackupTarget:E: -Include:C:
   ```

3. Type **Y** to begin the backup operation.

   The tool creates a shadow copy of the volume and then creates a block copy of the
   volume, as shown in Figure 4-2. A simple log file relating to the operation is created, and
   this is stored in C:\Windows\Logs\WindowsBackup\.

The WBAdmin utility saves the image backup in a WindowsImageBackup folder on the
target drive.

After you have created a backup, you can list backup images created on the system by using
the following command.

```
WBAdmin get versions -backupTarget:E:
```

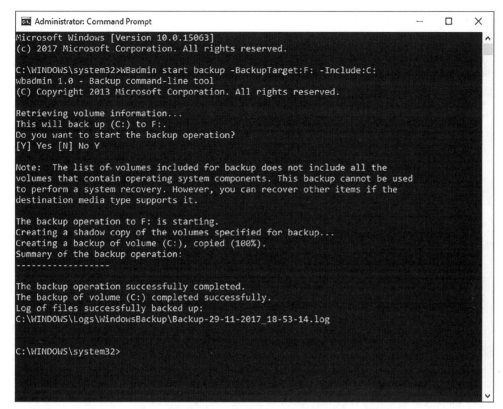

FIGURE 4-2 WBAdmin Command-Line Tool

RESTORING DATA USING WBADMIN

To recover from a backup that you have previously created with WBAdmin, boot to a Windows RE Command Prompt, and type **WBAdmin get versions backuptarget:d:** to provide the version information of the available backups. (You might need to change the drive letter to correspond to your system). For example, to recover a backup of volume E from May 31, 2017, at 17:12, type the following command at a command prompt and then press Enter.

```
WBAdmin start recovery -version:05/31/2017-17:12 -itemType:Volume -items:\\?\
Volume{a6f2e427-0000-0000-0000-501f00000000}\ -BackupTarget:D: -RecoveryTarget:E:
```

> **NOTE** **DRIVE LETTERS MIGHT VARY**
>
> The WBAdmin start recovery command is only supported in Windows RE and not in a normal Windows 10 administrative command prompt. Be careful because the drive letters of the mounted volumes can be different in Windows RE from those in Windows 10. You might need to replace the drive letters in your WBAdmin start recovery options.

Configure File History

File History is a file recovery method that provides users with a very easy and user-friendly method of retrieving files after they have been accidently deleted or modified. Once enabled, File History will automatically create a backup of all user files that have been modified on an hourly schedule. So long as the backup destination location does not become full, the File History can continue to store changes indefinitely.

To turn on File History, follow these steps:

1. Launch Settings, click Update & Security, and select Backup.
2. Click the Plus (+) icon labeled Add A Drive.
3. File History will search for drives.
4. In the Select A Drive dialog box, select the external hard drive that you want to use for File History.
5. On the Back Up Using File History page, verify that the Automatically Back Up My Files toggle is On.

Once enabled, File History will save copies of your files for the first time. This will happen as a background operation, and you can continue to work normally.

File History saves your files from your user profile and all the folders located in your libraries, including OneDrive, that are synced to your device if OneDrive is used. You can manually include or exclude folders on the Backup Options page. To manually include additional folders to be monitored by File History, you need to perform the following steps:

1. Open Settings, click Update & Security, and select Backup.
2. Click the More Options link.
3. On the Backup Options page, click Add A Folder.
4. Select the folder that you want to back up and click Choose This Folder as shown in Figure 4-3.
5. Ensure that the folder is listed in the list of folders under Back Up These Folders.
6. Close the Backup Options page.

There are two other methods for adding a folder to the File History list of folders:

- **Add folders to one of the existing libraries already backed up by File History**   File History will protect these folders.

- **Use File Explorer**   Select the folder, click History in the Home ribbon, and then click the Include It In Future Backups link.

You can configure many of the File History settings multiple ways, and you need to be familiar with each of them:

- File History in Control Panel
- Backup within the Settings app
- History item on the File Explorer ribbon

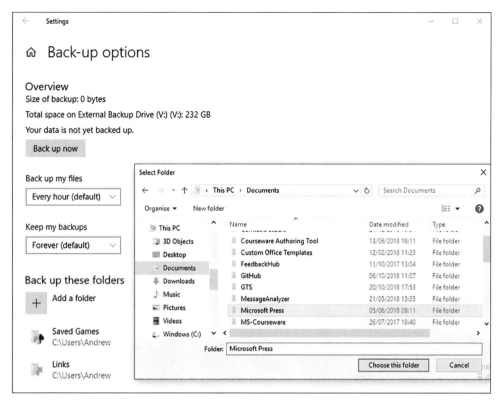

FIGURE 4-3 Configure File History Backup Options

Within the advanced settings screen of File History, accessed from the See Advanced Settings link on the Backup Options page, you configure the following:

- Modify the frequency of the File History backup from every 10 minutes to daily.
- Share the backup drive to other HomeGroup members.
- Open File History event logs to view recent events or errors.
- Define the length of time to keep saved versions of your files.
- Manually clean up older versions of files and folders contained in the backup to recover space on the backup drive. You could also use the command line tool FhManagew.exe to delete file versions based on their age stored on the File History target device.

> **NOTE   FILE HISTORY RESTORE POINTS**
>
> Previous Versions is a feature that uses the File History restore points and allows you to select one of the file version histories; it is accessed within File Explorer. Previous Versions is covered later in this chapter.

FILE HISTORY FILE RECOVERY

You can launch File History file recovery, as shown in Figure 4-4, in several ways:

- **History icon**   Open File Explorer and navigate to the folder that contains a modified or deleted file, and then click History on the Home ribbon. The File History page will open, and you can view the recoverable files.

- **Restore personal files**   Open File History in Control Panel and select the Restore Personal Files link on the left side.

- **Restore files from a current backup**   The Restore Files From A Current Backup link is at the bottom of the page within the following location: Settings\Update & security\ Backup\More options\Backup Options.

FIGURE 4-4 Restore your personal files using File History

When the File History page is in view, you can navigate through each restore point by using the left and right arrow buttons. Each restore point has a date and time to help you decide which version of the file or files to restore. You can select one or more files to revert and select which version of the file by navigating through the backups that have been made by File History. If you right-click the file or folder, you can preview the file to view the contents. If you want to proceed to recover the file, click the green button on the File History screen. The file or files selected will be restored, and File Explorer will open with the restored files displayed.

FILE HISTORY SUPPORT FOR ENCRYPTION

Protecting files and folders using Encrypting File System (EFS) is supported on NTFS when using Windows 10 Pro and Windows 10 Enterprise versions. File History supports backing up files that are encrypted using the EFS so long as the drive selected for the backup is formatted as a NTFS volume. Without NTFS, data cannot be encrypted using EFS. Therefore, if the destination drive does not use NTFS, File History will not back up encrypted files.

If you use BitLocker Drive Encryption to protect your data on your PC and use File History to back up this data to a removable drive, the data will no longer be protected. You should consider enabling BitLocker To Go on the removable drive to protect the contents. The File History is designed to back up on a per-user basis and is performed using the local user account, which means only files and folders that you have access to will be backed up.

> **NOTE TURN OFF FILE HISTORY**
>
> There is only one Group Policy Object (GPO) relating to File History, located at Computer Configuration\Administrative Templates\Windows Components\File History\Turn off File History. When enabled, File History cannot be turned on.

Restore previous versions of files and folders

Previous Versions has been reintroduced in Windows 10 and is a file and folder feature that enables users to view, revert, or recover files that have been modified or deleted by mistake. Previous Versions uses the File History feature or restore points created during backups in Backup And Restore (Windows 7). One of these features must be configured to use the Previous Versions feature.

After you have enabled File History or created a Backup And Restore (Windows 7) backup, you need to browse in File Explorer to the location where the modified or deleted files are stored. If one of these methods has "protected" the file or folders being browsed, the Previous Versions tab shown in File Explorer will list the available restore points for your data. Until one of these tasks has been performed, the Previous Versions tab will be empty.

VSS is used by Previous Versions to monitor and preserve copies of modified files on an automatic schedule. Earlier in the chapter, you saw that the Backup And Restore (Windows 7) tool also creates a restore point each time you create a backup. After the initial File History restore point has been created, subsequent restore points may take only a few minutes to complete.

> **NOTE PREVIOUS VERSIONS RESTORE POINTS**
>
> In the Previous Versions tab, a message is displayed, which states that the previous versions come from File History and restore points. The Previous Versions feature uses the restore points that are created by the Backup And Restore (Windows 7) tool and not the restore points that System Restore creates.

If you configure File History and also use the Backup And Restore (Windows 7) tool, multiple restore points will be available in the Previous Versions tab. The Previous Versions feature is available on all file systems if File History is used. The Backup And Restore (Windows 7) can only be used to back up data using New Technology File System (NTFS) volumes.

To revert files to a previous version, use the following steps:

1. Ensure that File History is turned on.
2. Create a folder on your computer, for example, **C:\Travel Plans\York**, and then create or save a text file called **Things to do** in the folder.

3. In File History, click Run Now.

4. Open Things to do, modify the contents, save, and exit the file.

5. In File History, click Run Now.

6. Right-click Things to do and select Restore Previous Versions.

7. On the Previous Versions tab, note that the Things to do.txt file has one previous version listed, which is the original file. Modify the file again. There will not be another Previous Version listed until the next Restore Point is created by File History.

8. To manually create a new Restore Point, return to File History and click Run Now. Return to the Things to do file and notice that it now has two file versions listed, as shown in Figure 4-5.

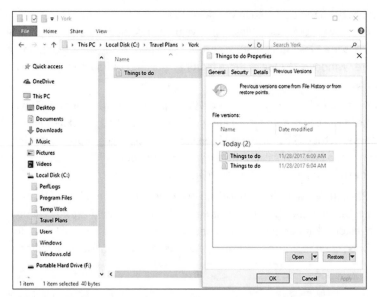

FIGURE 4-5 Restore previous versions of files and folders in File Explorer

9. Delete the Things to do.txt file.

10. To recover the last version of the file that was saved by File History, right-click the C:\Travel Plans\York folder and select Restore Previous Versions.

11. On the Previous Versions tab, select the Travel Plans folder, click the drop-down Open menu item, and select Open In File History.

12. File History launches. Double-click the folder that contained the deleted file.

13. Select the deleted file, and choose the green restore button.

14. Verify that the Things to do file has been restored to the C:\Travel Plans\York folder.

Recover files from OneDrive

OneDrive allows you to store your files online. You can sync files between your PC and One-Drive. You can access files from OneDrive.com from just about any device that is connected to the Internet. You can use the OneDrive Recycle Bin to recover files that you accidentally delete from your OneDrive account.

The OneDrive Recycle Bin can retain deleted items for between three and 30 days, if you are signing in using your Microsoft account. If you sign in with your Office365 account, deleted items are retained for up to 93 days. The actual retention period is dependent on the size of the Recycle Bin which is set to 10 percent of the total storage limit by default. If the Recycle Bin is full, old items will be deleted to make room for new items as they are added to the Recycle Bin and this may have an impact on the default retention period

To recover deleted files from your OneDrive.com, follow these steps:

1. Browse to your OneDrive.com, or right-click the cloud icon in the notification area and click View Online.

2. On the left side of the page, select the Recycle Bin.

3. If the Recycle Bin is not visible, click the three horizontal lines in the top left corner of the screen and select Recycle Bin.

4. Select the items that you want to recover.

5. Click Restore on the menu.

OneDrive will restore the items and they will be removed from the Recycle Bin.

At present, you are not able to modify the retention settings or increase the size of the Recycle Bin for OneDrive.com. If you use the Recycle Bin often and you are concerned about whether your deleted files will be protected by the Recycle Bin, you could consider increasing the space provided to the Recycle Bin by upgrading to a paid OneDrive storage plan such as Office 365 Personal. If space is limited, you could also review the items currently in the Recycle Bin and select items for permanent deletion to free up space, as shown in Figure 4-6.

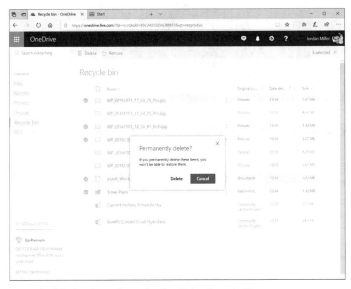

FIGURE 4-6 Permanently deleting items from the OneDrive Recycle Bin

When you delete files using the OneDrive.com interface or from your OneDrive folders within File Explorer, the deleted files will be automatically synchronized to the OneDrive.com Recycle Bin and the File Explorer Recycle Bin (or Trash if you are using OneDrive on a Mac). If you use the Restore All or Empty Recycle Bin options, you need to be aware that these tasks are irreversible.

The Search feature within OneDrive.com is a powerful method of locating files stored in your OneDrive. Search results do not include items in the OneDrive Recycle Bin or the File Explorer Recycle Bin.

ONEDRIVE DOCUMENT VERSION HISTORY

For Office documents, such as Microsoft Word and Microsoft Excel, OneDrive.com maintains previous versions of these documents where available. To view the available versions stored in OneDrive, navigate to the Office file, right-click it, and choose Version History. OneDrive will open the file in a new browser tab. You can then see the list of available versions on the left pane, and you can review the contents of each file as shown in Figure 4-7.

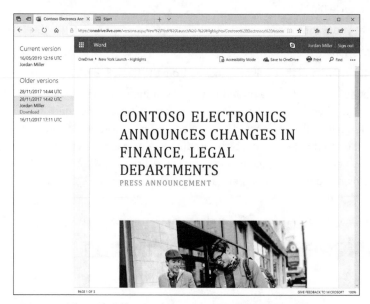

FIGURE 4-7 Microsoft Office previous versions available in OneDrive

The older versions are listed together with the date and time when the file was last saved. If you select an older version of the document from the list of older versions in the left pane, OneDrive will open the older file in the tab, and it will display the name of the modifier. You can choose to Download or Restore this older version from the link displayed in the left pane.

Recover Windows 10

Windows 10 is a reliable operating system. However, occasionally, you will encounter problems with your users' devices that require you to perform some sort of operating system recovery. The severity of the problem will determine your particular course of action, and because of this, Microsoft has provided a number of recovery tools in Windows 10.

Some of these are relatively benign and enable you to investigate and resolve the underlying problem with little effect on the operating system. Others are more intrusive and can result in resetting the operating system to an earlier point in time or even to its initial state. These recovery tools include:

- Recovery drive
- System Restore
- Windows Recovery Environment (Windows RE)
- Reset this PC
- Fresh Start
- System image restore
- System repair disk

Configure a recovery drive

Most Windows 10 PCs will have a recovery partition, which contains a full image of the system. If your computer does not start properly, you can use the recovery partition to start up.

The contents of the recovery partition can also be copied to a removable storage device so that if your recovery partition becomes inaccessible or corrupted, you will still be able to recover your system.

Disk drive space on many small form factor devices and tablets is often smaller than available on a laptop or PC. This can limit the availability for an original equipment manufacturer (OEM) to include a recovery partition on devices shipped with Windows 10. If there is no recovery partition, you can still create a bootable Universal Serial Bus (USB) flash drive–based recovery drive; you can use this drive to boot into the Recovery Environment (RE). You will then need to access a system image that you have created or that is provided by the OEM.

To create a recovery drive, follow these steps:

1. Search for Recovery Drive and select Create A Recovery Drive.
2. Accept the User Account Control (UAC) prompt, providing the necessary credentials, if required.
3. Select the Back Up System Files To The Recovery Drive option.
4. Click Next. Windows 10 will prepare the recovery image.
5. If you have not already connected a backup device to the system, on the Connect A USB Flash Drive page, connect a drive that has at least 16 GB capacity.
6. On the Select The USB Flash Drive page, select the drive for the recovery drive, as shown in Figure 4-8, and click Next.

7. On the Create The Recovery Drive page, read the warning that the USB drive contents will be deleted, and click Create. The Creating The Recovery Drive page appears with a progress bar, which will indicate which phase of the process is being performed. The process can take up to 30 minutes, depending on the performance of the PC and the media. The tool performs the following actions:

- Prepares the drive
- Formats the drive
- Copies Recovery Drive utilities
- Backs up system files

8. On the last page, click Finish.

When the recovery drive has been provisioned on the removable media, if your device has a recovery partition, you will see a link to delete the recovery partition from your PC. This relates to the Windows 10 device recovery partition and not the newly created recovery drive. If you want to free up the space on your device, you need to select this option. It is important to store the recovery drive in a safe place because you will not be able to recover your device if you have lost the recovery drive and you have deleted the recovery partition.

FIGURE 4-8 Creating a recovery drive

NOTE   SDHC MEMORY CARDS

Some devices will support the use of Secure Digital High-Capacity (SDHC) memory cards. The Recovery Drive Wizard can use a SDHC card as an alternative to using a USB flash drive.

You should carefully label your Recovery Drive media after they have been created. Note that a 64-bit (x64) recovery drive can only be used to reinstall a device with 64-bit architecture. The Windows 10 Recovery Drive cannot be used to repair earlier versions of Windows.

Configure System Restore

You might have used System Restore in a previous version of Windows, such as Windows XP or Windows 7, to restore a computer that has become unstable. System Restore has been retained in Windows 10, and it offers a familiar and reliable method of recovering systems by restoring the operating system to a restore point created during a period of stability.

Once enabled, System Restore will automatically create restore points at the following opportunities:

- **Whenever apps are installed**   If the installer is System Restore compliant.
- **With updates**   Whenever Windows 10 installs Windows updates.
- **Based on a schedule**   Windows 10 includes scheduled tasks, which can trigger restore point creation.
- **Manually**   You can create a System Restore from the System Protection screen.
- **Automatically**   When you use System Restore to restore to a previous restore point, Windows 10 will create a new restore point before it restores the system using the selected restore point.

To turn on System Restore and manually create a System Restore point, follow these steps:

1. Open Control Panel and click System and Security.
2. Click System, and then in System, select the System Protection link in the left pane. The System Properties dialog box appears with the System Protection tab open.
3. To turn on the System Restore feature, select the Local Disk (C:) (System) drive, and then click Configure.
4. On the System Protection For Local Disk (C:) dialog box, select Turn On System Protection.
5. Under Disk Space Usage, move the slider for the Max Usage to allow room on the restore points to be saved (five percent is a reasonable amount), as shown in Figure 4-9.
6. Click OK twice.

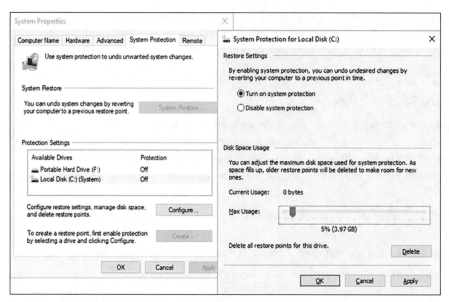

FIGURE 4-9 Configuring System Restore properties

You can also use PowerShell to configure System Restore. Some of the available commands that you need to review include:

- **Enable-ComputerRestore**   Enables the System Restore feature on the specified file system drive
- **Disable-ComputerRestore**   Disables the System Restore feature on the specified file system drive
- **Get-ComputerRestorePoint**   Gets the restore points on the local computer
- **Checkpoint-Computer**   Creates a system restore point

The following command enables System Restore on the C: drive of the local computer:

```
PS C:\> enable-computerrestore -drive "C:\"
```

> **NOTE   SYSTEM RESTORE REQUIRES NTFS AND USES VOLUME SHADOW COPY SERVICE**
>
> System Restore uses the Volume Shadow Copy Service (VSS) and is only available on drives that are formatted with NTFS.

If the amount of space allocated for the restore points becomes full, System Restore will automatically delete the oldest restore points. If you require more restore points to be available, you need to allocate a larger proportion of the hard disk to the feature.

Once the system has created restore points, you are protected, and the system should be recoverable.

To recover your system, you can launch the System Restore Wizard from either:

- **System Protection**   If your system will allow you to sign in to Windows, you can launch System Restore from the Windows 10 graphical user interface (GUI).

- **Windows Recovery Environment (Windows RE)**   If the system will not allow you to sign in, you can boot to the Windows RE and launch the System Restore Wizard from the Advanced options.

> *NOTE* **WINDOWS RE**
>
> Windows RE is built on Windows Preinstallation Environment (Windows PE), which is a cut-down version of Windows that offers only limited functionality.

IDENTIFYING AFFECTED APPS AND FILES

When using System Restore to restore the computer to an earlier state, the wizard will allow you to can scan the restore point and advise you which apps and files will be affected by performing the operation.

1. Search for System and click the System Control Panel item.

2. On the System page, select the System Protection link in the left pane. The System Properties dialog box appears with the System Protection tab open.

3. Click System Restore.

4. On the Restore System Files And Settings page, click Next.

5. On the Restore Your Computer To A State It Was In Before The Selected Event page, choose the restore point that you want to be restored, as shown in Figure 4-10.

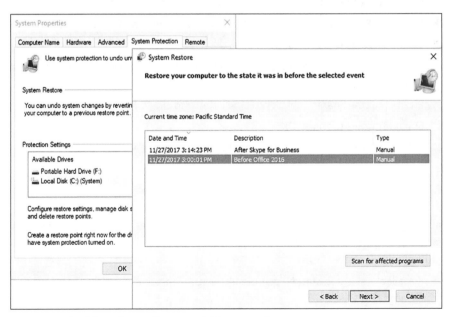

FIGURE 4-10 Applying a System Restore point to your system

6. Optionally, click Scan For Affected Programs, or click Next.

7. On the Confirm Your Restore Point page, click Finish.

8. On the warning screen, click Yes.

9. The System Restore will now prepare your computer and restart. The System Restore process can take some time to complete.

10. When the process is complete, the system will restart, and you can sign in to Windows.

11. You will be presented with a summary of the system restore status, and a confirmation that your documents have not been affected.

12. Click Close.

> **NOTE** **SYSTEM RESTORE WITHIN WINDOWS RE**
>
> When using System Restore within Windows RE—as a protection against unauthorized access to the system—you need to select a user account and provide the user's password before you can use the System Restore feature.

MODIFYING THE TASK SCHEDULE

After you have enabled the System Restore feature, you can modify the default task schedule for when you want automatic restore points to occur by modifying the SR scheduled task as follows:

1. Search for a Task and click the Task Scheduler item.

2. In the Task Scheduler Microsoft Management Console (MMC), expand the node on the left to locate Task Scheduler Library\Microsoft\Windows\SystemRestore.

3. Double-click the SR task in the middle pane.

4. On the SR Properties (Local Computer) dialog box, click the Triggers tab.

5. On the Triggers tab, click New.

6. In the New Trigger dialog box, configure the schedule that you require. For example, you can configure Windows to create a daily System Restore point at noon.

7. Ensure that the Enabled check box is selected and click OK.

8. On the Triggers tab, click OK.

9. In the Task Scheduler MMC, the trigger is now displayed and enabled.

10. Close the Task Scheduler MMC.

Launching Windows RE

To launch the Windows RE and use safe mode or other advanced troubleshooting tools, you can attempt to start Windows 10 in advanced troubleshooting mode by using one of the following options:

- If available, select Restart Now under Advanced Startup in the Recovery section of the Settings app.

- Restart the device using the Recovery Drive.
- Boot the device using Windows 10 installation media and select the Repair Your Computer option.
- Press the Shift key and select the Restart option on the Start menu.

In addition to the methods above, Windows will automatically start in the WinRE after detecting the following issues:

- Two consecutive failed attempts to launch Windows
- Two consecutive unexpected shutdowns that occur within two minutes of boot completion
- A Secure Boot error
- A BitLocker error on touch-only devices

Once Windows 10 boots to the advanced troubleshooting mode, you need to click Troubleshoot, then on the Advanced Options screen, you can access some or all the following options, as shown in Figure 4-11:

- **System Restore** Use a System Restore point to restore Windows.
- **Uninstall Updates** Remove quality or feature updates.
- **System Image Recovery** Recover Windows using a system image file.
- **Startup Repair** Fix problems that are preventing Windows from starting.
- **Command Prompt** Used for advanced troubleshooting.
- **Startup Setting** Change Windows startup behavior.

If your system has a unified extensible firmware interface (UEFI) motherboard, you will also be offered an additional option:

- **UEFI Firmware Settings** Used to modify UEFI settings.

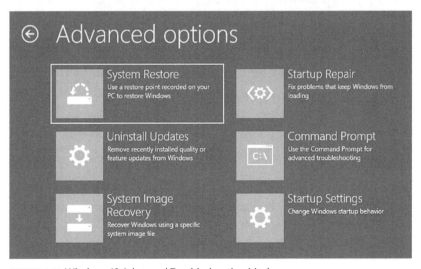

FIGURE 4-11 Windows 10 Advanced Troubleshooting Mode

The advanced troubleshooting mode shown in Figure 4-11 allows you to select the Startup Settings, which restarts Windows in a special troubleshooting mode that might be familiar to users of other versions of the Windows operating system. Selecting the Startup Settings troubleshooting mode presents you with the following options:

- **Enable Debugging** Start Windows 10 in troubleshooting mode, monitoring the behavior of device drivers to help determine if a specific device driver is causing Windows 10 to behave unexpectedly.

- **Enable Boot Logging** Windows 10 creates and writes to a file named Ntbtlog.txt to record the device drivers installed and loaded during startup.

- **Enable Low-Resolution Video** Start Windows 10 in a low-resolution graphics mode.

- **Enable Safe Mode** Windows 10 starts with a minimal set of drivers, services, and applications to allow you to troubleshoot the system using the GUI. Safe mode does not include network connectivity.

- **Enable Safe Mode With Networking** Safe mode with networking enables network connectivity.

- **Enable Safe Mode With Command Prompt** Safe mode using a command prompt window rather than the Windows GUI.

- **Disable Driver Signature Enforcement** Allows you to load device drivers that do not have a digital signature.

- **Disable Early Launch Anti-Malware Protection** Start Windows 10 without the early launch antimalware functionality running. This mode is useful for identifying whether early launch antimalware is affecting a driver or app from being loaded.

- **Disable Automatic Restart After System Failure** Stops Windows 10 from automatically restarting after a system failure occurs.

You can cancel and reboot your system normally by pressing Enter. To select an option that you require, you need to press the number key or function key F1–F9 that corresponds to the list of items as shown in Figure 4-12.

If you press F10, you are taken to another screen with the option to launch the recovery environment. This option reboots the system and returns you to the Advanced Options screen, as shown previously in Figure 4-11.

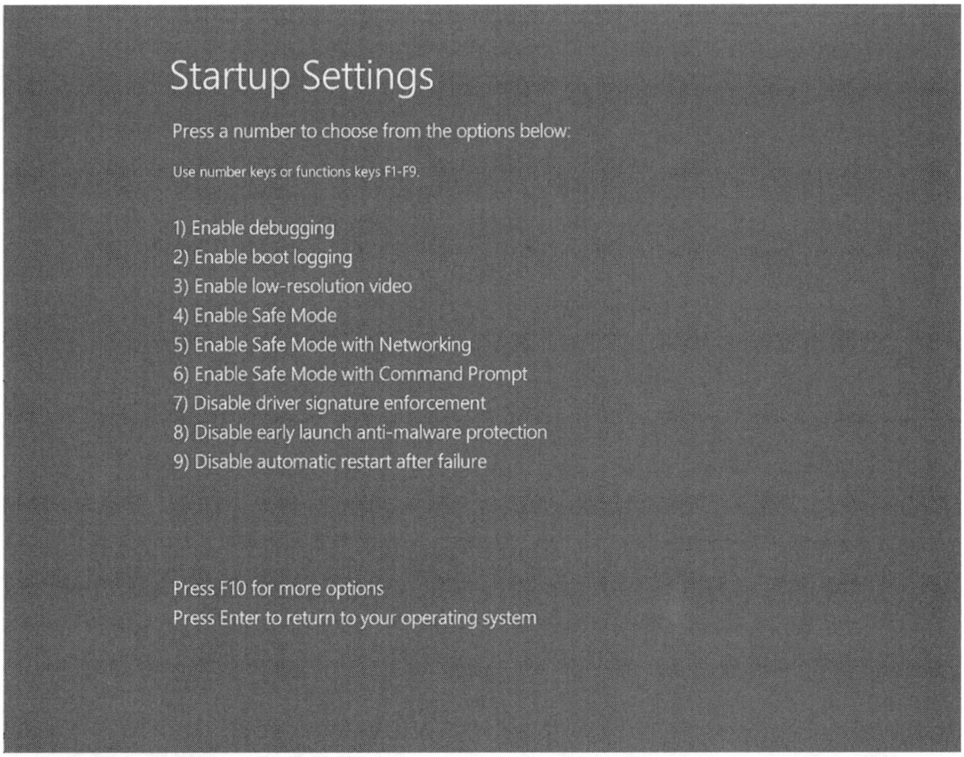

Startup Settings

Press a number to choose from the options below:

Use number keys or functions keys F1-F9.

1) Enable debugging
2) Enable boot logging
3) Enable low-resolution video
4) Enable Safe Mode
5) Enable Safe Mode with Networking
6) Enable Safe Mode with Command Prompt
7) Disable driver signature enforcement
8) Disable early launch anti-malware protection
9) Disable automatic restart after failure

Press F10 for more options
Press Enter to return to your operating system

FIGURE 4-12 Windows 10 Startup Settings

> **NOTE** **LAST KNOWN GOOD CONFIGURATION**
>
> Windows 10 does not support the Last Known Good Configuration startup option that was present in Windows 7 and other versions of Windows.

Reset This PC

If other methods of recovering your system fail or your problems reoccur, you can revert your system to the state similar to how it was when you purchased it or when Windows 10 was first installed. Typical issues that prevent the use of other tools mentioned in this chapter might include a damaged hard drive or a malware attack that encrypts the drive.

Windows 8 first introduced the option to refresh or recycle your computer; Windows 10 has improved the performance and reliability of this feature. You will see the words *recycle* and *reset* used interchangeably by Microsoft to mean the same thing, although the Windows interface options typically use the term *reset*. The Reset This PC option consolidates the two options (Refresh Your PC and Reset Your PC) that were available in Windows 8 and Windows 8.1.

For enterprise users who suffer from an unstable or corrupted system, often the quickest remediation is to deploy a fresh system image from the deployment server to the device. Home users and small organizations can utilize a similar solution, but rather than use a deployment server on the network such as Windows Deployment Services (Windows DS), Windows 10 is able to re-image the device itself. Selecting the Reset This PC option effectively reinstalls the Windows 10 operating system and allows you to either keep your files or remove everything.

To start the recovery process, follow these steps:

1. Launch the Settings app.

2. Click Update & Security.

3. Select Recovery.

4. On the Reset This PC page, click Get Started.

   The screen will be dimmed, and you will be presented with the options shown in Figure 4-13 as follows:

   - **Keep My Files**   Removes apps and settings but keeps your personal files

   - **Remove Everything**   Removes all your personal files, apps, and settings

5. Select Keep My Files.

   A warning appears informing you that your apps will be removed; it lists any apps that will need to be reinstalled.

6. Click Next.

   On the Ready To Reset This PC page, you are reminded that resetting the PC will remove apps and reset all settings back to defaults.

7. Click Reset to restart the PC and allow the reset process to begin.

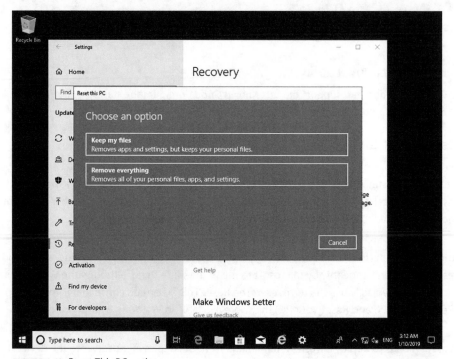

FIGURE 4-13 Reset This PC options

After the reset process has completed and you've signed in, you will have a list of removed apps on the desktop. This file, called Removed Apps, is discussed more in the next section.

> **NOTE** **RECYCLE THE DEVICE**
>
> If you want to recycle a device, you can use the Reset This PC option to make the device available for use by someone else. If you choose to Remove Everything, the device reverts to out-of-box experience (OOBE) state. You can then use a deployment process, such as Windows Autopilot, to configure the device for reuse in your organization—with minimal user intervention.

If you selected to Remove Everything, then you are also asked if you want to clean the drive(s), too. Cleaning the drive helps to ensure that your content is not recoverable by the new owner of the device. This option is ideal if you are seeking to recycle your PC and want to make it difficult for someone to recover your removed files. When the system reset is complete, you are offered the OOBE. You must configure the device, install any apps, and modify any settings that you would like.

Perform a Fresh Start

Windows 10 also provides another way to reset the system called Fresh Start. Fresh Start performs three actions:

- Reinstalls Windows 10 while retaining your data
- Removes all installed apps and bloatware
- Installs the latest security updates

You can access the Fresh Start feature using the following steps:

1. Launch Windows Security, which is a built-in Microsoft Store app.

2. Select Device Performance And Health and then under Fresh Start, click Additional Information.

3. On the Fresh Start page, click Get Started and accept the UAC prompt.

   The screen will be dimmed, and you will be presented with the warning, as shown in Figure 4-14.

FIGURE 4-14 Fresh Start options

4. To proceed, click Next.

5. Fresh Start will then display a list of apps that will be removed. Fresh Start saves a list of apps removed, called Removed Apps, which will be found on the desktop once the process is completed.

6. Click Next.

7. On the Let's Get Started page, click Start.

8. The PC is then reset, which can take up to 20 minutes.

> **NOTE**   **PREVIOUS VERSION OF WINDOWS WILL BE REMOVED**
>
> When performing a Fresh Start, if the device was recently upgraded to Windows 10, you won't be able to go back to the previous version of Windows.

When the device restarts after the Fresh Start has completed, you can sign in with the same username and password, and all your data will be retained. Any applications that you use must be reinstalled. Crucially, any apps that came preinstalled on your system by the OEM will have been removed. If you need access to the list of removed apps, a file is created during the process, which can be found on the desktop after you sign in to the device. Within the Fresh Start page in Windows Security, you will see a history of when the Fresh Start feature has been used and a link to the list of Removed Apps.

Creating a system image backup

As already mentioned, included with Windows 10 is the Backup And Restore (Windows 7) tool, which you can use to back up and restore selected files and folders. You can also use this tool to create a system image of your computer.

To create a system image backup, follow the steps:

1. In Settings, select Update & Security and then click the Backup tab.

2. In the Details pane, click Go to Backup And Restore (Windows 7)

3. On Backup And Restore (Windows 7), click Set Up Backup.

4. On the Select Where You Want To Save Your Backup page, choose the location and click Next.

5. On the What Do You Want To Back Up page, click Let Me Choose and then click Next.

6. Select any folders that you want to back up, but make sure you select the Include A System Image Of Drives check box, as shown in Figure 4-15.

7. On the Review Your Backup Settings page, click the Change Schedule Link.

8. On the How Often Do You Want To Back Up page, leave the Run Backup On A Schedule (Recommended) check box selected, and choose when you want the backup to be performed.

9. Click OK.

10. On the Review Your Backup Settings page, click Save Settings And Run Backup.

11. The backup will begin.

FIGURE 4-15 Performing a system image backup

> **NOTE** **ADVANCED BACKUP SCHEDULING**
>
> Backup And Restore (Windows 7) allows you to create a simple backup schedule. If you modify the Automatic Backup task in Task Scheduler, you can specify a more complex backup schedule, for example, to back up multiple times per day, or to back up when your workstation is in the locked state.

USING SYSTEM IMAGE RECOVERY

When you use the System Image Recovery process within Windows RE, Windows 10 replaces your computer's current operating system state with the system image that has been created by the Backup And Restore (Windows 7) tool.

You should only use System Image Recovery if other recovery methods are unsuccessful because it will overwrite data on your computer. During the restore process, you can't choose individual items to restore. All the apps, system settings, and files are replaced. Any data files stored locally on your computer that you have created or modified since the system image was created will not be available after you use the System Image Recovery unless you have saved them onto another location, such as OneDrive.

To recover a device with a system image, follow these steps:

1. Launch Settings, and then click Update & Security.

2. Select Recovery, and then, under Advanced Startup, click Restart Now.

3. In Windows RE, on the Choose An Option page, select Troubleshoot.

4. On the Troubleshoot page, select Advanced Options.

5. On the Advanced Options page, select System Image Recovery. Allow the system to reboot, and Windows will prepare for System Image Recovery.

6. On the System Image Recovery page, select your user account.

7. On the System Image Recovery page, enter your password and click Continue.

8. On the Re-Image Your Computer page, verify the system image is correctly selected, as shown in Figure 4-16, and click Next.

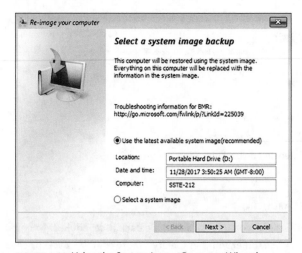

FIGURE 4-16 Using the System Image Recovery Wizard

9. On the Choose Additional Restore Options page, click Next and then click Finish to start the restoration process.

10. In the Re-Image Your Computer dialog box, read the warning, and then click Yes. The Re-Image Your Computer process will now proceed.

11. Once competed, Windows will need to restart. Click Restart Now, or you can wait and allow Windows to automatically restart. When Windows restarts, you will be presented with the sign-in screen.

Creating a system repair disk

In addition to a system image, you can use the Backup And Restore (Windows 7) tool to create a system repair disk. You can use a system repair disk to recover Windows 10 in the event of a drive or other catastrophic failure.

A system image can be incorporated into any backup when using the Backup And Restore (Windows 7) tool. However, creating a system repair disk requires that you manually create a repair disk, as follows:

1. Open Backup And Restore (Windows 7) in Control Panel.
2. Insert a blank writable CD or DVD into your device.
3. On Backup And Restore (Windows 7), click the Create A System Repair Disc link.
4. On the Create A System Repair Disc page, click Create Disc.
5. Click Create disc, as shown in Figure 4-17.

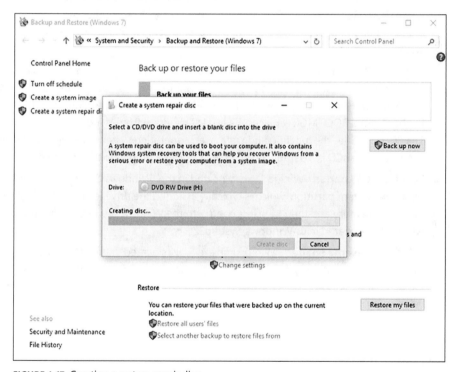

FIGURE 4-17 Creating a system repair disc

The system repair disc is useful if Windows 10 will not automatically boot in the advanced startup options. In this situation, insert the system repair disc and your computer will boot from the recovery media automatically. If it doesn't, you might need to change the boot order.

Troubleshoot the startup process

Windows 10 has an efficient and reliable startup architecture. It is rare that you will need to get involved in resolving startup problems. However, when startup problems do occur, they can be difficult to resolve unless you understand the underlying process.

Components of the startup architecture

There are four main components in the startup architecture. These are:

- **Windows Secure Boot** All computers are potentially vulnerable to malicious software, such as computer viruses. This is especially true during the early startup phases when the operating system's protective components may not yet be available. To mitigate this issue, Windows 10 implements Secure Boot. If your computer supports the Unified Extensible Firmware Interface (UEFI), you can enable Secure Boot in your computer's UEFI settings. Once enabled, when the computer starts and before control is transferred to the operating system, each piece of software is checked for a valid digital signature. Only software deemed safe is loaded, including all low-level operating system drivers and files.

- **Windows Boot Manager** This consists of a single file, BOOTMGR, which resides in the root directory of the active disk partition. This partition is not assigned a drive letter. The Windows Boot Manager, BOOTMGR, reads the Boot Configuration Data (BCD) from the boot store. BOOTMGR replaces the NTLDR program from Windows XP and earlier. The BCD identifies the location and state of any operating systems installed on the local computer. The BCD is a database. Windows XP used a simple text file called Boot.ini.

- **Windows OS Loader** Winload.exe is located in the \Windows\System32 folder on the operating system partition, which is typically assigned the drive letter C. Winload.exe initializes memory and then transfers control to the Windows kernel; this is a file called Ntoskrnl.exe located in C:\Windows\System32.

- **Windows Resume Loader** Winresume.exe is also located in the \Windows\System32 folder on the operating system partition. If the boot store identifies that there is a hibernation image (hiberfil.sys) on the local computer, then BOOTMGR has passed control to Winresume.exe rather than Winload.exe. Winresume.exe then returns the computer to its pre-hibernation state.

> **NOTE** **PARTITIONING**
>
> Your computer typically has at least two partitions on its installed hard disk. Both will be primary partitions. The first partition will be marked as active and will contain the files necessary to perform the initial startup of the operating system; this partition, or drive, is often referred to as the System partition (although it contains the boot store and low-level boot files). The second partition automatically is assigned the drive letter C and contains the operating system; it is often referred to as the Boot partition. You might also have a recovery partition, and possibly even a vendor-specific recovery partition.

The Windows 10 startup process

When you start a computer installed with Windows 10, as shown in Figure 4-18, the following process occurs:

1. **Power-on self-test** When you power up your computer, the UEFI or, on older computers, the Basic Input Output System (BIOS), performs a number of fundamental checks. This is referred to as the power-on self-test (POST).

   The critical check that the POST performs is to verify the presence and accessibility of a configured boot device, such as a hard disk. The hard disk must contain a valid master boot record (MBR). The MBR enables the computer to identify and access partition information on the attached disk. The computer accesses the primary active partition (which contains the Windows 10 boot sector) and loads BOOTMGR.

2. **Read the boot configuration data** BOOTMGR accesses the BCD from the system partition. This enables BOOTMGR to determine the location of any installed operating systems and, where necessary, to display a startup menu on computers configured with multiple operating systems (referred to as dual-boot or multiboot systems). BOOTMGR also determines whether the computer has a hibernation file.

3. **Winload.exe or Winresume.exe** If a Hiberfil.sys file exists, BOOTMGR passes control to Winresume.exe to restore the operating system from the pre-hibernation state. If no Hiberfil.sys file exists, BOOTMGR passes control to Winload.exe.

   Winload.exe initializes memory and scans the computer's registry to locate device drivers configured with a Start value of 0. These include low-level hardware components, such as hard disk controllers and peripheral bus components. Winload.exe then scans the registry for device drivers assigned a Start value of 1.

   Finally, control is passed to the operating system Kernel, Ntoskrnl.exe, and all drivers in memory; the Kernel is then initialized.

4. **Load drivers** After the kernel initializes, any remaining required drivers are loaded and initialized.

5. **Session Manager** The Kernel loads the Windows Session Manager (Smss.exe), which among other things, initializes the Windows subsystem (Csrss.exe). The display will now switch from character mode to graphical mode.

6. **Sign in** After the Windows subsystem loads, the Winlogon service starts. This displays the sign-in page, and the local user can sign in to the computer.

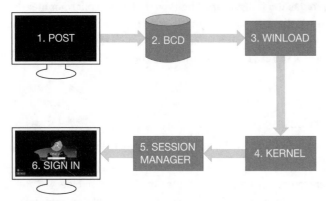

FIGURE 4-18 The Windows 10 startup process

Available options for startup recovery

If your computer does not start properly, or at all, you can choose from a number of repair and recovery tools, depending on the particular situation. These tools are:

- **Windows RE** If your computer won't start, then start from the product DVD and select Repair Your Computer In Setup. You can then access the full set of recovery tools in Windows RE, including System Restore, System Image Recovery, Startup Repair, Command Prompt, and Startup Settings. Generally, if the problem is related to low-level startup files, such as the boot sector, BOOTMGR, and the BCD, choosing the Startup Repair option is generally successful in fixing startup problems.

- **Advanced Startup Settings** If the startup problem lies elsewhere than with the startup files, you should be able to successfully start your computer in Safe Mode. Start from the product DVD, and in Setup, click Repair Your Computer. From the Advanced options menu, select Startup Settings, and then choose Safe Mode. Advanced Startup Settings include:

  - Enable Debugging
  - Enable Boot Logging
  - Enable Low-Resolution Video
  - Enable Safe Mode
  - Enable Safe Mode With Networking
  - Enable Safe Mode With Command Prompt
  - Disable Driver Signature Enforcement
  - Disable Early Launch Antimalware Protection
  - Disable Automatic Restart After Failure

- **System Configuration tool** If your computer starts, but with errors, you can access Safe Mode by running the System Configuration tool (Msconfig.exe). On the Boot tab, shown in Figure 4-19, select the appropriate Safe Boot option. Note that the computer remains in Safe Mode until you return to System Configuration to revert to Normal startup on the General tab.

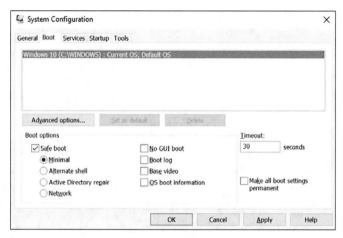

FIGURE 4-19 System Configuration tool

- **Automatic Failover** If your computer experiences startup problems, assuming that your computer still has the (default) recovery partition, Windows will failover to Windows RE from this recovery partition.

The boot store

The boot store contains information that enables the low-level startup components of Windows 10 to locate any installed operating systems on the attached hard disk(s). Generally, it is not necessary to make changes to the BCD. However, it is important that you know how to make changes in case you must troubleshoot the startup environment.

Typically, you make changes to the BCD by reconfiguring Windows. For example, you might use the System Configuration tool to force Safe Mode. You might decide to make changes to the Startup And Recovery settings to choose the default operating system (assuming several are installed). Both these changes are made in the user interface but are reflected in the BCD. However, you can also work directly with the BCD using a number of command-line tools. For example, Figure 4-20 shows the output from the **BCDEdit.exe /Enum** command; this command enumerates and displays all boot store entries.

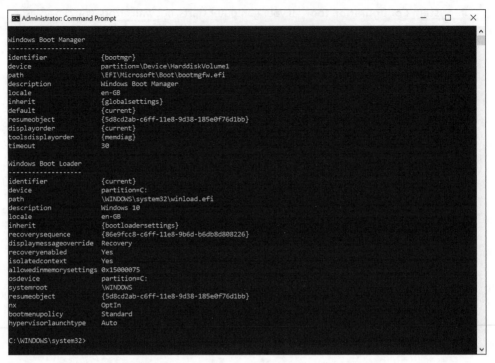

FIGURE 4-20 Output from BCDEdit.exe

MODIFYING THE BOOT STORE

There are a number of tools with which you can directly edit the BCD. These are:

- **BCDEdit.exe** You can use BCDEdit.exe from an elevated command prompt. It enables you to

  - Add BCD store entries
  - Modify BCD store entries
  - Delete entries
  - Export the BCD
  - Import into the BCD
  - List entries
  - Query entries
  - Make global changes
  - Change the default time-out

NEED MORE REVIEW? BCDEDIT COMMAND-LINE OPTIONS

You can find more information about the syntax of the BCDEdit.exe command on the Micro-soft website at *https://docs.microsoft.com/en-us/windows-hardware/manufacture/desktop/ bcdedit-command-line-options.*

- **Bootrec.exe** You can use Bootrec.exe to manually rebuild the BCD based on a scan that the program performs. You must run Bootrec.exe in Windows RE in the Command Prompt tool. There are a number of parameters that you can use:
  - **/FixMbr** Resolves MBR corruption issues
  - **/FixBoot** Corrects boot sector corruptions
  - **/ScanOS** Scans the hard disk(s) for Windows installations and displays any not listed in the BCD
  - **/RebuildBcd** Scans the hard disk(s) for Windows installations and prompts you to add any discovered to the BCD

Managing Devices and Device Drivers

For hardware to function properly, it requires special software designed for Windows 10 to communicate with it. This software is referred to as a device driver. When Windows 10 detects new hardware, the system automatically attempts to install one of the built-in drivers included as part of the operating system. These drivers are either located within the Windows 10 Driver Store, or you can download them through Windows Update. A common reason for a computer to fail to start, or to start with errors, is because a device driver is faulty or corrupted.

INSTALL DEVICES

New and updated hardware device drivers are regularly submitted to Microsoft by the equipment vendor for testing and cataloging. If the Windows Update feature is enabled, Windows 10 automatically detects the presence of new device drivers, downloads them, and installs them.

New hardware is typically installed automatically when it's added to Windows 10; the operating system detects and identifies the new hardware through the Plug and Play feature. Windows 10 supports new hardware connected through a variety of connection methods, including USB (1.0 through 3.1), Wi-Fi, and Bluetooth. In addition to backward compatibility for existing and earlier hardware, emerging technologies, such as near-field communication (NFC) and Miracast for wireless displays, also have built-in support in Windows 10.

For advanced users or for managing or troubleshooting a hardware device issue, you can use Device Manager. Device Manager provides information about each device, such as the device type, device status, manufacturer, device-specific properties, and device driver information.

There are multiple ways to load the Device Manager, including:

- Right-clicking the Start button and selecting Device Manager
- Typing **Device Manager** into Search
- Opening Control Panel, selecting Hardware And Sound, and then selecting Device Manager

The Device Manager default view (devices by type) is shown in Figure 4-21.

You can expand and explore each node in Device Manager and then select a device. All devices have properties, and these can be viewed by right-clicking the desired device and selecting the properties.

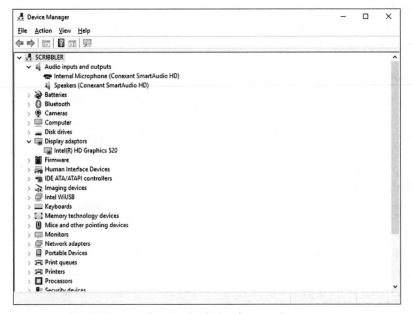

FIGURE 4-21 Device Manager showing the devices by type view

The Properties dialog box for a device is shown in Figure 4-22.

If you added a new peripheral and Windows 10 does not immediately recognize it, first check that the device is connected properly and that no cables are damaged. You should ensure that the external device is powered on and not in sleep or standby mode. You can also open Device Manager and launch the Scan For Hardware Changes Wizard from the Action menu, which will locate previously undetected hardware and then configure it for you.

FIGURE 4-22 Device Properties

UPDATE DEVICE DRIVERS

Most computers that you'll work with have different hardware components, such as mother-boards, disk controllers, graphics cards, and network adapters. Fortunately, Windows 10 is designed to work with an extensive list of hardware devices, and it benefits from Plug and Play, which tries to detect new devices automatically and then installs the correct driver software. If Windows has a problem with a device, you must troubleshoot the cause. This can involve locating the correct or updated device drivers and installing them.

Windows 10 automatically attempts to install a device driver and if one is not available locally, it attempts to locate one through Windows Update. For most systems, devices and their associated drivers remain constant and require no further administrative effort. In the following instances, you might need to update, disable, or reinstate a previous driver.

- Windows 10 detects that a newer driver is available through Windows Update.
- You want to install a newer device driver manually, typically obtained from the manufacturer's website.
- The device is not performing or functioning correctly with the current driver.
- A new or beta version of a driver is causing stability issues.

To update a specific driver, select the device in Device Manager and select Update Driver Software from the context menu.

Windows 10 offers you two choices for updating the driver:

- Search Automatically For Updated Driver Software
- Browse My Computer For Driver Software

Typically, most users allow Windows to locate, download, and install an updated device driver automatically if one is available through Windows Update. This is the default method.

If you have the installation media that came with the hardware, you can use the browse feature to locate the correct driver. The Windows 10 Update Driver Software Wizard can automatically search through the subfolders in the media and locate all the relevant drivers for the device.

If you have already downloaded a specific device driver from the manufacturer, for example, a video driver from NVIDIA or AMD/ATI, you might need to run the driver installation wizard included in the download files, which includes additional software besides the device driver.

If Windows determines that the current driver is the most up to date or best driver available, you can confirm the version number of the driver by viewing the properties of the driver in Device Manager. If you have a more recent driver that you want to use, you must manually uninstall the current driver and then manually install the more recent driver.

DISABLE INDIVIDUAL DRIVER UPDATES OR WINDOWS UPDATES

Sometimes it is important to remove a device driver completely from the system. It might be corrupted or incompatible with your system. If Windows determines that the driver is valid and up to date, it is impossible to use another device driver while the current driver is present. To uninstall an unwanted device driver, use the following steps:

1. Open Device Manager.

2. Locate the device with the problem driver, right-click it, and choose Uninstall Device.

3. In the Uninstall Device dialog box, click Uninstall.

If the item relates to an unwanted Windows Update, use the following steps.

1. Open Settings, click Update and Security, and on the Windows Update tab, click Update History.

2. Click Uninstall updates. In Control Panel, on the Installed Updates page, locate and uninstall the unwanted update by selecting it from the list and then clicking Uninstall.

If the driver is reluctant to be uninstalled, try restarting the computer and attempting the procedure again. Only as a last resort should you try to delete the software manually. You can use the PnPUtil.exe command-line tool and remove the .inf files that are associated with the device as shown.

```
PnPUtil.exe -a -d <path to the driver> \<drivername>.inf
```

The use of the PnPUtil.exe command-line tool is discussed later in this chapter.

> **NOTE** **DRIVER INSTALLATION AND REMOVAL ARE ADMINISTRATIVE FUNCTIONS**
>
> You must use administrative privileges to install or uninstall a device or driver package by using Device Manager.

Because different hardware types have different functions and features, review the tabs in the properties screen. Not all devices have the same tabs, and some devices do not offer the ability to view or modify the device driver.

TURN ON OR OFF AUTOMATIC DEVICE DRIVER INSTALLATION IN DEVICE INSTALLATION SETTINGS

Sometimes installing an updated driver can cause your computer to lose functionality, and you might decide to uninstall the driver. Windows 10 automatically attempts to reinstall the driver, which is not desirable. In this situation, you might want to turn off the automatic device driver installation setting by using the following steps.

1. Open Control Panel, and under Hardware And Sound, click Devices And Printers.

2. Under Devices, right-click the icon that represents your computer (it should have your computer name), and click Device Installation Settings, as shown in Figure 4-23.

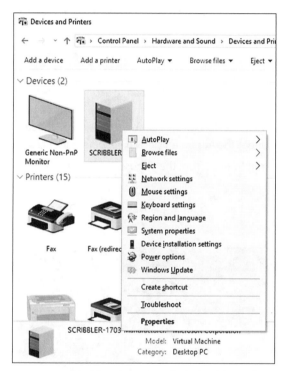

FIGURE 4-23 Disabling the automatic device driver software installation

3. In the Device Installation Settings dialog box, choose No (Your Device Might Not Work As Expected). (Yes is the default setting.)

4. Click Save Changes.

PERFORM A DRIVER ROLLBACK

Sometimes a driver problem can cause the system to become unstable. In Device Manager, you can roll back an updated driver to its previous version. If the system allows you to start normally, you can perform this task by using the following steps:

1. Open Device Manager.

2. Right-click the device that you want to roll back and then click Properties.

3. In the Properties dialog box, click the Drivers tab and then click Roll Back Driver.

4. In the Driver Package Rollback dialog box, click Yes.

The Driver Package Rollback feature can only be used to revert to a previously updated driver. If you have not installed a later driver, the option in Device Manager will be unavailable.

> *NOTE* **NO DRIVER ROLLBACK FOR PRINTERS**
>
> **Although Printers and Print queues appear in Device Manager, you cannot use Driver Package Rollback for these devices.**

If your system is unstable or won't start up properly because of a faulty driver, such as a video driver, you might need to restart the computer in Safe Mode to access Device Manager and perform the driver rollback. Windows 10 automatically detects startup failures and should boot into the advanced startup menu. To access Safe Mode, open Settings, click Update & Security, and then select the Recovery tab. Under the Advanced startup heading, click Restart now.

1. When your PC restarts, select Troubleshoot from the Choose An Option menu.

2. Select Advanced Options.

3. Select Startup Settings and click Restart. You see the Advanced Boot Options screen, as shown in Figure 4-24.

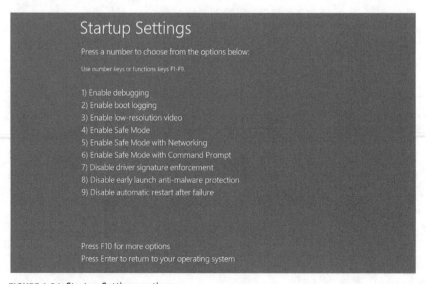

FIGURE 4-24 Startup Settings options

4. Select Safe Mode by pressing the 4 key.

5. Sign in to the system and roll back the driver as described earlier.

The rollback feature remembers only the last driver that was installed and doesn't keep copies of multiple drivers for the same device.

Resolve driver issues

One of the most common issues with device drivers relates to users attempting to install a driver designed for an earlier operating system or a different architecture. In some cases, on previous versions of Windows, it might have been possible to install a Windows 7 driver on a Windows 8–based computer, but this is not a supported operation for Windows 10 and should be avoided in a production environment. As is the case with other software installations, you can't use a 32-bit driver for a 64-bit resource. You can't use a 64-bit driver to communicate with a 32-bit resource either.

DISABLE UPDATES

Sometimes a specific update or driver will not be compatible with your system. Although all updates and drivers should be thoroughly checked before they are made available for installation, it is almost impossible to test every combination of software and hardware that can coexist on a computer. In some configurations, the new software might produce unsatisfactory results. You saw earlier that one method to avoid this situation is to turn off updates completely.

Disabling automatic driver updates might have a more widespread effect than you want, especially if you only need to disable or prevent the installation of a single driver. To enable you to block a specific update, Microsoft has released the Show Or Hide Updates troubleshooter package, available from the Microsoft Download Center at *https://support.microsoft.com/kb/3073930*.

This troubleshooter, shown in Figure 4-25, searches for available drivers and Windows updates and then enables you to hide them, which prevents Windows from automatically installing them.

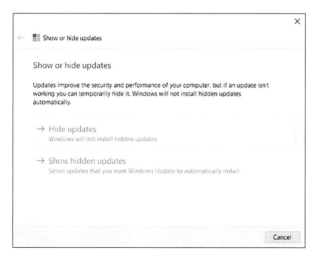

FIGURE 4-25 Show Or Hide Updates troubleshooter

Each time you experience an issue with a driver or update that you don't want installed, you can run this troubleshooter and select the updates that you want to disable.

> **NOTE DEVICE MANAGER ERROR TROUBLESHOOTING**
>
> Device Manager marks a device that is not operating normally with a yellow exclamation point. When troubleshooting a device, you can check the error that Device Manager reports. For a detailed list of errors that Device Manager reports, see the article at *https:// docs.microsoft.com/en-gb/windows-hardware/drivers/install/device-manager-error-messages*.

USE DRIVER VERIFICATION TOOLS

If you encounter issues with drivers that seem to relate to malware or missing drivers, you can use a command-line tool called Sigverif.exe, which checks whether any drivers have been installed on the computer that have not been signed. The check can take several minutes to complete. To run this tool, perform the following steps.

1. Open a command prompt. (Standard user privilege level is OK.)

2. Type **sigverif.exe** and press Enter. The File Signature Verification Tool appears.

3. Review the Advanced options.

4. Click Start and view the results, as shown in Figure 4-26.

FIGURE 4-26 File Signature Verification tool output

The sigverif.exe tool is useful if you need to locate an unsigned driver. However, there is a more powerful driver verification tool, Driver Verifier, which is built into Windows 10.

EXAM TIP

In the advanced settings of the Signature Verification tool is the file name of the log file; this is a good thing to know for the exam. Review the log file found at %SystemRoot%\Sigverif .txt after the operation has completed.

With the enhanced kernel mode operation and reliance on signed drivers, Windows 10 should be less prone to frequent Stop errors. Although less likely, even signed drivers can cause problems, especially if you have an exotic combination of hardware inside your computer. If you do encounter instability, use the built-in Driver Verifier to discover whether a faulty driver is causing the problem.

Driver Verifier Manager can help you troubleshoot, identify, and resolve common device driver problems, and you can then remove, reinstall, or roll back the offending driver with Device Manager.

To run the series of driver tests, follow these steps:

1. Open a command prompt (Admin), using administrative privileges.
2. Type **verifier.exe** and press Enter. The Driver Verifier tool appears.
3. Review the settings in the tool. Depending on which option you choose, you might need to restart your computer for the tool to recognize all loaded drivers.
4. After you have selected drivers to be tested, restart the computer, restart the application, and then select Display Information About The Currently Verified Drivers.

Driver Verifier Manager tests each specified driver at startup and then enables you to perform a live test of each loaded driver by running a range of tests, as shown in Figure 4-27. If it detects a problem, the tool can identify the driver, and then you can disable it.

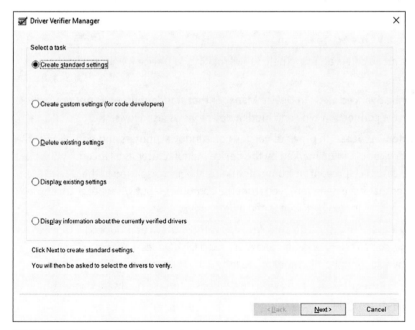

FIGURE 4-27 Driver Verifier Manager tool

VIEW DEVICE SETTINGS

Device drivers provide Windows 10 with the information required to populate the device details that you find in Device Manager. If only a few details are available to view, the device might have been installed using the built-in driver. You might be able to install a driver from the manufacturer's website, which will give additional information through Device Manager.

The default Device Manager screen enables users to work directly in the Properties dialog box of a device and provides information about the device that the hardware and device driver provide. The following is a review of Device Manager features that you can use to explore the available information, so that you can configure the driver settings.

In Device Manager, explore these four menu options:

- **File**   This menu enables you to exit the console and optionally delete the record of the console customizations you make to the console settings.

- **Action**   This menu enables you to access the action-specific tasks relating to the highlighted hardware, including Update Driver Software, Disable, Uninstall, Scan For Hardware Changes, Add Legacy Hardware, Properties, and Help.

- **View**   This menu enables you to change how the console view displays advanced information relating to the devices listed in Device Manager. Some hardware is also hidden from normal view, and this option can be set to show hidden devices. The Customize option enables you to show or hide items within the console. You can view devices by

  - Device type or connection

  - Resources by type or connection

- **Help**   This menu offers access to help topics relating to Device Manager and the console.

There are several advanced views in Device Manager that standard users do not normally use. These include the connection type and hidden device views, as follows.

- **Show Hidden Devices**   In previous versions of Windows, printers and non–Plug and Play (PnP) devices could be marked by the device manufacturer as a NoDisplayClass type of device, which prevents it from automatically being displayed in the Device Manager. Devices that have been removed from the computer—but whose registry entries are still present—can also be found in the hidden devices list.

- **Devices By Type**   This is the default view, and it shows devices grouped by familiar device name, such as Network Adapters, Ports, and Disk Drives. Each node can be expanded by selecting the > symbol to the left of the node name.

- **Devices By Connection**   You can view devices based on the hardware connection, such as physical or virtual.

- **Resources By Type**   Use this option to view resources organized by how they connect to system resources, including Direct Memory Access (DMA), Input/Output (IO), Interrupt Request (IRQ), and Memory. Unless your BIOS allows you to declare that you are not using a Plug and Play–compliant operating system, you will not be able to modify these settings.

- **Resources By Connection**   This view is for advanced users only and is not particularly useful on a modern system. Viewing the device hardware resources by DMA, IO, IRQ, and Memory were useful for earlier versions of Windows prior to the introduction of Plug and Play, which allowed the operating system to manage automatically the resources required by devices.

SUPPORT FOR OLDER HARDWARE

Some of the advanced settings in Device Manager are seldom used but have been retained for backward compatibility with older devices that do not support Plug and Play. Modern hardware peripherals must support Plug and Play, which allows Windows 10 to assign hardware resources automatically to new devices. If you look on the Resources tab of a device Properties dialog box in Device Manager, you see that a check box is selected indicating that Windows 10 is using automatic settings, as shown in Figure 4-28. The setting is unavailable and not changeable unless you disable the BIOS/UEFI setting, which declares that the operating system is Plug and Play–compliant.

FIGURE 4-28 Automatic resource allocation

The Plug and Play standard for connecting devices to Windows is nearly two decades old. Some hardware still exists that requires the administrator to install it manually. In Device Manager, the Add Hardware Wizard enables you to install hardware that does not support Plug and Play. To install such hardware, perform the following steps.

1. Open Device Manager.

2. On the Action tab, click Add Legacy Hardware.

3. On the Welcome To The Add Hardware Wizard page, click Next.

4. Select one of these options:

   - Search For And Install The Hardware Automatically (Recommended)

   - Install The Hardware That I Manually Select From A List

5. Follow the wizard prompts to finish the configuration of the hardware and provide the driver when requested.

> **NOTE** **NON-PNP (OLDER) DEVICES ARE NOT SHOWN IN WINDOWS 10**
>
> Since Windows 8 and Windows Server 2012, non-PnP devices have not been represented in Device Manager as viewable nodes.

DRIVER SIGNING

One of the reasons Windows 10 is more secure than earlier versions of Windows is that kernel mode drivers must now be submitted to and digitally signed by the Windows Hardware Developer Center Dashboard portal. Windows 10 will not load kernel mode drivers that the portal has not signed. To ensure backward compatibility, drivers that are properly signed by a valid cross-signing certificate will continue to pass signing checks on Windows 10.

Windows 10 also introduces a new Universal Windows driver, which is designed to work on all OneCoreUAP-based editions of Windows, such as Windows 10 for desktop editions (Home, Pro, Enterprise, and Education), Windows 10 Mobile, and Windows 10 Internet of Things Core (IoT Core).

A Universal Windows driver has access to the trusted kernel and has a very limited range of the interfaces that are available to a Windows driver. OEMs can supplement the driver functionality by including additional software, but this will be external to the driver. Windows 10 security is more robust by locking down the kernel to signed drivers and encouraging developers to use the Universal Windows driver model.

If you have a specific need to install an unsigned driver—for example, if you are a developer and work with drivers, and you want to test the driver functionality without having to sign the driver digitally each time—you can invoke a special boot-time configuration setting that bypasses the security the Windows 10 driver enforcement model provides. To load an unsigned driver (not recommended), you can follow these steps:

1. Sign out of Windows 10.
2. On the sign in screen, click the Power button, hold down the Shift key, and click Restart.
3. On the Choose An Option screen, choose Troubleshoot.
4. Choose Advanced Options.
5. On the Advanced Options screen, select Startup Settings and click Restart.
   Advanced Boot Options appears.
6. Choose Disable Driver Signature Enforcement, as shown in Figure 4-29.

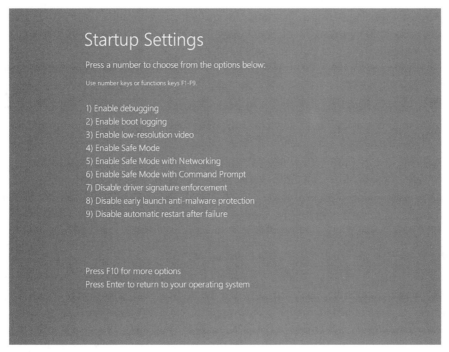

FIGURE 4-29 Disable Driver Signature Enforcement

7. Install the unsigned driver and then restart the computer.

Manage driver packages

When device drivers are created by the original equipment manufacturer (OEM), they are deployed with the hardware in a driver package that includes all the files and information required for Windows 10 to communicate with the hardware. You see how driver packages are managed and how to install, provision, and import driver packages on Windows 10 devices.

USE THE DRIVER STORE

You saw earlier that the driver package can include an information file (.inf file), any files that the .inf file references, and a .cat file that contains the digital signature for the device driver. Windows 10 uses the Driver Store to hold device drivers that have been installed or pre-staged.

All Windows 10 kernel mode drivers must be digitally signed by the Windows Hardware Developer Center Dashboard portal. Windows 10 will prevent the loading of new kernel mode drivers that are not signed by the portal. This is an important change from previous versions of Windows and will make the operating system more secure. Previously, it could be possible for a hacker to gain unauthorized access to a system by using a flaw in an unsigned device driver. Ensuring that all drivers are digitally signed will remove the ability for a hacker to add or modify device driver contents.

If you are creating a custom installation image, or if you build and deploy many computers, you can speed up the driver installation process by pre-loading the Windows 10 driver store with the specific drivers for the peripheral devices that your devices will be using. When Windows 10 finds the drivers it needs in the driver store (located in %SystemRoot%\System32 \DriverStore), it uses these local drivers and does not download them from Windows Update.

Pre-installing a driver is a two-stage process, and the first stage must be carried out with administrator credentials. You need to add the driver package to the driver store and then ensure that the hardware is attached; Windows 10 then automatically locates and installs the local driver.

There are a few ways to deploy drivers to the Driver Store, and the most appropriate method will depend on your physical network infrastructure, network connectivity, and level of administrative privileges on devices, among other things.

> **NOTE AVOID DELETING FILES FROM THE DRIVER STORE**
>
> You should take care not to delete driver packages manually from the Driver Store. Doing so can cause an inconsistency among the INF file, the Driver Store catalog, and the driver in the Driver Store. For more information, go to *https://docs.microsoft.com/windows-hardware/ drivers/install/how-devices-and-driver-packages-are-uninstalled.*

USE PNPUTIL.EXE TO MANAGE DRIVER PACKAGES

To pre-stage the installation of a specific hardware device, you can install a driver manually before connecting the device by using the PnPUtil.exe command-line tool. This could be useful when distributing a laptop to a remote user who you know has a local printer or scanner. Standard users cannot normally install device drivers, but if the driver package is already in the Driver Store, this is possible.

Run the PnPUtil.exe command by using administrative privileges. You can use it to manage the Driver Store; you can add, delete, and list driver packages. You saw earlier that a driver package consists of all the information Windows 10 requires to install and trust the driver, including the following:

- **Driver files**   Dynamic link library (DLL) files with the .sys file extension.

- **Installation files**   Text files containing all the information needed to install a driver. These .inf files include information, such as driver name and location, driver version information, and registry information. These files are copied to the %SystemRoot%\Inf directory during installation. Every installed device must have an .inf file.

- **Driver Catalog file**   Contains a cryptographic hash of each file in the driver package. These hashes are used to verify that the package was not altered after it was published (created). Digitally signing the catalog file proves the file has not been altered because only the digital signature owner can sign the file.

- **Additional files**   These are files such as a device installation application, device icon, device property pages, and additional files.

For enhanced security, Windows 10 now uses a single kernel model across all editions of Windows 10, and Windows 10 now encourages the use of a new universal driver model. This universal .inf file is required when deploying device drivers to an offline system image, such as when building a Windows 10 Mobile system (which does not support Plug and Play).

The syntax for the PnPUtil.exe command-line tool is as follows.

```
PnPUtil.exe a <path to the driver> \<drivername>.inf
```

The full list of parameters is shown in Table 4-2.

TABLE 4-2 PnPUtil.exe parameters

PARAMETER	DESCRIPTION
-a	Adds a driver package to the Driver Store.
-d	Removes a driver package from the Driver Store.
-e	Lists the driver packages that are currently in the Driver Store.
-f	Forces the deletion of the specified driver package from the Driver Store; cannot be used with the -i parameter.
-i	Installs the driver package on matching devices that are connected to the system. Cannot be used with the -f parameter.
/?	Displays help.

An example command to add the .inf? file specified by MyDevice.inf to the Driver Store (located at %SystemRoot%\System32\DriverStore) is:

```
PnPUtil.exe -a C:\Temp\MyDevice.inf
```

In addition to the PnPUtil.exe tool, you can use the following Windows PowerShell cmdlets:

- **Get-PnpDevice**   Displays information about PnP devices
- **Get-PnpDeviceProperty**   Displays detailed properties for a PnP device
- **Enable-PnpDevice**   Enables a PnP device
- **Disable-PnpDevice**   Disables a PnP device

An example Windows PowerShell command to enable the device with an instance ID of 'USB\VID_5986&;PID_0266&;MI_00\7&;1E5D3568&;0&;0000' is as follows:

```
PS C:\> Enable-PnpDevice -InstanceId 'USB\VID_5986&;PID_0266&;MI_00\7&;1
E5D3568&;0&;0000'
```

For more information about, or for the syntax of, any of the Windows PowerShell cmdlets, you can use the **Get-Help** *<cmdlet name>* cmdlet, such as the following.

```
Get-Help <cmdlet name> -Examples
```

DOWNLOAD DRIVER PACKAGES

Drivers are packaged together; each driver package consists of all the software components that are needed for your device to work with Windows.

Most drivers are obtained directly by using built-in tools such as Windows Update. However, if you are provisioning systems, you might want to deploy the PC with the required drivers already imported and configured.

Device drivers can be accessed to perform a malicious attack on your systems. Therefore, you should ensure that driver packages are sourced only from reputable locations, such as the manufacturer's own website. You should avoid third-party driver repository websites because some sites repackage drivers and include spyware or freeware products in the installation files.

The built-in Windows 10 driver packages are often just the core drivers created by your device manufacturer and provided by Microsoft through the Windows Hardware Quality Labs (WHQL), which tests and digitally signs the drivers. Video drivers often include additional software support and hardware functionality. For example, drivers sourced directly from NVIDIA or AMD for their graphics cards include the NVIDIA Control Panel or the AMD Catalyst control panel, respectively.

If you are seeking the most up-to-date or even a beta version of a device driver, you must download this directly from your device manufacturer. In most cases, you will not need to upgrade your device driver after Windows 10 is installed. If everything is working properly, you probably don't need to install extra hardware drivers.

If you are a gamer, it can be beneficial to ensure that your graphics card drivers are using the latest versions, so that they support the latest PC games.

You should consider downloading new driver packages in the following scenarios.

- **If you play PC games**   Install the latest graphics drivers directly from your graphics card manufacturer because they are often required to play the latest games. Newer versions can also improve graphics performance.

- **When you need a hardware utility**   Install the latest version if the manufacturer-provided driver package includes a hardware utility, such as a network configuration tool or ink monitor for your printer.

- **To resolve a bug**   Bugs can be found in released drivers and will often be fixed in the most up-to-date version.

- **To install hardware manually**   If Windows Plug and Play does not automatically detect and install the hardware, you might need to download the driver package from the manufacturer and install the device driver.

ADD PACKAGES USING DISM

The Deployment Image Servicing and Management (DISM) tool is now included as part of the Windows 10 operating system. It is useful for offline image servicing. DISM is a command-line tool that you can use to maintain images and apply them with Windows Updates. It is also used to add and remove Windows features, including language packs, and to manage device drivers.

If you have a custom Windows 10 image, you can use DISM to modify it, and the changes will be visible when you next deploy the image. This can be useful when you know that a driver has been updated since you built the deployment image. Using DISM to inject the new driver saves you from having to rebuild the whole image. Using DISM is similar to using a file compression tool, such as WinRAR, whereby you add or remove new files and then WinRAR reseals the .wim, .vhd, or .vhdx file so that it is ready for deployment.

When you use DISM to install a device driver to an offline image, the device driver is added to the Driver Store. When the image is booted, Plug and Play (PnP) runs, looks for drivers in the store, and associates them with the corresponding devices on the computer on which they're being installed.

To add drivers to an offline image by using DISM, use these steps:

1. Right-click the Start button and select Command Prompt (Admin).

2. Establish the name or index number for the image that you are servicing by typing:
   ```
   Dism /Get-ImageInfo /ImageFile:C: est\images\install.wim
   ```

3. Mount the offline Windows image by typing the following.
   ```
   Dism /Mount-Image /ImageFile:C: est\images\install.wim /Name:"Windows Offline
   Image" /MountDir:C:est\offline
   ```

4. You can now add the driver, located in the C:\Drivers folder, to the image by typing:
   ```
   Dism /Image:C: est\offline /Add-Driver /Driver:C:\drivers\New_driver.inf
   ```

5. If you have additional drivers in a folder, you can use the **/Recurse** option, which installs all the drivers from a folder and all its subfolders. To do this, type:
   ```
   Dism /Image:C: est\offline /Add-Driver /Driver:c:\drivers /Recurse
   ```

6. You can review the drivers in the Windows image by typing:

```
Dism /Image:C:est\offline /Get-Drivers
```

In the list of drivers, notice that the added drivers have been renamed Oem*.inf. This ensures that all driver files in the driver store have unique names. For example, the New_Driver1.inf and New_Driver2.inf files are renamed Oem0.inf and Oem1.inf.

7. To complete the operation, commit the changes and unmount the image by typing:

```
Dism /Unmount-Image /MountDir:C:\test\offline /Commit
```

> **NEED MORE REVIEW? DISM**
>
> For a detailed reference for the DISM command-line options, you can visit the Microsoft website at *https://docs.microsoft.com/en-us/previous-versions/windows/it-pro/windows-8.1-and-8/hh825099(v=win.10)*.

MANAGE DRIVER PACKAGES WITH DISM

During the life of a Windows 10 installation, the system downloads and installs multiple versions of device driver packages over time. For devices with small hard drive capacity, be aware of how to locate and delete outdated driver packages that the system retains.

You can use the built-in Disk Cleanup tool to remove device driver packages that have been kept after newer drivers are installed.

To clean up old device drivers by using the Disk Cleanup tool, perform these steps:

1. Click the Start button, type **Disk Cleanup,** and then select the Disk Cleanup app.

2. In the Drive Selection dialog box, select (C:) and click OK.

3. On the Disk Cleanup results screen, select Clean Up System Files.

4. In the Drive Selection dialog box, select (C:) and click OK.

5. On the Disk Cleanup results screen, select Device Driver Packages and click OK.

6. On the Are You Sure You Want To Permanently Delete These Files page, click Delete Files.

All driver packages that were installed during the Windows 10 setup process are stored in a directory called WinSxS, the side-by-side component store. This folder contains driver packages and operating system components, so that you can add devices later without having to supply device drivers. If disk space is limited, you can purge the WinSxS directory contents; doing so can be helpful because it could occupy a significant amount of disk space.

To analyze the Windows Component Store for driver packages and other files that can be deleted, you can use the DISM command by using the following steps:

1. Right-click the Start button, select Windows PowerShell (Admin), and type the following:

```
DISM /Online /Cleanup-Image /AnalyzeComponentStore
```

The tool analyzes your system. Typical results are shown in Figure 4-30.

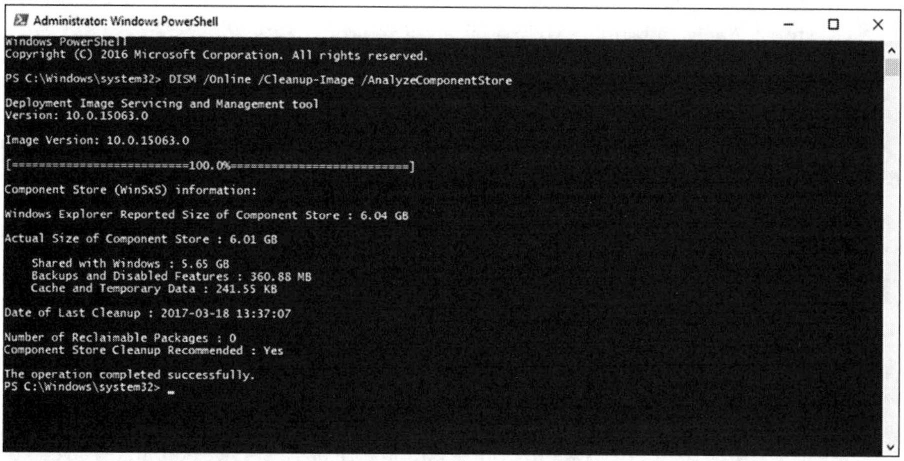

FIGURE 4-30 Analyzing the Component Store (WinSxS) with DISM

2. When the analysis is complete, you can initiate a cleanup of the Windows Component Store by typing the following command:

DISM /Online /Cleanup-Image /StartComponentCleanup /ResetBase

> **IMPORTANT   DO NOT DELETE THE WINSXS FOLDER**
>
> Do not manually delete the WinSxS directory or its contents to reclaim the space because Windows creates many hard links from files in the WinSxS folder to locations in system folders.

Managing Services

Another possible cause of startup problems in Windows 10 is services; these are software components that function with the operating system and usually require no user intervention. Usually, services start before a user signs in to a Windows computer.

If your computer experiences problems when starting, you can use the following tools to help to identify whether the issue relates to operating system services:

- **Event Viewer**   If services have problems, then generally, errors are written to the Windows log files. You use the Event Viewer tool to access these log files. Event Viewer is discussed in more detail later in this chapter.

- **Log files**   Outside of the built-in capabilities of the Windows logs, you can also enable additional logging within specific Windows components or within a particular app. For instance, you can enable more detailed logging of the startup process by selecting Boot Logging in the Advanced Startup Options menu.

- **Stop codes** Windows 10 is very robust and system crashes are rare. However, when they occur, you can use the stop codes generated to help to identity the cause. These stop codes might suggest that a service is the root cause of a system crash.

- **Notifications** Within the Action Center, you can view notifications from Windows about system events, including possible problems.

If your computer does not start as a result of an issue with services, you can attempt to resolve the problem in a number of ways. These include:

- **Safe Mode** Start your computer in Safe Mode; this reduces the number of services running and might enable you to start your computer successfully. Once started, you can then investigate the possible causes using the tools listed above.

- **Windows RE** Start your computer into Windows RE and then select the Command Prompt tool. Using commands such as **Net.exe** and **Sc.exe** enables you to manually control service behavior.

- **MSConfig.exe** The System Configuration tool has a Services tab that you can use to control service startup. You can choose to disable specific services from this console. You can also focus only on those services that are not built in to Windows, as shown in Figure 4-31.

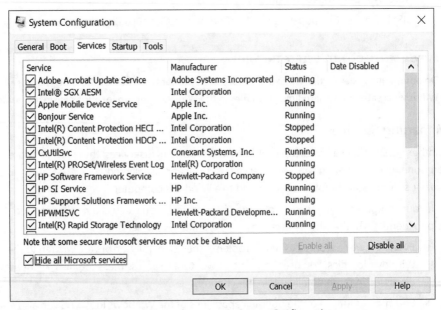

FIGURE 4-31 Viewing the non-Microsoft services in System Configuration

Skill 4.2: Manage updates

Keeping computers safe and protected from external threats such as malware and hackers is a big challenge. In earlier versions of Windows, you could decide whether the operating system was automatically updated with the latest features, security updates, and fixes through the Windows Update feature. Some users chose to disable automatic updates, and these computers are vulnerable to attack. With over a billion Windows devices worldwide, even if this number is a small percentage of the total, it might mean millions of devices were unprotected.

Windows 10 changes the game with regard to updates and security because it will continually and automatically benefit from new updates rolled out through Windows Update. To enhance the security protection delivered in Windows 10, the consumer can no longer turn off security updates. Enterprise users will have some leeway on the timing of updates and upgrades, and they can still choose to test updates and deliver them internally, using Windows Server Update Service (WSUS) or other management tools to keep their devices updated. For organizations that require deployment of a static installation of Windows 10 that will not have upgrades, Microsoft ships a special build of Windows 10, which is discussed later in this skill.

This skill covers how to:

- Select the appropriate servicing channel
- Configure Windows Update options
- Check for updates
- Validate and test updates
- Troubleshoot updates

Select the appropriate servicing channel

In order to keep your Windows computers running efficiently and securely, it is important to install updates from Microsoft when they become available. In the past, these updates were designed primarily to fix identified problems or security vulnerabilities. However, with Windows 10, Microsoft has introduced a new update model: Windows as a service.

With Windows as a service, updates are designed not only to resolve perceived defects in software, but also to add new features to the operating system. Instead of releasing new versions of Windows every few years, Microsoft now provides continual updates—updates that provide new features—to Windows 10.

As an IT professional supporting Windows 10 users, it's important that you know how to manage updates within your organization. A significant part of this understanding is based on understanding the new Windows as a service model.

Windows as a service

Windows as a service is more about Windows deployment than it is updating; in other words, the update mechanism is used to deliver, or deploy, new builds of Windows instead of relying on more traditional deployment methods.

As an organization, this means that instead of planning and performing operating system upgrades, such as from Windows 7 to Windows 10, you use Windows Update to continually introduce new Windows 10 features as the operating system evolves.

Microsoft now deploys the following types of updates:

- **Feature updates**   These add significant functionality to the Windows 10 operating system, and to date, these updates have been deployed twice a year—spring and fall. These updates are usually identified by their year and month. For example, this book and its companion exam, are based on Windows 10 1809, which shipped in September 2018. Other feature updates include Windows 10 1703, Windows 10 1709, and Windows 10 1803.

- **Quality updates**   These provide reliability and security updates and fixes. Microsoft deploys these updates monthly on the second Tuesday of the month. They are cumulative, meaning that even if you miss an update, by applying a subsequent update, you receive all previous updates.

Users of Windows 10 Home editions have no control over how their computers receive these updates. However, users in business and educational organizations who are using Windows 10 Pro, Windows 10 Enterprise, or Windows 10 Education editions can control their update experience using

- **Servicing channels**   Microsoft provides several servicing channels. These channels determine when updates are applied to a computer. These channels are
    - Windows Insider Program
    - Semi-Annual Channel
    - Long-Term Servicing Channel

- **Deployment rings**   You can define deployment rings by using Group Policy Objects (GPOs) or Microsoft Intune. These deployment rings use a selected servicing channel and additional Windows settings to determine when updates apply. By configuring groups of computers with matching settings, you can control updates to that group.

Select the servicing channel

To configure the appropriate servicing channel for a device, use the following procedure:

1.   Open Settings.
2.   Select Update & Security and then, on the Windows Update tab, click Advanced Options.

3. As shown in Figure 4-32, under the Choose When Updates Are Installed heading, select the appropriate servicing channel. Options are

- Semi-Annual Channel
- Semi-Annual Channel (Targeted)

4. You can also choose to defer the application of both Feature and Quality updates by selecting a value from the appropriate drop-down menu. You can defer feature updates for up to 365 days. You can defer quality updates for up to 30 days.

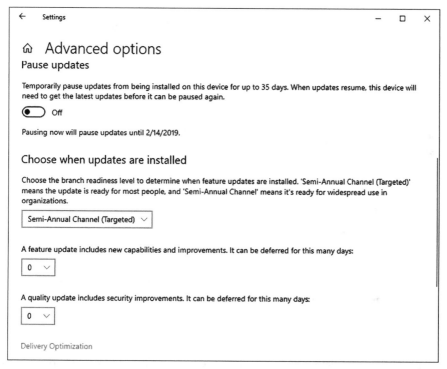

FIGURE 4-32 Windows Update Advanced Options

> **NOTE   SERVICING DURATION**
>
> All releases of Windows 10 have 18 months of servicing across all editions. September feature updates for Windows 10 Enterprise and Education editions have 30 months of servicing from initial release.

The Windows Insider Program enables users of Windows 10 to gain an insight into features update before they're released. They can also provide feedback to Microsoft during their evaluation of those feature updates. To opt in to the Windows Insider Program channel, use the following procedure:

1. Open the Settings app.

2. Select Update & Security and then select the Windows Insider Program tab.

3. As shown in Figure 4-33, on the Windows Insider Program tab and under the Get Insider Preview Builds heading, click Get Started.

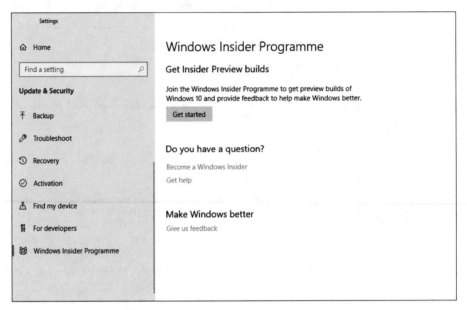

FIGURE 4-33 Windows Insider Program

Using deployment rings

By selecting an appropriate servicing channel, and then configuring feature update and quality update deferral values, you can create deployment rings. You might decide that you require a test group of computers that get updates early. You may also decide to create a group of computers that receive updates reasonably quickly after release. After testing, you might then want to enable the bulk of your remaining computers to receive the updates. You could achieve this by using the deployment rings described in Table 4-3.

TABLE 4-3 Suggested deployment rings

RING	CHANNEL	FEATURE DEFERRAL	QUALITY DEFERRAL	EXPLANATION
Test	Windows Insider Program	0 days	0 days	Enables you to evaluate and test pre-release updates before they are deployed to your other devices. During this phase, you can begin to identify any potential issues with the updates.
Early	Semi-Annual Channel (Targeted)	0 days	0 days	Enables you to evaluate released updates on a small subset of your devices. This enables you to identify any possible problems before you deploy updates to the rest of your computers.
Standard	Semi-Annual Channel	90 days	15 days	For most of your users, the deferment values ensure that you have had adequate time to test updates and to identify possible problems.
Slow	Semi-Annual Channel	365 days	30 days	This ring might be used to ensure that updates are applied as long as possible after their release. Devices configured into this ring might be running critical apps or services.

To configure deployment rings for Active Directory Domain Services (AD DS) domain-joined devices, use GPO settings. These settings are discussed in the next section. To configure deployment rings for non-domain-joined devices, use Microsoft Intune. You can configure the deployment rings using the Microsoft 365 Device Management portal, as shown in Figure 4-34. Details about this process are beyond the scope for this book, as they are not covered in the MD-100 Windows 10 exam. Note, in the Microsoft 365 Device Management portal, deployment rings are referred to as update rings.

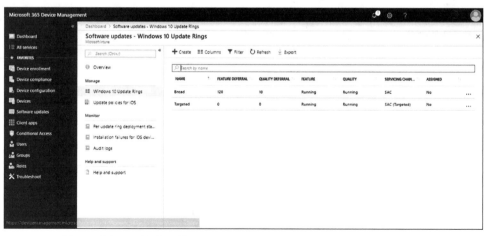

FIGURE 4-34 Microsoft Intune Update Rings

Configure Windows Update options

After you have planned your deployment rings, you must configure the Windows Update settings. You can do this either on a per-computer basis, by using the Settings app, or by using GPOs to configure AD DS domain-joined computers.

Configuring settings on an individual computer

To configure the Windows Update settings on an individual computer, open the Settings app and select Update & Security. You can then configure the following settings.

WINDOWS UPDATE

Select the Windows Update tab, as shown in Figure 4-35.

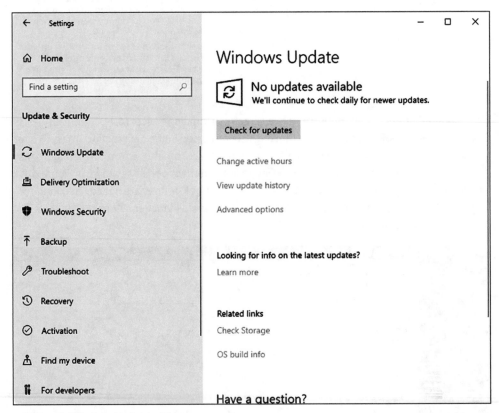

FIGURE 4-35 Windows Update settings

You can then configure active hours, view update history, and configure advanced options (discussed above).

- **Change Active Hours** This setting allows the user to identify the period of time when they expect the device to be in use. Automatic restarts after an update will occur outside of the active hours. The default is 8 AM to 5 PM.

- **View Update History** Provides access to the links to uninstall updates and to access recovery options. You can also see a list of recent updates, as shown in Figure 4-36. To uninstall updates, click the link and select the update you want to remove.

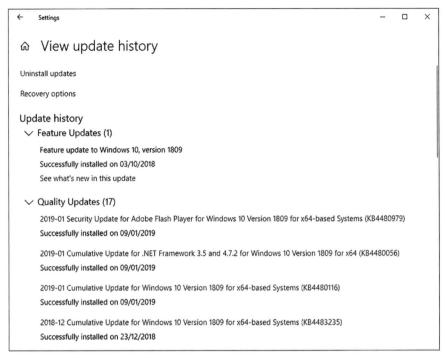

FIGURE 4-36 Viewing update history

- **Advanced options** On the advanced options page, shown in Figure 4-37, you can configure the following properties:
    - **Give Me Updates For Other Microsoft Products When I Update Windows** Users can choose to include updates for other Microsoft products in addition to Windows, and use the users' sign-in info to automatically sign back in to the device to complete the installation following an update.
    - **Automatically Download Updates, Even Over Metered Data Connections** Enables users to ensure they receive updates, even when connected using cellular data.
    - **Update Notifications** Allows Windows to display a notification when a restart is required following updates.
    - **Pause Updates** Enables the user to turn off updating for a period of up to 35 days.

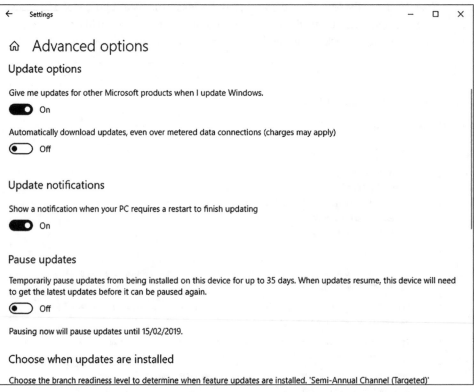

FIGURE 4-37 Changing advanced Windows Update options

The remaining settings were discussed earlier in this skill.

DELIVERY OPTIMIZATION

In Windows 10, you have several options regarding how Windows updates and Microsoft Store apps are delivered to the computer. By default, Windows obtains updates from the Microsoft Update servers, computers on the local network, and on the Internet. Windows Update Delivery Optimization allows the application of updates more quickly than previous versions of Windows. Once one PC on your local network has installed an update, other devices on the network can obtain the same updates without downloading directly from Microsoft.

This process is similar to popular peer-to-peer file sharing apps. Only partial file fragments of the update files are downloaded from any source, which speeds up the delivery and increases the security of the process. If you allow delivery optimization to take place, you then can choose from the following options how your PC will obtain updates and apps from other PCs:

- **PCs On My Local Network**   Windows will attempt to download from other PCs on your local network that have already downloaded the update or app.

- **PCs On My Local Network, And PCs On The Internet**   Windows will attempt to download from the PCs on your local network, and Windows also looks for PCs on the Internet that are configured to share parts of updates and apps.

If Delivery Optimization is enabled, your computer can also send parts of apps or updates that have been downloaded using Delivery Optimization to other PCs locally or on the Internet. To enable Delivery Optimization, from Settings, in Update & Security, select the Delivery Optimization tab, as shown in Figure 4-38.

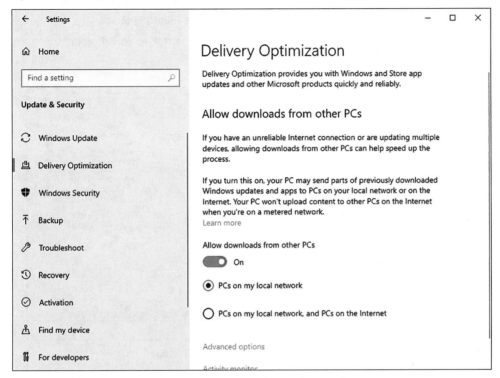

FIGURE 4-38 Editing the Delivery Optimization settings for Windows Update

Note that there are additional delivery optimization settings that you can configure by using GPO settings. These settings are discussed in the next section.

Configuring settings using GPOs

Although you can configure all your computers running Windows 10 manually, it is far easier and quicker to use Group Policy to configure your domain-joined computers. You can configure the following Windows Update settings using GPOs:

- Computer Configuration\Administrative Templates\Windows Components\Windows Update as shown in Table 4-4.

- Computer Configuration\Administrative Templates\Windows Components\Data Collection And Preview Builds as shown in Table 4-5.

- Computer Configuration\Administrative Templates\Windows Components\Delivery Optimization as shown in Table 4-6.

- Computer Configuration\Administrative Templates\Windows Components\Windows Update\Windows Update for Business as shown in Table 4-7.

To set a GPO to configure Windows Update, complete the following steps:

1. On a domain controller, open Group Policy Management.

2. Right-click a suitable GPO and then click Edit.

3. In the Group Policy Management Editor, shown in Figure 4-39, navigate to the appropriate node and edit the appropriate setting(s) as per the following tables.

4. Close the editor when you are finished. The GPOs will refresh to domain-joined computers.

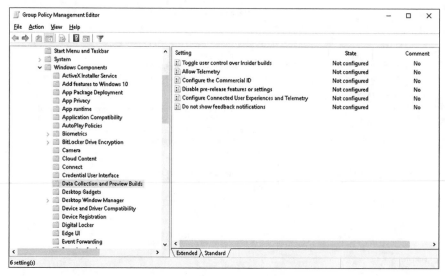

FIGURE 4-39 Editing Data Collection and Preview Builds GPO settings

TABLE 4-4 Windows 10 GPO settings in the Windows Update node

GPO SETTING	DESCRIPTION
Turn Off Auto-Restart For Updates During Active Hours	Allows you to specify the active hours during which the PC won't restart.
Specify Active Hours Range For Auto-Restarts	Allows you to specify the maximum number of hours that active hours can be set. This time can be set between 8 and 18 hours.
Specify Deadline Before Auto-Restart For Update Installation	Allows you to enforce a restart between 2–14 days after a restart is scheduled.
Configure Auto-Restart Reminder Notification For Updates	Allows you to specify when auto-restart reminders are displayed.

(Continued)

GPO SETTING	DESCRIPTION
Turn Off Auto-Restart Notifications For Update Installations	Allows you to turn off all auto restart notifications.
Configure Auto-Restart Required Notifications For Updates	Allows you to specify how the restart notifications are dismissed. By default, this is automatic after 25 seconds.
Configure Automatic Updates	Configure whether Windows Update can enable automatic updates on your computer. If this setting is enabled, you must select one of the four options in the Group Policy setting (note there is no option 1): ■ 2 = Notify for download and auto install ■ 3 = Auto-download and notify for install ■ 4 = Auto-download and schedule the install ■ 5 = Allow local admin to choose setting If you select option 4, you can also modify a recurring schedule; otherwise all installations will be attempted every day at 03:00.
Specify Intranet Microsoft Update Service Location	Configure whether Windows Update will use a server on your network to function as an internal update service.
Do Not Allow Update Deferral Policies To Cause Scans Against Windows Update	Allows you to prevent update deferral policies to cause scans against Windows Update.
Remove Access To Use All Windows Update Features	Enabling this policy removes user access to Windows Update scan, download, and install features.
Specify Engaged Restart Transition And Notification Schedule For Updates	Enabling this policy allows you to configure settings related to PC restart following a period of time when auto restart settings have been configured.
Do Not Include Drivers With Windows Updates	If you enable this policy setting, Windows Update will not include drivers with Windows quality updates.
Configure Auto-Restart Warning Notifications Schedule For Updates	Controls when users receive notification reminders and warnings to restart their devices following an update installation.
Update Power Policy For Cart Restarts	For EDU devices that remain on charging carts overnight to receive updates to reboot during the scheduled install timeframe.
Defer Windows Updates\Select When Feature Updates Are Received	Controls the type of feature updates to receive and when based on branch readiness level.
Defer Windows Updates\Select When Quality Updates Are Received	Controls the type of quality updates to receive and when to receive them based on branch-readiness level.

There are seven GPO settings that relate to the Windows 10 Preview Builds, as described in Table 4-5.

TABLE 4-5 GPO settings in the Data Collection And Preview Builds node

GPO SETTINGS	DESCRIPTION
Toggle User Control Over Insider Builds	Determines whether users can access the Insider build controls in the Advanced Options for Windows Update.
Allow Telemetry	Determines the amount of diagnostic and usage data reported to Microsoft by Preview Build users, as follows. ■ 0= Security (Enterprise, EDU, Server, and IoT Operating Systems will send minimal telemetry data to Microsoft) ■ 1= Basic (Limited amount of diagnostic and usage data) ■ 2= Enhanced (Sends enhanced diagnostic and usage data). ■ 3= Full (Sends enhanced diagnostic and usage data plus additional diagnostics data during a crash).
Configure The Commercial ID	Allows you to define the identifier used to uniquely associate the device for when telemetry data is being sent to Microsoft.
Configure Authenticated Proxy Usage For The Connected User Experience And Telemetry Service	Allows you to block or allow the Connected User Experience and Telemetry service from automatically using an authenticated proxy to send data back to Microsoft.
Disable Pre-Release Features Or Settings	Determines the level to which Microsoft can experiment with the product to study user preferences or device behavior as follows: ■ 1 = Allows Microsoft to configure device settings only. ■ 2 = Allows Microsoft to conduct full experimentations.
Configure Connected User Experiences And Telemetry	Forward Connected User Experience and Telemetry requests to a proxy server.
Do Not Show Feedback Notifications	Allows you to prevent devices from showing feedback questions from Microsoft.

The third table of GPO settings allows you to modify the Delivery Optimization settings in Windows 10, so that you can fine tune and regulate the peer caching of updates.

TABLE 4-6 GPO settings in the Delivery Optimization node

GPO SETTINGS	DESCRIPTION
Absolute Max Cache Size (In GB)	Allows you to limit the maximum size in GB for the Delivery Optimization cache. The default size is 10 GB.
Enable Peer Caching While The Device Connects Via VPN	Can allow the device to participate in Peer Caching while connected via VPN to the domain network to download from or upload to other domain network devices, while either on the VPN or via the corporate network.
Download Mode	Configure the use of Windows Update Delivery Optimization for downloads of Windows apps and updates as follows: ■ 0=HTTP only: No peering ■ 1=LAN: HTTP blended with peering behind the same NAT ■ 2=Group: HTTP blended with peering across a private group ■ 3=Internet: HTTP blended with Internet Peering ■ 99=Simple: Download mode with no peering ■ 100=Bypass mode: Do not use Delivery Optimization and use BITS instead

(Continued)

GPO SETTINGS	DESCRIPTION
Group ID	Used to create a group ID to which the device belongs. Used to limit or to group devices.
Max Cache Age (In Seconds)	Specifies the maximum time in seconds that each file is held in the Delivery Optimization cache after downloading successfully. Default setting is 3 days.
Max Cache Size (Percentage)	Specifies the maximum cache size that Delivery Optimization uses as a percentage of available disk size. Default is 20%.
Maximum Download Bandwidth (In KB/S)	Specifies the maximum download bandwidth that the device can use across all concurrent download activities using Delivery Optimization.
Max Upload Bandwidth (In KB/S)	Defines the maximum upload bandwidth that a device will utilize for Delivery Optimization.
Minimum Background QoS (In KB/S)	Specifies the minimum download QoS (Quality of Service or Speed) for background downloads. Default is 500 KB/s.
Allow Uploads While The Device Is On Battery While Under Set Battery Level (Percentage)	Specify the value between 1 and 100 to allow the device to upload data to LAN and Group peers while on battery power. The device can download from peers while on battery regardless of this policy.
Minimum Disk Size Allowed To Use Peer Caching (In GB)	Specifies the required minimum disk size for the device to use Peer Caching. Default is 32 GB.
Minimum Peer Caching Content File Size (In MB)	Specifies the minimum content file size in MB enabled to use Peer Caching. Default value is 100 MB.
Minimum RAM Capacity (Inclusive) Required To Enable Use Of Peer Caching (In GB)	Specifies the minimum RAM size in GB required to use Peer Caching. Default value is 4 GB.
Modify Cache Drive	Specifies the drive Delivery Optimization will use for its cache.
Monthly Upload Data Cap (In GB)	Specifies the maximum total bytes in GB that Delivery Optimization is allowed to upload to Internet peers in each calendar month. Default value is 20 GB.
Maximum Download Bandwidth (Percentage)	Specifies the maximum download bandwidth that Delivery Optimization uses. The default value is 0.

Windows Update for Business settings in GPO enable you to control which deployment ring your users' computers are configured for. By using these settings, you control which servicing channel your users' devices use, and deferment values for both feature and quality updates.

TABLE 4-7 GPO settings in the Windows Update for Business node

GPO SETTINGS	DESCRIPTION
Manage Preview Builds	You can control whether your users' computers can be configured into the Insider Build servicing channel. Enable this value to configure the device into the Windows Insider Program.

(Continued)

GPO SETTINGS	DESCRIPTION
Select When Preview Builds And Feature Updates Are Received	This value enables you to select the servicing channel. You can choose between: ■ Preview Build – Fast ■ Preview Build – Slow ■ Release Preview ■ Semi-Annual Channel (Targeted) ■ Semi-Annual Channel You can then also select a deferment value.
Select When Quality Updates Are Received	If you enable this value, you can then define a deferment value (in days) for quality updates.

Check for updates

It is not usually necessary to check for updates manually. However, you can easily do so by opening the Settings app. In Update & Security, on the Windows Update tab, shown in Figure 4-40, click Check For Updates. Windows connects to Windows Update and retrieves a list of any pending updates.

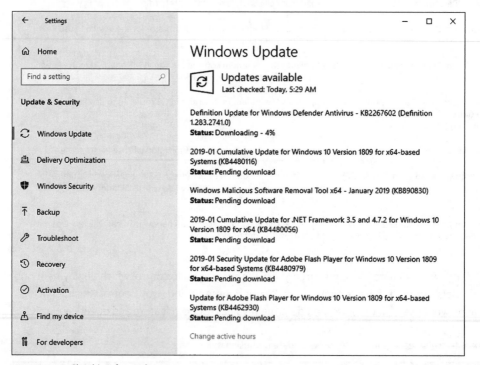

FIGURE 4-40 Checking for updates

NOTE **CAUTION**

If updates are available, they will automatically start to download and install, even if you have configured settings in GPO to only notify for download and install.

Validate and test updates

It is important that you know how Windows updates might affect your users' devices. Consequently, you should take the time to validate and test updates before making them available across your organization.

We have already discussed how using a servicing channel together with deferment values can be used to create the notion of deployment rings. Using deployment rings gives you an opportunity to obtain and test forthcoming updates before ongoing deployment.

In addition, you can consider using additional services to deploy Windows updates rather than relying solely on the Windows Update servers. Table 4-8 describes the additional options.

TABLE 4-8 Options for deployment of updates

GPO SETTINGS	DESCRIPTION
WSUS	This is a Windows Server 2019 server role. WSUS downloads updates from the Windows Update server(s). You can then configure how these updates are propagated to your client computers. This gives you time to test and validate updates.
Windows Update For Business	Essentially, you can consider this to be similar to WSUS. However, it is maintained in the cloud by Microsoft and is available for devices running Windows 10 Pro or Windows 10 Enterprise.
System Center Configuration Manager (SCCM)	If you already have SCCM for managing deployment, you can also use it to manage updates. SCCM gives you great control and flexibility in managing updates.
Microsoft Intune	Intune is a cloud-based device and app management tool. It's especially useful for managing non-domain-joined devices. With Intune, you can approve updates, deploy updates, and remove updates.

When testing updates, it's important that you make sure that all devices, peripherals, and apps will work with the new updates. This is particularly relevant when considering the deployment of feature updates.

Troubleshoot updates

If a machine is not receiving updates and you have checked the Settings app and Group Policy settings to ensure that updates are not deferred or paused, you should verify that the two services in Windows relating to Windows Update are running.

The first is the Windows Update service, which checks which updates have been installed locally and what is available on the update servers. The Windows Update service also handles the download, installation, and reporting of the state of updates.

Background Intelligent Transfer Service (BITS) is a supplemental service that handles the transfer of update files in the most efficient manner. Both services need to be running for Windows Update to function correctly.

You can also use the Windows Update troubleshooter. This is located on the Troubleshoot tab in Update & Security in the Settings app, as shown in Figure 4-41.

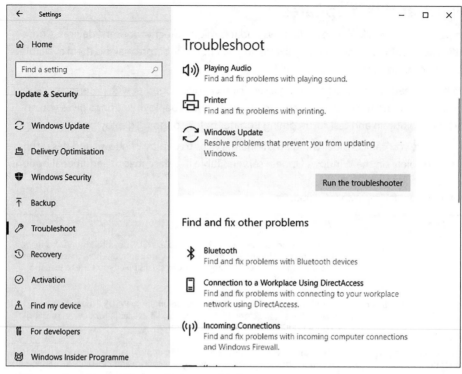

FIGURE 4-41 Running the Windows Update troubleshooter

Click Run The Troubleshooter. Windows attempts to check the required services and attempts to connect to the Windows Update server. If Windows identifies problems, as shown in Figure 4-42, it might make recommendations on how best to resolve the issue(s).

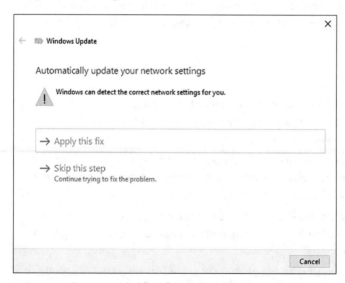

FIGURE 4-42 Recommended fixes for Windows Update problems

Roll back updates

With the rhythm of regular updates becoming the method of keeping devices secure and up to date, there might be instances when an update causes problems and you need to consider removing the update completely by rolling it back. You might have experience with driver rollbacks; the same concept is used for rolling back Windows updates.

Sometimes you need to remove a single Windows update. You can perform this task in a number of ways–through Control Panel, the Settings app, or the command prompt.

UNINSTALL A WINDOWS UPDATE BY USING CONTROL PANEL

If you prefer to use Control Panel, you can see an Installed Updates list in Control Panel by following these steps:

1. Click the Start button and type Control Panel, click Control Panel.
2. Open Programs > Programs And Features.
3. Click View Installed Updates.
4. Select an update that you want to uninstall.
5. If Windows allows you to uninstall it, Uninstall appears on the toolbar.
6. In the Uninstall An Update dialog box, click Yes to confirm.
7. Accept the UAC if prompted. A restart might be needed to complete the removal of the update.

UNINSTALL A WINDOWS UPDATE IN SETTINGS

The Settings app ultimately opens the same Installed Updates list in Control Panel. Perform these steps if you prefer to use the Settings app.

1. Open the Settings app and click Update & Security.
2. Click Windows Update and then click Update History. A list of your installed Windows Updates appears.
3. Click Uninstall Updates at the top of the screen. The link opens the Control Panel > Programs> Programs and Features > Installed Updates page.
4. Select an update that you want to uninstall. If Windows allows you to uninstall it, Uninstall appears on the toolbar.
5. In the Uninstall An Update dialog box, click Yes to confirm.
6. Accept the UAC if prompted. A restart might be needed to complete the removal of the update.

UNINSTALL A WINDOWS UPDATE BY USING THE COMMAND PROMPT

Sometimes you will want to remove the same update from multiple devices. After you have tested the command-line tool on your test device, you can use the command prompt or Windows PowerShell to script the command and distribute it to multiple devices by using Group Policy or Windows PowerShell.

You can use the Windows Management Instrumentation (WMI) command-line utility to generate a list of installed Windows Update packages on a Windows 10–based device, as shown in Figure 4-43.

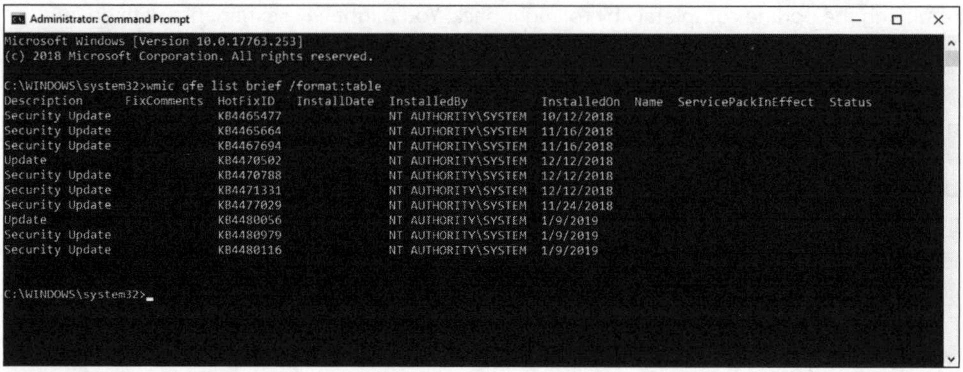

FIGURE 4-43 Command Prompt running the wmic qfe list command

To generate the list of installed Windows Update packages on your device, open a command prompt, (or Windows PowerShell) and type the following command.

```
wmic qfe list brief /format:table
```

When you have identified an update that you want to remove, you can use the Windows Update Stand-Alone Installer (Wusa.exe) command-line tool to uninstall updates by providing the package number (from the Microsoft Knowledge Base) of the update to be uninstalled. The syntax for the tool is as follows.

```
wusa.exe /uninstall /kb:<KB Number>
```

Substitute *<KB Number>* in the command with the actual KB number of the update you want to uninstall. The WMIC and WUSA commands work in either the command prompt or Windows PowerShell.

Skill 4.3: Monitor and manage Windows

After your computers are installed with Windows 10, it will be necessary to monitor and manage them. Windows 10 provides many tools with which to monitor your computers, including the Event Viewer, and a number of performance-monitoring tools, including Resource Monitor and Performance Monitor.

In addition to monitoring your computers, it is important you are familiar with how to manage important elements of the operating system, including printers and printing, indexing, and services.

> **This skill covers how to:**
> - Configure and analyze event logs
> - Manage performance
> - Manage the Windows 10 environment

Configure and analyze event logs

A key built-in security tool in all Windows operating systems are event logs, which are accessed in the Windows Event Viewer and provide information regarding system events that occur. Event logs are generated as a background activity by the Event Log service and can include information, warning, and error messages about Windows components and installed applications and actions carried out on the system.

Understand event logs

You can start Event Viewer, as shown in Figure 4-44, by typing **eventvwr.msc**.

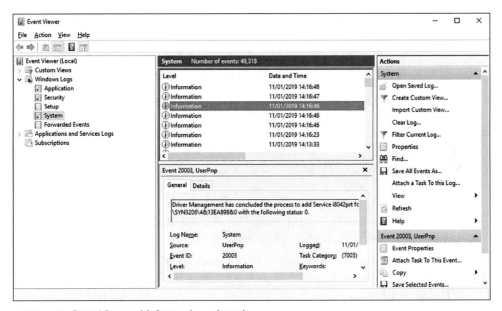

FIGURE 4-44 Event Viewer with System log selected

Upon opening, the console retrieves the events that have occurred on your computer and displays them. You can configure the Event Viewer to work with event logs from remote computers; you must enable remote management in your firewall.

There are two types of log files.

- **Windows logs**   Includes Application, Security, Setup, System, and Forwarded Events
- **Applications and services logs**   Includes other logs from applications and services to record application-specific or service-specific events

Because logs are created as part of the operating system, they can provide forensic-level metadata that can help you understand problems that are difficult to diagnose, using real-time analysis of the system.

The Windows logs are described in more detail in Table 4-9.

TABLE 4-9 Built-in Windows logs

LOG	DESCRIPTION	LOG FILE LOCATION	DEFAULT LOG SIZE
Application	Events logged by installed applications.	%SystemRoot%\System32\Winevt\Logs\Application.Evtx	20,480 KB
Setup	Records events logged by Windows during setup and installation.	%SystemRoot%\System32\Winevt\Logs\Setup.Evtx	1,028 KB
Security	Contains auditable events such as logon, logoff, privilege use, and shutdown.	%SystemRoot%\System32\Winevt\Logs\Security.Evtx.	20,480 KB
System	Contains events logged by Windows 10. This is the main system log.	%SystemRoot%\System32\Winevt\Logs\System.Evtx	20,480 KB
Forwarded Events	Used when event forwarding is operational. This log records forwarded events from other computers.	%SystemRoot%\System32\Config\ForwardedEvents.Evtx	20,480 KB

The default Windows 10 event log maximum file size is 20 MB. If your system reaches this maximum size, new events will overwrite old events.

Open Event Viewer and take some time to familiarize yourself by reviewing some logs. There are several levels of events, with meanings as follows.

- **Information**   These logs provide information about changes related to a component or system process, usually a successful outcome.
- **Warning**   These events are not critical, although they could lead to more serious problems and should be investigated.
- **Error**   Events warn you that a problem has occurred.
- **Critical**   These events are the most severe and could lead to failure or loss of function. They are highly significant and indicate that a problem is occurring or has occurred.

- **Audit Success/Failure**   If you have enabled auditing, these log entries appear in the security log.

In Event Viewer, select each of the Windows logs and look at the types of events that have been generated. The Actions pane on the right side provides tools and wizards to help you work with logs, including saving a log, clearing/deleting entries in a log, opening a previously saved log, and attaching a task to an event.

Create a custom view

When you explore Event Viewer, you might find so many entries that it is hard to locate specific issues. You'll want to remove entries, but you should not clear a log on a production machine without first saving the log. A better method of removing log entries, such as informational or warning log entries, is to create a custom view that shows only specific events. This acts like a saved filter that you can invoke.

To create a custom view in Event Viewer that displays only Critical events in the System log, follow these steps:

1. Open Event Viewer.
2. On the Action menu, click Create Custom View.
3. On the Filter tab, select the Critical check box in Event Level.
4. In By Log, use the Down arrow and expand Windows Logs; select only the System check box and then click OK.
5. Type a name, such as **System-Critical** for the log name, and click OK.
6. The custom view immediately refreshes and displays log entries that match the criteria.
7. Your custom view filter—in this case, named System-Critical—is located in the left pane under the Custom Views node.
8. Close Event Viewer.

With all events, you can double-click the event log entry to reveal its Properties dialog box. The Event Properties dialog box provides you with additional detailed information together with a Copy button so that you can copy the event data to the Clipboard and then work with the data or seek help. Event descriptions have become easier to understand than in previous versions of Windows. The experience of reading event log entries will also help build your understanding.

Configure event subscriptions

You can configure Event Viewer to gather other computers' event logs. Manually connecting to other computers on a regular basis can be cumbersome. You can automate the collection of event logs from other computers by creating event subscriptions.

All computers participating in a subscription must be configured to allow remote administration. This is achieved by enabling the Windows Remote Management service on the source computer. On the collector computer, start the Windows Event Collector service, which enables the computer to collect events from remote devices. To configure the computers to collect and send events, perform the following two short procedures.

VIEW SUBSCRIPTIONS

To enable the collector computer to view subscriptions:

1. Open an elevated command prompt.
2. Type **wecutil qc** and press Enter.
3. Type **Y** and press Enter to start the Windows Event Collector service. Windows Event Collector service announces it was configured successfully.
4. Close the command prompt window.

To enable remote collection of events on the source computer, follow these steps:

1. Open an elevated command prompt.
2. Type **winrm quickconfig** and press Enter.
3. Type **Y** and press Enter; repeat when prompted. The WinRM firewall exception is now enabled.
4. Close the command prompt window.

You can create two kinds of subscriptions: collector-initiated and source computer–initiated. The subscriptions are described in Table 4-10, with some of the key terms related to event subscriptions.

TABLE 4-10 Event subscription terms

TERM	DESCRIPTION
Subscription	A group of events you configure based on specific criteria you create is called a subscription. Subscriptions enable you to receive events from other computers, called sources.
Source	The event source computer is the computer that provides you with events on your network. The source computer can be a PC or a server.
Collector	The event collector computer is the computer on which you view the collected events. The collector computer can be a PC or a server.
Collector-initiated subscription	In a collector-initiated subscription, the subscription must contain a list of all the event sources that need to be added one at a time. This is used on small networks because each must be configured manually.
Source computer–initiated subscription	The source computer transmits local events to the collector computer. This is a push type of arrangement, often configured using Group Policy.

CREATE A SUBSCRIPTION

To create a collector-initiated subscription, follow these steps:

1. Open Event Viewer.
2. Click the Subscriptions node.
3. If the option to start the Windows Event Collection Service dialog box appears, click Yes.

4. In the Action pane, click Create Subscription.

5. Type a name and a description for the subscription, as shown in Figure 4-45.

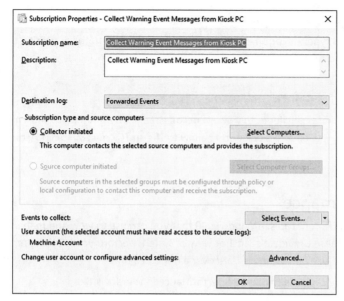

FIGURE 4-45 Creating an event subscription

6. Under Subscription Type And Source Computers, click Collector Initiated and click Select Computers.

7. In the Computers dialog box, click Add Domain Computers, select the computer to be polled for subscriptions, and click OK.

8. Under Events To Collect, click Select Events and define the event criteria—such as event levels, log type, and event source—that will be used to match and collect events. Click OK.

9. Click OK to save and make the subscription active.

   The new subscription is listed in the main pane of the Subscriptions node.

If you want to view events on other computers on your network, you can do so without creating a subscription. This is useful for ad hoc monitoring, for example, to see whether a particular event has occurred.

Access event logs remotely

When you need to quickly view event logs on a remote computer, you don't need to create a subscription. Instead you can view the event logs directly. To view event logs on a remote system, follow these steps:

1. Open Event Viewer.

2. Right-click Event Viewer (Local) in the left pane and choose Connect To Another Computer.

3. When the Select Computer dialog box opens, click Another Computer and enter the name, type the domain name or IP address of the computer, or click Browse to search for the computer on your network.

4. If you need to specify logon credentials, select the Connect As Another User check box. Click Set User and type the logon credentials for a local administrator or user on the remote device and then click OK.

> **NOTE   VIEW EVENTS ON REMOTE COMPUTERS**
> You must have administrator privileges to view events on a remote computer. You must also configure Windows Firewall on all participants to allow traffic on TCP port 80 for HTTP or on TCP port 443 for HTTPS.

Manage performance

There are a number of different tools in Windows 10 that you can use to view and manage performance. Some of these provide a snapshot view of system performance. Others provide a means to collect and analyze performance data over a period of time.

You can use the following tools to manage performance in Windows 10:

- Task Manager
- Resource Monitor
- Performance Monitor

Monitor performance using Task Manager

If you have used an earlier version of Windows, you probably have used Task Manager. This is one of the most useful tools available in Windows for gaining an immediate insight into how a system is performing.

ACCESS TASK MANAGER

The Task Manager built into Windows 10 shows you which processes (tasks) are running on your system and, importantly, shows the system resource usage that directly relates to performance. If a particular task or process is not responding or continues to run after you have closed the application, you can use Task Manager to view this behavior and force the offending process to end.

When troubleshooting, you might find that some users are comfortable using Task Manager to review the system status and end problematic tasks.

If you are moving to Windows 10 from Windows 7 or earlier, notice that Task Manager has been redesigned extensively and is now much more user-friendly, informative, colorful, and slightly less technical.

To open Task Manager, right-click the Start button and then click Task Manager. There are several other ways to open Task Manager, including

- Pressing Ctrl+Shift+Esc
- Right-clicking the taskbar, Cortana, or the Task View button and then clicking Task Manager

By default, the Task Manager opens to show only the running applications, as shown in Figure 4-46. While using this view, you can highlight any of the listed applications and click End Task to stop a running app.

FIGURE 4-46 Task Manager

If you click More Details, Task Manager reopens and displays seven tabs, which enable you to review specific areas of your computer activity. The tabs are described in Table 4-11.

TABLE 4-11 Task Manager tabs

TASK MANAGER TAB	DESCRIPTION
Processes	Shows all running apps and background processes
Performance	Shows real-time statistics for CPU, memory, disk, Ethernet, Bluetooth, and Wi-Fi usage
App History	Shows historical data for universal and modern apps usage for the previous month
Startup	Lists the apps that start when the computer boots
Users	Lists all the users currently logged on to the computer locally and remotely
Details	Shows detailed statistics on all running and suspended processes
Services	Displays all running and stopped system services

Each tab offers you a different view of the system. Most users might be interested only in the simple view, whereas most IT professionals will only use the detailed version of Task Manager.

USING THE PERFORMANCE TAB

The Performance tab provides a graphical, real-time, statistical view for CPU, Memory, Disk, and Ethernet. If you have multiple Ethernet devices, such as Wi-Fi, these are listed. Figure 4-47 shows the Performance tab with Disk 0 selected. In the lower pane, below the graphics, you see additional information, such as read/write speed, capacity, and average response time. If you are connected to Wi-Fi and click Ethernet, you see the adapter name, Service Set Identifier (SSID), Domain Name Service (DNS) name, connection type, IPv4 and IPv6 addresses, and signal strength.

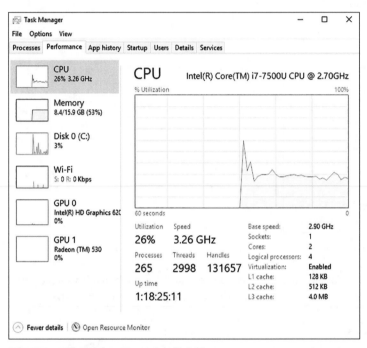

FIGURE 4-47 The Performance tab in Task Manager

At the bottom of the Performance tab is an Open Resource Monitor link to the management console.

Monitor performance using Resource Monitor

The Resource Monitor displays more information and activity statistics relating to your system resources in real time. It is similar to Task Manager, but it also enables you to dive deeper into the actual processes and see how they affect the performance of your CPU, disk, network, and memory subcomponents.

Open the Resource Monitor by using the link on the Performance tab of Task Manager or search for Resource on the Start button. The executable for Resource Monitor is Resmon.exe, which you can run from a Run dialog box or command prompt.

When you open Resource Monitor, you see an overview of your system with graphs for each area of the system subcomponent. Four further tabs are available: CPU, Disk, Network, and Memory. The statistics tracked on the Overview tab include the following:

- % CPU Usage
- CPU Maximum Frequency
- Disk I/O Bytes Per Second
- Disk % Highest Active Time
- Network I/O Bytes Per Second
- % Network Utilization
- Memory Hard Faults Per Second
- % Physical Memory Used

Review each tab; each subcomponent offers additional components, as shown in Table 4-12.

TABLE 4-12 Resource Monitor components

SYSTEM COMPONENT	ADDITIONAL SUBCOMPONENTS
CPU	Processes Services Associated Handles Associated Modules
Memory	Processes Physical Memory
Disk	Processes With Disk Activity Disk Activity Storage
Network	Processes With Network Activity Network Activity TCP Connections Listening Ports

In each data collector, you can sort the output by clicking the column title. If you select one or more processes in the topmost section, selecting the check box on the left side creates a filter for the items across all four tabs. The selected item is highlighted in orange, so that you can see how the item compares to the overall output, as shown in Figure 4-48.

The Resource Monitor is useful for troubleshooting performance issues that relate to high resource usage, and you need to establish which process is using a more than normal amount of resource such as memory.

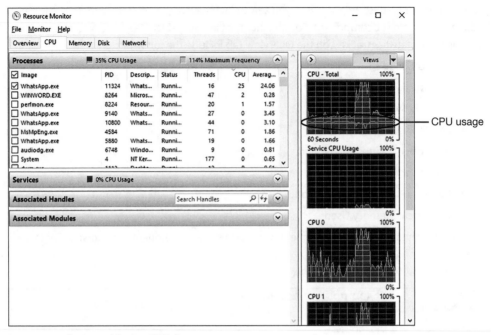

FIGURE 4-48 Resource Monitor CPU view

For more advanced analysis, you can right-click any column and choose additional columns by choosing Select Columns. Each tab has associated columns; the CPU panel offers the following additional columns.

- **Average Cycle** Average percentage of CPU cycle time for the process (over a 60-second interval).

- **Cycle** Current percentage of CPU cycle time the process is using.

- **Elevated** The elevation status of the process. (If this is Yes, it is an elevated process.)

- **Operating System Context** The operating system context in which the process is running.

- **Platform** The platform architecture that the process is running.

- **User Name** The name of the user or service that is running the process.

If you want to freeze the screen so that you can analyze the display or capture an image, you can click the Monitor menu item and select Stop Monitoring.

Monitor performance using Performance Monitor and Data Collector Sets

You can use the Performance Monitor Microsoft Management Console (MMC) snap-in to monitor and track your device for the default set of performance parameters or a custom set you select for display. These performance parameters are referred to as counters.

Performance Monitor graphically displays statistics and offers real-time monitoring and recording capabilities. By default, the update interval for the capture is set to one second, but this is configurable.

You can use the tool to record performance information in a log file so that it can be played back and used as part of your overall benchmarking process on a system being tested, or when collecting information to help you troubleshoot an issue. You can also create alerts that notify you when a specific performance criterion, such as a threshold or limit, has been met or exceeded.

The easiest way to learn how to use Performance Monitor is to run one of the two built-in collector sets and review the results.

- **System Diagnostics**   Data Collector Set collects the status of local hardware resources and configuration data, together with data from the System Information tool.
- **System Performance**   Data Collector Set reports the status of local hardware resources, system response times, and processes.

RUN THE PERFORMANCE MONITOR DATA COLLECTOR

To run the System Performance data collector and view the report, follow these steps:

1. Type **Performance** into Start and click Performance Monitor in Control Panel.
2. On the navigation pane, select Data Collector Sets\System and click System Performance.
3. On the toolbar, click the Run icon (green triangle). The collector runs for 60 seconds and then stops.
4. After the collector has stopped, in the navigation pane, select Reports and expand System.
5. Click the chevron arrow next to System Performance and then click the Report icon related to the collector you just ran. The latest report should be listed at the bottom. The System Performance Report appears in the results pane.
6. Review the System Performance Report and then close Performance Monitor.

When you review the report, as shown in Figure 4-49, you can see how extensive and detailed the monitoring is. The report is saved and can be printed and refreshed to provide an up-to-date report, which you can compare to other reports.

The diagnostic or performance-monitoring data collector sets are very useful when identifying the cause of performance deterioration, which might be a warning sign of potential malfunction or failing hardware.

You can manually configure Performance Monitor to report on one or many parameters you select for display. You choose the counters that relate to the hardware and software installed on your system. If you add new hardware, such as a new network card, Performance Monitor updates the set of performance counters for the new resource.

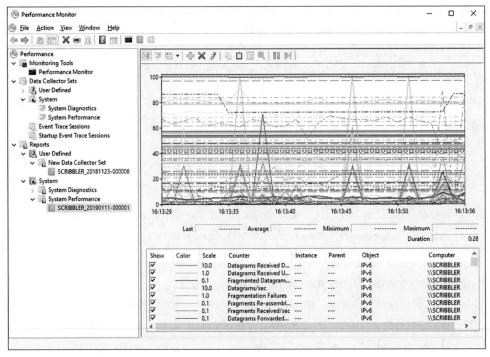

FIGURE 4-49 Viewing a report in Performance Monitor's reporting node

USE PERFORMANCE MONITOR

To use Performance Monitor, you start with a blank canvas and add items that you want to monitor. There are three components that you can add as follows.

- **Performance objects** These relate to any system component that enables monitoring, such as
    - **Physical** The memory, the processor, or the paging file
    - **Logical component** For example, a logical disk or print queue
    - **Software** For example, a process or a thread
- **Performance object instances** These represent single occurrences of performance objects. You can choose individual instances, or you can track all instances of an object.
- **Performance counters** These are the measurable properties of performance objects, such as the Bytes Sent/Sec for the Ethernet Controller as shown in Figure 4-50.

After some counters have been selected, a moving graphical display shows the activity relating to the counters selected. You can locate the color of the line from the key at the base of the graph and hide/show any counter by clearing the check box on the left of the counter.

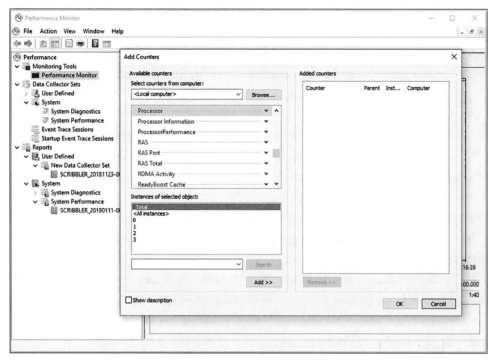

FIGURE 4-50 Adding objects and counters to Performance Monitor

A selection of the most common performance objects that you might want to monitor are summarized in Table 4-13.

TABLE 4-13 Commonly tracked performance objects

PERFORMANCE OBJECT	DESCRIPTION
Memory	Monitors memory performance for system cache, physical memory, and virtual memory
IPv4	Monitors IPv4 communications
LogicalDisk	Monitors the logical volumes on a computer
Network Interface	Monitors the network adapters on the computer
PhysicalDisk	Monitors hard disk read/write activity and data transfers, hard faults, and soft faults
Print Queue	Monitors print jobs, spooling, and print queue activity
Processor	Monitors processor idle time, idle states, usage, deferred procedure calls, and interrupts

Because the monitoring is performed in real-time, the effect of monitoring many counters can have an impact on the host system performance, which could distort the usefulness of the performance information. Therefore, you should test the number of counters and the frequency of data collection and witness the impact. To add new values to the Performance Monitor chart, follow these steps:

1. Click the Start button and type **perfmon**. Performance Monitor opens.

2. Click the Performance Monitor node in the left pane. The default counter for % Processor Time appears.

3. On the toolbar, click the plus (+) symbol to add an additional counter.

4. In the Available Counters area, expand PhysicalDisk, and click % Idle Time.

5. In the Instances Of Selected Object box, click 0 C:, click Add, and click OK.

6. Right-click % Idle Time and then click Properties.

7. In the Color box, click blue, and then click OK.

8. Leave Performance Monitor open.

To create a new Data Collector Set based on a template, in Performance Monitor, follow these steps:

1. In the left pane, expand Data Collector Sets and then click User Defined.

2. Right-click User Defined, click New, and then click Data Collector Set.

3. On the Create New Data Collector Set page, type **Disk Activity**, and click Next.

4. In the Template Data Collector Set box, click Basic and click Next.

5. Click Next to accept the default storage location.

6. Select Open Properties For This Data Collector Set and click Finish. The Disk Activity Properties dialog box appears and has six tabs.

7. Review the General, Directory, Security, Schedule, Stop Condition, and Task tabs and click OK.

8. In the right pane, double-click Disk Activity. Three types of logs are shown in the right pane:

   - **Performance Counter** Collects data that is viewable in Performance Monitor

   - **Configuration** Records changes to registry keys

   - **Kernel Trace** Collects detailed information about system events and activities

9. In the right pane, double-click Performance Counter.

10. Select the Processor Counter and click Remove.

11. Click Add and then click PhysicalDisk in Available Counters.

12. Click Add and then click OK.

13. In the left pane, right-click Disk Activity and then click Start.

14. On the Disk Activity node, a small play icon appears for 60 seconds.

15. When Data Collector Set has stopped recording, right-click Disk Activity and then click Latest Report.

16. Review the report, which shows the data that the data collector set collected.

17. Close Performance Monitor.

Monitor system resources

Every computer system has a performance threshold that, if pushed beyond this level, will cause the system to struggle to perform optimally. If you overload the system, it eventually slows down as it attempts to service each demand with the available resources. Most systems include a capable processor and sufficient amount of RAM for everyday or general needs. Memory is automatically reclaimed from apps that are closed. However, when apps or web browser tabs are left open, and more apps are then opened, the overall ability for the system to perform is degraded.

UNDERSTAND BASELINE PERFORMANCE VS. REAL-TIME MONITORING

You have seen that with tools, such as Performance Monitor, Resource Monitor, and Task Manager, you can monitor your system activity and understand how demands on processor, RAM, networking, and disks affect your computer system. Real-time monitoring information is useful for instant diagnosis. Also, creating a baseline for your computer's performance can generate a system-specific report that can be useful to show what your performance statistics look like during normal or heavy use.

If you intend to ship a device to a user who will use the device extensively for system-intensive tasks, such as video editing or computer-aided design, it might be useful to create a performance baseline for the device so that you can establish how the system performs normally and when under heavy load. This will be useful to confirm that the device specification is suitable for the user. Also, this will be helpful if the user reports performance issues because you can run another performance baseline and compare the two baselines to evaluate whether the system environment has changed. For example, perhaps the user now regularly multitasks with additional new apps on the system that use additional memory.

In this scenario, when an issue or symptom occurs, you can compare your baseline statistics to your real-time statistic and identify differences between the two instances. When you can diagnose the issue, you can recommend a solution, such as to add more memory.

The most appropriate tool to record a baseline in Windows 10 is Performance Monitor; it will help you review and report on the following areas in your system:

- Evaluate your system workload
- Monitor system resources
- Notice changes and trends in resource use
- Help diagnose problems

CREATE A PERFORMANCE BASELINE

To create a performance baseline that monitors key system components you can use to measure against a future performance baseline, follow these steps:

1. Click the Start button and type **perfmon**. Performance Monitor opens.
2. Click the Data Collector Sets node in the left pane.
3. Click User Defined, right-click User Defined, click New, and then click Data Collector Set.

4. In the Create New Data Collector Set Wizard, on the How Would You Like To Create This New Data Collector Set page, in the Name box, type **Initial PC Baseline**.

5. Click Create Manually (Advanced) and then click Next.

6. On the What Type Of Data Do You Want To Include page, select the Performance Counter check box and then click Next.

7. On the Which Performance Counters Would You Like To Log page, in the Sample Interval box, type **1** and then click Add.

8. Include the following counters.

   - Memory > Pages/Sec
   - Network Interface > Packets/Sec
   - PhysicalDisk > % Disk Time
   - PhysicalDisk > Avg. Disk Queue Length
   - Processor > % Processor Time
   - System > Processor Queue Length

9. Click OK and then click Finish.

10. Right-click Initial PC Baseline and then click Start.

11. Simulate load on the system by starting several programs, including Internet Explorer, Word 2016, Microsoft Excel 2016, and Microsoft PowerPoint 2016.

12. Close all Microsoft Office apps, close Internet Explorer, and stop the Initial PC Baseline data collector set.

13. To view the baseline report, in Performance Monitor, expand the Reports\User Defined node\Initial PC Baseline and click the report to open it.

14. Print the report or view the report and record the values for the following counters.

   - Memory > Pages/sec
   - Network Interface > Packets/Sec
   - PhysicalDisk > % Disk Time
   - PhysicalDisk > Avg. Disk Queue Length
   - Processor > % Processor Time
   - System > Processor Queue Length

Troubleshoot performance issues

In normal operating conditions, the majority of users rarely experience performance issues with their devices after they have been configured with the necessary security, antimalware, productivity, and specialist software. Out of the box, Windows 10 is optimized for general user environments.

Over time, the device might gradually seem to become slower. If the user notices this decreased system performance, he or she might request help from the help desk.

You can avoid some performance degradation by performing regular maintenance, such as using the Disk Cleanup utility to remove temporary or unwanted files. Windows 10 does a good job at self-healing and maintaining the system and schedules many maintenance tasks to run automatically for you.

If poor performance occurs, investigate and troubleshoot the reason to establish whether there is a bottleneck—perhaps a memory-hungry app, multiple startup programs, or even malware. Another gradual but common occurrence is when a system runs out of disk space, especially because the majority of devices are now using solid-state drives (SSDs) that are typically smaller-capacity drives.

When looking at the factors that might influence your PC, consider some of the following.

- Windows 10 architecture: x86 or x64
- Processor speed, processor quantity, onboard cache memory, and cores
- Physical hard disks input/output speed, buffer size, and defragmentation state
- Memory: capacity, speed, and type
- Graphics card: throughput, memory, onboard processing speed, quantity, and drivers
- Network interface throughput, onboard processing capability, quantity, and drivers
- Application number, type, available optimizations, and architecture
- System, peripheral, and application drivers

Understand how system bottlenecks can occur, how to diagnose a system that is suffering from a performance bottleneck, and how to respond and recover from the problem. Some common performance bottlenecks that are useful to know about when troubleshooting are shown in Table 4-14.

TABLE 4-14 Performance bottlenecks

PERFORMANCE COUNTER	BOTTLENECK
LogicalDisk\% Free Space	If this is less than 15 percent, you risk running out of free space for Windows 10 to use to store critical files.
PhysicalDisk\% Idle Time	If this is less than 20 percent, the disk system is overloaded. Consider replacing with a faster disk.
PhysicalDisk\Avg. Disk Sec/Read	If the number is larger than 25 milliseconds (ms), the disk system is experiencing read latency; suspect drive failure (or a very slow and/or old disk).
PhysicalDisk\Avg. Disk Sec/Write	If the number is larger than 25 milliseconds (ms), the disk system is experiencing write latency; suspect drive failure (or a very slow and/or old disk).

(Continued)

PERFORMANCE COUNTER	BOTTLENECK
PhysicalDisk\Avg. Disk Queue Length	If the value is larger than 2 times the number of drive spindles, the disk might be the bottleneck.
Memory\% Committed Bytes in Use	If the value is greater than 80 percent, it indicates insufficient memory.
Memory\Available Mbytes	If this value is less than 5 percent of the total physical RAM, there is insufficient memory, which can increase paging activity.
Processor\% Processor Time	If the percentage is greater than 85 percent, the processor is overwhelmed, and the PC might require a faster processor.
System\Processor Queue Length	If the value is more than twice the number of CPUs for an extended period, you should consider a more powerful processor.
Network Interface\Output Queue Length	There is network saturation if the value is more than 2. Consider a faster or additional network interface.

Manage Windows 10 environment

In this section, you will learn how to manage printers, control and configure indexing, evaluate system stability, and configure and manage services.

Monitor and manage printers

Windows 10 provides some additional options for you to manage your printing compared to previous versions of Windows. A new Print Management desktop app and the new Printers & Scanners options in the Settings app provide basic printer management such as Add, Remove, and Set As Default Printer.

You still have previous printer tools in the Devices And Printers section of Control Panel or from the link at the bottom of the Printers & Scanners options in the Settings app. The Devices And Printers Control Panel item is the same interface as in previous versions of Windows 7. This section focuses on the new features relating to Printer With Windows 10, but for the exam, you should also review the older printer tools.

MANAGE PRINTERS BY USING PRINT MANAGEMENT

A new Print Management console is available for you to manage your device printers from a single management console. Print devices connected to your PC can be shared, and you can manage the properties of the device. The Print Management MMC, as shown in Figure 4-51, is included in the Administrative Tools of Windows 10 Pro and Enterprise editions, and it lists all printers, drivers, and other print servers that you are connected to.

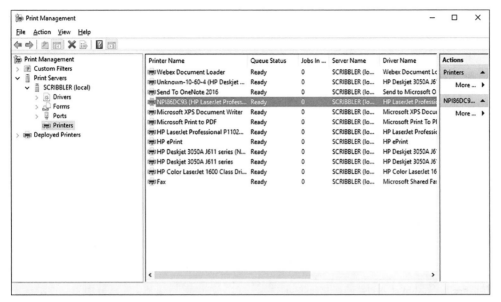

FIGURE 4-51 Managing printers

You can also launch the Print Management console by typing **Printmanagement.msc** in the Start menu.

The Print Management console offers you a single location to perform the following printer-related management tasks:

- Add and delete print devices
- View printers and print servers
- Add and remove print servers
- Add and manage print drivers
- Deploy printers using Group Policy
- Open and manage printer queues
- View and modify status of printers
- Use the filter feature to view printers based on filters

If you right-click a printer, you are presented with a list of some action items that can be performed on the selected printer. These can include the following tasks:

- Open Printer Queue
- Pause Printing
- List In Directory
- Deploy With Group Policy
- Set Printing Defaults
- Manage Sharing
- Print Test Page

- Enable Branch Office Direct Printing
- Properties
- Delete
- Rename
- Help

> **NOTE** **REMOTE PRINTERS**
>
> You can use the Print Management console to manage both local and remote printers. Devices And Printers in Control Panel can only manage locally connected printers.

MANAGE PRINTERS BY USING WINDOWS POWERSHELL

More than 20 Windows PowerShell cmdlets can be used to manage printers. Some of the most common cmdlets are shown in Table 4-15.

TABLE 4-15 Windows PowerShell printer cmdlets

CMDLET	DESCRIPTION
Add-Printer	Adds a printer to the specified computer
Add-PrinterDriver	Installs a printer driver on the specified computer
Add-PrinterPort	Installs a printer port on the specified computer
Get-PrintConfiguration	Gets the configuration information of a printer
Get-Printer	Retrieves a list of printers installed on a computer
Get-PrinterDriver	Retrieves the list of printer drivers installed on the specified computer
Get-PrinterPort	Retrieves a list of printer ports installed on the specified computer
Get-PrinterProperty	Retrieves printer properties for the specified printer
Remove-Printer	Removes a printer from the specified computer
Remove-PrinterDriver	Deletes printer drivers from the specified computer
Remove-PrintJob	Removes a print job on the specified printer
Rename-Printer	Renames the specified printer
Restart-PrintJob	Restarts a print job on the specified printer
Resume-PrintJob	Resumes a suspended print job
Set-PrintConfiguration	Sets the configuration information for the specified printer
Set-Printer	Updates the configuration of an existing printer
Set-PrinterProperty	Modifies the printer properties for the specified printer

To list all the available cmdlets, type the following command into a Windows PowerShell console:

```
Get-Command -Module PrintManagement
```

Configure indexing options

To maintain the performance of Windows 10 search, the system automatically indexes data on your computer in the background. This data includes user-generated files, folders, and documents. Most users will never modify the default indexing settings, but you can add new areas to be indexed and exclude others. Common locations include your user profile areas and app data that you access frequently, such as Office apps.

If you store a lot of data in a storage space or a removable drive, you can add this location to Indexing Options to significantly speed up the performance of future searches in this location.

To view your existing indexing locations, type **Index** on the Start screen and click Indexing Options in Control Panel to see the Indexing Options dialog box shown in Figure 4-52.

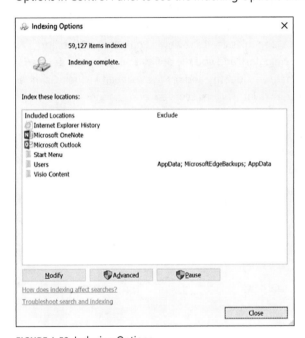

FIGURE 4-52 Indexing Options

You can use the Modify button to add or remove locations. In the Indexed Locations dialog box, you see the summary of locations. If you click Show All Locations, Windows 10 displays all the hidden locations, and this enables you to fine-tune the indexing to specific subfolders, if necessary. To select the Downloads and Documents folders within your profile, select the arrow next to the Users folder and then locate and select Downloads and Documents in your user profile.

After you apply changes to indexing, the indexing process doesn't happen immediately; rather, it runs as a background task whenever your machine is running but not being used.

While the indexing process is incomplete, the message in the dialog box indicates that Indexing Speed Is Reduced Due To User Activity. When the process has finished, the message states Indexing Complete.

Be careful not to index everything on your disk. A large index can affect the search performance negatively.

In the Indexing Options dialog box, the Advanced button enables you to configure Index Settings and specify File Types to be excluded. You can include or exclude encrypted files, treat similar words as different words, delete and rebuild the index (useful if you suspect search is not working), and change the index location from the default C:\ProgramData\Microsoft.

On the File Types tab, you can exclude file types from the index and configure whether the index searches in the file contents or just in the file properties. You can also manually add new file types that have not been automatically included to index.

Evaluate system stability by using Reliability Monitor

Members of the desktop support team often report that it is difficult to ascertain the precise nature of calls that relate to poor performance or system instability. Reliability Monitor is an excellent tool for these situations because it enables you to review a computer's reliability and problem history and offers both the help desk and you the ability to explore the detailed reports and recommendations that can help you identify and resolve reliability issues. Changes to the system such as software and driver installations are recorded, and changes in system stability are then linked to changes in the system configuration.

To launch Reliability Monitor, type **reliability** in the Start screen and click View Reliability History in Control Panel, or type **perfmon /rel** at a command prompt. The tool displays a summary of the reliability history for your system, as shown in Figure 4-53.

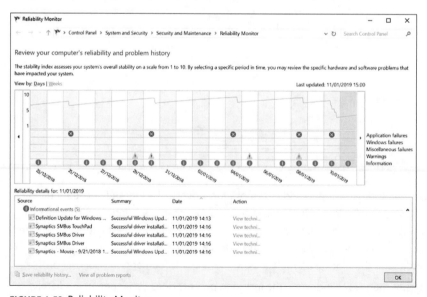

FIGURE 4-53 Reliability Monitor

The top half of the Reliability Monitor screen shows a line graph with a scale of 1 to 10 and date timeline along the bottom axis. You can toggle the view from weeks to days. The graph rises and sinks over time, and at the low points are colored markers in red, blue, or yellow. Below the graph are the details that relate to system configuration changes, such as software and driver installations. When system changes result in a negative system stability, such as an app crashing or a service stopping, there might be a relationship between the two, and these can be further explored. The graph gradually reaches the maximum level of 10 if the system does not experience negative system stability over a prolonged period.

Reliability Monitor is enabled by default in Windows 10. Reliability Monitor requires the Microsoft Reliability Analysis task, RacTask, to process system reliability data, which is a background process that collects reliability data. RacTask can be found in the Task Scheduler library under the Microsoft\Windows\RAC node.

The Reliability Monitor main features include:

- **System stability chart**   Provides summary of annual system stability in daily/weekly increments. The chart indicates three levels of stability data: information, warning messages, and critical errors.

- **Records key events in a timeline**   Tracks events about the system configuration, such as the installation of new apps, operating system patches, and drivers.

- **Installation and failure reports**   Provides information about each event shown in the chart, including:

    - Software Installs/Software Uninstalls

    - App Failures

    - Hardware & Driver Failures

    - Windows Operating System Failures

    - Miscellaneous Failures

Because the tool offers a rolling view of reliability history, you can retain a copy of a point-in-time report. Click the Save Reliability History link to save complete details at periodic time points, such as annually. System builders and repair shops often use the report to demonstrate computer stability for future reference.

At the bottom of the Reliability Monitor screen are two additional links that list all computer problems and attempt to locate problem solutions from the Internet. The Problem Reports And Solutions tool helps you track problems that are reported and checks for all available solution information to problems.

Configure and manage services

A service can best be described as a software component that interacts at one level with device drivers and, at another level, with app-level components. In a sense, services sit between apps and hardware devices and are considered a core part of the operating system, controlling user requests, through apps, to hardware resources.

These operating system services provide discrete functions in Windows 10 and require no user interaction. You can manage services in a number of ways, including from the command prompt, by using Windows PowerShell, and by using the management console.

USING THE SERVICES MANAGEMENT CONSOLE SNAP-IN

The most straightforward way to manage services is to use the Services management console snap-in, as shown in Figure 4-54.

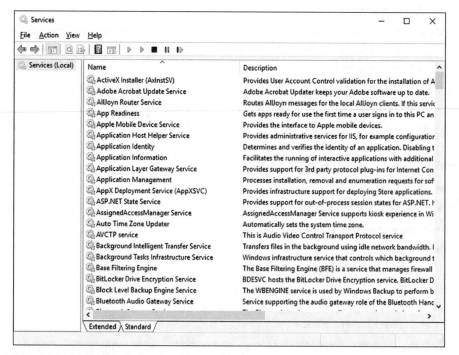

FIGURE 4-54 Managing services

You can use this console to view and manage services in the operating system. For example, to manage the status of a service (assuming it is not running), right-click the service and then click Start. If you want to stop or restart a running service, right-click the running service and then click either Stop or Restart.

You can also manage the settings of a service by double-clicking the desired service. In the Properties dialog box for the named service, as shown in Figure 4-55, you can then configure the properties shown in Table 4-16.

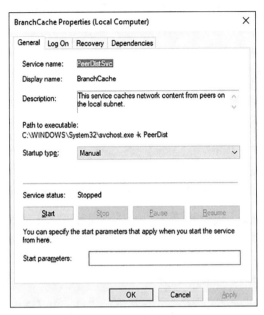

FIGURE 4-55 Managing a specific service

TABLE 4-16 Configurable options for a Windows 10 service

TAB	OPTIONS AND EXPLANATION
General	■ Service name. You cannot change this value, but it is useful to know what name Windows assigns to the service so that you can reference it when using a command-line tool or Windows PowerShell. ■ Startup type: Disabled, Manual, Automatic, Automatic (Delayed Start). This option enables you to determine the startup behavior of the service. ■ Start parameters. You can add properties to configure the service behavior when it starts.
Log On	Log on as Local System Account or This Account. Some services run in the context of the Local System Account. Others must be configured to use a specific, named account (for example, when communicating across the network with another service). You can create special local user accounts for the purpose of running services. When you define a specific user account and change the user password, you must update the password information on the Log On tab for the services that use that account.
Recovery	You can configure what happens when a service fails to start or crashes. Specifically, you can configure Windows 10 to attempt a restart of a service if it fails to start on the first attempt. On second attempts, you can choose another option, such as Restart The Computer. Available options for failures are Take No Action, Restart The Service, Run A Program, and Restart The Computer. If you select Run A Program, you can configure additional options for the path and name of the program, plus any runtime switches you want to apply.

(Continued)

TAB	OPTIONS AND EXPLANATION
Dependencies	Some services depend on other services, or groups of services, to run. In this way, Windows 10 can start efficiently by making sure only the required services are in memory. You cannot make changes on this tab, but it is informative to know whether a service has dependencies, especially when a service is failing to start properly.

USING COMMAND-LINE TOOLS

You can also use the command line to investigate and troubleshoot service startup. Table 4-17 shows some of the more common command-line tools you can use to work with services. To use these commands, open an elevated command prompt.

TABLE 4-17 Managing services from the command line

COMMAND	EXPLANATION
Net start	When used without arguments, lists the running services. When used with the name of a service, the service, if not running, is started. For example, **net start workstation** starts the Windows workstation service.
Net stop	Must be used with the name of a running service. For example, **net stop workstation** will stop the Windows workstation service.
Sc query	Displays a list of services.
Sc stop	Enables you to stop a named service. For example, to stop the spooler service, run: **Sc stop spooler**
Sc start	Enables you to start a named service. For example, to start the spooler service, run: **Sc start spooler**

You can also use Windows PowerShell to manage services. This is particularly useful because you can use Windows PowerShell to administer other computers remotely, including their services. In addition, you can script Windows PowerShell cmdlets, enabling you to store common administrative tasks for future use. Table 4-18 shows the cmdlets you can use to manage services in Windows 10. Open an elevated Windows PowerShell window to use these cmdlets.

TABLE 4-18 Managing services with Windows PowerShell

CMDLET	EXPLANATION
Get-service	Lists available services. To get a list of running services, use the following cmdlet: **Get-Service	Where-Object {$_.status -eq "running"}**
Stop-service	Enables you to stop the named service(s). For example: **Stop-service - name spooler**
Start-service	Enables you to start the named service(s). For example: **Start-service - name spooler**
Restart-service	Enables you to stop and start the named service(s). For example: **Restart-service - name spooler**
Set-service	Enables you to reconfigure the startup and other properties of the named service. For example, to change the display name of the Workstation service, use the following cmdlet: **set-service -name lanmanworkstation -DisplayName "LanMan Workstation"**

USE THE SYSTEM CONFIGURATION TOOL

If you are experiencing problems with starting your Windows 10 device, and you suspect a service might be the cause of the problem, you can control which services start when you start your computer by using Safe Mode. This reduces the set of services that start to the minimum required to run Windows.

You can force your computer into Safe Mode during startup or use the System Configuration tool, Msconfig.exe. To access the System Configuration tool, run **msconfig.exe**. You can then configure your computer's startup behavior. Configurable options are described in Table 4-19.

TABLE 4-19 System configuration options

TAB	OPTIONS AND EXPLANATION
General	■ Select Normal Startup to configure normal operations on your computer. ■ Choose Diagnostic Startup to load a minimal set of devices and services. ■ Choose Selective Startup to be more selective about what is initialized during startup.
Boot	■ You can enable Safe Mode by clicking Safe Boot. Then you can choose additional options: Minimal, Alternate Shell, and Network. You can also start without the GUI, enable a boot log, and configure startup to use a base video driver and configuration. ■ The Advanced Options button enables you to restrict Windows to using fewer logical processors and a reduced amount of memory. These options are useful for re-creating a computer configuration in which a specific problem was experienced. ■ If multiple operating systems are installed on your computer, they are listed on this tab, enabling you to select between the available operating systems. ■ You can choose to make your boot selections permanent, but you should exercise caution with this option in case the settings you have selected are inappropriate.
Services	The Services tab displays the available operating system services and enables you to configure their startup behavior. For example, you can disable any services that you suspect might be causing issues with your computer. To disable a service, clear the check box next to its name.
Startup	The Startup tab enables you to access the Startup tab in Task Manager to control the startup behavior of apps.
Tools	The Tools tab provides a consolidated list of available system tools, including: Change UAC Settings, System Properties, Computer Management, Device Manager, and the Registry Editor.

Thought experiments

In these thought experiments, demonstrate your skills and knowledge of the topics covered in this chapter. You can find the answers to these thought experiments in the next section.

Scenario 1

You want to use the Backup And Restore (Windows 7) tool to create a backup of your files contained on your computer to a removable USB hard drive or SDHC memory card. You want to create a custom schedule. Answer the following questions relating to the Backup And Restore (Windows 7) tool:

1. What is the default backup schedule for the Backup And Restore (Windows 7) tool?

2. How would you modify the schedule so that you can be more specific? For example, you want to back up the data every 30 minutes.

3. What triggers are available that could be used to begin the backup task?

4. You no longer want to use Backup And Restore (Windows 7) tool for your Windows 10 Pro tablet. What built-in backup tool could you use instead? How could the data be safeguarded from theft?

Scenario 2

You have been asked to review the backup and restore options available within Windows 10 and OneDrive.com. Your manager is developing a backup strategy and wants to ensure that files are backed up and users can easily access the backed-up files for at least six months. Backups will be stored offsite. Answer the following backup-related questions.

1. How would relying on the OneDrive Recycle Bin feature affect the backup strategy?

2. You want to examine how the Previous Versions feature found in File Explorer works, but you cannot see any Previous Versions listed. How do you enable Previous Versions?

3. Could the Previous Versions feature found in File Explorer offer backup and recovery of files as part of the backup strategy?

Scenario 3

Your company has recently upgraded half of its computers from Windows 7 to Windows 10 Pro. Staff members use Office and a web-based line-of-business application. The help desk manager has received several complaints from users who state a variety of problems following the upgrade, including that the following:

-   Their computers are slow
-   Apps stop responding
-   Websites are slow to load

The remaining Windows 7–based computers do not exhibit the same issues. You need to offer the help desk some advice on how to diagnose these problems and recommend how to resolve them as soon as possible.

Answer the following questions from the help desk:

1. Why might the computers be slow after the upgrade?

2. Which tool could you recommend to assist the help desk support members verify which apps are freezing?

3. You suspect that the network card could be a performance bottleneck. How could this suspicion be tested?

4. How would a network card bottleneck present itself?

Scenario 4

You work as a desktop support technician. Your Windows 10 deployment for 5000 devices is now complete, and you are now busy supporting your users. Answer the following questions about using advanced management tools and techniques for your organization:

1. You find that you are repeatedly performing the same management task on multiple computers. At the moment, you use several customized Microsoft Management Consoles to perform the required tasks. How could you achieve this more easily?

2. A number of users are experiencing problems with their computers. You determine that the issue relates to a service that occasionally stops and is then restarted. Where can you track information about this problem?

3. What command-line tools can you use for managing services?

Thought experiment answers

This section provides the solutions for the tasks included in the thought experiment.

Scenario 1

1. The default backup schedule for the Backup And Restore (Windows 7) tool is every Sunday at 7 PM.

2. You need to edit the AutomaticBackup task in the WindowsBackup node found in Task Scheduler and configure the task to repeat every 30 minutes by editing the trigger.

3. The triggers available for the task to begin include the following: On A Schedule, At Log On, At Startup, On Idle, On An Event, At Task Creation/Modification, On Connection/Disconnect To A User Session, and On Workstation Lock/Unlock.

4. You would suggest using File History. This feature allows the backup of files and folders to a removable drive—for example, a USB drive or SDHC memory card—that may be used with the device. Optionally, the external storage may be encrypted using BitLocker To Go or EFS.

Scenario 2

1. The OneDrive Recycle Bin is not a backup facility. It will only retain files that have been deleted for a maximum of 93 days. This is less than the 6 months required by the backup strategy.

2. You would need to turn on the schedule to create restore points using either File History or the Backup And Restore (Windows 7) tool. Once the Backup And Restore (Windows 7) tool creates a backup, or when File History runs, previous versions of files will be available on the Previous Versions tab.

3. Previous Versions could provide the longevity of access to the backed-up files if the backup storage location does not become full. To ensure that the Previous Versions complied with the backup strategy, you would need File History or the Backup And Restore (Windows 7) tool to save the image to a remote storage location, such as a networked attached drive.

Scenario 3

1. Answers might vary. Several potential areas need to be investigated. The original computers should have met the minimum specification for Windows 10 to upgrade from Windows 7. The computers might be quite old and contain components that are slow in comparison to modern hardware, such as older hard drives without cache, or slow RAM memory. The BIOS or motherboard firmware might be old and need updating. The hardware device drivers might not have been updated to the latest versions for Windows 10.

2. Recommend to the help desk that it suggest using Reliability Monitor to review the stability history of the computers that are reporting app freezing. The Reliability Monitor report should identify the failing app and how often it is failing; also, the report should identify potential solutions. You should also be able to see whether other failures are occurring that might relate or contribute to the app failure.

3. Answers might vary. You could review the network card driver version and see whether there are any known issues relating to the network card and Windows 10 on the manufacturer's website. You could use Performance Monitor to review the performance for the Network Interface counter and monitor the Output Queue Length.

4. Network-related activities, such as web browsing and opening and saving resources across the network, would be slower than normal. If there is network saturation, the report should indicate that the queue length is more than 2, meaning that the network card cannot process network packets quickly enough.

Scenario 4

1. You could create Windows PowerShell scripts, as required, that contain the required management cmdlets. Because Windows PowerShell supports remoting, it is easy to run the script against remote computers at the same time. You must, however, ensure that the execution policy for each computer supports the running of PowerShell scripts and that Windows PowerShell remoting is enabled.

2. Use the System log in Event Viewer. You can group events based on source; in this instance, the source is Service Control Manager.

3. You can use Windows PowerShell to manage services. Also, the SC.exe and Net.exe command-line tools can be used.

Chapter Summary

- Windows 10 File History is the preferred backup option that performs automatic back-ups of files every hour to a non-local storage.

- Previous Versions is a feature that allows you to recover deleted or modified versions of your files directly from File Explorer rather than via a backup or File History.

- OneDrive offers you a Recycle Bin, which allows you to recover files you've deleted from OneDrive folders and syncs with the File Explorer Recycle bin.

- OneDrive can provide a history of older versions of Office documents that are stored within OneDrive, so that you can access, restore, and download previous versions of your files.

- A Windows 10 recovery drive can be used to recover your system in the event of failure.

- System Restore is useful for restoring the operating system to a previous point in time. For example, you can restore to a point prior to when your computer became unstable.

- Windows RE enables you to access the advanced startup options to troubleshoot Windows 10 startup issues.

- You can use Reset this PC to recycle a computer for use by another user or to revert the computer to its OOBE state if you experience serious problems with the computer.

- Fresh Start within Windows Security enables you to keep your personal files and some Windows settings but remove all apps, including third-party apps that are pre-installed on your device.

- Restore points are created when the Backup and Restore (Windows 7) tool creates a backup image. You can use a system image to recover Windows 10 if Windows 10 becomes unstable (for example, if your hard drive has failed and other recovery meth-ods have failed).

- Driver Rollback allows you to revert to a previous device driver after your system begins to suffer the effects of upgrading to a new device driver that is poorly performing.

- Windows 10 Home users have Windows Updates automatically downloaded and installed on their devices. Windows 10 Pro, Education, and Enterprise customers can defer feature updates for up to 365 days, and they can defer quality updates for up to 30 days.

- Windows 10 Pro, Education, and Enterprise customers can pause quality updates for up to 35 days.

- Windows Update Delivery Optimization is a method of peer-to-peer sharing of Windows update files. This feature significantly reduces the time that a Windows 10 device is vulnerable from zero-day malware attacks. Peer caching can occur between other users on the local network or optionally across the Internet.

- Administrators can use Group Policy to centrally configure and manage Windows Update behavior, location of WSUS servers, and Windows Update Delivery Optimization settings.

- If a driver update causes system stability issues, you can uninstall the update, and if necessary, you can disable the automatic application of the update.

- Event logs automatically record system activity such as logons, application errors, and services stopping and starting.

- If you enable remote management, you can pull event logs from remote computers by using event subscriptions.

- Windows 10 includes several tools to view system performance, including Task Manager, Performance Monitor, and Resource Monitor.

- In Performance Monitor, you can create benchmarking reports by creating your own user-defined collector sets and running them to generate a performance baseline.

- Windows 10 introduces the option, to manage your default printer by setting the default to the last printer you used, rather than the printer at your current location.

- The built-in Search feature uses the background indexing service to index areas of your hard drive automatically, including files stored in your user profile.

- Reliability Monitor provides a graphical history of your computer's reliability and offers solutions to resolve issues.

Index

Symbols

B

C

Plug into learning at

MicrosoftPressStore.com

The Microsoft Press Store by Pearson offers:

- Free U.S. shipping

- Buy an eBook, get three formats – Includes PDF, EPUB, and MOBI to use with your computer, tablet, and mobile devices

- Print & eBook Best Value Packs

- eBook Deal of the Week – Save up to 50% on featured title

- Newsletter – Be the first to hear about new releases, announcements, special offers, and more

- Register your book – Find companion files, errata, and product updates, plus receive a special coupon* to save on your next purchase

Discounts are applied to the list price of a product. Some products are not eligible to receive additional discounts, so your discount code may not be applied to all items in your cart. Discount codes cannot be applied to products that are already discounted, such as eBook Deal of the Week, eBooks that are part of a book + eBook pack, and products with special discounts applied as part of a promotional offering. Only one coupon can be used per order.

Hear about it first.

Since 1984, Microsoft Press has helped IT professionals, developers, and home office users advance their technical skills and knowledge with books and learning resources.

Sign up today to deliver exclusive offers directly to your inbox.

- New products and announcements

- Free sample chapters

- Special promotions and discounts

- ... and more!

MicrosoftPressStore.com/newsletters

 Pearson